Special Populations in the Community

Advances in Reducing Health Disparities

Editors

Juliann G. Sebastian, PhD, RN, CS
Associate Professor and Assistant Dean
for Advanced Practice Nursing
University of Kentucky
College of Nursing
Lexington, Kentucky

Angeline Bushy, PhD, RN, CS
Professor
Bert Fish Endowed Chair
Community Health Nursing
University of Central Florida
Daytona Beach, Florida

AN ASPEN PUBLICATION®
Aspen Publishers, Inc.
Gaithersburg, Maryland
1999

Library of Congress Cataloging-in-Publication Data

Sebastian, Juliann.
Special populations in the community: advances in reducing health
disparities/Juliann G. Sebastian, Angeline Bushy.
p. cm.
Includes bibliographical references and index.
ISBN 0-8342-1364-8 (alk. paper)
1. Poor—Medical care—United States. 2. Health services
accessibility—United States. 3. Poor—Health and hygiene—United
States. I. Bushy, Angeline. II. Title
RA445.S443 1999
362.1'086'9420973—dc21
99-23669
CIP

About Aspen Publishers • For more than 35 years, Aspen has been a leading professional
publisher in a variety of disciplines. Aspen's vast information resources are available in both
print and electronic formats. We are committed to providing the highest quality information
available in the most appropriate format for our customers. Visit Aspen's Internet site for more
information resources, directories, articles, and a searchable version of Aspen's full catalog,
including the most recent publications: **http://www.aspenpublishers.com**
Aspen Publishers, Inc. • The hallmark of quality in publishing
Member of the worldwide Wolters Kluwer group.

Editorial Services: Denise Hawkins Coursey
Library of Congress Catalog Card Number: 99-23669
ISBN: 0-8342-1364-8

Printed in the United States of America

1   2   3   4   5

Table of Contents

Contributors

Lu Ann Aday, PhD
Professor of Behavioral Sciences and
Management and Policy Sciences
University of Texas School of Public
Health
Houston, Texas

Dyanne D. Affonso, PhD
Professor and Principal Investigator
Department of Family Health Care
Nursing
School of Nursing
University of California
San Francisco, California

Charles C. Berry, PhD
Adjunct Professor of Community and
Family Medicine
Department of Community and Family
Medicine
University of California
San Diego, California

Kenneth L. Bettenhausen, PhD
Assistant Professor
Graduate School of Business
University of Colorado at Denver
Denver, Colorado

Joyceen S. Boyle, RN, PhD, FAAN
Professor and Chair
Department of Community Nursing
School of Nursing
Medical College of Georgia
Augusta, Georgia

Shelia L. Broyles, PhD
Assistant Research Psychologist
Department of Pediatrics
University of California
San Diego, California

Angeline Bushy, PhD, RN, CS
Professor
Bert Fisher Endowed Chair
Community Health Nursing
University of Central Florida
Daytona Beach, Florida

William V. Chambers, PhD
Adjunct Associate Professor
University of Alabama in Huntsville
College of Nursing
Huntsville, Alabama

Hazel W. Chappell, MSN, RN
Faculty, College of Nursing
University of Kentucky
Lexington, Kentucky

Angela Cole, BSN, RN
Public Health Program
Emory University
Georgia Migrant Health Care Task Force
Georgia Department of Human Services
Division of Public Health
Atlanta, Georgia

Henry Cole, EdD
Professor
College of Education
University of Kentucky
Lexington, Kentucky

Lynda H. Crawford, MN, RN
Assistant Professor of Nursing
Nell Hogson School of Nursing
Emory University
Atlanta, Georgia

Shelly S. Crow, MS, RN
Second Chief
Hickory Ground
Muscogee (Creek) Nation
Okmulgee, Oklahoma

Mary DeLetter, PhD, RN
Associate Nurse–Executive Research
Department of Veterans Affairs Medical
    Center
Assistant Professor
College of Nursing
University of Kentucky
Lexington, Kentucky

Linda Diaconis, MS, RN
Doctoral Student
University of Maryland at College Park
College of Education
Villa Julie College
Union Memorial Hospital Baccalaureate
    Nursing Program
Baltimore, Maryland

Connie Dickey, MSN, RN
Clinical Specialist
Baptist Hospital of East Tennessee
Knoxville, Tennessee

John P. Elder, PhD, MPH
Professor of Public Health
School of Public Health
San Diego State University
Adjunct Professor of Pediatrics
Department of Pediatrics
University of California
San Diego, California

Jimmy Ferrell, PhD
Associate Professor
Division Chair, BSN Nursing
Mary Black School of Nursing
University of South Carolina–
    Spartanburg
Spartanburg, South Carolina

Gail C. Frank-Spohrer, DrPH, RD
Professor of Nutrition
Nutritional Epidemiologist
Department of Family and Consumer
    Sciences
California State University
Long Beach, California

Rodney D. Fulton, MS, MEd
Research Associate
College of Nursing
Montana State University
Bozeman, Montana

Blair D. Gifford, PhD
Assistant Professor
Graduate School of Business
University of Colorado at Denver
Denver, Colorado

Katherine Young Graham, PhD
Professor and Chair
Department of Community Health Care
  Systems
School of Nursing
University of Washington
Seattle, Washington

Lou Gramling, PhD
Assistant Professor
Mental Health—Psychiatric Nursing
School of Nursing
Medical College of Georgia
Augusta, Georgia

Susan Hedrick, PhD
Associate Research Career Scientist
Health Services Research and
  Development Field Program
US Department of Veterans Affairs
  Medical Center
Associate Professor
Department of Health Services
University of Washington
Seattle, Washington

Donna Hodnicki, PhD
Associate Professor
Director, MSN Program
Department of Nursing
Georgia Southern University
Statesboro, Georgia

Pamela Kidd, RN, PhD
Associate Professor
College of Nursing
University of Kentucky
Lexington, Kentucky

June Kunimoto, PHN
PHN Supervisor, Island of Hawaii
Public Health Nursing Branch
State of Hawaii Department of Health
Hilo, Hawaii

**Jeanette Lancaster, PhD, RN,
  FAAN**
Sadie Heath Cabaniss Professor of
  Nursing and Dean
School of Nursing
University of Virginia
Charlottesville, Virginia

Dona J. Lethbridge, PhD, RN
Associate Professor
University of Alabama in Huntsville
College of Nursing
Huntsville, Alabama

James E. Lubben, MPH, DSW
Professor
School of Social Research and Public
  Policy
Department of Social Welfare
University of California at Los Angeles
Los Angeles, California

M. Katherine Maeve, RN, PhD
Assistant Professor
Department of Community Nursing
Medical College of Georgia
Augusta, Georgia

Linda J. Mayberry, PhD
Assistant Adjunct Professor
Department of Family Health Care
  Nursing
School of Nursing
University of California
San Francisco, California

Nancy McCain, DSN
Associate Professor
Adult Health Nursing
School of Nursing
Virginia Commonwealth University
Richmond, Virginia

Thomas L. McKenzie, PhD
Professor of Physical Education
Department of Exercise and Nutritional
 Sciences
San Diego State University
San Diego, California

Robert McKnight, MPH, ScD
Associate Professor
Department of Preventive Medicine and
 Environmental Health
Director, Southeast Center for
 Agricultural Health and Injury
 Prevention
University of Kentucky
Lexington, Kentucky

Martha A. Miser, PhD
Adjunct Professor of Social Work
Whittier College
Whittier, California

Ailee Moon, PhD
Assistant Professor
School of Social Research and Public
 Policy
Department of Social Welfare
University of California at Los Angeles
Los Angeles, California

Rachel Beaty Muller, RN, MSN
Doctoral Student
School of Nursing
Medical College of Georgia
Augusta, Georgia

Philip R. Nader, MD
Director
Division of Community Pediatrics
Professor of Pediatrics
Department of Pediatrics
University of California
San Diego, California

Maggie T. Neal, PhD, RN
Assistant Professor
University of Maryland at Baltimore
School of Nursing
Baltimore, Maryland

Susan Neibacher, MSW
Executive Director
Care for the Homeless
New York, New York

Samson Omotosho, MA, RN
Doctoral Candidate
University of Maryland at Baltimore
School of Nursing
Baltimore, Maryland

Marcie Parker, PhD, CFLE
Family Social Science Department
University of Minnesota
St. Paul, Minnesota

Peggy L. Parks, PhD
Assistant Professor
University of Maryland at Baltimore
School of Nursing
Baltimore, Maryland

Jane W. Peterson, RN, PhD
Professor and Anthropologist
Seattle University School of Nursing
Seattle, Washington

Larry Piercy, MS
Agricultural Extension Safety Specialist
College of Agriculture
University of Kentucky
Lexington, Kentucky

Marcus Plescia, MD, MPH
Assistant Professor of Family Medicine
Department of Family Medicine
Carolinas Medical Center
Charlotte, North Carolina

Eileen Jones Porter, PhD, RN
Assistant Professor
Sinclair School of Nursing
University of Missouri–Columbia
Columbia, Missouri

Kathleen B. Powell, PhD, RN
Director
Nursing Special Projects
Children's Hospital
Birmingham, Alabama

Keith G. Provan, PhD
Professor
School of Public Administration and
  Policy
University of Arizona
Tucson, Arizona

James F. Sallis, PhD
Professor of Psychology
Department of Psychology
San Diego State University
Assistant Adjunct Professor of Pediatrics
Department of Pediatrics
University of California
San Diego, California

Juliann G. Sebastian, PhD, RN, CS
Associate Professor and Assistant Dean
  for Advanced Practice Nursing
University of Kentucky
College of Nursing
Lexington, Kentucky

Suann Sheptak, MS
Data Management Specialist
Department of Family Health Care
  Nursing
School of Nursing
University of California
San Francisco, California

June Shibuya, PHN
Program Coordinator, Makura Project
Public Health Nursing Branch
State of Hawaii Department of Health
Hilo, Hawaii

Yvonne M. Sterling, RN, DNSc
Professor and Coordinator
Louisiana State University Medical
  Center
School of Nursing Graduate Program
New Orleans, Louisiana

Hal Strelnick, MD
Associate Professor of Family Medicine
Department of Family Medicine
Montefiore Medical Center
Bronx, New York

David L. Strickland, MA
Instructor of Sociology
Social Science Division
East Georgia College
Swainsboro, Georgia

W. Jay Strickland, PhD
Assistant Professor of Sociology
Department of Sociology and
  Anthropology
Georgia Southern University
Statesboro, Georgia

Therese Sullivan, PhD, RN
Chair and Professor
Department of Nursing
Carroll College
Helena, Montana

Timmy Thompson
Heleshaya (Medicine Man)
Hickory Ground
Muscogee (Creek) Nation
Okmulgee, Oklahoma

Kimberly Townley, PhD
Associate Professor
College of Human Environmental
  Sciences
University of Kentucky
Lexington, Kentucky

Margaret Smith Ulione, RN, PhD
Assistant Professor
Barnes College of Nursing
University of Missouri–St. Louis
St. Louis, Missouri

Valentine M. Villa, PhD
Adjunct Assistant Professor
School of Social Research and Public
  Policy
Department of Social Welfare
University of California at Los Angeles
Los Angeles, California

Steven P. Wallace, PhD
Associate Professor
School of Public Health
University of California at Los Angeles
Los Angeles, California

G. Robert Watts, MPH, MS
Assistant to the Executive Director
Care for the Homeless
New York, New York

DeLois P. Weekes, RN, DNS
Associate Professor and Associate Dean
Boston College School of Nursing
Chestnut Hill, Massachusetts

**Clarann Weinert, SC, PhD, RN,
  FAAN**
Associate Professor
College of Nursing
Montana State University
Bozeman, Montana

Roma D. Williams, PhD, CRNP
Associate Professor
University of Alabama at Birmingham
School of Nursing
Birmingham, Alabama

Donna Marie Wing, EdD, RN
Associate Professor
University of Tulsa School of Nursing
Tulsa, Oklahoma

Martha Worcester, PhD
Associate Professor
School of Health Sciences
Seattle Pacific University
Seattle, Washington

Foreword

Jeanette Lancaster, PhD, RN, FAAN

It really is not true that "all men (and women) are created equal." Some people have far more resources. Those people who have more advantages are born in countries that support freedom among its people; they are born to families who have the psychological and physical resources to support the children's growth and development; and they are born with an adequate genetic make-up to grow, develop, learn and achieve. Unfortunately, in the United States as well as all other countries, some people are born with and into better sets of circumstances.

Similarly there are visible health disparities among people. Of particular concern to health care providers, social service workers, and politicians among others, is the growing numbers of what are termed "vulnerable or special populations." The word "vulnerable" is derived from the Latin verb *vulnerare* which means to 'wound'[1.p.65] .Vulnerability is generally thought to mean susceptibility to health problems, harm or neglect. There is typically an implied danger or threat to the vulnerable person. This threat can be real or perceived. Some groups are more vulnerable or at risk for physical, psychological or social health disruptions. Generally, when we think of vulnerable or special at risk populations we include those who are poor, homeless, chronically ill or disabled, people with AIDS, members of abusing families, pregnant adolescents and their infants, frail elderly people, immigrants and refugees, and those who are mentally ill.

There are also some segments of society, in addition to the groups listed above, that have special needs and may be at greater risk for health disruption. These are the very young and the very old. Both of these groups tend to rely on others for much of their care. Adolescents are more vulnerable than children and young adults because of their tendency to engage in risky behavior and their belief in their immortality. Women are more likely than men to suffer from depression, eating disorders, and domestic injuries. Similarly, several racial and ethnic groups are vulnerable. For example, African Americans and Hispanics have higher rates of hypertension, diabetes, cancer, and infant mortality.

In a somewhat different way of looking at vulnerability, it is known that people with higher levels of both education and income tend to have better health. Vulnerability is also situational. That is, the same person may react differently to the same stressor at different times depending on the strength of the person's resources and support. It is important to remember that in most instances, people do not cause themselves to be vulnerable. Their vulnerability is not a personal deficiency. Rather it represents the interaction effects of many factors over which the individual may have little or no control.

Ecological thinking is useful when thinking about the concept of vulnerability. Simply stated, all people are open systems in constant interaction both with their own inner environment and the external environment in which they live and survive. At times, people may succumb to external environmental stressors more readily if their internal environments are also in chaos.

If we observe that not all members of special or vulnerable populations succumb to the negative factors affecting them, what then makes the difference? Clearly, some people can pull together more personal, family, and other social supports. Also as discussed in Part III, hardiness influences how members of special populations deal with the forces around them. Some people are more resilient than others; they have greater personal strength and more support from others. Resilience may be influenced by attitudes and perceptions. If people think they are healthy, capable and in general an average and competent person, then they may be able to cope more effectively. In reality, they may not have the same capacity as others, yet their own perception influences whether they can cope or will succumb to stressors.

As is so ably pointed out in Part IV, intervening in vulnerability is not a solo endeavor. Since vulnerability occurs from a number of interacting forces and factors, developing resiliency also requires the interaction of many forces. Individuals, families, groups and communities must work together to strengthen people so they can avoid becoming members of special populations.

As will be discussed in this insightful book, a great deal needs to be learned about how to effectively reduce disparities in the health status of members of special populations in comparison to the population as a whole. This change will require concentrated, focused, and systematic efforts on the part of the affected individuals and their families as well as on the part of their communities, states, and the nation. This is no simple matter.

Change of this consequence and magnitude requires policy changes which are based on sound research that identifies causes of vulnerability and then tests interventions. Collaboration and new partnerships will be central to this change, and Part IV describes how and why these partnerships and collaborations must occur. In short, this book both describes and explains the problem related to meeting the health needs of special populations and also provides a range of actions that can help achieve solutions.

REFERENCE

1. Rogers, A.C. Vulnerability, health and health care, *Journal of Advanced Nursing,* 1997;26:65–67.

Preface

Juliann G. Sebastian, PhD, RN, CS

Angeline Bushy, PhD, RN, CS

NOT ALL segments of the population have benefited equally from expenditures on health care in the United States despite the fact that the proportion of the gross domestic product spent on health care has increased throughout the century. The beginning of the twenty-first century brings with it a mandate to health care providers, policy makers, administrators, insurers, and consumers to work together in designing ways to ensure equity and parity in health care delivery. Certain subsets of the population experience wide disparity in access to health services, outcomes of health care, and higher relative risk of poor health than the population as a whole. At the same time, demographic shifts are occurring both in the United States and globally that will result in these populations becoming the majority within the twenty-first century.[1] Their needs must be effectively addressed to ensure a global populace with a high quality of life.

The United States federal government addressed these issues in President Clinton's initiative to reduce racial and ethnic disparities in health[1] and in the *Health United States, 1998*[2] report that highlights the causal relationships between socioeconomic status and health. *Healthy People 2010* will focus on reducing disparities in access, outcomes, and risk across population groups in this country.

The purpose of this book is to highlight work that is being done to understand the health care needs and effective health care strategies for special population groups. These groups are more vulnerable to poor health outcomes than the population as a whole because they have greater relative risk resulting from limited resources. Aday[3] notes that the critical resources for good health include social and environmental resources, human capital, and biological and genetic predispositions. The authors of the chapters in this volume address these resources from the perspectives of strengthening factors that build resilience and working in partnership with families and communities to identify and meet health care needs. These chapters focus on culturally appropriate strategies for making health care more acceptable to many special population groups. Health care providers face a challenge to work collaboratively with communities to design service delivery systems that effectively blend unique cultural, social, and economic strategies to ensure good health outcomes for special populations. This book advances the state of knowledge in this area.

The book is intended to be a useful adjunct to graduate courses in public health, health education, nursing, medicine, pharmacy, health administration, social work, allied health disciplines, and other areas in which students are planning health professions careers working with special populations. Each part contains an introduction outlining the conceptual framework that links the chapters in the part, key terms, and discussion questions. The chapters themselves are primarily drawn from several issues of *Family and Community Health* that focused on these topics. As editors of this book of readings, it is our hope that the excellent work contained in this volume will enrich and expand analyses of ways to reduce health disparities in this country.

REFERENCES

1. Hamburg M. Eliminating racial and ethnic disparities in health: response to the Presidential Initiative on Race. *Public Health Rep.* 1998; 113:372–375.
2. National Center for Health Statistics. *Health, United States, 1998*. Hyattsville, Md: Public Health Service; 1998.
3. Aday LA. *At Risk in America: The Health and Health Care Needs of Vulnerable Populations in the United States*. San Francisco: Jossey-Bass; 1993.

Theoretical Underpinnings of Vulnerability and Approaches to Special Populations

Definitions and Theory Underlying Vulnerability

Juliann G. Sebastian, PhD, RN, CS

WHILE HEALTH status in the United States has improved throughout this century, and has continued to improve during the 1990s, disparities in health status still exist across various segments of the population. The antecedents of these disparities are rooted in economic and social circumstances. The most recent federal report on health of the country, *Health, United States, 1998*[1] documents the impact of income and education on health. Those with lower incomes and fewer years of education do not fare as well in terms of morbidity, mortality, injuries, exposure to environmental hazards, and access to health care as do people with more financial resources and higher educational backgrounds.

Clinton's 1998 Presidential Initiative on Race documents the disparities in health status between certain racial and ethnic groups and the rest of the United States population. For example, the infant mortality rate for whites declined from 7.3 per 1,000 live births to 6.3 per 1,000 live births between 1990 and 1995, representing a 14% decline in infant mortality.[2] This is a record low level of infant mortality and represents substantial progress in a leading public health indicator. The infant mortality rate for African Americans also declined by 14% during this time period. However, with rates of 16.9 per 1,000 live births in 1990 and 14.6 per 1,000 live births in 1995, African Americans have a very high infant mortality rate and one that is over 100% higher than that of whites. Infant mortality among Hispanics actually increased from 7.5 per 1,000 live births to 7.6 per 1,000 live births in that same time period.

Studies have shown that it is not race that is the primary contributor to these poor outcomes, but lower socioeconomic status. For example, Kochanek and colleagues[3] evaluated the gap in life expectancies between African Americans and whites in the United States and concluded that the gaps were related to socioeconomic status rather than to race. Thus, members of certain subsets of the population are at higher risk, or are more vulnerable to poor health than the population as a whole and these vulnerabilities have much to do with economic and social circumstances. The view that health is an outcome of both personal assets, such as heredity and lifestyle, and social and environmental context (eg, access to health care, healthy living and working environments, access to nutritious foods) is not a new one,[4] but is receiving increasing attention in policy and research arenas.

President Clinton's goal for the United States is elimination of "the disparities in six areas of health status experienced by racial and ethnic minority populations while continuing the progress we have made in improving the overall health of the American people."[2(p372)] These six areas are: infant mortality, cancer screening and management, cardiovascular disease, diabetes, human immunodeficiency virus (HIV) infection and acquired immune deficiency syndrome (AIDS), and immunizations. Together, these six areas focus on several of the major causes of disease, disability, and mortality.

Healthy People 2000[5] called for reduction in health disparities between the majority population and special populations in the United States. These special populations have poorer health outcomes than the majority and are at higher risk of developing poor health. Special populations were identified in *Healthy People 2000* as those with low income, disabilities, and minority groups. Clinton's 1998 Initiative on Race further specified high priority special population groups by focusing attention on African Americans, American Indians, Pacific Islanders, Hispanics, and Alaskan Natives.[2] Both this initiative and *Healthy People 2010* emphasize even more strongly the need to reduce health disparities between special populations and the US population as a whole. This part of the book focuses on what is meant by vulnerability to poor health and both the processes that contribute to poor health outcomes and those that serve as buffers, or protective factors.

DEFINITIONS

Vulnerability can be defined as susceptibility to negative events. In the context of health care, vulnerable populations are those subsets of the population with a higher than average risk of developing health problems.[6,7] Vulnerable populations are "social groups who have an increased relative risk or susceptibility to adverse health outcomes."[8(p69)] This definition suggests that more than personal factors are involved in increased risk levels. Societal and environmental contributions are key to conceptualizing vulnerability. A "victim blaming" perspective on vulnerability would lead to very different social and health policies than would an ecological perspective that takes into account personal, interpersonal, and system contributors to vulnerability.[7,9] Numerous antecedents to vulnerability exist, leading to a conceptual model of vulnerability that is more consistent with the web of causation described in epidemiologic approaches to health and illness. Most striking is the role that social, economic, and cultural factors play in developing either vulnerability or resilience.

CONCEPTUAL MODELS

Aday[6] delineated a conceptual model outlining the antecedents to vulnerability (see Part IV). She argued that the interaction between individual assets, social assets, and demographic factors contributes to a higher likelihood of poor health in the United States. Age, race, ethnicity, and sex are the key demographic variables associated with variations in health status. In some cases these variations result from genetic predispositions (eg, breast cancer), while in others (eg, race and ethnicity) they may be part of an intricate set of socioeconomic variables correlated with poor health. Individual

assets (human capital) include those skills and resources that contribute to one's ability to be economically self-sufficient, such as education and employment. Social assets (social capital) refer to characteristics of one's social network that provide emotional and instrumental support, such as family structure, friendship ties, neighborhood connections, and religious organizations. Aday's model focuses attention on the role that internal and societal resources play in development of health risks.

Aday's "differential vulnerability hypothesis" refers to the higher risk of health problems and poorer health outcomes that result from the convergence of these three sets of resources. The important underlying concept in Aday's formulation is that vulnerability to poor health does not represent a personal deficiency on the part of members of these special populations. It reflects the interaction effects of many factors over which individuals have little control and therefore indicates that society as a whole has a responsibility to provide unique and customized services to prevent illness and promote health in these populations. This is consistent with the ecological health model described by Dever et al.[9]

Flaskerud and Winslow[8] expand Aday's model by focusing on the interaction between resources at a broad level, increased relative risk, and subsequent health status as measured by morbidity and mortality rates. They argue that resource availability is the key issue correlated with health-related vulnerability. They conceptualize resources in terms of socioeconomic and environmental resources. In their model, socioeconomic resources include human capital, social networks and support, and social status. Environmental resources include both access to health care and the quality of care rendered. Limitations in resources needed for good health and quality of life lead to higher risks than average for health problems and to increases in morbidity and mortality in special population groups. In Flaskerud and Winslow's model, research, clinical practice, and policy interventions should be aimed at breaking the links between resource limitations and effects on relative risk and subsequent health outcomes.

Sebastian[7,10] emphasizes the dynamics that take place in the links between resource availability and health outcomes. In her model, resource limitations are related to disenfranchisement and marginalization, disadvantage, and reduced personal control over health. Population subgroups such as the homeless, ethnic minority groups, immigrants, frail elderly, and poor women and children have been marginalized and disadvantaged in contemporary society. Special populations may be marginalized in terms of health policies due to their limited visibility and the difficulty associated with developing policies that respond to the complexities of health needs that are interwoven with many social and economic issues. For example, medically indigent families, who are commonly among the working poor, may be less visible and less likely to be accounted for in health utilization statistics because they do not access health services since those services are unaffordable to them. Similarly, it is difficult to estimate health need among homeless populations because they are mobile and do not have permanent residences.

Marginalization interferes with developing coherent health policies and with partnering with members of these populations to develop services that are culturally, socially, and economically appropriate, leading to disadvantage in terms of access to health services. One example that counters this trend is the development of the State Children's Health Insurance Program,[2] which is designed to increase access to health services by children in working poor families. Vulnerable populations seem to have less control over their own health practices than the population as a whole. They may live and work in more hazardous environments and may find it necessary to choose between paying for basic needs such as shelter or clothing and buying nutritious foods or medications. Theoretically, it may be that marginalization, disadvantaged status, and reduced personal control over health are the underpinnings of vulnerability. However, not everyone experiences negative outcomes under these circumstances, and in fact, some individuals and families demonstrate a remarkable resilience to these challenges to health.

This leads naturally to an evaluation of the clinical, social, and policy interventions that empower members of special populations to be better able to promote their own health and prevent illness. The chapters in this part focus on the dynamics of vulnerability and resilience. They highlight the fact that not all members of special populations succumb to the negative impact of resource problems. Many are able to marshall internal resources and family and other social support to find meaning in difficult circumstances and to prevent further poor health outcomes.

PART I: OVERVIEW

The conceptual thread tying the three chapter in this part together is the strength that people bring to bear in overcoming the potentially adverse outcomes of vulnerability. This is important for two reasons. First, vulnerability can become a label and self-fulfilling if health professionals do not fully appreciate the complex interactions of individual and societal factors that contribute to poor health outcomes. Health professionals should work together with members of special populations to identify the strengths and meanings that people bring to these situations in order to build on those strengths and provide culturally appropriate care. This leads to the second point, which is the emphasis that the next century seems likely to bring to partnering with communities and clients to design the most appropriate and accessible health services possible. The chapters in this part provide a starting point for analysis about ways to redesign health services to build on clients' cultural preferences. Drawing on Aday's model, the populations described in these chapters built on their inner resources (ie, part of the human capital concept) to find meaning in adversity, and to forestall further poor outcomes.

The chapter by Neal et al describes how parents of ill children find meaning in the experience of caring for those children. Neal et al's work makes an important contribution to advancing knowledge about how people facing adverse circumstances develop and sustain resilience. Their work also emphasizes the concept that vulnerability to poor health is not an irreversible circumstance, but responds instead to a variety of interventions, one of which is strengthening the "human capital" or inner resources of those in difficult circumstances. The chapter by Porter shows how families whose children are at high risk of lead poisoning are able to overcome that risk due to interventions that they themselves have initiated. Finally, the chapter by Powell describes how children at high risk for violence draw on personal and social assets to overcome those risks. In each of these chapters, personal action and reflection by members of high-risk, vulnerable populations are the keys to avoiding negative health outcomes. Health professionals have much to learn from members of vulnerable populations in terms of using personal strengths as a strategy for health promotion and illness prevention.

SUMMARY

Vulnerability to poor health outcomes is higher for certain subsets of the population because of a complex interplay between biologic, genetic, social, and economic factors. These factors interact within a "web" of causality to create a lower threshold for tolerating risks to health. Additionally, the accumulation of multiple risk factors makes poor health outcomes more likely for members of these special populations. In the United States, a national effort has been initiated to reduce the disparity in health outcomes between the population as a whole and subsets of the population. The chapters in this part of this book address some of the theoretical issues associated with vulnerability to poor health outcomes.

DISCUSSION QUESTIONS

1. Analyze the personal, social, and economic resources available to populations with whom you work. Determine those actions you can take to partner with members of those populations to jointly define assets available to them and to use those assets and strengths to promote health and prevent illness. What barriers can you anticipate to working together to build on assets? How might those barriers be overcome?

2. Analyze the major causes of morbidity and mortality in your community. Determine if disparities exist between some population groups in your community and the population as a whole. What do you think are the sources of these disparities? What can be done at a local level to reduce disparities?

3. How can you work with populations experiencing major health problems to facilitate finding meaning in illness? How can you help people with chronic health problems promote high quality of life?

4. Together with colleagues from at least several other disciplines, analyze how an interdisciplinary approach to working with vulnerable populations can contribute to improved health outcomes. How would adding consumers and community agency representatives to the discussion shift the actions that might be taken?

REFERENCES

1. National Center for Health Statistics. *Health, United States, 1998*. Hyattsville, Md: Public Health Service; 1998.

2. Hamburg M. Eliminating racial and ethnic disparities in health: response to the Presidential Initiative on Race. *Public Health Rep*. 1998;113:372–375.

3. Kochanek KD, Maurer JD, Rosenberg HM. Why did black life expectancy decline from 1984 through 1989 in the United States? *Am J Public Health*. 1994;84(6):938–944.

4. Bollini P, Siem H. No real progress towards equity: health of migrants and ethnic minorities on the eve

of the Year 2000. *Soc Sci Med*. 1995;41(6):819–828.

5. US Department of Health and Human Services. *Healthy People 2000: National Health Promotion and Disease Prevention Objectives*. Washington, DC: Government Printing Office;1991.

6. Aday LA. *At Risk in America: The Health and Health Care Needs of Vulnerable Populations in the United States*. San Francisco: Jossey-Bass; 1993.

7. Sebastian JG. Vulnerability and vulnerable populations. In: Stanhope M, Lancaster J, eds. *Community Health Nursing: Promoting Health of Indi-*

viduals, Aggregates, and Communities. 4th ed. St. Louis: Mosby; 1996.

8. Flaskerud JH, Winslow BJ. Conceptualizing vulnerable populations health-related research. *Nurs Res.* 1998;47(2):69–78.

9. Dever GEA, Sciegaj M, Wade TE. Creation of a social vulnerability index for justice in health planning. *Fam Community Health.* 1998;10(4): 23–32.

10. Sebastian JG. Vulnerability and vulnerable populations: community health nursing issues for the twenty-first century. In: Stanhope M, Lancaster J, eds. *Community Health Nursing: Promoting Health of Individuals, Aggregates, and Communities.* 5th ed. St. Louis: Mosby. In press.

"I Was Scared . . .": Voices of Vulnerable Parents

Maggie T. Neal, PhD, RN

Peggy L. Parks, PhD

Linda Diaconis, MS, RN

Samson Omotosho, MA, RN

What can cause more fear than being poor when Being Poor is the father of Being Scared?

An African saying

SIGNIFICANT NUMBERS of parents and children in the United States live with limited financial resources, which increases their chances of being vulnerable to social deprivation, educational disadvantage, loss of job or income, poor nutrition, poor child-rearing conditions and practices, and poor health and illness, as well as robberies, murders, and property damage.[1] When some families are exposed to potential risk or harm they quickly rebound, recover, and may even grow stronger from adversity. They may be thought of as resilient. Factors that contribute to resilience are "I have" (external supports and resources), "I am" (internal personal strengths), and "I can" (social

Partial funding for this project was provided by an award to the first two authors from Designated Research Initiative Funds at the University of Maryland School of Nursing.

Fam Community Health 1997;19(4):49–63
© 1997 Aspen Publishers, Inc.

and interpersonal skills).[2] Phenomenologically, resilience is connected with rebounding or springing back. Movement associated with resilience engenders power, buoyancy, and elasticity of spirit.[3] Theoretically, resilience is the capacity of a person, family, or community to prevent, minimize, overcome, or adapt successfully to challenging and threatening consequences of adversity.[2,4] Feelings, such as being frightened, are part of the experience of being vulnerable to negative outcomes related to high-risk conditions.[2] However, being scared does not mean that the individual has succumbed to adversity. In order to understand an experience that results in an unexpected outcome, one must know the meaning that individuals make of the experience, their way of thinking about it. Resilience has been called a "way of thinking."[5] Phenomenologic inquiry, a research method that allows researchers to understand the meaning that people make of their experiences, was chosen to understand parental resilience.

The conceptualization of resilience was used to think about the participants in this study. Some of the factors that promote resilience are forming trusting relationships, having role models, receiving encouragement to be autonomous, being able to manage feelings and impulses, having good communication skills, and being able to problem solve. Furthermore, factors such as pride, hope, faith, and an appealing temperament are important. While a variety of factors may promote resiliency, all need not be present to be resilient.[2,4]

The research question for this study was how do potentially resilient parents who were identified as vulnerable because of limited financial resources respond when confronted with the reality of their ill child's needs? Because it is not possible to estimate the number of people who overcome or are transformed by adversity, we must assume that every parent with whom we have contact as health care providers has the potential to be resilient when presented with adverse experiences associated with their child's illness. Are the parents scared because of limited financial resources? Do parents fear that children can easily succumb to an illness and die? Are parents scared of the possibility of losing their child who is so valued? Are they scared of losing control of their parenting practices? Or, do they simply fear failing in the responsibility they assign themselves as parents for their children? We believe in the infinite potential of the parent and hope that our practices as health care providers would be transformed by understanding the meaning of these experiences to parents.

THE INQUIRY PROCESS

Phenomenology

Phenomenology, a qualitative research approach, allows scientists to uncover the meaning that people make of the experiences they have, without testing predetermined hypotheses. Phenomenologists often use ordinary language (texts) as the basis for learning about how people interpret their lived experiences.[6–8] Usually, participants are interviewed and the process begins with the request, "Tell me about your experience." The interviewer follows the person's lead and pursues the experience for every detail. These in-depth, open-ended interviews are tape recorded and later transcribed. The transcribed text is treated as symbolic of the meaning the person makes of the experience as interpreted by the phenomenologist. The analysis of text is a tedious and time-consuming process of examining the text by repeatedly asking, "What meaning do these words have for this person?" When repeated meanings emerge from the text in the interviews of one participant and across participants, themes or patterns are created. The text is reexamined many times as themes are named to represent common or shared experiences found in the text of the participants. This process results in receiving an understanding that was beneath the surface level of the participant's words,[7] yet was known and real to them.

Selection of parents

Parents from two ambulatory health clinics in an urban area were recruited with the assistance of two expert nurse clinicians. The nurses identified exemplary parents whose children had experienced chronic or episodic illnesses. After explaining the study to the parents, all agreed to participate and signed a statement of informed consent. These four mothers and one mother–father couple are described using pseudonyms:

June (age 41, Caucasian), the mother of an 8-month-old child with special needs, experienced the death of a low-birthweight infant 11 years prior. She has responsibility for a child whose physical condition calls for vigilance and con-stant care. She answered the call. Metaphorically, life for June is a spiral of hope, fear, and worry.

Tina (age 29, African American), the mother of two young daughters, aged 4 and 6, is with them constantly, mostly in a basement apartment in subsidized housing. From this home she has heard gunshots and knows "drugs are everywhere . . . you see a whole lot of drug traffic." She lives in a place where rearranging the furniture, instead of escaping, is the strategy. One of her children's chronic illnesses was a strand in a complex web of circumstances that entraps her. Life for Tina is longingly looking out a window but not venturing much beyond that view.

Tressa (age 28, African American), the mother of an infant and a 9-year-old child, is going places. She says, "Now I'm goin' to school for nursing. I work as a nursing assistant." She has family support to help her reach the destination. Parenting is an important part of her identity. According to Tressa, "They always first." Parenting is tied up in a complex context of relationships among mothers. When one of her children is sick, it's "scary," but she is not frozen; she takes action. She is in charge of parenting, and the man she lives with is the father of one of her children. Life for Tressa is like a bus trip slowed by frequent stops.

Angela (age 22, African American) lived with her mother until she had her baby, now 9 months old. Her employment was interrupted for 2 months of maternity leave, and she paid a neighbor for child care when she was working. The baby and the absence of the father triggered an increase in maturation in this mother. Life for Angela is "baby and me."

Shirley and Norman (ages 29 and 27, Caucasian) have two children, aged 7 months and 4 years, and live with the father's parents. They are partners in an intense and consuming life of parenting in which one child was enough and two are too many. One of the children's recurrent ear infections and crying meant sleep deprivation and misery for these parents. They received medical care from authorities who sometimes used language the parents did not understand. Both parents spoke with pride about what they did with the children and what the children have accomplished. Without financial resources, life for Shirley and Norm is not moving.

Generation of text and textual analysis

The parents were interviewed for approximately 1 hour in the clinics. The semistructured interviews were tape recorded and later transcribed. Parents were asked to describe becoming and being parents as well as experiences about when their children were ill. The texts from the transcripts were interpreted by all four authors. As a group, we read and talked about each passage of text from the five interviews. Shared meanings of two interviews emerged from the texts, and these themes were modified when the last three interviews were interpreted. We developed connections among the themes and wrote interpretive summaries of each interview and each theme. This analytic process was like the unfolding of a lotus flower so the fullness and beauty of the text could be seen and

appreciated. *Being scared*, an experience that each parent talked about, emerged as a lens through which we saw these four themes:

1. being there with the power of knowing,
2. being there and taking action,
3. being the only one there, and
4. being there with the support of others

DISCOVERIES

When parents talked about caring for their children during times of illness, we heard their fear. When describing what it felt like when her child became ill, Tressa said it was "scary cause you don't know what it is; there's nothin' you can do about it" and resigned herself to the powerlessness of not knowing. In contrast, Angela said, "I knew I had to take her to the emergency room, but I was kind of scared." She used her fear and intuition as an impetus for taking action. Having to go to the emergency room meant that she recognized both the severity of the problem as well as the security that comes when fears are relieved.

When afraid, turning to others for support was a response that empowered parents to face adversity and risk, to be resilient. Sharing fears with others, like sharing caregiving activities, lightened the parents' burdens. June, the mother of a child with special needs, is afraid that if she is not with her child at all times she will lose him. She says, "I think with him, he was just so special, you know, I was scared to leave him. I didn't want to leave him anywhere. He's got to be stuck with me because I'm scared something'll happen to him with his condition and all."

Being afraid occurred for these parents in the context of caring for their children. These parents stay connected with their children in spite of the accompanying fear and anxiety. The agony of being scared seems to come with the package of being a vulnerable parent. Though scared, they take action; they do what they have to do! Even in the face of limited financial resources, they do not abandon their caring responsibilities. It is not surprising that these parents were identified by experienced nurses as parents who were good parents.

Being there with the power of knowing: "I knew I had to take her to the ER . . ."

Parents had multiple ways of knowing that gave them the power to provide care for their children. Among these were intuition or experience, family members, and information from health care providers. Attentive knowers learned through observation and sensing; they created an increased awareness through interactions with others.[9] Parents were intensely connected to their children. Knowledge of the child's normal patterns and watchfulness were ways of being there and recognizing changes that were signs of illness.

Intuitive or experiential knowing

Being there intuitively means the parent is intimately connected to the child. Parents know or can feel in their bones what they need to know in order to provide the care their children need when they are ill. During an illness or when the child is perceived as being ill, the parent's first knowledge of the illness is intuitive. As

Tressa says, "A lot of it just come to you. You just know [what to do]." Through watching, listening, and connecting, the parent immediately grasps the nature of the unfolding situation. Angela told us, "It seems like everything else is common sense, you know." Knowledge of the child's normal patterns and watching helps them be there intuitively and recognize changes that signal an illness. When Shirley was asked how she knew when her child was becoming ill, she stated that the child is "mostly restless, not what [he] usually does when they're around or whatever. Usually just still, quiet." Similarly, in another situation, Norm recognized his child's illness by being aware of the child's patterns. "He won't sleep, constantly waking up at nights. Crankiness and crying. You can tell when he's sick, cause normally, he's very social, but when he starts getting sick, he don't want to eat or drink." Tressa said, "I touched her and she was hot, 106, and that was scary." Like health care providers, parents recognize the child's fever as a signal of impending danger. In addition, the parents are scared of the challenge they face if the illness turns out to be something very serious. Fever, like a child's unexplained cry, is one of the experiences that brings the reality of parenting directly in the face of these vulnerable parents. Because their child's survival is perceived as threatened, their parental resilience is also challenged. Though parents go through many episodes of fever with every child, these parents face this fear and uncertainty yet remain hardy and gain strength from being responsible. As Angela explained, "I want to come home . . . I mean I can still go out occasionally, but not like I used to and I don't even want to do that because I know I have more responsibility."

Sometimes the parent feels he or she knows the nature and cause of the illness. For example, Tina said, "I had an idea it was sinus. . . . I think it's by living in the basement cause if we go somewhere, she don't have nose bleeds the whole time there. As soon as we come home, and it be chilly in there, and I turn the heat on, that's when her nose'll start."

By living through these experiences, the parents' intuition becomes so strong that it moves them to action, almost as though they were propelled. Frequently the parents' trust in their own intuition was validated by the positive outcome of acting on the feelings of what was the right thing to do for the child. Goleman asserted that persons with a natural attunement to their "heart's voice—the language of emotion"[10(p29)] are more adept at articulating the protective wisdom of the unconscious. He argues that all emotions are impulses to act. "The very root of the word *emotion* is *motere*, the Latin verb 'to move,' plus the prefix 'e' to connote 'mov[ing] away,' suggesting that a tendency to act is implicit in every emotion."[10(p6)]

Knowing from family members

All the mothers said they learned parenting skills from persons they knew and trusted who already had children. Angela provided an example:

One time she was taking a nap and she was asleep for a long time, so I called my mother and I asked her why she sleeps so long. But I mean she was okay and everything but I just wanted to know why she was sleeping so long. She said some babies sleep long and some babies don't. Maybe she was worn out or something.

Mothers, in particular, sought out their own mothers or sisters as a trusted source of knowing about children. Emphasizing this point, June told us, "We've always been around my mom. My grandmother, she would babysit for me when I'd work . . . but my mom, she's always been there." This tie was maintained whether they lived independently or with their mothers. These connections are clearly a source of strength and affirmation.

Knowing from health care providers

Parents experienced the information given by health care providers in both positive and negative ways. There were situations where the parents' knowing from health care providers was hindered by the use of language they did not understand. In sharing the child's medical record, June confided, "I really don't know, really understand a whole lot, uh, in my own terms . . . but when they're talking to me like in these terms now, I have to sort of like look them up myself to see what they're talking about. But they'll usually explain it to me." Parents, however, wanted information shared by health care providers in simple terms that they understood. Medical jargon was counterproductive to a trusting relationship and did not help them know how to provide good care. In fact, it may be a way of controlling and keeping parents out.

Alliances with health care providers, when effective, serve to improve parenting skills while building confidence in the responsibilities the parents are assuming. Sharing her experience of hospital staff, June recounted, "I learnt a lot while he was in the hospital. How to hold him; what to do with him if he did do that; how to squeeze his throat."

Being there and taking action: "It scared me after I got to my senses what I'd done"

All parents provided examples in which they acted quickly when the children became sick. If it was not within their own power to change the situation at home, they elected to take the child to the emergency room, clinic, or hospital. For all the parents, actively watching, protecting as a guardian, taking charge of situations, holding, nurturing, and teaching seemed natural parts of being a parent.

Actively watching

Actively watching is a practice of attending through listening, observing, and connecting. However, it involves more than watching with the eyes, listening with the ears, and touching with the hands. Based on what is learned from the watchfulness, the parent is empowered to act. The following text is an example of how Angela's watching led to action: "I knew I had to take her to the emergency room. . . . I felt like I never did this before, suppose I don't do it right. Suppose something happens on the way there and little things like that, I was scared."

In one situation, active watching is described by the grandmother. She tells about visiting her grandson in the hospital: "I went in to see him one time. He was out of the incubator at the time, and he had a big lump on his little head like this, and I went to the nurse and said the IV was wrong, and it was just as purple and blue and red. And that nurse tried to tell me that it was a bone, I said that isn't a bone."

These parents describe such intimate caregiving acts as watching their child's breathing, which gives us a clear sense that they may be breathing together. As van Manen explained, "in my relation to my children, I embody my fatherhood, such that I look with fatherly eyes at . . . the skin injury my child incurred while playing, or the feverish color of my child in his sickbed, etc. And this 'seeing' prompted me to do something, to act the way a father should."[6(p105)] Parents' connections with their children allow them to quickly recognize incremental changes or potentially harmful situations. This recognition combined with intimacy can evoke strong feelings of fear and uncertainty. In some situations the parents' fear of losing the child motivated their active watchfulness.

Protecting

There is a sense of the parent's need to stand guard over the child or the situation. In observing her child's computed tomography scan procedure, Tina stated, "I wanted to know what was going on."

For June, her sense of guardianship during her child's hospitalization had greater import than that of the institution. She attributed his recovery directly to her attending to his nutritional needs, as she explained:

[The hospital staff] kept him on the tubes, but they were dietary. Instead of trying to feed him, they would keep him on the tubes. And when I took him to [another hospital], I was there every meal time. Every time he fed, I was there. Twelve hours after he was there, he was completely off of everything, you know. And a week and a half after he was there, he came home. He's been doing good ever since.

The guardianship extends into the future for these parents who face many impending uncertainties. June, the mother of a child with special needs, commented, "I think that's [to be like other kids] what everyone thinks about something like this. Is he going to fit in? He's goin' to be laughed at or picked on." These parents, mostly mothers, help us encounter the rich meaning of being a parent: the fear of difference, the desire for a child to succeed, and the overwhelming feeling of being scared when the child is ill.

Taking charge

The parent as guardian takes charge with boldness, knowing that consequences of not acting might have long-term effects for them and their children. June, who acted boldly by removing her child from the hospital, later reflected on the results of her action, "It scared me after I got to my senses what I'd done, but I wasn't sorry that I did it." Parents took such heroic actions in the interest of their child that they in retrospect scared themselves. At the time the action was being taken, the only and overriding consideration was the child's well-being.

From these experiences of taking action parents develop a transformative power. Taking action is a way of responding, made possible through the intimacy of connection and the responsibility that the parent assumes. These parents tell us they have become more responsible. Angela expressed it this way: "It [the child's birth] settled me down quite a bit. Cause I was at the point where I just didn't really care anymore. But since he's been here, I'm like two different people. I have somebody that needs me."

These parents shoulder more than the responsibility of good parenting. Lost in the demands of the child, self-interests are often sacrificed. We found the parents consumed by the burdens of the child's needs. Norm stated, "Kids are always first." Likewise, Tressa said, "If I have 10 dollars and he [the child] needs milk, and I want something, he gotta get the milk. So, I sacrifice. They always first." We found the intensity of the relationship with the child became so consuming that there was often a blurring of boundaries between the child and parent. Sometimes a mother crossed the boundary between responsibility and self-sacrifice.

Holding, nurturing

Parents do a variety of activities with their children on a daily basis. They act as "healers"; they read to their children; they do other activities that promote the child's development. June spent extensive time with her child following the protocols of an intervention. She said, "I have to do his therapy during the day with his hands and his feet . . . mostly circulation in his hands, bending of fingers, bending of his feet, the toes, because he can't do it himself."

We found these parents spent time with their children. They taught them and prepared them for school. When asked to describe a day with her child, Angela said, "It's holding, nurturing, feeding, and bathing." These are typical actions for parents to take as they connect with their children and experience the realities of being responsible for a child's care.

Being the only one there: "She needs me, I need her"

Being with young children is an intense and consuming relationship that had the potential for overtaking parents' lives. Two of the mothers in this study had such a strong connection with their child that the usual margins separating mother and child were blurred. The other fills a void of unmet needs. Angela accentuated, "She needs me. I need her." Several mothers referred to how the intensity of the mutual needs created a sense of isolation. For some mothers the presence of the child gave them important reasons to live; "I have somebody that needs me." In these situations, the mothers became a constant and sole companion. June described her child as "just so special . . . I was scared to leave him anywhere."

For the parent the child is someone special who might be open to tremendous risks if left alone when ill. The vulnerable parent therefore wants to be in the constant presence of the child. As van Manen said, "It is not enough to just give birth to a child; in order to be a parent one has to live as a parent side by side this child as well. . . . We may describe the parenting relation as one of togetherness, homeness, being there for the child, intimacy, closeness."[6(p108)]

Mother as constant companion

There are moments when these mothers described themselves in ways that suggest they were "one with" their child. They also described themselves in ways that reflect isolation. June poignantly said, "He's all I have. I spend all my time with him. . . . He doesn't stay with a sitter. He has never been to one, because I have a problem with him eating. When I'm gone he won't eat right, so I have to kinda stick around."

The mothers were tethered to their children, who were the center of their lifeworld. Self-interests are lost in the demands of the child. Integral with parental caring seems to be an intimacy so close that it appears as if both child and parent are of one flesh. This fundamental existential of lived body was explained by van Manen: "I experience my children as utterly separate from me and yet as physically close. For many people, there is a deep significance in the knowledge that parents and children are of one flesh. And in the physical holding and parental embrace we know our children in a profoundly symbiotic way. We also sense in the lived bodily encounter a primordial sense of security for the child."[6(p105)] Parental caring by these parents was profoundly close.

Mother as abandoned mother

Failure of connection with men was pervasive, either by choice or abandonment. These women did not live in the shadows of a man, although there clearly were shadows of men in their lives. When asked about the children's father, Tina responded, "Living with his girlfriend." Angela told us,

It seems like soon as her father went away, I had her for a reason, because I would need somebody there with me. She need me. I need her. Whenever I be needing somebody and I be like well, you know she don't answer me back or whatever but she might cry or something like that. Cause her father wasn't around for her. Let me see, she's 9 months, about 3 months of her life it was just me.

In the single-parent home the mother serves as both parents. They do it all themselves. Tina said, "It's hard. But we makes it." Rather than turning to male partners for help with child rearing, mothers, sisters, and grandmothers are frequently the significant other that provides support, modeling and actual care. They also turn to the child for support and nurturance in a reciprocal way.

Mother in need of mothering

Value of friendship and support among women—sisters, mothers, grandmothers—is evident. They are there for each other. They speak for and support each other's voice; they help each other, they encourage action, and they often pose questions and interpret when professionals speak as confusing and distancing experts. Tressa gave a specific example of how she continued to be mothered by her own mother. "Well, she brought everything to me, I didn't have to do anything."

As a way of gaining some relief from the parenting responsibilities—"the only

break momma gets"—Shirley and her children spent the weekends with her mother, and "Grandmom takes over." Child-rearing activities continue from one generation to the next, a way of staying connected and maintaining relationships.

Being there with the support of others: "It was a relief once I was there [the ER]"

Parents were able to be there for their child with the support of others. They expressed the need of not going it alone in situations of uncertainty and high stress. This support came from diverse sources. Support for the parent could be emotional support from a partner, information from health care providers, baby-sitting by a day-care mother, living arrangements provided by parents, and financial support from government agencies. What appears to be most meaningful across all participants was the intergenerational connections of mothers, sisters, and grandmothers.

Support from partners

Shirley and Norm actually completed one another's sentences throughout the interview. When the interviewer commented on the fact that they always brought their child to the clinic together, the mother responded, "Sometimes when they say a big word or something, I don't understand what they're saying and he'll just explain it to me and what it means and all." In this family, parenting practices were complementary. Tressa, when asked what it is like to take care of her children, responded, "[Caring for children] is hard, it's hard, but his father helps a lot." The realities of parenting, when shared with a partner, seemed to be less burdensome.

Support from health care providers

Angela, concerned about the outcome of her pregnancy, told what it was like for her to visit the prenatal clinic: "So when I used to come over here [the clinic], some of the nurses, well, one nurse I had, she was my normal nurse, she was always trying to comfort me and tell me nothing's wrong. . . . But every time I would come over to this clinic, I mean they were always giving me donuts and drinks and everything."

June was grateful for the information and support provided by health care team members. She stated, "The ladies here [the clinic] told me if I needed them to help me that I could ask for the records and to bring them to them, and they'll help me with them."

Support from babysitters

Vulnerable parents face additional challenges to the basic demands of providing care to their children. For example, Angela said, "At first, I couldn't find a babysitter and I was scared that I wasn't going to be able to go back to work." The structure of this statement also signifies the priority that parents usually give to their children over and above other important issues in their lives. The statement presupposed that a parent has to give priority to staying home to care for a child rather than going back to work, in spite of her already limited financial resources. No matter how scary the alternative might be, the vulnerable parent had made up her mind to live with the decision as long as

she could take care of her child. Finding suitable child care enabled Angela to return to work. Surprisingly small details make quite a difference in supporting what parents are sometimes able to do.

Support from government agencies

All the participants in the study received medical assistance. Parents who lived in situations of limited financial resources were able to provide care for their children because of the financial support from outside sources.

Prenatal care was made possible for Angela through the efforts of health care providers within her community. She said, "I was on maternity leave and I didn't have any health insurance and when I came over here [the clinic], they told me they could help me get some insurance, help me get medical assistance."

Resources from various public agencies meet (or do not meet) parents' needs in different ways. For Tina, the government provided housing in a basement apartment. She said, "I'm on subsidized housing and . . . paying low income." The irony is that the housing environment was so damp that it endangered her child's health. She wanted to move but had few choices. She hoped that the nurse practitioner would help her relocate to a safer environment.

Support from family

Family members, especially the women, became strong advocates for one another. They took charge and acted when the need arose. Angela described how her family supported her when she was in labor: "My sister ran out of the house and asked [the neighbor] if he could take us to the hospital. By the time my mother had got off work and she came down there and she was like, 'You're not going home. You're going to stay down here, you're going to walk around.' She made me walk around the whole hospital until I got down to 8 centimeters."

Mothers told us how their mothers helped. They did what their mothers did and asked, "What am I supposed to do?" when their children were sick. These parents were there with their children, and they know their mothers were there too. The African aphorism "It takes a whole village to raise a child" was a way of recognizing that support from many sources was necessary for those who care for children. Parents relied on a community of family members and others to be there to help them in caring for their children.

TOWARD AN UNDERSTANDING

"Understanding begins . . . when something addresses us."[11(p299)] The issue that addresses health care professionals is how to connect with parents when their children are ill. Compelling messages from the parents in this study emerged as admonitions for health care providers. An *admonition* is a counsel against a fault, error, or oversight. These are the admonitions:

Be connected

As health care providers, we need to respect the parents' knowledge as expert, because the parent as primary caregiver has seen the child in situations where we have not. While expert "medical knowledge" of diseases is familiar to health care providers, the parents hold the expert knowledge of the day-to-day realities of the child. This compels us to be connected with the parent and share each other's knowledge.

Affirm the caregivers

Parents seek affirmation as good parents and take obvious pride in their children's accomplishments. They are truly interested in "doing the right thing by the child" and there is evidence of continuity of family practices. Parents experience frustration and powerlessness, however, at some situations in which they find themselves: undesired housing or living arrangements, illnesses, lack of employment opportunities, and sometimes abandonment. In the face of adversity, parents make caring choices for their children that should be respected and affirmed. Usually they seek affirmation from a family member, the maternal grandmother of the child or health care providers, and occasionally the father of the child.

Work in partnerships

In their work with parents, health care professionals need to build partnerships founded on strengths of acceptance, respect, and understanding. On the one hand parents portrayed a belief that what was said and done by health care practitioners was not to be questioned. On the other hand, their stories related struggles between doing what they thought was best for the child and complying with the health care system. As health care providers, we must

- resist the temptation to think that we "know what is best" for the parents;
- truthfully share our knowledge (and lack of knowledge) in ways that are understood so that parents are in a position to make choices;
- resist the temptation to act upon stereotypic assumptions about the parents instead of the realities of the parents' lives;
- contextualize our work with caregivers around ways that account for their naturally occurring support systems in the caregivers' families and communities;
- respect and affirm the connection between the parent and child as a crucial element of our partnership with parents; and
- relinquish the illusionary power of being in control and acknowledge our own vulnerability in knowing that our observations and interventions are always fallible, frequently incomplete, and often uncertain.

Working in partnership with parents as experts is important to the process of creating a place for parents to be empowered to act. Gadamer reminded us that the purpose of expert knowledge is "to govern action, to discover the point at which one is to act."[11(p314)]

Encounter the parents' ways of knowing

"Standing beside" is one way of acknowledging the fear and situation of the parent. The parents' response to a child's needs by being there calls us to respond in the same way. When a parent says, "I was scared," health care practitioners are challenged to listen to those feelings and recognize that the emotion of fear needs to be addressed before the practitioner can begin to demystify the medical jargon or high-technology procedures. When parents operate on an intuitive rather than rational basis we must be more creative in our approach as we address their fears and how they know. Thus, we confirm their intuitive way of knowing as we work in partnership with them. We need to affirm them as parents so they can be resilient and actualize their potential as responsible parents.

• • •

In this study, we had the privilege of listening to the stories of vulnerable parents who seemed resilient. They helped us understand how they acted and were transformed when they experienced the adversity of their children's illnesses. We heard their fears and how they drew from inner sources of power (I am, I can) and from external sources of support (I have). Insights from this study revealed how resilience factors are related and used for action and transformation. I am, I have, and I can reveal how parents own their experiences. This ownership that is known, consciously and unconsciously, demands transformative actions. The process happens in the presence of being scared and in intimate connection with their children. From this phenomenologic study we came to understand that resilience factors, which are positive, have oppositional negatives lurking in the parents' lives. Having support available from others was in opposition to being alone. Being compelled to take action was in opposition to feeling immobilized. Breaking unspoken rules of the health care system was in opposition to not challenging its authority. While parents may be resilient, the opposition of the resilience factors is present but not visible.

As we view the strength of parents, we stand in awe of what they know and how they know it. Statements from the mothers such as, "A lot of it just come to you. You just know," "I was constantly learning from them," and "I used to call her for every little thing" point to intuition, experience, and consultation as three outstanding sources of knowing that parents use. A family member, the child's maternal grandmother, was most frequently consulted by the mothers in this study. The task of practitioners is neither to disregard nor replace those resources. Rather, health care workers need to explore, assess, extend, reinforce, and supplement them. Many circumstances will call parents to act or take charge in the care of their child. The parents should be prepared and encouraged to do this boldly. As researchers and clinicians, we should encourage parents to continue to be watchful as this will help them confidently and effectively take charge.

Understandings from this study have implications for clinical practice. As practitioners, we need to seek, respect, consider, and affirm the parents' caring, knowledge, skills, and choices. Initiating services that enhance connection and working in partnerships with the parents promote quality care for children. Holding the belief that parents are the experts rather than mere receivers of ready-made options affirms the ownership of their parenting experience. This could lead to restructuring health care and education so people have successful experiences as owners of their own health and learning.

There are many unanswered questions that emerged from this study. The study did not include parents who were vulnerable and not doing well. How might their experiences illuminate what we learned from the resilient parents? The depth of our understanding about being scared could profit from additional interviews. How might our research lead to a better balance between the emotional and cognitive aspects of being health care providers to parents? Finally, these parents taught us about the importance of ownership; how did they come to be this way and how do expert nurses partner with them? The interviews with these parents did not focus on the resources of the family and community, although these emerged from the text. What kinds of community resources are important for parents who have diverse levels of family support? How do community resources help parents be resilient and meet the challenges of adversity?

REFERENCES

1. Bureau of the Census. *Statistical Abstracts of the United States: 1994*. 114th ed. Washington, DC: US Dept of Commerce; 1994.

2. Grotberg E. *A Guide to Promoting Resilience in Children*. The Netherlands: Bernard van Leer Foundation; 1995.

3. *The Compact Edition of the Oxford English Dictionary.* New York, NY: Oxford University Press; 1971.

4. Zimmerman MA, Arunkumar R. Resiliency research: implications for schools and policy. *Social Policy Rep.* 1994;3(4):1–18.

5. Grotberg E. *Sixth Action Update.* Birmingham, Ala: Civitan International Research Center; 1995.

6. van Manen M. *Researching Lived Experience.* Albany, NY: State University of New York Press; 1990.

7. Nancy JL. Sharing voices. In: Ormiston GL, Schrift AD, eds. *Transforming the Hermeneutic Context: From Nietzsche to Nancy.* Albany, NY: State University of New York Press; 1990.

8. Dreyfus HL. *Being-in-the-World: A Commentary of Heidegger's Being and Time, Division I.* Cambridge, Mass: MIT Press; 1991.

9. Moch SD. Personal knowing: evolving research and practice. *Schol Inquiry Nurs Pract Int J.* 1990;4:155–165.

10. Goleman D. *Emotional Intelligence.* New York, NY: Bantam Books; 1995.

11. Gadamer HG; Weinsheimer J, Marshall DG, trans. *Truth and Method.* New York, NY: Continuum; 1994.

CHAPTER 2

Parental Actions To Reduce Children's Exposure to Lead: Some Implications for Primary and Secondary Prevention

Eileen Jones Porter, PhD, RN

ACCORDING TO THE Agency for Toxic Substances and Disease Registry,[1] lead is ranked first among the top 10 hazardous substances. Because lead is pervasive in the environment,[2] children are *at risk* for lead exposure, and they are particularly *vulnerable* to the toxic effects of lead.[2,3] While their bones and vital organs are still developing, they have rapid mineral turnover[2]; therefore, compared with adults, children have a greater potential for lead absorption, and they actually absorb more of the lead that they ingest.[4] In particular, children under 3 years of age[5] are a "vulnerable popula-

This research was supported in part by the Outagamie-Winnebago Lead (OWL) Program, sponsored by the Winnebago County Health Department and the Outagamie County Department of Health and Human Services, with funds from the State of Wisconsin and the Centers for Disease Control and Prevention. OWL Program staff who contributed to this study were Deborah Hummel, RN, MSN, Program Coordinator; Linda Hauessinger, RN, BSN; Virginia Betley, RN, BSN; and Bonnie Johnson, RN, BSN. The author is grateful to Dolores J. Severtson, BSN, RN, who served as a research assistant.

Fam Community Health 1997;20(2):24–37
© 1997 Aspen Publishers, Inc.

tion group at-risk."[6] They are physiologically vulnerable to lead's adverse effects, and their hand-to-mouth behavior increases the risk of ingesting lead in its various forms.[5]

Because lead exposure is a multifaceted phenomenon with "complex and interrelated pathways from . . . sources to children,"[2(p6)] prevention also must be a multifaceted effort. In the literature, the primary and secondary prevention efforts of public health workers, primary care providers, and property owners have been emphasized.[7-16] Generally, parents have been cast in passive roles— either as recipients of preventive information[13,16] or as sources of data about the child's possible exposure.[14,17] Parental efforts to decrease exposure have been considered chiefly in the context of tertiary prevention; for instance, Binns et al noted that lead-poisoned children may "benefit if parents are able to decrease lead exposure."[8(p170)]

However, in the presence of a lead source, the occurrence of exposure (and the eventual development of lead poisoning), may be influenced by parents' steps to interrupt or prevent exposure. For instance, if a child plays in lead-contaminated soil, a parent can supervise handwashing to decrease the chance for exposure through ingestion behaviors such as sucking the fingers.[18] Indeed, the professional interventions of anticipatory guidance and parental education are based upon the tenet that "parents can prevent the exposure of their children to lead."[9(p180)]

To teach parents how to maintain or improve their strategies to reduce lead exposure, practitioners need information about parents' current preventive actions. However, there has been minimal study of parents' preventive actions or the intentions that underlie their actions. It is not known whether parents' intentions are consistent with standard recommendations for reducing lead exposure, such as removing lead sources and interrupting pathways through which lead is delivered to children.[2,5,7] It is important to identify parents' actions, to determine their underlying intentions and to compare these intentions with professional recommendations. Health workers could utilize such information in teaching parents about prevention of childhood lead exposure.

To effectively guide parents' preventive actions, health workers need to be aware of factors that could influence parents' efforts. To attain a thorough epidemiologic understanding of lead exposure, researchers must understand the demographic circumstances of at-risk, vulnerable children who are not lead poisoned.[3,5,16] However, researchers have focused on variables associated with elevated blood lead levels (BLL 10 μg/dL).[8,10,14-18] Demographic characteristics, such as family income, may be associated with parental steps to reduce exposure, but predisposing factors such as knowledge, attitudes, and beliefs also may be associated with such behaviors.[19] For instance, parents may be more likely to try to reduce lead exposure if they know about lead's health risks, or if they believe that their children's exposure is excessive. Compared with parents of older children, parents of infants and toddlers may be more likely to take preventive action, if they are aware of the greater risks of lead exposure at younger ages.

Intensive study of parental involvement in reducing childhood lead exposure is needed to guide preventive strategies and to counterbalance the emphasis in the literature on professional interventions. Accordingly, the purposes of this study were to explore factors that may be associated with parental actions to reduce lead exposure in vulnerable, at-risk children who are not lead-poisoned and to identify the specific intentions undergirding parental actions to reduce lead exposure.

METHOD

Sample

Data reported in this article were obtained as part of a larger study of lead-exposure patterns among children who attended six public lead-screening clinics. The clinics were conducted by the Outagamie-Winnebago Lead (OWL) Program in Wisconsin.[20] A power analysis was done to determine the minimum sample size needed for the chi-square statistic. Because there were limited data concerning relationships among the study's variables (possible lead exposure and related parental knowledge, beliefs, and actions), the author sought a small effect size (.2). When power is .80, the sample size needed is 210, when $p = .05$ and u = 2.[21]

Nonprobability convenience sampling was undertaken. As parents registered their children at a lead-screening clinic, project staff explained the study and provided written information about it. Of 291 children who were registered, the parents of 274 (94.1%) children agreed to participate. After giving informed consent and while waiting for the blood test, parents completed a questionnaire concerning each child. Because this particular study pertained to children who were not lead-poisoned, the three children (1.2%) with elevated BLL (10 µg/dL)[6] were excluded from the sample. The BLLs of the 271 children in the sample were < 5 µg/dL, $n = 224$ (82.6%); 5–9 µg/dL, $n = 51$ (18.8%); and not obtained, $n = 6$ (2.2%). Other pertinent demographic data are shown in Table 2–1. The sample's ethnic diversity was consistent with that of Outagamie and Winnebago counties, as documented in the 1990 census.[22]

Instrument

The measurement goals were to obtain data by parental report concerning
- actions taken to reduce lead exposure;
- factors possibly related to these actions, such as knowledge of lead's risks and beliefs concerning the child's degree of exposure;
- the child's possible exposures; and
- demographic variables.

Consistent with these goals (and those of the larger study), a Lead Exposure Questionnaire (LEQ) was developed.[20] (Procedures used to estimate content validity, to attain acceptable readability, and to pilot the LEQ are described elsewhere.[20]) The

Table 2–1. Demographic characteristics of the sample (N = 271)

Variable	n	%
Family income		
> 100% poverty level for family size	218	80.4
< 100% poverty level for family size	48	17.8
Not reported	5	1.8
Location of home		
Rural*	169	62.4
Urban†	99	36.5
Not reported	3	1.1
Type of dwelling		
Owned or mortgaged home	220	81.2
Rented home or apartment	48	17.7
Not reported	3	1.1

*Rural = working farm, open countryside, or city of less than 2,500 persons.
†Urban = suburb or city with more than 2,500 persons.

LEQ included forced-choice questions on demographic factors, such as family income, type of dwelling (rented or owned),[16] and home location (rural or urban).[23] There were closed questions about possible exposures, such as living in a home built before 1960 that had peeling interior paint or playing in the soil near an older building.[7,14,17,18] With response options of "yes," "no," and "not sure," parents were asked:

- Do you think that your children are being exposed to too much lead?
- Are you taking special steps to reduce your children's exposure to lead?
- Before coming to this clinic, did you have information about the possible risks of lead to your children?

Finally, parents were asked to list any steps they were taking to reduce their children's exposure.

Quantitative data analysis

To determine factors associated with parental actions to reduce their children's exposure to lead, the author conducted chi-square tests with predisposing (cognitive) variables, demographic variables, and indicators of possible lead exposure. Cognitive variables that may have predisposed parents to action were prior knowledge of lead's risks to children and a belief that the child's exposure was excessive. These demographic variables were analyzed: family income (above or below poverty level for family size), home location (rural or urban), and type of dwelling (rent home or own home).

To reflect the children's lead exposure status, the author used two measures. Age (range: 6 months–9 years, M = 4.6, SD = 1.9) was used as a measure of vulnerability to lead poisoning. For reasons previously explained, age was categorized as 36 months or less (*n* = 89; 32.8%) and over 36 months (*n* = 178; 65.7%). As a measure of exposure risk, the sample's norm-referenced, summative scale of possible lead exposure was used. This scale, the Outagamie-Winnebago Lead Program lead exposure risk scale (OWLRISK), was developed from the 14 indicators of possible exposure reported by the parents of more than 25% of the children.[20] The indicators (Table 2–2) were related to these general categories:

- the neighborhood (eg, living near a busy highway),

- the home or other domiciliary structure (eg, exterior remodeling of the child's pre-1960 day-care center),
- the family (eg, parent with a lead-related job, such as welding), and
- the child's ingestion behaviors in the presence of a lead source (eg, playing in the soil near a pre-1960 building).

This scoring system was used for parents' responses concerning the child's contact with each indicator of possible lead exposure: "yes" = 3, "not sure" = 2, and "no" = 1. To determine each child's OWLRISK score, scores for the 14 items were summed. For OWLRISK (M =

Table 2–2. Indicators of possible lead exposure*

Source	*n*	%
Lives in a home built before 1960 (*n* = 172, 63.5%)		
Dust accumulates on woodwork	145	53.5
Interior has been remodeled since family moved to the home	119	43.9
Exterior paint is chipping or peeling	89	32.8
Interior paint is chipping or peeling	86	31.7
Some broken plaster	86	31.7
Interior being remodeled	75	27.7
Adult with whom child is in contact has lead-related job or hobby	105	38.8
Family lives near busy street	102	37.6
Family lives near busy highway	88	32.5
Child plays in the soil near a pre-1960 building	161	59.4
Lives in home with plumbing of lead pipes or solder joints, or lives in pre-1960 home that may have lead pipes; drinks hot or boiled tap water	95	35.1
Lives in pre-1960 home, regularly visits pre-1960 structure, or lives with an adult with a lead-related job and		
habitually puts open mouth on toys	93	34.3
habitually sucks own fingers	68	25.1
Eats paint, dirt, or sand	84	31.0

*Reported by the parents of > 25% of the sample

24.898, range = 28.00, SD = 6.12), the alpha coefficient was .728.[20] For this study, 271 OWLRISK scores were categorized as above the mean (n = 134) or below the mean (n = 137).

SPSS-X was used to calculate descriptive statistics and perform chi-square tests. The preestablished alpha level was .05. To estimate strength of relationships,[24] measures of association were used[25]; because all variables were nominal, phi (ϕ) was used for 2 × 2 tables, and Cramer's V (V) was used for rectangular tables.[25]

Qualitative data analysis

To identify the intentions underlying parents' steps to reduce lead exposure, the author used a qualitative strategy to analyze parents' written descriptions of their actions. The method was grounded in Husserl's phenomenologic philosophy,[26] in which it is assumed that experiences are structured by goal-oriented (or intentional) actions.[27] Giorgi's[28] four-step phenomenologic method was used. Based upon Husserl's philosophy, its purpose is to obtain a "consistent statement"[26(p11)] about an experience; it is appropriate for analysis of textual data.[26] Actions to reduce lead exposure were documented by 46 parents. Some parents cited more than one action, so the dataset consisted of 67 phrases. The first step was to study the dataset and develop a congruent perspective concerning the data. Next, meaning units, or "spontaneously perceived discriminations"[26(p11)] within the dataset, were specified; then the meaning units were used to categorize each parent's re-

sponse. The final step was to create a synthesis from the meaning units to reveal the insights that emerged from the analysis.[28]

RESULTS

Frequencies and demographic comparisons

Frequency data are shown for the variables of parental action and the two predisposing factors (Table 2–3). Compared with parents who reported that they had tried to reduce exposure, nearly twice as many parents reported that they had not done so. A majority of parents said that they had prior information about lead's risks to children. Most parents did not believe that their children's exposure was excessive. However, because the "unsure" responses constituted about a quarter of the sample, this category was included in all cross-tabulations of this variable.

Demographic factors were minimally associated with the two predisposing factors and parental action. Compared with urban parents, rural parents were not as likely to report having prior information about lead's risks (χ_2 = 3.29, df = 1, p = .070, ϕ = .12) and more likely to be taking steps to reduce exposure (χ_2 = 4.13, df = 1, p = .042, ϕ = .13); however, these associations were quite weak. The relationship between home location (rural or urban) and parental belief concerning exposure was not significant. Home ownership was related to parental belief about exposure (χ_2 = 7.60, df = 2, p = .022, ϕ = .17). Compared with owners, renters were more likely to be uncertain

Table 2–3. Frequency data for predisposing variables and parental action

	Response, n (%)		
	Yes	**No**	**Unsure**
Predisposing variables			
Has prior information on lead's risks to children	171 (63.1)	79 (29.1)	21 (7.8)
Believes child is "exposed to too much lead"	51 (18.8)	149 (55.0)	71 (26.2)
Parental action			
Taking "steps to reduce child's exposure to lead"	81 (29.9)	161 (59.4)	29 (10.7)

about the degree of exposure; owners were more likely to believe that exposure was not excessive. Family income was not related significantly to parental belief, and neither home ownership nor family income was significantly related to parental knowledge or action. Concerning demographics related to OWLRISK, the sample's normative measure of possible lead exposures, urban children were more likely than rural children to have scores above the mean ($\chi_2 = 7.37$, df = 1, $p = .007$, $\phi = .17$). Relationships between OWLRISK and the variables of home ownership and family income were not significant.

Relationships between parental action and predisposing variables

There was a moderate association between the predisposing variable of having prior information about lead risks and taking steps to reduce exposure ($\chi_2 = 27.70$, df = 1, $p = .000$, $\phi = .34$); parents who reported that they were informed were more likely than the other parents to report that they were taking action. A substantial association was found between reporting action to reduce exposure and the predisposing variable of belief that exposure was excessive. Compared with parents who did not believe that exposure was excessive, parents who reported this belief were much more likely to be trying to reduce exposure ($\chi_2 = 45.96$, df = 3, $p = .000$, $\phi = .44$).

Although parental action was related to both predisposing variables (prior information and belief that exposure was excessive), a significant relationship was not found between these two variables. However, it was feasible that prior information could have accounted for some of the covariation between the variables of belief and action. So, the relationship between action and belief was examined again, controlling for prior information. An interaction effect was found. Compared with the association between belief and action for the entire sample ($\phi = .44$, as reported previously), the association was stronger for parents who reported having prior information on lead's risks ($\phi = .47$) and weaker for parents who denied having such information ($\phi = .29$).

Lead exposure status

Scores on OWLRISK, the normative scale of lead exposure risk, were associated with parents' beliefs that exposure was excessive and with parental actions to reduce exposure. Parents whose children scored above the mean on OWLRISK were more likely to believe that exposure was excessive or to be unsure about the degree of exposure (χ_2 = 44.22, df = 2, p = .000, V = .404). There was a significant relationship between parental action and OWLRISK (χ_2 = 5.65, df = 1, p = .017, ϕ = .14). Compared with children whose parents were not taking action, children whose parents were taking action were more likely to have scored above the mean. The relationship between OWLRISK scores and prior parental information about lead risks was not significant (χ_2 = 1.76, df = 1, p = .185, ϕ = .08).

The measure of vulnerability for lead poisoning (the child's age) was not significantly related to the predisposing variables or to parental action to reduce exposure. Compared with parents of older children, parents of children 36 months of age or less were no more likely to report (a) being knowledgeable of lead's risks, (b) believing that the child's exposure was excessive, or (c) taking action to reduce exposure.

However, because children who have had multiple exposures to lead may be more vulnerable to its effects,[3] these analyses were repeated for the subsample of children (n = 134) with multiple exposures—those who scored above the mean on OWLRISK. For this subsample, the parents of younger children (n = 46) were no more likely than parents of older children (n = 88) to report prior knowledge of lead's risks (χ_2 = 2.36, df = 1, p = .125, ϕ = .14); a belief that exposure was excessive (χ_2 = 4.44, df = 2, p = .109, V = .18); or action to reduce exposure (χ_2 = 1.57, df = 1, p = .210, V = .12).

Intentions underlying parental actions

To identify the intentions underlying parental actions to reduce lead exposure, the author used Giorgi's phenomenologic method[28] to analyze parents' written explanations of their actions. Three intentions were identified as meaning units, and each parent's explanation was categorized as representative of a meaning unit (see Exhibit 2–1):

1. to create a living situation in which lead is not a threat to the child (n = 5);
2. to alter the home environment where lead may be present (n = 33); and
3. to protect the child from direct contact with a possible lead source (n = 29).

Finally, a synthesis of the three meaning units was created by comparing and contrasting parental intentions. Each intention was understood as a linkage between two of these key concepts: the child, the lead source, and the child's environment. This synthesis was expressed in a Model of Parental Control of Childhood Lead Exposure (Fig 2–1). Some parental actions were centered around the child–environment interaction. These steps were intended to create a living

Exhibit 2-1 Parents' Explanations of Steps Being Taken To Reduce Children's Exposure to Lead: Categorized by Intention

Intention 1: To create a living situation in which lead is not a threat to the child:
Painting house with water-soluble paint
Replumbing (x 3)
Living in newer house

Intention 2: To alter the home environment where lead may be present:
Putting filters on water system (x 5)
Covering lead paint with new paint (x 5); new paint on woodwork; repainting (x 5)
Removing old paint (x 2)
Remodeling (x 2); remodeling to remove or cover lead sources (x 2)
Cleaning [the older home] as much as possible (x 2); keeping [paint] chips cleaned up

Intention 3: To protect the child from direct contact with a possible lead source
Limiting amount of tap water (x 2)
Trying to let tap water run awhile before using (x 4)
Drinking bottled water (x 3)
Washing toys
Keeping child out of house for [repainting/remodeling] (x 2)
Trying to keep child out of area being remodeled
Minimizing child's exposure to old homes and areas
Making sure child does not bite on painted wall and woodwork

situation in which lead was not a threat to the child; one parent explained that the family lived "in a newer house." When concern was focused upon a particular lead source, parents tried to alter the environment where lead could exist; for instance, some parents installed water filters. Finally, other parents identified a potential or actual lead source that could affect the child, and they took steps to protect the child from the lead; one parent was "mak[ing] sure they don't bite on paint[ed] wall and woodwork."

DISCUSSION

In this study of 271 children who were not lead-poisoned, interesting relationships were found between several variables and parents' reports that they had taken action to reduce exposure. Associated with parental action to reduce lead exposure were two variables that could predispose parents to action: prior information about lead's risks and a belief that the children were being exposed to excessive lead.

Several methodological aspects of this descriptive study are limits upon its generalizability. First, the frequency and variety of parental actions may have been underreported because examples of relevant actions were not included on the LEQ. Some parents may not have reported housekeeping activities that actually were controlling lead exposure, if they were not aware of the possible beneficial effects. Data were obtained from parents whose children did not have elevated lead levels; comparative study should be done with parents whose children have elevated levels.

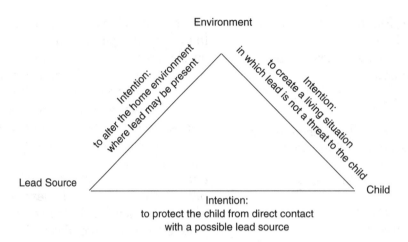

Environment

Intention: to alter the home environment where lead may be present

Intention: to create a living situation in which lead is not a threat to the child

Lead Source

Child

Intention:
to protect the child from direct contact
with a possible lead source

Fig 2-1. Model of parental control of childhood lead exposure.

Consistent with phenomenologic methodology,[26,28] a theoretical framework was not adopted to guide this study. Variables such as prior knowledge, beliefs about the degree of lead exposure, and action to reduce lead exposure may be viewed as similar to key constructs of the Health Belief Model (HBM).[29] However, the study's thrust was descriptive, rather than predictive as in the HBM tradition.[30] Rather than focusing upon parents' current subjective status[30] (eg, their perceived motivation to reduce lead exposure as a result of attending the screening clinic), the author addressed their historic and ongoing experience as parents. Although associations were described between parents' actions and related beliefs and prior knowledge, the study was not designed to predict their actions. Other researchers could test the HBM if they chose to predict parents' preventive actions in particular situations; study of parents' perceived self-ef-

ficacy[31] in controlling exposure would be valuable.

Although the study has limitations, its findings are evidence of the importance of providing information to parents about lead's risks. Indeed, Glotzer and Weitzman emphasized that "families of all children, including those with BLL < 10 μg/dL, should receive anticipatory guidance regarding the hazards and likely sources of lead exposure."[32(p631)] In this study, parents of more than one third of the children denied having such information prior to the screening clinic, although parents who choose to attend such clinics may be more informed than those who do not attend. Because of the variation in sources of potential exposure, health care providers must ensure that the information provided is directly relevant to the child's likely sources of exposure.

A strong relationship was demonstrated between parental belief that children were being exposed to too much lead and parental actions to reduce exposure. This finding may be specific to this sample, but community health workers should investigate it within their jurisdictions. When warranted by the regional prevalence of certain lead sources, interventions could be designed to foster specific parental beliefs about lead exposure. For instance, media campaigns could be designed to emphasize the prevalence of specific environmental lead sources.

In this sample, parental belief that exposure was excessive was not related to knowledge of lead's risks. Because both predisposing variables influenced parental action, their relationship should be explored further, and other similar variables need to be studied. Compared with knowledge of lead's risks, knowledge of potential lead sources may be more central to parents' belief that exposure is excessive. Accordingly, practitioners' counseling should be case-specific; parents may need assistance in identifying potential lead sources in the child's environment.

The children whose parents were concerned about excessive exposure were more likely to have above-average scores on a sample-specific scale of possible exposure. Evidence of this relationship was anticipated, because parents who reported a general concern about excessive exposure would be likely to give more affirmative responses to specific questions about exposure sources. Parental action also was associated with above-the-mean scores on the sample's scale of lead exposure. For this sample, there was consistency between parents' reports concerning the children's exposure status, their beliefs about it, and their actions in relation to it.

For both the entire sample and for children with above-average scores on the lead exposure scale, age was not significantly related to prior information about lead's risks, to belief that exposure was excessive, or to parental action. Because children under age 3 are a vulnerable population group at-risk for lead exposure, health workers should determine if parents of younger children in their communities have the knowledge they need to reduce exposure. If not, health workers could create appropriate interventions; for instance, parents of toddlers could be taught to wash the child's hands often if lead dust is prevalent in the child's environment; such interim control measures have been found to be successful in reducing lead levels.[33]

Most parents of children with multiple lead exposures reported that they were taking action to reduce exposure before they came to the clinic. About 20% of the children had BLLs ranging from 5 to 9 μg/dL, approaching 10 μg/dL. Although the extent to which the parents' actions had moderated the BLL is unknown, this possibility must be considered; when an older home is well maintained, BLL can be low, even when lead is present.[33] Parents' actions may influence whether a lead source becomes an actual risk to the child's health.

The perspective that parents may be key actors in the prevention of childhood lead exposure is important, because it undergirds a nontraditional understanding of the phenomenon of lead poisoning. Researchers have been puzzled when children with similar exposures do not have comparable BLLs.[14,23,33,34] Variations in BLL usually have been "attributed to the degree of environmental lead exposure"[23(p281)] or to demographic characteristics, such as ethnicity or income.[12,23] Few scholars have cited parents' preventive actions as possible influences on BLL.

However, as demonstrated here, it is important to consider exposures, demographic characteristics, and parental actions as influences upon BLLs. In this study, for example, urban parents were more likely than rural parents to have information about lead risks, but they were less likely to be taking action to reduce exposure. However, on the average, urban children had higher OWLRISK scores; they had more possible lead exposures than did the rural children. Community health workers need to obtain and use such data to target preventive interventions effectively within diverse communities. It is critical to appraise children's exposures in the context of both demographic parameters and data relevant to parents' preventive actions.

Parental action to reduce lead exposure is a probable contributor to the public's health, but its impact cannot be revealed unless data about parental actions are obtained during screening opportunities. The typical lead screening tools[5] consist of questions about lead sources; the underlying assumption is that if a lead source is found, a risk for lead poisoning has been identified. For example, practitioners are to ask if the child lives in an older home with peeling paint[5]; an affirmative answer means a risk for lead poisoning. However, if parents have tried to control this exposure, the degree of risk from the source may have been minimized, and the BLL may not be elevated. In such cases, the lead source itself is not a valid indicator of the construct "lead poisoning risk." An affirmative response to any question concerning lead exposure, in the absence of an elevated BLL, results in a reduced specificity of the screening tool. Accordingly, lead screening procedures should be modified. To gather a "careful and explicit lead exposure history,"[16(p71)] practitioners should do more than assess possible lead exposures. They also should assess parental knowledge of lead sources and beliefs about the degree of the child's exposure; providers also should determine whether parents are taking steps to reduce possible exposure.

The Model of Parental Control of Childhood Lead Exposure is presented for the "confirmation or criticism"[28(p19)] of other researchers, as is to be done with a phenomenologic synthesis. The model's configuration is that of the epidemiologic triad, but its elements are comparable to those of a hazard control model: source, environment, and worker.[35] A hazard control model is designed to emphasize the impact of each element,[35] but the Model of Parental Control of Lead Exposure was configured to highlight linkages between its three elements (lead source, environment, and child). The model is a depiction of these relationships, which are grounds for parents' intentional actions to reduce lead exposure. Therefore, the model may be an appropriate framework for interventions to foster parental control of childhood lead exposure. The intentions can be used as guides in teaching parents how to protect their children from direct contact with lead. A field study of parents' experience of controlling lead exposure should be done to further explore these intentions and to identify other intentions to incorporate into the model.

• • •

The three parental intentions described in this study are correspondent with the public health goal of interrupting pathways through which lead can be delivered to children.[2,5,7] However, the potential effectiveness of each parental action can be appraised only in relation to that child's specific exposures; this is an important topic for further research. Even when the appropriateness of an action is in question, however, practitioners should consider the thrust of the underlying intention. Parents who *intend* to protect their child from lead sources can be affirmed in that goal and guided to select actions consistent with that intention.

When evaluating a child's lead poisoning risk, practitioners should consider lead sources as relative phenomena that occur within a fluctuating context of parental knowledge, parental beliefs, and parental actions. The most effective strategy in controlling BLL is to prevent an initial elevation.[36] To promote parental prevention of childhood lead exposure, professionals should seek to understand the factors associated with parents' actions and acknowledge the intentions underlying those actions.

REFERENCES

1. Lybarger JA, Spengler RF, DeRosa CT. *Priority Health Conditions.* Washington, DC: Agency for Toxic Substances and Disease Registry; 1993.
2. National Academy of Sciences, Committee on Lead in the Human Environment. *Lead in the Human Environment.* Washington, DC: NAS; 1980.
3. Agency for Toxic Substances and Disease Registry. *The Nature and Extent of Lead Poisoning in Children in the United States: A Report to Congress.* Atlanta, Ga: ATSDR; 1988.
4. Environmental Protection Agency. *Air Quality Criteria for Lead.* Research Triangle Park, NC: Office of Health and Environmental Assessment; 1986. EPA Report no. EPA/600/8-83/028aF.
5. Centers for Disease Control and Prevention. *Preventing Lead Poisoning in Young Children.* Atlanta, Ga: CDC; 1991.
6. Porter EJ. Administrative diagnosis—implications for the public's health. *Public Health Nurs.* 1987; 4:247–256.
7. Morgan LL. Children and lead: a model of care for community health and primary care providers. *Fam Community Health.* 1996;19(1):42–48.
8. Binns HJ, LeBailly SA, Poncher J, Kinsella R, Saunders S, the Pediatric Practice Research Group. Is there lead in the suburbs? Risk assessment in Chicago suburban pediatric practices. *Pediatrics.* 1994;93:164–171.
9. Committee on Environmental Health, American Academy of Pediatrics. Lead poisoning: from screening to primary prevention. *Pediatrics.* 1993; 92:176–183.
10. Schirmer J, Anderson H, Peterson DE. Childhood lead exposure in Wisconsin in 1990. *Wisconsin Med J.* 1991 (Jan);31–34.
11. Pope AM, Snyder MA, Mood LH. *Nursing, Health, and the Environment: Strengthening the Relationship to Improve the Public's Health.* Washington, DC: National Academy Press; 1995.
12. Bar-on ME, Boyle RM. Are pediatricians ready for the new guidelines on lead poisoning? *Pediatrics.* 1994;93:178–182.
13. Harvey B. Commentary: should blood lead screening recommendations be revised? *Pediatrics.* 1994;93:201–204.

14. Rooney BL, Hayes EB, Allen BK, Strutt PJ. Development of a screening tool for prediction of children at risk for lead exposure in a Midwestern clinical setting. *Pediatrics*. 1994;93:183–187.

15. Sargent JD, Brown MJ, Freeman JL, Bailey A, Goodman D, Freeman DH. Childhood lead poisoning in Massachusetts communities: its association with sociodemographic and housing characteristics. *Am J Public Health*. 1995;85:528–534.

16. Gellert GA, Wagner GA, Maxwell RM, Moore D, Foster L. Lead poisoning among low-income children in Orange County, California: a need for regionally differentiated policy. *JAMA*. 1993;270:69–71.

17. Schaffer SJ, Szilagyi PG, Weitzman M. Lead poisoning risk determination in an urban population through the use of a standardized questionnaire. *Pediatrics*. 1994;93:159–163.

18. Bellinger D, Leviton A, Rabinowitz M, Needleman H, Waternaux C. Correlates of low-level lead exposure in urban children at 2 years of age. *Pediatrics*. 1986;77:826–833.

19. Green LW, Kreutzer MW, Deeds SG, Partridge KB. *Health Education Planning: A Diagnostic Approach*. Palo Alto, Calif: Mayfield; 1980.

20. Porter EJ, Severtson D. Indicators of possible lead exposure among children attending public lead screening clinics: implications for primary prevention. *Public Health Nurs*. 1997;14:12–19.

21. Cohen J. *Statistical Power Analysis for the Behavioral Sciences*, ed 2. Hillsdale, NJ: Lawrence Erlbaum Associates; 1988.

22. US Bureau of the Census. *1990 U.S. Census Data. Database: C90STF1A*. (Summary Level: State-County) [On-line];1992 (last update, Dec 1996). http://venus.census.gov/cdrom/lookup.

23. Brody DJ, Pirkle JL, Kramer RA, et al. Blood lead levels in the US population: phase 1 of the third National Health and Nutrition Examination Survey (NHANES III, 1988 to 1991). *JAMA*. 1994;272:277–283.

24. Duggan TJ, Dean CW. Common misinterpretations of significance levels in sociological journals. In: Miller DC, ed. *Handbook of Research Design and Social Measurement*. Newbury Park, Calif: Sage; 1991.

25. Bohrnstedt GW, Knoke D. *Statistics for Social Data Analysis*. Itasca, Ill: FE Peacock; 1982.

26. Husserl E; Gibson WRB, trans. *Ideas: General Introduction to Pure Phenomenology*. New York: Macmillan; 1963.

27. Kohak E. *Ideas and Experience*. Chicago, Ill: The University of Chicago Press; 1978.

28. Giorgi A. Sketch of a psychological phenomenological method. In: Giorgi A, ed. *Phenomenology and Psychological Research*. Pittsburgh, Pa: Duquesne University Press; 1985.

29. Becker MH. *The Health Belief Model and Personal Health Behavior*. Thorofare, NJ: Charles B. Slack; 1974.

30. Thomas LW. A critical feminist perspective of the health belief model: implications for nursing theory, research, practice, and education. *J Prof Nurs*. 1995;11:246–252.

31. Rosenstock IM, Stetcher UJ, Becker MH. Social learning theory on the health belief model. *Health Educ Q*. 1988;15:175–183.

32. Glotzer DE, Weitzman M. Commonly asked questions about childhood lead poisoning. *Pediatr Ann*. 1995;24:630–639.

33. Kimbrough RD, LeVois M, Webb DR. Management of children with slightly elevated blood lead levels. *Pediatrics*. 1994;93:188–191.

34. Nordin JD, Rolnick SJ, Griffin JM. Prevalence of excess lead absorption and associated risk factors in children enrolled in a Midwestern health maintenance organization. *Pediatrics*. 1994;93:172–177.

35. Weeks JL, Levy BS, Wagner GR. A public health approach to preventing occupational diseases and injuries. In: Weeks JL, Levy BS, Wagner GR, eds. *Preventing Occupational Disease and Injury*. Washington, DC: American Public Health Association; 1991.

36. Swindell SL, Charney E, Brown MJ, Delaney J. Home abatement and blood lead changes in children with class III lead poisoning. *Clin Pediatr*. 1994;33:536–541.

CHAPTER 3

Correlates of Violent and Nonviolent Behavior among Vulnerable Inner-City Youths

Kathleen B. Powell, PhD, RN

AMERICA TODAY IS experiencing a major epidemic of death and trauma from violence. Homicide has become the 10th leading cause of death in the United States and the 6th leading cause of years of potential life lost. Among young people 15 to 24 years of age, homicide is the second leading cause of death, surpassed only by unintentional injuries. Furthermore, the homicide rate among young males in the United States is roughly 20 times higher than homicide rates in most other industrialized nations.[1-3]

Youths in minority communities are at particular risk for homicide. Among African American male youths, homicide is seven to eight times higher than among Caucasian males, and homicide rates for African American female youths are

This study was supported in part by the Southeast Child Safety Institute at Children's Hospital and by Grant R49/CCr403641 from the US Department of Health and Human Services, Centers for Disease Control and Prevention—National Center for Injury Prevention to The University of Alabama at Birmingham, Injury Control Research Center.

Fam Community Health 1997;20(2):38–47

three to four times higher than among Caucasian females.[4]

The urgent need to prevent destruction of young lives by violence has led to a proliferation of antiviolence interventions for children, youths, and their families. However, many of these programs were created without scientific underpinnings.[5] This study serves to strengthen the theoretic understanding of violent and nonviolent behavior.

REVIEW OF LITERATURE

Recent studies have focused on determinants of violent behavior. Increased fighting and weapon carrying have been associated with age, male gender, African American and Hispanic ethnicity, substance use, gang membership, exposure to violence, victimization, hopelessness, and low academic performance.[6-10] Poverty has often been recognized as a factor that contributes to violent behavior.[4,11,12] Poverty leads to life circumstances that deny youth opportunities such as a social support system, effective role models, educational opportunities, and a hopeful future.

Yet, some youths raised under these same conditions show amazing resiliency in overcoming negative life circumstances without turning to violence. Influences in their lives appear to act as buffers against the negative social forces they encounter. This can in some instances be attributed to the presence of protective or mediating factors, which, according to Rutter,[13] serve to moderate, buffer, insulate against, and thereby mitigate the impact of risk on adolescent behavior. It is most likely that these adolescents' exposure to risk is countered by exposure to protective or mediating factors that buffer the risk and that foster resiliency.

The conceptual role of mediating factors is to help explain that many adolescents do not succumb to violence, or are less involved with it than their peers, or if involved, seem to abandon it more readily than others.[14] The role of these protective or mediating factors and their impact in preventing violent behavior have received little attention from researchers and are promising areas for research.[15,16]

This study examined the concepts of social support, religiosity, and participation in extracurricular activities as protective factors. Although other studies have noted relationships between these areas and resiliency, general well-being, or health-promoting behaviors in adolescents, their relationship as potential mediators of violent behavior has not been reported.[17-23]

RESEARCH QUESTIONS

The following research questions directed the study:

- Is there a relationship between nonviolent behaviors and social support?
- Is there a relationship between nonviolent behaviors and exposure to violence?
- Is there a relationship between nonviolent behaviors and religiosity?
- Is there a relationship between nonviolent behaviors and gang membership?
- Is there a relationship between nonviolent behaviors and participation in extracurricular activities?

- Is there a set of variables associated with nonviolent behaviors?

METHODS

This cross-sectional research study was conducted in a Southeast city with a population of 265,968. Youths within this area are particularly vulnerable to violence due to the incidence and intensity of violent crime around them. The city has been ranked as one of the five worst cities, with a population of over 250,000, in relation to rapes and murders.[24] High-risk geographic areas within the city were further identified utilizing data collected by Reynolds and associates,[25] which examined demographic variables related to violent youth firearm injuries. In addition, the metropolitan city school system examined each of the 79 schools under its jurisdiction. Every school's risk status for violence was considered based on the number of student conduct code violations documented for that school year. Based on these two considerations, students attending two middle schools and two high schools were identified as vulnerable targets, along with students from two elementary schools that feed into the target middle schools. Permission to conduct the study was obtained from the Institutional Review Board at the University of Alabama in Birmingham and the city school system.

Fifty percent of the classes of 5th, 7th, 9th, and 11th grades from these six target schools were randomly chosen to make up the study population. A stratified grade sample was selected in order to examine the relationship between age and violent behavior. All students enrolled in the randomly selected classes were invited to participate in the study. The researcher visited randomly selected student classrooms, explained the purpose of the study, answered student questions, and distributed consent forms to be signed by the student and parent or legal guardian. All students who returned signed consent forms were eligible to participate in the study. Of 1,286 students who were invited to participate in the study and who received consent forms, 521 students returned signed consent forms, were present on testing days, and completed questionnaires (a 41% response rate).

The questionnaire was read aloud to 5th and 7th graders in the event that the 5th-grade reading level of the instrument had not been attained. Ninth and 11th graders silently read the questionnaire and responded at their own pace. Physically and mentally challenged students were identified by school personnel and attended to on an individual basis.

Representativeness of the sample was assessed by comparing the demographics of the study population with that of the selected target schools and with that of the other 79 schools within the city school system. Comparison between the study sample and the sociodemographic characteristics of the target schools indicated that the sample was representative of these schools (Table 3–1).

INSTRUMENTATION

Based on a literature review, an instrument was developed by combining previously used scales that were found to be reliable with similar populations and investigator-developed questions. The instrument was assessed for content validity by a group of experts and piloted for use in the selected city school system with a group similar in demographics to the target groups. Following completion of pilot testing, internal consistency measures were determined for scales.

The questionnaire addressed
- demographic information;
- exposure to violence;
- violent and nonviolent behavior;
- religiosity;
- social support;
- gang membership; and
- participation in extracurricular activities.

Exposure to violence was determined by dichotomizing the responses of nine questions that assessed exposure to violence. Each positive response produced a score of 1, and a total sum score reflected an overall exposure to violence score.

Violent and nonviolent behavior was determined by dividing students into four mutually exclusive, violence-related categories:
- *Group 0 (most nonviolent)*—students who were not involved in a physical fight in the past 12 months and did not carry a weapon in the past 30 days.
- *Group 1 (nonviolent)*—students who were involved in a physical fight at least once in the past 12 months, but did not carry a weapon in the past 30 days.
- *Group 2 (violent)*—students who carried a weapon (handgun or other guns; knife or razor; club stick, bat, or pipe) at least once in the past 30 days, but were not involved in a physical fight in the past 12 months.
- *Group 3 (most violent)*—students who both carried a weapon in the past 30 days and were involved in a physical fight in the past 12 months.

Religiosity was assessed with two self-report items. One of the items measured attitudes or importance of religion in the respondent's life, while the other mea-

Table 3–1. Demographic characteristics of population

Variable	Sample, %	Target schools, %	Other city schools, %
Ethnicity			
African American	95.91	93.80	91.55
Caucasian	1.95	1.99	7.95
Other	2.14	0.43	0.49
Gender			
Male	37.84	49.83	50.00
Female	62.16	50.16	50.00
Participation in reduced-price or free lunch program	62.98	70.83	70.00

sured frequency of attendance at religious services.

Social support was measured with a scale that ranked various individuals' helpfulness in providing care and emotional support if the respondent needed it. This scale lists 16 sources of social support, which fall into three main categories:

1. peer support, including support from same- and opposite-sex friends;
2. family support, including support from relatives; and
3. adult support, including support from teachers, coaches, etc.

A total score for social support was derived by summing individual rankings (ranging from 0–5) on 16 items yielding a range of 0 to 80. Family social support was determined by summing individual rankings on eight items, producing a range of 0 to 40. Adult social support considered rankings of five items with a range of 0 to 25, and peer social support summed rankings of three items yielding a range of 0 to 15. Internal reliability of this scale was .77 as determined by Cronbach's alpha.

Gang membership was assessed by two self-report items that explored respondent's current and prior gang membership status and the involvement in gangs by friends and family members.

Participation in extracurricular activities was assessed with a 16-item scale used to indicate participation, within the past 12 months in a variety of activities, including academic clubs, sports, or community organizations. Total score was determined by summing the number of activities in which subjects participated. The internal consistency of this scale was .71, as determined by Cronbach's alpha.

DATA ANALYSIS

Initial descriptive statistics were calculated to determine prevalence data. Derived variables were created and compared across violence categories; and analysis of variance (ANOVA) was utilized to compare differences across groups. All variables were then entered into a backward elimination multiple logistic regression analysis, and a model with adjusted odds ratios was derived.

RESULTS

Seventy-nine percent of respondents were categorized as nonviolent, with 48% falling into group 0 (most nonviolent) and 31% into group 1 (nonviolent). The remaining 20% were categorized as violent, with 7% falling into group 2 (violent) and 13% into group 3 (most violent).

Demographics, except for age and gender, were not significantly related to violent behavior. Age was significant with younger teens exhibiting more nonviolent behaviors. The majority of female respondents (70%) fell into group 0, the most nonviolent category, while the majority of males (60%) fell into group 3, the most violent category. As violent behavior increased, the percentage of male involvement increased.

Overall, social support did not prove to be significantly related to violent behavior. When social support subscales were examined, peer and family support remained insignificant. However, adult social support emerged as a variable significantly related to violent behavior.

ANOVA revealed a statistically significant relationship $(f = 43.71)$ $(df = 3, 514)$ between violence categories and exposure to violence. Exposure was significantly different between each of the violence groups, with the total amount of exposure increasing steadily as participation in violence increased.

Violence categories were found to be significantly associated with religiosity on bivariate analysis. Although one aspect of religiosity, church attendance, was removed in the logistic regression analysis, the other aspect, attitude toward religion, remained a significant factor in the final model.

A statistically significant difference $(f = 41.12)$ $(df = 3, 514)$ was also noted between violence categories and gang membership. While only 10% of nonviolent respondents reported involvement as gang members, 30% to 50% of the violent respondents reported positive gang membership status. A significant statistical difference was also observed between the violence categories and the number of gang members among family and friends $(f = 17.30)$ $(df = 3, 508)$. The percentage of subjects reporting family and friend gang members increased steadily as violent behavior increased. Utilizing ANOVA, no statistically significant difference at the $\alpha = .05$ level was found between violence categories and participation in extracurricular activities.

In an attempt to identify a set of variables associated with violent behavior, the author entered all independent variables into a logistic regression analysis using a backward elimination procedure. This analysis generated model statistics and adjusted odds ratio that derived an equation that proved effective in predicting nonviolent and violent behavior 90% of the time. Church attendance, extracurricular activity participation, and family social support were backed out of the model. All other variables remained significant at the $\alpha = .05$ level (Table 3–2). Adult support, age, and religion emerged as protective factors or mediators against violence and are indicated by negative beta values. Other variables represent risk factors, or factors that contribute to violence, and are represented by positive beta values.

DISCUSSION

Demographic findings of this study are consistent with other research studies that identify 15- to 19-year-old youths as those at highest risk for violent injury[25,26] and male gender as a risk factor for violent behavior.[26–28]

The absence of a statistically significant relationship between family support and violent behavior is unexpected since most research cites family support as a factor that may mediate risk in this population.[29,30] This could be related to a methodological issue because in this study, family support encompassed a wide range of individuals. However, it is interesting to note that a strong relationship was found between violent youth and the number of family and friends who participated in gangs.

Table 3–2. Variables in regression equation

Variable	Beta	Standard error	p	Odds ratio	95% Confidence interval
n = 521					
Adult support*	−0.1172	0.0401	0.00	0.1106	.032, .189
Age*	−0.4379	0.12	0.00	0.3546	.119, .590
Violence exposure	0.9987	0.1772	0.00	1.7148	1.368, 2.062
Friend or family gang members	0.4201	0.1935	0.03	0.5221	.143, .901
Gang membership	0.9521	0.3369	0.00	1.5911	.931, 2.251
Peer support	0.1452	0.0651	0.03	0.1562	.029, .284
Religion*	−0.4692	0.2409	0.05	0.3745	0.98, .847
Gender	1.5885	0.4983	0.00	3.8962	2.920, 4.873

*Protective factors or mediators against violent behavior.

The consistency of peer support across violence categories is not surprising because approval of peers is commonly sought among this age group. In fact, this finding is supported by literature that suggests that antisocial children who lack social approval among one peer group will band together to form deviant groups that share commonalities.[31,32]

The relationship observed between violence categories and adult support indicates that adult support from a source outside of the family may mediate risky violent behavior. Other researchers have noted that relationships with adults who model positive social behavior may act as a protective factor for children who are at risk for violence.[31,32] In this study, potentially influential adults included teachers, school counselors, principals and assistant principals, clergy, and other adult friends.

Exposure to violence findings are also consistent with those noted by other researchers who identify violent youth as those most likely to be injured or to injure others through violent acts.[6,33] Due to the nature of this cross-sectional data, it is not possible to determine if exposure to violence evokes violent behavior or if violent behavior leads to an increase in exposure to violence.

The relationship observed between religiosity and nonviolent behavior has been noted by other researchers who cite commitment to conventional institutions, such as church, as a mediating factor for risk behavior.[20] It has been suggested that participation in these institutions fosters the behaviors promoted by them, although church attendance did not remain significant in the final logistic model of this study. Youths who value the importance of religion may also share comparable beliefs regarding the value of human life.

The statistically significant difference found between violence categories and gang membership has been substantiated by other studies that note relationships between violent injuries and gang activity.[7,34,35] The relationship noted in this study, however, does expand the field of gang-related research by identifying a relationship between living, noninjured, nonincarcerated youth and violent behavior.

The absence of a statistically significant difference between violent categories and extracurricular activities is unexpected since other researchers have inferred that extracurricular activities may mediate risky behaviors.[36–39] The scale that assessed involvement in this study was broad and encompassed school activities, sports, church, community or civic activities, and employment. It is possible that only selected activities act as mediating factors within this population.

A set of variables associated with nonviolent behaviors emerged upon logistic regression. Adult social support, importance of religion, female gender, and younger ages were found to be mediators of violent behavior while peer social support, gang membership, family or friend gang members, and exposure to violence were found to be risk factors for violent behavior.

This study supports risk factors for violence that have been documented by previous studies including older youth, male gender, exposure to violence, and association with gangs. It also suggests that the existence of certain factors, adult support and religion, can be effective in promoting nonviolent behavior in a group of vulnerable inner-city youth.

• • •

Study findings must be interpreted in light of certain limitations. Foremost, this study used a cross-sectional research design that prevents the inference of causality. The study subjects were predominantly African Americans and were restricted to those attending school on the day of data collection, which limits the generalizability of findings. Lastly, the results are based on self-reporting data with no corroborative information.

The results of this study provide some implications for practice that may be helpful in developing violence intervention programs. It supports the premise that protective factors can be effective forces in reducing risk for violence. Therefore, violence intervention programs should be designed in a framework that can simultaneously reduce risk and promote protection. Since the presence of a relationship with a positive adult may prove instrumental in mediating violent behavior, this study supports schools and churches investing in individuals who exhibit and promote nonviolent attitudes and behaviors, as well as continuing education opportunities for those individuals aimed at enhancing effective communication. It suggests that younger teens, particularly males, should be targeted in an attempt to prevent them from becoming violent. Interventions should consider developmental "windows of opportunity," points at which prevention programs may make a difference. Finally, it supports the premise that community programs should be the central focus point for intervention efforts. Schools and churches provide two avenues for reaching youth, but success of interventions will be enhanced if resources within the community are working together to meet the same goal.

Future studies should expand research to include youth in urban and suburban areas, those not attending school, and those with other ethnic backgrounds in order to determine generalizability of the results. Males should be further studied since they are at highest risk for violence and are slightly underrepresented in this study. The study of resiliency factors in vulnerable youths also needs to be expanded to identify other variables amenable to intervention such as school achievement and self-esteem.

There is a need for greater research in the area of resiliency. In a real sense, resiliency research is an evaluation of what is "working right" in the lives of these youths. The identification of these mediators of violence or determinants of nonviolence lend support to the need for violence intervention programs that are community based and cross all levels of life.

REFERENCES

1. Mortality trends and leading causes of death among adolescents and young adults—United States, 1979-1988. *MMWR*. 1993; 42:459–462.

2. Rachuba L, Stanton B, Howard D. Violent crime in the United States. An epidemiologic profile. *Arch Pediatr Adolesc Med*. 1995;149:953–960.

3. Rosenburg M. Violence in America: an integrated approach to understanding and prevention. *J Health Care Poor Underserved*. 1995;6:102–110.

4. Novello A. Violence is a greater killer of children than disease. *Public Health Rep*. 1991;106:231–233.

5. Hill HM, Soriano FI, Chen SA. Social and cultural factors in youth violence. In: *Report of the American Psychological Association Commission on Violence and Youth*, vol. I. Washington, DC: APA; 1993.

6. Durant R, Cadenhead C, Pendergrast R, Slavens G, Linder C. Factors associated with the use of violence among urban Black adolescents. *Am J Public Health*. 1994;84:612–617.

7. Lyon J, Henggler S, Hall J. The family relations, peer relations, and criminal activities of Caucasian and Hispanic American gang members. *J Abnormal Child Psychol*. 1992;20:439–449.

8. Orpinas P, Basen-Engquist K, Grunbaum J, Parcel G. The co-morbidity of violence-related behaviors with health-risk behaviors in a population of high school students. *J Adolesc Health*. 1995;16:216–225.

9. Sosin D, Koepsell T, Rivara F, Mercy J. Fighting as a marker for multiple problem behaviors in adolescents. *J Adolesc Health*. 1995;16:209–215.

10. Valois R, Vincent M, McKeown R, Garrison C, Kirby S. Adolescent risk behaviors and the potential for violence: a look at what's coming to campus. *J Amer College Health*. 1993;41:141–147.

11. Roberts C, Quillian J. Preventing violence through primary care intervention. *Health Care Issues*. 1992;17:62–70.

12. Spivak H, Hausman A, Prothrow-Stith D. Practitioners' forum: public health and the primary prevention of adolescent violence—the violence prevention project. *Violence Victims*. 1989;4:203–211.

13. Rutter M. Psychosocial resilience and protective mechanisms. In: Rolf J, et al, eds. *Risk and Protective Factors in the Development of Psychopathology*. Cambridge, UK: Cambridge University Press; 1990.

14. Jessor R. Risk behavior in adolescence: a psychosocial framework for understanding and action. *J Adolesc Health*. 1991;12:597–605.

15. Becker JV, Barham J, Eron LD, Chen SA. Present status and future directions for psychological research on youth violence. In: *Report of the American Psychological Association Commission on Violence and Youth*, vol. I. Washington, DC: APA; 1993.

16. Jenkins E, Bell C. Adolescent violence: can it be curbed? *Adolesc Med.* 1992;3:71–86.

17. Yarcheski A, Scoloveno M, Mahon N. Social support and well-being in adolescents: the mediating role of hopefulness. *Nurs Res.* 1994;43:288–292.

18. Seifer R, Sameroff A, Baldwin C, Baldwin A. Child and family factors that ameliorate risk between 4 and 13 years of age. *J Am Acad Child Adolesc Psychiatry.* 1992;31:893–903.

19. Resnick M, Harris L, Blum F. The impact of caring and connectedness on adolescent health and well being. *J Pediatr Child Health.* 1993;29:S3–S9.

20. Donovan J, Jessor R, Costa F. Adolescent health behavior and conventionality–unconventionality: an extension of problem-behavior theory. *Health Psychol.* 1991;10:52–61.

21. Federal Advisory Panel on Health Promotion Strategies for High-Risk Youth. Designing health promotion approaches to high-risk adolescents through formative research with youth and parents. *Public Health Rep.* 1993;108:68–77.

22. Luthar S, Zigler E. Vulnerability and competence: a review of research on resilience in childhood. *Am J Orthopsychiatry.* 1991;61:6–22.

23. Bernard B. Fostering resiliency in kids: protective factors in the family, school, and community. *Prevention Forum.* 1992;12:1–16.

24. Smolowe J. Danger in the safety zone. *Time.* 1993;142:29–33.

25. Reynolds D, King WD, Brissie R. *Firearm Mortality in Jefferson County, Alabama Youth: A Six-Year Review.* Presented at the meeting of the American Academy of Pediatrics; Washington, DC; October 1993.

26. Christoffel K. Pediatric firearm injuries: time to target a growing population. *Pediatr Ann.* 1992; 10:52–61.

27. Behaviors related to unintentional and intentional injuries among high school students–United States, 1991. *MMWR.* 1992;41:760–765, 771–772.

28. Hausman A, Spivak H, Prothrow-Stith D. Adolescents' knowledge and attitudes about and experience with violence. *J Adolesc Health.* 1994;15: 400–406.

29. Kafka R, London P. Communication in relationships and adolescent substance use: the influence of parents and friends. *Adolescence.* 1991;26:587–597.

30. Wills T, Vaccar D, McNamara G. The role of life events, family support, and competence in adolescent substance use: a test of vulnerability and protective factors. *Am J Psychol.* 1992;20:349–374.

31. Pepler D, Slaby RG. Developmental perspectives on youth and violence. In: *Report of the American Psychological Association Commission on Violence and Youth*, vol. I. Washington, DC: APA; 1993.

32. Prothrow-Stith D, Quaday S. The effect of violence on learning. In: Gehahan S, ed. *Hidden Casualties: The Relationship Between Violence and Learning.* Washington, DC: National Consortium for African American Children, Inc. and the National Health & Education Consortium; 1995.

33. Cairns R, Coleman-Miller B, Greenwood P, et al. Violence prevention strategies directed toward high-risk minority youths. *Public Health Rep.* 1991;106:250–254.

34. Hutson H, Anglin M, Pratts M. Adolescents and children injured or killed in drive-by shootings in Los Angeles. *N Engl J Med.* 1994;330:324–330.

35. Ryan M, Leighton T, Pianim N, Bongard F. Medical and economic consequences of gang-related shootings. *Am Surgeon.* 1993;59:831–833.

36. Fertman C, Chubb N. The effects of a psychoeducational program on adolescents' activity involvement, self-esteem, and locus of control. *Adolescence.* 1992;27:517–526.

37. Lorion R, Saltzman W. Children's exposure to community violence: following a path from concern to research to action. *Psychiatry.* 1993;56:55–65.

38. Shilts L. The relationship of early adolescent substance use to extracurricular activities, peer influence, and personal attitudes. *Adolescence.* 1991; 26:613–617.

39. Zimmerman M, Maton K. Life-style and substance use among male African-American urban adolescents: a cluster analytic approach. *Am J Community Psychol.* 1992;20:121–137.

Families with Special Health Problems

The Need for Cultural-Linguistic Competent Care for Families with Special Health Problems

Angeline Bushy, PhD, RN, CS

THE DOMINANT culture of white Anglo Americans is expected to be in the minority sometime in the next century but it is impossible to predict precisely when this will happen. Predominant minorities in the United States at this time include African Americans, Latino/Hispanics, Asians, Pacific Islanders, and Native Americans (Indians), including Native Alaskans and Hawaiians. Diversity is accelerated even more by the numerous immigrants arriving in our nation. Significant differences exist among and within the various groups in their beliefs, health behaviors, and extent of acculturation into mainstream society. Diversity goes beyond obvious racial and ethnic features. In fact, Anglo American health professionals may find some white middle-class citizens have beliefs quite different from their own. Even in a homogeneous community, there is diversity among the residents stemming from their life experiences and exposures to other cultural groups. No one can predict the long-range impact of these projected population and cultural trends. Pessimists speculate the changing social fabric will lead to ethnic tension with divisions between old and young, rich and poor. Even though there are data to support this rather bleak forecast, it must be stressed that dire predictions do not always come to fruition. Insidious driving and restraining forces often impact society in unanticipated ways. Furthermore, some are adapting well to the increasing diversity. For instance, there are increasing numbers of marriages between people of color and whites as are the number of children with mixed-racial origins. Latinos, too, are marrying across ethnic lines with greater frequency, further diluting Hispanic ethnic identities.[1-5]

Regional variations exist, with some areas having a significant minority population while other communities remain quite homogeneous. For example, several counties in the southeastern states are composed predominantly of African Americans, several counties in the plains states with an Indian reservation have high numbers of Native Americans, while Mexican American Hispanics predominate in a few counties located in southwestern states. Such variations reinforce the need for caregivers to develop skills to effectively care for persons who are of a minority background, especially if they also are vulnerable and at risk for health problems or have special health care needs.

In spite of biomedical innovations that have been developed in the 20th century, epidemiologic reports reveal that disparities exist in the health status of minorities compared with the general population. Infant mortality among the African Americans and Native Americans, for example, is twice that of whites

in the first year of life. Hispanics and American Indians are twice as likely as whites to have diabetes. This particular chronic condition leads to other more serious and costly medical problems such as blindness, amputations, kidney disease, stroke, and heart attack. Other minority disparities include significantly higher incidences of cervical and prostate cancer, cardiovascular disease, human immunodeficiency virus/acquired immune deficiency syndrome (HIV/AIDS), and incomplete immunizations. The US Office of the Surgeon General is concerned, and objectives focusing on the disparities are cited in *Healthy People 2010*.[5]

Racial and ethnic minorities often exhibit features of vulnerable, at-risk populations with special needs. Specifically, they are more likely to have a low economic status, fewer years of formal education, a higher incidence of chronic health problems, fewer years of life, and poorer pregnancy outcomes. Further, they encounter a variety of access barriers to health-related services. Minorities are more likely to work in low-paying jobs that often do not offer fringe benefits, and in particular, health care insurance. In some cases an employer may provide coverage for employees but not their families. Even if health care is available at no cost, the person may not be able to take the necessary time off from work to see a health care provider.[6-8]

Each community is different with respect to epidemiologic characteristics. In respect to community health outcomes, these usually are quantified as life expectancy, mortality, morbidity, or disease etiology rates. As for quality of life measures, these offer other kinds of information and usually are described in terms of socioeconomic status, standard of living, job satisfaction, lifestyle, and housing situations. As separate descriptors, the two types of data do not present a complete picture of what is occurring in a community. Together, however, epidemiologic data and quality-of-life measures can provide a more comprehensive view of the community's health status and care-seeking behaviors.[9-12]

THE CULTURAL-LINGUISTIC COMPETENCY CONTINUUM

Considering changing demographic patterns, there is an obvious need for health professionals to develop the essential competencies to work with persons of diverse backgrounds. Cultural-linguistic competence can be described as a continuum of interpersonal skills ranging from ethnocentrism on the one extreme to enculturation at the opposing end of the spectrum. Developing proficiency with these skills is an ongoing process and everyone progresses at their own pace.[13-17]

More specifically, *ethnocentrism* refers to the prejudicial belief that one's own group determines the standards for behavior by which all other cultural groups are to be judged. At this level, behaviors and beliefs of other cultural groups are devalued or treated with suspicion or hostility by the provider. The next level on the continuum is *cultural awareness,* described as an appreciation of and sensitivity to another's values, beliefs, practices, lifestyle, and problem-solving preferences. Next comes *cul-*

tural knowledge, and this infers that the caregiver gleans insights about the society's organizational patterns. Subsequently, the person seeks information on strategies to provide care that is acceptable by members of the group.

Progressing along the skills continuum, the professional experiences *cultural change*, which tends to occur after having more intense contact with those of another group. Until quite recently, *cultural competence* was described as the most sophisticated skill on the continuum. At this level the provider not only is aware, sensitive, and knowledgeable about another culture but also has a repertoire of skills to render care that is deemed appropriate by a client of minority origins. Quite recently, the term *linguistic competence* has come into use. This includes complex skills that require a person to integrate another society's linguistic preferences when providing care. *Enculturation,* at the opposite end of the continuum, alludes to an outsider fully internalizing the values of a foreign culture. However, complete cultural assimilation can hinder objectivity about a group's practices because the person has become an intimate member.

Developing any kind of competence is a nonlinear process. Individual progression is dependent on life experiences, frequency of exposure to other societies, and receptivity to learning about cultural differences. As with other interventions, cultural-linguistic competencies are refined as a caregiver moves from novice to expert.[9-11]

In the preceding discussion several terms have been repeatedly used, specifically culture, race, and ethnicity. In day-to-day conversations the three often are interchanged but the concepts have different meanings. Race refers to skin color and the associated biologic markers that define group membership, specifically Caucasian, Mongolian, Native American, and Negroid. Biologic markers include features such as the color and thickness of skin, hair texture, physical development patterns, and susceptibility to certain diseases. In our diverse society, it is becoming more difficult to differentiate genetic features because of the mixed interracial origins of people coupled with multiple contextual variables such as socioeconomic status, nutrition, lifestyle, and climatic influences.

Ethnicity refers to the "commonness" among a group stemming from a shared history. It is sustained by race, religion, and national origin but can be influenced by education, socioeconomic factors, access to transportation, technology, and exposure to other groups. There are wide variations and not all members of a society express the same degree of ethnicity. For example, the Bureau of the Census uses a group classification of "Hispanic" that is subdivided into white and nonwhite categories. The term *Hispanic* refers to a language commonly used in nations that were colonized by Spain several hundred years ago. These nations are located in Europe as well as in North, South, and Central America; the Caribbean; and the Philippine Islands. All use a common language, Hispanic; albeit in a local dialect. In the United States, the cultural and ethnic diversity among Hispanics is especially obvious. They represent all regions of the world. Each ethnic group has its own unique cultural, ethnic, racial, and linguistic nuances. Ethnic and cultural variations can be obscured by skin color, and stereotyping is a consequence of not recognizing individual preferences.[18-20]

The culturally and linguistically competent provider recognizes biologic variations among subpopulations in a given community. For instance, if there is a segment of African Americans or Native Americans in a community, the caregiver learns about physical variations and symptoms associated with their common health problems such as sickle cell anemia, osteoporosis, diabetes, hypertension, breast cancer, sudden infant death syndrome, and cirrhosis from substance abuse, as well as particular occupational or trauma-related injuries they may experience.

The term *culture* essentially refers to the values, ideals, and belief systems that emerge over time among a group of individuals. Often, but not always, the group shares a common ethnicity or race. Cultural beliefs guide in defining an individual's roles and responsibilities in usual and unusual life events such as birth, child rearing, health, illness, and death. Intergenerational transfer of a society's world view begins early in life through the verbal and nonverbal actions and behaviors of caregivers. Appropriate and inappropriate behaviors are learned through routine and day-to-day human interactions and by observing others deal with such events. Other dimensions of culture, race, and ethnicity that have particular relevance to vulnerable and special populations include their social organizations, assigned roles, naming, linguistic patterns, perceptions of space and distance, time orientation, control of the environment, and self-care and healing behaviors. Each of these dimensions will be examined more in detail within subsequent paragraphs.

Social organizations

The family is the basic unit of society, and cultural values influence how it is to be organized and the roles of each member. The concept of family is difficult to define. For example, in some societies family is defined as an extensive kinship network comprised of many blood relatives along with those acquired through marriage. Other societies refer to all maternal aunts as "mother" and all paternal uncles as "father." Some Native Americans refer to all members of their clan as "cousins," and a few tribes have an adoption ceremony to incorporate an outsider with whom they have a strong emotional bond into their family. The adoptee subsequently is referred to as brother, sister, son, or daughter by other family members. Along with highly structured nuclear families, and loosely organized extended families, other arrangements the health professional may encounter are same-gender couples with and without children, grandparents raising grandchildren, blended-families extending from divorce and remarriage, communal living arrangements, and cohabitating widowed elderly persons. Therefore, a culturally competent caregiver will ask the person who constitutes his or her "family" system, and include these individuals in planning, implementing, and evaluating care.

Assigned roles

Roles and their associated behaviors are culturally prescribed, such as what is or is not expected of children and the value placed on the elderly within a society. More precisely, in a persistent poverty community, education may be relegated second place to the support of the family. Sometimes this is the first evidence by school officials reporting consistent student absences or tardiness. On closer examination, the provider may find parents are keeping the child out of school in order to help care for younger siblings or to work in the fields when the weather lends itself to harvesting. Gender role behaviors, too, are culturally defined and influence a family's health care–seeking behaviors. For instance, the decision maker regarding personal health problems among some African American families is a highly regarded elderly female. In some Latino communities, on the other hand, such decisions emanate from the dominant male in the extended family. Sometimes a family member having more years of education than other members, especially in a health-related field, becomes the designated decision maker. With immigrants, it often is someone who understands and is able to translate English, albeit, he or she is familiar with only a few words. In many instances, young children serve as the family interpreter. Health professionals should be aware, however, that most cultures have parameters as to who can discuss particular topics regarding health- and illness-related topics.

Role behaviors also dictate individual involvement in the treatment of sick family members. For example, in some societies only older females in the immediate family, specifically a mother or wife, can provide direct physical care. Other societies condone "machismo," sometimes evidenced by a male being highly suspicious of another male who interacts with his spouse and other females in the extended family. Sometimes, the male dominance extends to male health professionals who provide care to "their women," even during pregnancy and childbirth. Consequently, this particular male is often cited by some Latino women as a barrier to their obtaining prenatal and preventive health care.

In other instances, the entire extended family actively participates when one member is ill. This health care–seeking behavior has particular implications when a person arrives at a health care facility accompanied by many extended family members. A culturally competent provider might designate a specific waiting room to accommodate the family to avoid disrupting others on the unit, assign a less congested room, extend visiting privileges, negotiate with the family to rotate visiting times, or integrate the activities of an indigenous or spiritual healer to augment contemporary medicine. In other cases, it may mean allowing the family to bring food to the client that was prepared at home because they believe it is essential for restoring health or healing.

Culturally steeped expectations such as these can lead to contention between the family and health care providers should the latter not be aware of a client's preference. If caregivers are not culturally and linguistically competent, they may not even be aware of the disparities; hence, the client usually will choose the path of least resistance. That is to say, the client will verbally agree with the provider but do what has always been done by the family in similar situations. Subsequently, the family may express dissatisfaction with services to other community members but not to the health care provider.

Naming

Cultural preferences influence naming and how a person is referred to. More specifically, some Latino societies use surnames from mothers, grandmothers, and fathers in a sequence that can vary from time to time and from person to person. In some Asian societies, the family surname comes before a birth name. In respect to Native Americans, they are named shortly after birth, but some select another name during a ceremonial rite of passage. Immigrants who have names difficult to pronounce or spell may shorten their legal titles or select commonly used English ones to facilitate entry into mainstream society. Culturally based naming practices can lead to errors stemming from conflicting information found in official records with a client's word-of-mouth report. Individual preferences related to name and title should be determined and respected by the linguistically competent provider. To ensure accuracy, the client's pronunciation and spelling should carefully be cross-referenced with the written information in the health record. Subsequently, a caregiver must ensure that the "right" treatment is administered to the "right" person and recorded in the "right" record.

Linguistic patterns

Linguistic competence infers that a caregiver has a good understanding of societal communication patterns and is able to integrate that information when rendering care to individuals of other backgrounds. To reiterate, communication refers to the use of language, vocabulary, grammar, voice qualities, intonation, rhythm, speed, pronunciation, physical gestures, and silence. The English language has a variety of pronunciations for some words and assorted nonverbal nuances vary among regions and other English-speaking nations. Consequently, similar to Hispanics, two people speaking in English may not completely understand, or may even misunderstand each other. Communication barriers are intensified among people who speak different languages and can be especially frustrating when caring for a person who is seriously injured or in need of urgent attention.

The spoken word

Regardless of the setting, a caregiver ideally should know the language spoken by all clients. This may not be not a realistic expectation. Taking a foreign language course can be helpful. However, such offerings usually present a classic form of grammar and teach pronunciations not used in day-to-day communication, especially among those with less formal education. Further, dialects tend to be discouraged in a formal language course. Consequently, being able to read

and write a foreign language does not always assure that a caregiver is able to communicate effectively with persons who speak in a dialect form. Augmenting the spoken word with gestures and pictures is a useful strategy but sometimes a translator still is needed to interpret what has been said by both parties.

Linguistically competent health professionals are aware that communication is based on cultural rules that dictate who can, or cannot, discuss certain topics regarding personal health matters. Often parameters are delimited based on age, gender, family position, and the health problem of concern. In some societies, children and males are not allowed to talk about reproductive issues. In other cultures, male health professionals should not speak to women unless the women are appropriately attired, which may mean their faces or other body parts first being covered by particular garments. If knowledge is limited about anatomy, physiology, and the disease process or if medical jargon and acronyms are used by the speaker, the translator may not be able to understand what was being said. Translators should be objective and able to deliver an accurate interpretation of what was stated by both parties. The provider, in turn, must use language that both the client and the translator can understand.

Linguistic competence implies that the care provider is familiar with another person's unwritten code of social courtesies. For example, an elderly Latino man who speaks very little English arrives at a clinic to see the physician for lower abdominal pain. A young female health professional enters the treatment room with the intention of completing a routine intake assessment. Upon greeting the man, she begins the conversation by focusing on his presenting symptoms using a direct question approach. The client is startled by the interrogative nature of the questions asked by a complete stranger. For him, this action is construed as disrespectful, especially since the caregiver is younger and of the opposite gender.

In some other cultures, a typical response to direct questions about symptoms of an illness is telling a "life story" that metaphorically depicts the problem as it impacts the person. Some condone talking extensively about circumstantial themes related to the event, expecting the caregiver to glean the essence of their health problem. Others enumerate all of the preceding day's or week's events, interspersing symptomatology development, leading up to the present time. Obviously, it takes time to interpret another person's linguistic preferences, and there is no single approach to initiating conversation. To effectively communicate the provider must first establish mutual rapport, be sensitive to individual cultural and linguistic preferences, and allocate adequate time to meet a client's expectations in the discussion.

Nonverbal communication

Nonverbal communication, too, is culturally steeped. For example, a person speaking very softly with a slightly bowed head and downcast eyes is a sign of respect and deference among some Native Americans. To some people, those behaviors could demonstrate shyness, slyness, or dishonesty. Conversely, direct and prolonged eye contact by an adult male could be indicative of self-confidence or even aggressiveness, especially among some white, middle-class Americans. Head nodding is another behavior often misinterpreted by caregivers when speaking to elderly immigrants of Asian origins. The gesture does not necessarily mean the person understands what is being said. Rather, it might be indicative of great respect for the speaker even though the client does not understand a word of what is being said. These are a few of the many culturally steeped linguistic patterns the professional may encounter when caring for minorities. A linguistically competent caregiver is sensitive to cultural nuances among vulnerable clients, who also are of another background.

The following suggestions may help the professional to communicate more effectively with persons of another ethnic or cultural background:

- Speak slowly, respectfully, and at a calm normal volume. A raised voice can be threatening or offensive to someone of another culture.
- Give verbal instructions slowly. Periodically assess if the person comprehends what has been discussed.
- Do not use multisyllable words, medical jargon, or acronyms.
- Remember that adults learn most effectively when new information is presented in segments and over several time periods. Ask how the person learns best (ie, words, pictures, or hands-on demonstration). Incorporate those preferences when working with the client and family.
- Request that the individual repeat, in his or her own words, what was

heard in order to assess the level of understanding.

- Respect and protect the person's dignity. Regardless of culture or ethnicity, most people sense when the speaker is reassuring and has a well-meaning intent.
- Remember that an attitude of acceptance and tolerance goes a long way in establishing rapport with a person and the groundwork for subsequent communication.
- Remember that people who are illiterate are extremely sensitive to the manner in which others respond to them. Therefore, when presenting information that seems elementary, control facial expressions that could be interpreted by the individual and family members as impatience, annoyance or amusement.

The written word

A useful strategy for the caregiver is to write specific verbal directions describing the client's treatment plan. However, inadequate literacy skills pose serious challenges for many individuals that health professionals encounter. Surprisingly among all nations in the world, the US literacy rate dropped from 1st place in the 1960s to 49th place in 1997.[4,5] Functional literacy infers an ability to read and write at least at a fifth grade level. Of all adults in the United States, about 90 million (48%) possess inadequate literacy skills. Of these, about half are functionally illiterate (21%) or have marginal literacy skills (27%).

In more pragmatic terms, someone who is functionally illiterate is not able to read a newspaper, use a bus schedule, write a check, identify an expiration date on a driver's license, read street signs or a clinic appointment card, much less understand written information regarding a prescription or discharge plan. Most are not able to function in a job that requires even the most basic reading and writing skills. Health professionals should be aware, too, that adults with limited literacy skills are less likely to obtain preventive health care, adhere to recommended treatment regimens, and keep appointments and are more likely to delay seeking professional services until they are quite ill.

A stigma is associated with illiteracy, and many people hide the problem because they are ashamed or embarrassed. Of the illiterate, about 67% never tell their wives and 53% do not tell their children. Over time, many learn to recognize symbols and key words, rely on their children or a spouse who is able to read, and usually offer minimal information to others in day-to-day social interactions.[4,5]

Health professionals should not assume that a client can read even the most simply written document or be able to follow complex verbal instructions. Furthermore, some are not literate even if they have completed high school. Increasing numbers of elderly and families cannot afford eye care and glasses, and linguistically competent caregivers are aware that the print size used in written materials is very important in preparing educational materials targeting a vulnerable group. Likewise, the health care environment (clinic, institution) should be assessed to determine linguistic barriers. For instance, one should ask whether posters and pictures reflect the culture of the clientele, such as Mexican American Latinos, Native Americans, African Americans or Asians? Are these materials written in clients' primary language? Are consent forms and instructional materials written at levels that can be understood, perhaps even in another language? Linguistically friendly materials are less likely to frustrate consumers, especially those having inadequate literacy skills, and are indicative of cultural and linguistic competency.

Perception of space and distance

The manner in which space and body boundaries are perceived is culturally based and another important dimension of linguistic competence. Use of space is exhibited as "comfort zones" for different kinds of human interactions such as day-to-day business transactions, intimate situations, and when rendering care. Generally, compared to males, females do not have as many restrictions placed on them regarding space and touch but there are cultural variations. For instance, compared to Anglo Americans in day-to-day social interactions, some Latinos prefer less distance and often touch the person with whom they are interacting. In other societies, a common practice upon meeting a new acquaintance is lightly embracing another person of the same gender. This gesture is highly uncomfortable to some Anglo Americans who prefer more space and are unaccustomed to being touched, much less by someone they do not even know. A firm handshake is the accepted greeting among some European cultures. This gesture, too, surprises some mainstream

Americans. Preferences related to personal space also are evidenced as discomfort by patients during a physical examination or with other interventions that involve touching the body.

Time orientation

Time, and how it is perceived relative to daily life, varies from one group to another and among members. More specifically, societies tend to be past, present, or future oriented. It is with *utmost caution and at the risk of stereotyping* that general statements can be made regarding time orientation. In order to better illustrate dimensions of linguistic competency several examples are provided about time orientation but these should not be construed by the reader as the norm for a particular racial group.

For example, some middle-class Anglo Americans are future oriented; therefore, they are willing to work hard and delay gratification for some anticipated goal. This time perspective can influence lifestyle choices, such as adhering to a rigorous physical fitness program to eventually appear more attractive or increase their years of life. Another example is the pregnant woman who is highly committed to delivering her child using "natural processes." She attends Lamaze classes, exercises, and does everything that is said to be "right." Not achieving either of the idealized outcomes, namely gaining weight or having an emergency cesarean section, can lead to excessive stress and even depression in a future-oriented person.

A present-time orientation may be

seen in some African Americans and it, too, can influence their lifestyles and health behaviors. For example, an individual is aware that he or she has a chronic health condition that is difficult to control, such as hypertension or diabetes. Still, at a family gathering such as a reunion or holiday, he or she may eat particular ethnic foods because these traditionally are served at that particular event. Even though the foods are known to be high in salt, animal fat, and sugar content and that these factors contribute to increased symptomatology, the event has inherent emotions tied to it. In other words, those particular foods are part of the spirit of the happening. Hence these foods are eaten by an attendee, in spite of the acknowledged health consequences such as erratic blood sugar levels, increased blood pressure, or even congestive heart failure.

Cultures with a past orientation to time include some Native Americans, Alaskans, Asians, and Pacific Islanders having a world view that life is a circular phenomenon. For them, deceased relatives are part of the extended family and given great deference by the living. Family members in the non-earthly spiritual realm are believed to provide guidance to living relatives. Hence, it is not unusual for a client with a past-oriented perspective to incorporate healing practices that a deceased relative suggested for a health problem to the great bewilderment of a future-oriented caregiver.

Linguistically competent persons are aware that time orientation often is a source of misunderstanding when rendering care to persons of another background such as conflicting views regarding the precise time for a scheduled intervention. More precisely, when waiting for something to happen, time is perceived to pass very slowly as in the case of hospitalized persons who report their call lights were on for hours before a staff member finally responded to them. Another example is the client who expects to receive medications at the exact moment it is scheduled while the health professional adheres to the institution's policy for administering medications (ie, most medications can be administered within a window of time: one-half hour before to one-half hour after it is scheduled to be given).

Some societies espouse a range of time in which an individual can fulfill personal responsibilities. Conflicts can arise when clients are prioritized differently than the caregivers. This situation is exemplified by a client who does not adhere to scheduled appointments or the mother who does not follow through with her children's recommended immunizations. Linguistic competence infers learning about another person's frame of reference regarding time orientation and considering those preferences when implementing care. Strategies that may be useful in achieving this outcome include anticipating late arrivals for prescheduled appointments; not having formally scheduled appointments but using a number system as clients arrive in the clinic; providing services at nontraditional times such as evenings, weekends, or during communitywide events; and offering outreach services by linguistically competent caregivers at accessible community sites where the targeted population congregates.

Control of the environment

Understanding the degree of control that a society perceives to have over their environment and nature is another aspect of cultural-linguistic competency. More specifically, some cultures perceive humans as having mastery over nature, others believe they are dominated by it, and others live harmoniously with nature. Individuals who perceive they have mastery over nature are likely to believe they can overcome most natural forces, exemplified by a person having a strong conviction in the ultimate success of medicine and biotechnology. Hence, they may expect that a malignancy will be "cured" through surgery. Those believing they are subjugated to nature might be viewed as fatalistic or demonstrating "learned helplessness" behavior. This world view sometimes is evident in multigenerational impoverished families or women who do not leave abusive relationships. Over time, both groups come to believe they have little control over what happens to them. This cultural perspective may also offer insights to a caregiver regarding a client who does not adhere to prescribed treatments or perform routine preventive health care such as having a mammogram, pap smear, prenatal care, or immunizations; wearing a seat belt; or donning a cycle helmet. These world views could be factors in the health disparities that exist among the vulnerable and special populations such as African Americans being diagnosed later with breast cancer and having higher mortality rates.

Societies having a world view of living in harmony with nature believe that illness is the result of the two forces not being in balance. Those holding this perspective believe that Western medicine primarily relieves symptoms but does little to address the source of the problem. For them, disease is a manifestation of the individual not living in balance with his or her environment. Consequently, cultural-linguistic competence implies integrating contemporary medicine with traditional healing, such as incorporating an indigenous spiritual healer or self-care practice in the care plan. When harmony and balance are restored within the person, good health may be an outcome.

Self-care and healing behaviors

An important dimension of cultural-linguistic competence is acknowledging the use of ethnocultural self-care behaviors in society as a whole. Resources and rituals used for healing vary among groups and are influenced by environmental and economic factors. Even mainstream Americans use a wide range of alternative healers and healing practices. Some of the more popular are herbal, chiropractic, magnetic, massage, hydro and aroma therapies, spiritual and psychic healing, acupressure, osteopathy, meditation, visualization, and the use of veterinarian products. The culturally competent caregiver, therefore, should assume that most people, including health professionals, engage in some self-care practices, especially when feeling sick.[9–11]

Providers must accept that these behaviors probably will not be acknowledged. Still, if a client uses herbs, over-the-counter products, or eats certain foods to manage a health condition, these should be recognized. This, however, does not negate use of scientifically based interventions. Rather, it means assessing their benefits and risks and, if appropriate, integrating the self-care practice with prescribed interventions.

To elicit sensitive information of this nature the provider must reflect a nonjudgmental attitude when tactfully asking a client about self-care practices. Cultural-linguistic competence entails presenting scientific information that is compatible with a client's beliefs; if not, the person or the family probably will reject it. Although it may take more time in the beginning, in the long run a collaborative approach can reduce phone calls and office visits by clients due to misunderstood treatment plans.[9-11]

DEVELOPING CULTURAL AND LINGUISTIC COMPETENCY

Complete a cultural self-appraisal

Prior to becoming sensitive to and accommodating others' beliefs and values, providers should first understand their own backgrounds. Self-appraisal involves reflecting on the manner in which ethnocultural origins affect a person's beliefs, behaviors, and ways of interacting with diverse people on a professional and personal level. Self-awareness then can progress to developing sensitivity to minorities' expectations when ill. Ultimately, providers should develop competencies that will deflect potential cultural conflicts in day-to-day as well as highly unusual events.

Increase exposure to other cultures

After developing cultural self-awareness, the individual is able to extend to persons who are of another background. Information on diverse groups can be obtained from recreational and professional literature. An open and nonjudgmental attitude is critical in learning about other cultures. Talking with people having greater knowledge and experience about another culture is one strategy to learn about their world views. Health professionals should ask questions. Most people enjoy telling others about their culture if the inquiry is made with an intent to learn. If possible, seek explanations as to how and why specific rituals are used in certain situations. Then collaborate with the client to integrate those preferences with scientifically based interventions and to develop a holistic plan of care that is mutually acceptable.

Heighten community participation

Probably the most effective strategy is to actually interact with people of a particular background on their turf (natural environment) at social events as well as in their home. Even when highly involved and subsumed in a community's social and political activities, it is not likely that an outsider will learn all of the important facts about a different culture before making at least a few blunders. Rather, one learns gradually by working within a community over a period of time. Eventually, with a desire to learn, less obvious values and expectations become more obvious. For example, through formal and informal communication exchanges, the provider becomes aware of and sensitive to persons' manner of interacting with various kinds of health professionals, their self-care practices and use of alternative healers.

In order to overcome cultural barriers to health care, the professional must acquire ethnocultural knowledge that can explain why clients engage in certain practices to promote health or treat an illness. It can be difficult to learn about persons who are not part of a community's mainstream unless the individual actively seeks out those (sub)groups. Therefore, it is important to assess a catchment area to identify cultural subgroups within the larger community. Some underrepresented groups are easy to identify because they are isolated by a geographical boundary, biologic or racial features, lifestyle, attire, religion, political views, language, leisure activity, or occupation. There are, however, other groups that are not as obviously bound in a given region nor do they appear to have such distinct lifestyles. Essentially, cultural-linguistic competence involves a dedicated effort to learn about others by interacting with them in their natural settings—where they live, learn, work, play, and pray. Real-world experiences should subsequently be augmented with theoretical information about the world view of a particular group.

Recruit minorities to the health professions

A serious problem with cultural insensitivity in the health care system in general is attributable to low percentages of individuals of minority origins entering the health professions. Historically, schools preparing health professionals reflected a homogeneous student body, with a predominance of Anglo-Euro-American students. Currently, most educational programs are recruiting and retaining minority students with varying degrees of success. Current and projected demographic changes challenge educators of health professionals to produce culturally and linguistically competent clinicians and researchers. Who can better present the perspective of a vulnerable or special population than persons who are of that background? Minorities must, therefore, be encouraged to enter the health professions. Essentially, health professionals of minority backgrounds, especially in leadership roles, are in ideal positions to serve as role models to others in their community.

Measure consumer satisfaction

In addition to planning and delivering care, the cultural perspective must be taken into consideration when measuring consumer satisfaction, health outcomes, and appropriateness of services rendered. Acceptability and appropriateness of care imply that a particular service is offered in a manner that is congruent with the values of a targeted vulnerable group and perceived as desirable and familiar to persons receiving it. Culturally and linguistically competent strategies that evoke consumer satisfaction go beyond dietary and pastoral care preferences or manner of requesting analgesics. They include incorporating individuals' definition of health and illness and their self-care practices into health services. Ethnocultural factors also influence the appropriate time for seeking health care and the manner in which one interacts with a professional provider. Even if a service is available and accessible in a community, it may not be deemed satisfactory by a targeted population. Consumer satisfaction surveys, for instance, often incorporate rating scales of "satisfactory," "unsatisfactory," "acceptable," or "unacceptable." Yet, little attention is given to the reasons a group perceives it as such. Furthermore, developers of the tool may not even consider whether respondents are able to read or understand what such ratings refer to. Suffice it to say, traditional evaluation approaches often are not culturally or linguistically sensitive; hence, the data may not be valid or reliable. Both qualitative and quantitative methods should be used, with ongoing input from the members of a vulnerable or special population. Their input can ensure that the proper questions are asked, in the right manner, using linguistically sensitive terminology to measure the outcomes as these are defined by the group.[8,12]

PART II: OVERVIEW

Part II of *Special Populations in the Community: Advances in Reducing Health Disparities* includes a broad scope of topics on issues confronting culturally and ethnically diverse vulnerable populations and persons with special needs. Part II begins with a chapter by Ulione who speaks to the physical and emotional health in dual-earner families and the role social support has on health

outcomes. This is followed by Muller and Boyle's work that presents a poignant perspective about women who do sex and drugs. Broyles et al then discuss cardiovascular disease risk factors in Anglo and Mexican American children and their mothers. They focus on the eating and exercise behaviors of this particular minority group. Parker examines a less common chronic health condition, children with tuberous sclerosis, and family stress in caring for a sick child.

Worcester and Hedrick examine a dilemma confronting a growing vulnerable population in our society; the respite care needs for family caregivers of the frail elderly. Peterson, Sterling, and Weekes focus on African American families with children having a chronic illness and their perspective on access to health care. In this chapter, primary caretakers explain how they view asthma and strategies they have developed to access care for their children that fit their particular preferences. In a study by Kidd, Townley, Cole, McKnight, and Piercy, farm children and parental views regarding suitable chores for their children are discussed. They elaborate on the process parents use in teaching these responsibilities to their children. Strickland and Strickland examine access to health service and the coping strategies of lower income minority households in Georgia. The authors also provide a model of health service utilization that practitioners will find useful when rendering care to vulnerable clients. This part concludes with a discussion of less well known minority groups. Affonso, Mayberry, Shibuya, Kunimoto, Graham, and Sheptak speak to stressors for childbearing women on the island of

Hawaii, specifically those of Filipino, Japanese, Hawaiian, or part-Hawaiian background.

SUMMARY

Overall, the chapters in Part II reinforce that the United States has become a mosaic of many cultures. This trend is expected to continue well into the next millennium. Increasing ethnic, cultural, and racial diversity is a concern at all levels of the health care delivery system, i.e., federal, state, local, and even in the private sector. Demographic projections reinforce the urgent need for health professionals to be culturally and linguistically competent in order to respond to the diverse preferences of vulnerable groups to whom they render services. The chapters in this part offer a range of interventions to achieve this outcome and provide unique perspectives of select vulnerable communities with special health care needs.

DISCUSSION QUESTIONS

1. Differentiate and describe the interrelatedness of race, ethnicity, and culture with rural socioeconomic factors on the health status of minorities.
2. Identify a group that is vulnerable in your community. Describe why you believe the members are at risk for certain health problems. Are any interventions being implemented to address the particular concerns of the group? Elaborate on these.
3. Select a population with special health care needs in your community. What are the demographic features of the group, and what services are available to meet their particular needs?
4. Using epidemiologic reports from the Centers for Disease Control and Prevention or from the state Department of Health, identify the most prevalent health conditions in your catchment area that could be attributed to racial or ethnic genetic predisposition. Describe treatment protocols for these conditions and identify strategies to integrate the ethnocultural beliefs into client care plans.
5. How can a cultural assessment be incorporated into the existing client assessment protocols that are used in the health care setting where you practice?
6. Identify a plan of action to increase your level of cultural and linguistic competence. When caring for rural minority clients, where on the continuum do you believe you currently fall? Why do you believe this to be true? Cite examples. What changes will you need to make in order to progress to a more sophisticated competency level in your professional development?

REFERENCES

1. Ahmann E. "Chunky stew": appreciating cultural diversity while providing health care to children. *Pediatr Nurs*, 1994;20(3): 320–324.
2. Rosella J, Regan-Kubinski M, Albrecht S. The need for multicultural diversity among health professionals. *Nurs Health Care.* 1994; 15(5):242–246.
3. US Department of Health and Human Services. *Healthy People 2000: National Health Promotion and Disease Prevention.* Washington, DC: Government Printing Office; 1991.
4. US Department of Health and Human Services. *Health United States: 1997.* Hyattsville, Md: Author; 1998.
5. US Department of Health and Human Services. *Healthy People 2010.* (Draft copy). Hyattsville, Md: Author; 1998.
6. Andrews M, Boyle J. Competence in transcultural nursing care. *Am J Nurs.* 1997;97(8):16AAA–16DDD.
7. Barbee E. Racism in U.S. nursing. *Med Anthropol Q.* 1993;7(4):346–362.
8. Krieger N. Inequality, diversity and health: thoughts on "race/ethnicity," and "gender." *J Am Med Wom Assoc.* 1996; 51(4):133–136.
9. Bushy A. Social and cultural factors affecting health care and nursing practice. In: Lancaster J, ed. *Nursing Issues in Leading and Managing Care.* St. Louis, Mo: Mosby; 1998.
10. Bushy A. Cultural and ethnic diversity: cultural competence. In: Hickey J, Ouimette R, Venegoni C, eds. *Advanced Practice Nursing: Changing Roles and Clinical Application.* Philadelphia, Pa: J.B. Lippincott Company; 1999.
11. Bushy A. Vulnerability: an overview. In: Saucier-Lundy K, Jaynes, S, Hartman, S, eds. *Nursing in the Community: Continuity of Care of Individuals, Families, and Populations.* Sudbury, Mass: Jones & Bartlett Publishers; 1999.
12. Milburn N, Gary L, Booth J, Brown D. Conducting epidemiologic research in a minority community: methodological considerations. *J Community Psychol.* 1992;19(1):3–12.
13. Leininger M. *Transcultural Nursing: Concepts, Theories and Practice.* New York: NY: Wiley Medical Publishers: 1978.
14. Leininger M. *Cultural Diversity and Universality, A Theory of Nursing.* New York, NY: National League for Nursing Press; 1991.
15. Leininger M. Transcultural nursing education: a worldwide imperative. *Nurs Health Care.* 1994; 15(5):254–261.
16. Leininger M. Transcultural nursing research to transform nursing education and practice: 40 years. *Image: J Nurs Schol.* 1997;29(4);341–347.
17. Stanhope M, Knollmueller R. *Public Health and Community Health Nurse's Consultant: A Health Promotion Guide.* St. Louis, Mo: Mosby; 1997.
18. Degazone C. Cultural diversity in community health nursing practice. In: Stanhope M, Lancaster J, eds. *Community Health Nursing: Promoting Health of Aggregates, Families and Individuals.* St. Louis, Mo: Mosby; 1996.
19. Geissler E. *Pocket Guide: Cultural Assessment.* St. Louis, Mo: Mosby;1994.
20. Grossman D, Taylor R. Cultural diversity on the unit. *Am J Nurs.* 1995; 95(2):64–67.

CHAPTER 4

Physical and Emotional Health in Dual-Earner Family Members

Margaret Smith Ulione, RN, PhD

INCREASINGLY, mothers of preschool children are in the work force. Currently, 62% of women with preschool children are employed outside the home, creating significant numbers of dual-earner families.[1]

A dual-earner family is one in which the husband and wife are committed to both occupational work and family life together and in which each earner works at least 30 hours per week outside the home. While much has been written about how dual-earner family members cope with the stress and demands of their lifestyle, most of the research was done in the 1970s and 1980s. Little has been written recently in professional journals, but the popular periodicals continue to discuss the perils of the dual-earner family, especially the "exhaustion" of the dual-earner mom. Many dual-earner family studies focus on the negative consequences for the family of managing multiple roles. There is a gap in the literature

Fam Community Health 1996;19(3):14–20
© 1996 Aspen Publishers, Inc.

regarding dual-earner men's and women's physical and mental health and the factors that positively affect their health and well-being.

Nurses are in the forefront of health promotion. As leaders, nurses need to be aware of the stresses and coping responses of dual-earner family members and of the factors that promote health. Research that focuses on facilitating conditions or resources that help family members will enable nurses and other professionals to design policies and programs that reduce the burden of juggling multiple roles. The study described in this chapter sought to determine what factors were associated with positive emotional and physical health in dual-earner family members. This study focuses on either the husband or the wife from dual-earner families and not on a comparison of the two genders.

REVIEW OF THE LITERATURE

Several nursing studies have been conducted on women's multiple roles and how those roles affect their psychological and physical health. Woods[2] conducted a study to determine whether certain variables had an effect on the mental health of women in dual-career marriages. She investigated the influence of sex role orientation and social support on the mental health of dual-career women. Mental health was measured by the Cornell Medical Index MR scale. She found that women who had traditional sex role orientation, little task-sharing support from their spouses, and little support from confidants had poorer mental health than their counterparts.

This finding has been echoed by others. Vanfossen[3] found that spouse affirmation by men to women in a dual-earner family was a protective influence against depression in the women. Similarly, Ulbrich[4] found that women who had husbands who opposed their working reported more symptoms of depression than women whose husbands favored their employment. McEntee and Rankin[5] investigated whether multiple role demands could adversely affect health and found that multiple role demands, particularly child care, may have adverse effects on health, especially in the absence of good support systems. These findings suggest that social support buffers emotional ill health.

Coping appears to affect health.[6,7] Lazarus and Folkman[8] examined the effect of coping on mental and physical health in a sample of 150 community resident adults. They found that the variables of trust, appraisal, and coping explained the variance in psychological symptoms. Specifically, problem-focused or active coping strategies were associated with fewer psychological symptoms than were reactive or emotion-focused coping behaviors. Skinner and McCubbin[9] examined the coping behaviors of 69 dual-earner couples to determine which behaviors were the most adaptive. The strategies of compromise, prioritizing, reactive role behavior, and using external support systems were common to adaptive dual-earner couples. The research indicated that the healthiest behaviors were specifically planning family time together, modifying work schedules, and limiting job involvement to have time for the family.

Other researchers[10] have echoed Skinner and McCubbin's[9] findings that one of the healthiest factors in a dual-earner family is job flexibility. In fact, sociologists[11,12] suggest that in dual-earner couples the career roles and the family roles must complement each other if the family is to function smoothly.

METHODS

This study examines what variables are associated with optimum health in dual-earner family members. Specifically, are a person's resources, such as adaptive coping behaviors, job flexibility, and social support associated with optimum health?

Sample

A convenience sample of 131 was obtained through notices placed in licensed child care centers in two large metropolitan areas, one in the East and one in the Midwest. Criteria for inclusion in the study were that the respondent be a member of a dual-earner family; have no chronic illnesses; and, if female, not be pregnant. Of the 131 who responded to the survey, 72 (55%) were female and 59 (45%) were male. The age range for the subjects was from 21 to 52 years old (M = 34.2, SD = 4.7), and the children were between 4 weeks and 14 years of age.

All participants had completed high school; 33% had completed college, and 35% had attended graduate school. The majority of the sample (72%) were professionals according to the US Bureau of the Census[1] occupational classification system.

Data collection

The procedure for data collection in this study was similar to that of a mailed questionnaire; however, questionnaire packets were placed in child care centers for parents to pick up. Sixty child care centers were contacted from health department lists in the two large metropolitan areas. Of these 60, 20 centers agreed to participate in the study. In most of the centers a notice was posted at the entrance to the center soliciting volunteers for the study. The questionnaire packets were available near the notice for 2 weeks. The packet contained a stamped, self-addressed envelope for questionnaire return. The questionnaire consisted of demographic information, a coping scale, a social support measure, and a health profile. A mailed questionnaire method was used because the instruments requested personal information on how these families manage their lives and their state of health and one question regarding sexual activity. The personal nature of these questions might have made them difficult for the subjects to answer in person.

The available sample was approximately 1,994 individuals; 500 took questionnaires. One hundred and thirty-nine individuals sent back usable questionnaires; of these, 131 met the study criteria.

Instruments

Demographic data were obtained to ensure eligibility for inclusion in the study and to compare descriptive statistics of the sample. Information was obtained regarding the subjects' occupation, number of hours worked, the number of day care centers used, and satisfaction with day care. Data regarding the subject included age, gender, and education. The demographic variables chosen for study were drawn from previous research and the literature.

Coping was measured using Skinner and McCubbin's[9] Dual Earner Coping Scale (DECS). The DECS consists of 58 items regarding strategies dual-earner couples use to manage the demands of their lifestyle. Participants rate each item according to how well it describes their coping on a five-point Likert scale ranging from 1 = strongly disagree to 5 = strongly agree. Internal consistency reliability using Cronbach's alpha for the scale was .80 on this sample.

Job flexibility was measured by the Job Flexibility Scale (JFS), which has seven items with Likert-scale responses constructed for the present study. A review of the literature on dual-earner families revealed that several authors speculated that more flexible hours and personal benefit days may moderate the time demands on family members. The JFS consists of statements about occupation to which the subject responds on a five-point Likert scale from 1 = strongly disagree to 5 = strongly agree. Examples of the statements on the JFS are

- "It is easy for my spouse and me to schedule vacation time together."
- "I have no trouble taking all my vacation time."

- "I have several personal days as a benefit that I use when emergencies arise."

Internal consistency reliability using Cronbach's alpha was .72 on this sample.

Social support was measured using part 2 of Weinert's[13] Personal Resource Questionnaire (PRQ). The PRQ is a two-part questionnaire based on the relational dimensions of social support by Weiss.[14] Part 2 is a 25-item test with Likert-scale responses measuring the respondent's level of perceived social support ranging from 1 = strongly disagree to 7 = strongly agree. Cronbach's alphas for the total perceived social support scale ranged from .88 to .90. The Cronbach's alpha estimate on part 2 of the PRQ for the study sample was .92.

Physical health was measured using three of the four subscales of the Duke-UNC Health Profile (DUHP).[15] Emotional health was measured using the emotional function subscale of the DUHP. The DUHP was developed to help primary medical care service personnel assess the functional and feeling status of patients in a reliable and valid manner. The DUHP measures health along four dimensions: symptom status, physical function, social function, and emotional function. Cronbach's alpha estimates on the sample of 131 were .87 for the overall physical scale, .84 for the symptom subscale, .59 for the social subscale, .70 for the physical function subscale, and .85 for the emotional subscale.

RESULTS

The study used a descriptive survey design. Descriptive statistics were carried out for each of the study variables. Pearson product-moment correlations were calculated to determine relationships among variables in the study. Additionally, multivariate comparisons on the data were done using canonical correlation.

Correlations among the study's demographic variables and personal resources were calculated to explore the existence of relationships. Social support was positively correlated with both physical health ($r = .62$, $P < .01$) and emotional health ($r = .34$, $P < .01$). Adaptive coping was not correlated with either physical health or emotional health. Job flexibility was positively correlated with emotional health ($r = .24$, $P < .01$). Interestingly, in the demographic data, satisfaction with child care was positively correlated with emotional health ($r = .19$, $P < .05$). This was the only positive correlation in the demographic data. The results of the Pearson product-moment correlation appear in Table 4–1.

To determine how well an individual's resources predicted health, a canonical correlation was computed. A canonical correlation determines the overall relationship between two sets of variables and also indicates which individual variables contribute most to the relation between the two sets.

In this study the set of resource variables included coping, job flexibility, and social support, and the set of health variables was physical and emotional health. The set of resource variables was correlated with the set of health variables. There was one significant canonical correlation or variate (canonical $R = .73$, $P < .01$), with the resource set predicting 96% of the variance in the health set.

Of the resources that made up the resource set, social support was the most predictive variable, with job flexibility following second and coping third. In the health set, emotional health carried the most weight in the set, with physical health second. The results of the significant canonical correlation and related variates appear in Table 4–2.

Table 4–1. Pearson product-moment correlations among study variables

Variable	1	2	3	4	5	6
1. Physical health	1.00**					
2. Emotional health	.47**	1.00				
3. Social support	.62**	.34**	1.00			
4. Coping	.12	.17	.07	1.00		
5. Job flexibility	.13	.24**	.06	.12	1.00	
6. Satisfaction with child care	.10	.19*	.10	.10	−.01	1.00

*$P < .05$. **$P < .01$.

DISCUSSION

Results confirm the underlying assumption that coping, job flexibility, and social support are positively correlated with emotional and physical health. Health care professionals can influence the health of dual-earner family members by counseling them on ways to manage the stress in their lives. Specifically, professionals can discuss the importance of flexibility in dual-earner parents' jobs and explain ways to increase the family members' social support. A family's social support network can be increased through informal groups such as church-sponsored parents' groups or through more structured institutions such as the YMCA and area hospitals that offer parenting classes and structured play groups.

In this sample, satisfaction with child care was associated with optimum emotional health. Health care professionals can encourage parents who are experiencing stress related to child care to devote time to finding satisfactory child care, because that may decrease their stress. Female health care professionals can be role models for managing career-related stress by requesting high-quality on-site child care at places of employment or choosing employment based on the availability of high-quality child care.

While many health care jobs are inflexible, professional women can request that units self-staff and hire a certain number of per diem employees to cover staff personal days, which will impact job flexibility. In the area of social support, hospital-based and community-based health care professionals can call on the resources of pediatric nurses, pediatric nurse practitioners, pediatricians, and social workers for informational workshops on child illness and child rearing.

Table 4-2. Correlations and standardized canonical coefficients between resource and health variates and their corresponding canonical variates

| Resource and health variates | Dimension 1 | |
	Correlation	Standardized coefficient
Resource set		
Job flexibility	.41	.22
Social support	.98	.96
Coping	.33	-.07
Health set		
Physical health	.54	.00
Emotional health	.99	.99
Canonical correlation	.73	

Women in the health professions can be good role models for working women. According to this study, the healthiest women consciously compromised work for family while children were preschoolers. Perhaps both men and women should be encouraged to switch to a "mommy" or "daddy" track while the children are young and parenting and role stress are at their peak.

• • •

Dual-earner families with preschool children are under stress, but many families are both emotionally and physically healthy. These families use resources such as coping, job flexibility, and social support to manage their stress. As professionals and as colleagues of dual-earner family members, health care professionals can have a positive effect on the family through teaching, modeling, and changing environments to be supportive of these families.

REFERENCES

1. U.S. Bureau of the Census. *1990 Labor Force Statistics: 1990 Census of Population Social and Economic Characteristics, United States—1990 CP-2-1.* Washington, DC: U.S. Bureau of the Census; 1990.
2. Woods NF. Employment, family roles and mental ill health in young married women. *Nurs Res.* 1985; 34:4–10.
3. Vanfossen BE. Sex differences in the mental health effects of spouse and equity. *J Health Soc Behav.* 1981;22:130–143.
4. Ulbrich PM. The determinants of depression in two-income marriages. *J Marriage Family.* 1988;50: 121–131.
5. McEntee MA, Rankin EA. Multiple role demands, mind-body distress disorders and illness-related absenteeism among business and professional women. *Issues Health Care Women.* 1983;4:7–16.
6. Billings AG, Moos RH. Stressful life events and symptoms: a longitudinal model. *Health Psychol.* 1982;1:99–117.
7. Pearlin L, Schooler C. The structure of coping. *J Health Soc Behav.* 1978;19:2–21.
8. Lazarus R, Folkman S. *Stress, Appraisal and Coping.* New York, NY: Springer; 1984.
9. Skinner DA, McCubbin HI. *Coping in Dual Employed Families: Spousal Differences.* Paper presented at the Annual Meeting of the National Council on Family Relations; October 1982; Washington, DC.
10. Kanter KM. *When Giants Learn to Dance: Mastering the Challenges of Strategy, Management and Careers in the 1990s.* New York, NY: Simon & Schuster; 1990.
11. Staines GL. *The Impact of Work Schedule on the Family.* Ann Arbor, Mich: Institute for Social Research; 1983.
12. Pleck JH. The work-family problem: overloading the system. In: Floisha B, Goldman B, eds. *Outsiders on the Inside: Women in Organizations.* Englewood Cliffs, NJ: Prentice Hall; 1980.
13. Weinert C. Measuring social support: revision and further development of the Personal Resource Questionnaire. In: Waltz C, Strickland O, eds. *Measurement of Nursing Outcomes.* New York, NY: Springer; 1988:1.
14. Weiss R. The provisions of social relationships. In: Rubin D, ed. *Doing unto Others.* Englewood Cliffs, NJ: Prentice Hall; 1974.
15. Parkerson GR, Gehlback SH, Wagner ES, et al. The Duke-UNC Health Profile: an adult health status instrument for primary care. *Med Care.* 1981; 19:806–823.

CHAPTER 5

"You Don't Ask for Trouble": Women Who Do Sex and Drugs

Rachel Beaty Muller, RN, MSN

Joyceen S. Boyle, RN, PhD, FAAN

ALTHOUGH THE literature on human immunodeficiency virus (HIV) and its transmission has burgeoned with information about the disease process, treatment, and epidemiology, there is still little understanding of the social behavior of high-risk groups, especially those who exchange sex for drugs or money.[1] Interventions with clients at risk for HIV have involved education about risk behaviors and condom use; such measures are currently the most effective means to limit the spread of HIV. But attempts to change or influence sexual behavior must take into account the context in which behavior occurs as well as multiple social, cultural, and environmental factors.

The study described in this chapter focused on a group of women who exhibited high-risk behavior—women who en-

The authors acknowledge the contributions to this study by Gerald Bennett, RN, PhD, FAAN, who read and commented on earlier drafts of this article.

Fam Community Health 1996;19(3):35–48
© 1996 Aspen Publishers, Inc.

gaged in sex with multiple partners primarily for money to purchase drugs. The purpose of this research was to understand the context and experiences of a select group of high-risk women, all of whom were in jail on charges of prostitution or being a "public nuisance." In particular, data were elicited about the women's lifestyles, drug use, and sexual experiences, including the use of condoms.

RELATED LITERATURE

Although there are reports of changes in sexual patterns and knowledge related to HIV transmission, little is known about the specific factors that reduce risk and maintain changes in behavior.[2] Studies have indicated that attitudes, values, and beliefs among various cultural and ethnic groups must be taken into account when planning intervention strategies.[3-7] However, many of these studies have major shortcomings when findings are applied to the women in this study. Gender issues are problematic because many of the studies on risk behavior and HIV have examined sexual practices of gay men, and such findings cannot be generalized to women.[8]

The effects of an individual's consumption of alcohol and drugs are also of concern in HIV transmission. Studies have found increased risk behaviors with the use of drugs and alcohol.[9-11] A recent study assessing sexual behavior, sexually transmitted diseases, and cocaine use in inner-city women reported that each of the HIV-positive women acknowledged crack cocaine use.[12] Another recent study of women enrolled in an inner-city

drug treatment program concluded that drug use and HIV disease and acquired immune deficiency syndrome (AIDS) "permeate the subjects' sexual, familial, and household relationships."[13(p271)]

Heterosexual HIV transmission has accounted for the largest proportionate increase in reported AIDS cases, with women representing the larger proportionate increase.[14] Heterosexual contact has become the predominant mode of HIV exposure among women. Prostitutes and their sexual partners have been identified by the Centers for Disease Control[15] as being at increased risk for HIV infection. Many intravenous drug users report prostitution as a means of financial support for their drug use and thus are at risk for HIV infection from intravenous drug use as well as unprotected sex.[16,17] Exchanging sex for drugs or money with the concomitant higher risk for sexually transmitted diseases and HIV infection has also been observed in the crack cocaine culture.[18-22] In addition, prostitutes (as well as other women) are at risk if their steady, nonpaying sexual partners use drugs or engage in behaviors that are likely to expose them to sexually transmitted diseases.[17,23]

Several studies[16,23,24] suggest that many women at high risk do not take adequate protective measures when engaging in sexual activities with someone who is known to them. For example, condoms are not likely to be used by prostitutes with their nonpaying sexual partners. Similarly, heterosexual respondents who reported sexual behavior changes in response to the AIDS epidemic acknowledged continued unprotected intercourse.[25] In contrast, a number of studies[9,16,17] report that many prostitutes require the use of condoms by their customers, a practice that reportedly started in the 1970s in response to the risk of acquiring other sexually transmitted diseases, especially herpes.[9,16,17] Condom use appeared to act as a mechanism that separated a prostitute's professional practice from personal sexual relationships.[26,27]

Pressure from sexual customers as well as economic concerns of the more desperate and vulnerable women makes it difficult for them to comply with safer sexual practices. Women in a drug treatment program developed strategies to reduce the risk of sexually transmitted infections; however, they were unable to sustain risk-reduction efforts.[28] After reviewing studies on women and HIV infection, Smeltzer and Whipple[29] concluded that models for interventions must consider empowerment of women because "women who are most at risk of HIV infection are often disadvantaged and disenfranchised."[29(p255)] Personal empowerment has been suggested as an integral concept in attempting to help drug-dependent African American women.[30–33]

Interventions that address risk behaviors only at the individual level and teach strategies that attempt to change personal behavior without confronting issues and structures that foster risky behavior may be incomplete.[1] Individual behavior change may well be enhanced and supported by incorporating important population-level determinants of risk that include physical, cultural, and environmental considerations.[5,8] Poverty, lack of economic opportunity, discrimi-

nation, and sex inequality and their relationship to HIV risk behaviors have yet to be fully explored. Overall, the AIDS epidemic has been disastrous for poor minority women—in part because of the prevalence of intravenous drug use and crack cocaine in their communities.

METHODS

This study was conducted in a city jail located in a southeastern city in the United States. An ethnographic approach described by Spradley[34,35] was selected to meet the purpose of the study. Ethnography is ideal for the discovery of cultural meaning and facilitates description of the ways that social activities are conducted.[34] An ethnographic design facilitates an understanding of the participants' world and seeks to discover the implicit assumptions and cultural rules that guide behavior.

Data for the study were collected over a 3-month period using interviews and participant observation with 23 women during the time they spent in jail. The focus of the study, however, was on the experiences and context of the women's lives before their incarceration.

Sample

The convenience sample of 23 participants was selected from the jail population. All of the participants admitted to having several sexual partners and had received money or drugs from men for sexual activities. Some of the women reported serial monogamous sexual relationships in the past. Two male participants who were transvestite prostitutes were also interviewed. They reported that they considered themselves women, identified themselves socially by feminine names, dressed as women outside of the jail, were on hormone therapy before incarceration, and functioned as women with their "dates." The data provided by these two male participants about their sexual behavior were consistent with the data provided by the female participants. Although some of the women did not consider themselves prostitutes, all acknowledged being close to the prostitution subculture by virtue of their familiarity with "street life" (ie, knowing how to "sell" sex to obtain money). Drug use, predominantly alcohol and crack cocaine, was an integral part of their daily lives.

The sample consisted of 5 white and 18 African American participants from 18 to 49 years of age. Four of the women were married at the time of the study; 14 participants reported a mean income from prostitution as slightly over $1,500 per month. Of the 14 participants who reported prostitution as a steady means of income, 4 reported practicing prostitution less than 1 year; 5 had been prostitutes from 2 to 5 years, and 3 others had been "in the life" for 5 to 10 years. This study was conducted under conditions of informed consent. Participants were permitted to use initials rather than their full name on the consent form; all tapes were destroyed at the completion of the study.

Data collection and analysis

Data collection and analysis occurred simultaneously; Spradley's[34] approach to ethnographic interviews categorizes the data as they are collected. Interviews were conducted in a private area of the jail. All interviews were audiotaped. The interviews began with "grand tour" questions that elicited a broad view of the women's lives including drug use, sexual practices, and knowledge of HIV disease. The participants were asked such questions as, What can you tell me about AIDS? How do you protect yourself against AIDS? What does your man think about using a condom with him? How do you feel about using a condom? Later, as "insider" language was learned, the questions reflected this knowledge. Tell me how you use your "works." How do you choose your "running partners"? How do you get "paper" for your "stuff"? Tell me about your "old man" and your "friends on the side." What about "freaking and geaking"?

Questions were constructed to categorize data by developing taxonomies based on exclusiveness and inclusiveness. Contrast questions searched for attributes and relationships among the terms and elicited labels, definitions, or examples. Toward the end of each interview, further questions elicited details that had not been sufficiently described by the participants. Women who were knowledgeable about selected topics were interviewed several times to facilitate interpretation of data and expand the initial findings. The jail setting posed some limitations; a few women were released before they participated in additional interviews.

Tapes from 14 participants who reported income from prostitution were transcribed verbatim for analysis. The remaining tapes were scanned for corroborating and atypical data. All interviews were conducted by one of the investigators. The 14 transcripts were read by both investigators for initial insights about the women's lifestyles as well as how they viewed HIV disease and their descriptions of sexual practices and drug use. A total of 71 domains was identified in the initial analysis; these domains were then scrutinized to identify components to expand the description of the domain. For example, the domain "ways to get drugs" was explored to identify the different ways that participants used to obtain drugs. "Having it given to you," "freaking and geaking" (sex and drugs), "doing anything" (becoming a junkie), "stealing," "dating" (prostitution), and "roasting" (con games) were explored to expand the description of the domain. Then ethnographic themes were formulated to explain relationships among the domains.

Qualitative evaluation criteria as defined by Leininger[36] were used to enhance the rigor of this study. Credibility and confirmability were strengthened through repeated inquiry and exhaustive exploration of each domain until theoretical saturation was achieved. The experiences and relationships described by the participants were shared and corroborated by the participants after the initial analysis. This process was followed to ensure that the true significance of actions, symbols, and events was interpreted accurately and reflected the meaning and values of the participants. Meaning-in-context and saturation occurred through extended interviews over a significant period of time as well as fre-

quent reinterviewing and member checks with participants. Findings from this study may have transferability to other women in contexts and situations comparable to those described here.

The method, design, and rationale for conducting an ethnographic analysis have been reported in detail by Spradley.[34,35] Spradley[34] urged the use of the participants' own words and terminology to describe and understand the meaning of experiences. Whenever possible, we have tried to use participants' terminology if we thought it enhanced understanding; on the other hand, we tried not to go overboard with the use of what could be considered "street language." The four themes presented here examine relationships between sex and drugs, sex and money, women with multiple sexual partners, and lastly the use of condoms.

Limitations of the study include the sample and site of the research; only women who were incarcerated in the city jail could be sampled for theoretical saturation. In addition, the study was conducted in a small facility, and the sample was restricted to informants who happened to be incarcerated at the time of the interviews. The participants were asked to describe events that had occurred before their incarceration; there was no opportunity for the investigators to observe their behavior outside of the restricted jail environment.

FINDINGS

Doing sex and drugs

All of the participants reported the use of crack cocaine and multiple sexual partners. Sex and drug use were closely related; sex was used by the women to obtain drugs and to generate money for other needs. The women described an environment where drugs were readily available and everyone used them. The close link between drugs and sexual behavior was explicitly and graphically described by the participants. One participant described a scenario that illustrated how sex and drugs—in this instance crack cocaine—were intimately linked:

We all were in the room and this guy came in with some dope. So we went into the bathroom to cut it up. He asked me, "Who is the bitch with the green pants?" I said, "I don't even know her, she came here with X." So he said, "Go tell her I want to do something with her." I wouldn't tell her nothing, I just say he want to talk with her in the bathroom. She was one of the ones who said she wouldn't do that, but I knew the guy, right. She stayed in the bathroom and I could hear him say, "Look bitch, if you ain't going to do nothing, you can get out. Don't you want this rock?" She ended up doing it.

"Freaking and geaking" are activities that were described in a recreational context; for example, a party usually involved several persons participating in sexual activities while smoking large quantities of crack cocaine. "Freaking" refers to sexual activity; "geaking" is getting high and still wanting more drugs. Freaking and geaking fulfilled social and emotional needs as well as providing a way to obtain drugs. Ménage à trois was described as a common arrangement during these sessions. Freaking and geaking usually began in a social gathering among friends and over time, friends of friends or other acquaintances joined the group. The result was a mix of people participating in drug use and sexual activities in a casual way. One of the participants, a 23-year-old African American named "Star," described how freaking and geaking happens:

Like me and some friends get together. We might meet up with some men; might not even know them, you know how people is. They say, "We got something to get high with, y'all want to go freak and geak a little bit?" Or, me and my friend had a room, so we meet these guys; one had just picked up the other one who was a drug man. They go in the room and the first guy says, "Why don't you all get comfortable" and stuff like that. They start, for example, one of the guys like kinda talked to me and the other say nothing. My girlfriend she was pregnant, she was smoking but they didn't want her, they wanted me. So, we started, both of them steady giving me pieces, both of them wanted me, I was steady smoking. . . .

Other women started on drugs in a slightly different manner. At first they were able to buy cocaine themselves for their personal use. However, when they had no money or they wanted larger quantities of cocaine, freaking and geaking were easy and viable ways to obtain drugs, especially crack cocaine. It was generally understood by everyone that women could engage in sex to obtain drugs or money. Getting together with others led to participation in sexual activities and the use of drugs. These social aspects of freaking and geaking were important to women. Having sex for drugs (as opposed to money) was not viewed as prostitution or considered high-risk behavior by the participants because of the social aspects of the interaction. After all, they were just freaking and geaking with "friends."

Friends on the side

Some of the participants described a different kind of lifestyle, one that involved "friends on the side," or men with whom they had sex to supplement their income. Sometimes money exchanged hands, but it was just as common for the women to receive household goods such as groceries, diapers, clothes, or whatever else was needed. Often men would pay rent or utility bills or simply give the women money. Women with friends on the side were not involved in "street activities" or freaking and geaking. Usually, women who had friends on the side were older and more settled, although they occasionally used drugs. Having friends on the side to help pay the bills was not considered prostitution, and it certainly was not considered high-risk behavior by the participants. It was simply a way of making ends meet. One of the participants named Susie said, "I know girls that go out . . . it ain't no everyday thing like running the streets. A friend might come over and pick them up; they go do a little something and come back with some money. I don't call that prostituting." Because the women knew the men and considered them friends and important members of their support system, they did not believe that having sex with them involved risky behavior.

Many times the women knew that their "friends" were having sex with other women, but they still did not consider the men or themselves at risk for HIV infection. The men could usually be counted on for help when a woman needed it. Breaking off a sexual relationship with them would compromise a woman's financial stability and jeopardize her intimate relationships.

Multiple sexual partners

The participants classified the women they knew into seven categories:
1. just has relationships
2. whore
3. freak
4. junkie
5. has friends on side
6. con artist
7. prostitute (professional or part-time)

Each category identifies characteristics that illustrate the women's status and roles. The ways in which women classified their behaviors and the men with whom they associated were closely tied to decisions about condom use. The conventional definition of having sex for financial gain or even in exchange for drugs was not always considered prostitution. Although the participants had been arrested for prostitution or solicitation, many of them were offended when the term "prostitution" was applied to them.

Women who "just had relationships" were not paid for sex, because these kinds of relationships were based on emotional and social ties to their sexual partners. These relationships were seen as "normal," and women who "had relationships" were usually not involved in street life. "Whores" were differentiated from other women because they were not paid money or anything else in exchange for sexual favors. They were described as women who "gave it away." A whore was the kind of woman who engaged in sex because she thought it would make men like her. The participants considered whores to be at high risk for HIV infection, but they were not "real" prostitutes.

Women who participated in freaking and geaking, or "freaks," generally were not considered prostitutes. They were considered lucky to have friends that could help them obtain drugs. The recreational and social aspects of freaking and geaking were emphasized. One woman explained it this way: "It's all just fun and they want the drug. They going to do what they can to get that drug. Let's go have some fun. Freaking's all in the game with the geaking."

Junkies were freaks who would "do anything" even for a small amount of crack cocaine. A junkie was a step down from a freak in the social order. No participant in this study considered herself a junkie; junkies were described as "too far gone." All the participants maintained that they would never become a junkie because they could control their drug use. Women with "friends on the side" had regular steady relationships that provided support and security.

Another kind of woman with multiple sexual partners was called a "con artist." A con artist promised sexual services but did not follow through if at all possible. For example, con artists pursued targets that were unfamiliar with street life or men who were very drunk or high on drugs. A con artist would promise a man to "go out and get some drugs for a little fun," then take the man's money and not return.

Prostitutes were of two categories: professional and part-time. The women who said they were part-time prostitutes sold sex for money but said they were not financially dependent on prostitution. They only engaged in sex for money when they wanted drugs or to get something for their children. Prostitution was something they initiated, yet they had little control over the actual situation. For example, they did not feel comfortable in setting limits, such as asking the man to wear a condom, because they had not made careful plans for the sexual encounter. On the other hand, professional prostitutes considered that prostitution was "work," and they went about it in a methodical manner. They budgeted their time, not rushing customers but setting time limits. Prostitutes planned their workdays carefully, scheduling "regulars" during the day whenever possible and "turning tricks" at night. Drug use was considered a threat to protecting themselves from unscrupulous "johns," and its use exposed the women to the possibility of getting arrested. Rosie described her mistake: "We were fixing to do a rock and I thought, 'No—I'm going to take care of business first and then I'll get high.' When I get high, I don't pay attention to what I'm doing. So, it's my own stupid fault that I'm in jail."

A protocol was followed by professional prostitutes that they described as "get it on, get it off, get it down the road"—meaning take care of business first and get away from the scene. Professional prostitutes were always aware of the importance of maintaining control of the sexual encounter, especially the use of condoms. They reported that condoms were necessary if they wanted to continue their work. All of the prostitutes could describe the hazards of sexually transmitted diseases, including HIV infection, and they knew that condoms prevented these conditions. Even more importantly, the prostitutes believed they could control sexual encounters primarily by asking that men use condoms. They said that they valued their personal safety and health more than money or drugs. Trixie, a professional, described it this way: "I love myself. I'm the most important thing there is. I don't need your money. You can't pay me for my life. You can only pay me for what we're going to do right now. If you can't do it the way I want us to do it, we don't need to do it at all."

Sex and condom use

Women who described themselves as "prostitutes" were more likely to believe that they were at risk for diseases such as HIV infection. They would verbally acknowledge the need for condoms, but in the reality of street life, the use of condoms varied with the situation. If a woman engaged in sex on an occasional basis—"I am just going to do this for a little bit of money"—the activity might be viewed by society as prostitution, but the woman did not see herself as a "prostitute." Women with "friends on the side," women who sold sex on an occasional basis, and women who participated in social sex such as freaking and geaking were not seen as prostitutes. The participants said that women who were prostitutes "would sleep with anyone" or "do anything." Only three women in the sample admittedly met these self-defined criteria, even though others reported that they exchanged sex for money or drugs. Regardless of the nature of the sexual activity, the women reported that the use of condoms was not a routine practice. Most of the women could describe the awkwardness and discomfort they experienced when they had asked a man to use a condom. Table 5–1 shows the reasons women did not use condoms and illustrates how requesting condom use is transformed from a technically simple practice into a difficult task that is largely influenced, scheduled, and controlled by others.

Lack of comfort

Women said that they did not bring up the subject of condom use in their regular, established relationships because it would imply that they were questioning the man's integrity. Vicky described her reluctance to request condom use this way:

Maybe it's the world that I come from, how I was raised or something. It's always the woman. If you say we should use a condom, there's a fight—first of all. Everything drops, like a dump truck, dumped on you. You're doing something wrong. It [asking about condom use] always reflects on me, couldn't possibly be him. It's always me. His male ego. If push comes to shove, I wouldn't use condoms. Just forget it, because if you love each other and if anything happens, you don't mind.

Table 5–1. Reasons the women did not use condoms

Lack of comfort	Lack of desire	Characteristics of partners
Just don't talk about that kind of thing.	It's bad for business.	He's clean, not sleazy.
I was too young and didn't know about condoms.	Don't use one with my boyfriend.	He's good looking and honest.
He'll think I'm messing around with other men.	Don't care or I forget when I'm using drugs.	I trust him.
	It's not my responsibility to carry them.	
	I just don't have any use for them.	

Some women reported that when they first became sexually active, they did not know that condoms existed, much less how they were used. They said they were "too young"—that is, too inexperienced or unknowledgeable about how to interact with men. Even at present, they said they still felt awkward when talking about condoms or HIV disease with anyone.

Lack of desire

Women reported that they thought condoms were bad for business and social interactions. Taking the time to talk with a man about condoms and to negotiate for condom use during sexual encounters takes time in addition to social skills. Furthermore, the participants said that some men complained that they had decreased feelings with the use of condoms. If a woman wanted to use a condom during sex, the man would immediately be suspicious that she was a "prostitute" or that she "had VD [venereal disease]." If she asked a man to use a condom, the man would spread the ru-

mor that she was sick. Why would she be using a condom? She must have something! These suspicions on the part of both men and women had a destructive influence on personal relationships.

Who should actually provide the condom was another issue of concern. The women reported that professional prostitutes always carried condoms and that condoms were used by women who identified themselves as professional prostitutes. Other women, however, were reluctant to have condoms in their possession. Some men refused to purchase them, and most of the women said they dropped their request for condom use at the slightest resistance. Not insisting on a condom meant women could "ask for more" (ie, more money) for the sexual encounter.

Many women reported that they "dated" or "had friends on the side" most of the time. Maybe they even freaked and geaked, but these were not considered activities that put them at risk for HIV infection because they "weren't doing anything." When "boyfriends" were their sexual partners, women did not see any potential risk. Some women said that if they were heavily using drugs, it was easy for them to "forget" or not care about using condoms.

Characteristics of the partner

An important factor that influenced the use of condoms involved the characteristics of the intended sexual partner. Women reported that they relied on their ability to observe for cleanliness, illness, honesty, general appearance, and carriage, as well as other attributes. They were confident that they were not at risk for AIDS because they were selective about the personal characteristics of their partner. For example, trust and honesty were important when boyfriends and lovers were being assessed. When customers or "tricks" were evaluated, then personal appearance and cleanliness were the criteria to be considered. Except for the three women who acknowledged that they were professional prostitutes, the participants in this study did not see themselves at risk for HIV infection because they were not the kind of women who "had sex with men who were so out of control as to do anything." Men who were "out of control" were men who were "sleazy," not clean, or dishonest or who used drugs heavily.

One of the participants, an intravenous drug user, reported that she found it difficult to believe that she had tested seropositive for HIV infection. She said that she was not "sleazy"; she didn't "run in the streets" or "sleep with just anyone." She claimed that she had never

shared needles. In fact, she believed that she really was not HIV positive; she thought that the drugs she had taken contained impurities which caused an "instability" in her system, and that made her test seropositive. She consistently maintained that she could not have HIV disease because she and the men in her life were "not the type."

DISCUSSION

This study described how a group of women in jail explained their behaviors related to drug use and sexual practices. All of the participants reported the use of crack cocaine and multiple sexual partners. However, the manner in which drugs were obtained and used as well as the kinds of sexual relationships they engaged in varied considerably among the women. Sex was used to obtain drugs and other favors. Women in this study came from a drug-oriented and chaotic environment; they had devised a variety of strategies to take care of themselves. They had learned that sex enabled them to participate in social activities, obtain money and drugs, and engage in intimacy. The women acknowledged that risks were encountered when they engaged in sexual practices or used illegal drugs, and they might briefly consider these risks. However, in the reality of male-dominated street life, strategies that would ensure the use of condoms were difficult to implement without endangering relationships. These relationships were important to the women, because they had learned that sex enabled them to maintain intimate relationships with men who could help them financially or who could provide them with drugs. Most importantly, relationships with men provided women with a sense of emotional well-being. Asking a man to use a condom during sex would endanger the relationship, and it was obvious that "you don't go around askin' for trouble."

To the outsider, it may appear that women like those in this study live promiscuously with indiscriminate sexual encounters and widespread use of illegal drugs. Although sexual encounters and the use of drugs are common, this view is far too simplistic to explain the behavior of the women in this study. The use of drugs and sexual practices differed considerably according to the kinds of relationships women had with men. An important aspect of meaning for women in this study were relationships with men. It is around these different kinds of relationships that the women learned to organize their behavior and interpret their experiences.

IMPLICATIONS

Sexual practices and drug use were closely linked in this study of women at high risk for developing HIV disease. Sexual relationships and drug use provided women with opportunities for social interaction and intimate relationships that enhanced their self-esteem and sense of worth. Drug use and sexual practices, including the use of condoms, varied considerably according to the kinds of relationships engaged in by women. Professional prostitutes were willing to forgo establishing emotionally

based relationships with men and expected only financial remuneration for sexual favors. In contrast, other women in the study valued the sense of being wanted and an intimate relationship with a member of the opposite sex. Maintaining such relationships and their positive benefits was the most important cultural theme in this research project. Until women like those who participated in this study can satisfy their emotional needs outside of the context of drugs and sex, efforts to encourage such women to use condoms and take other precautions against HIV infection will be relatively unsuccessful.

Furthermore, the findings supported the notion that the women underestimated the probability of HIV infection posed by their personal behaviors, because they did not view unprotected sex with multiple partners as risky. Instead, the use of condoms was influenced by the emotional overtones attributed to relationships, personal characteristics of sexual partners, and the assumption that women could detect their partners' risk behaviors.

• • •

The findings from this research support studies[30,31,33,37] that suggest personal empowerment may be an integral concept in working with drug-dependent or poor minority women. Indeed, it may be the first step in helping women negotiate condom use or instigate other positive behavioral changes. Multidimensional approaches that include educational programs that acknowledge client experiences, values, and contributions are necessary if empowerment is a goal of these programs. Integration of health and social programs that address the larger context and the effects of unequal power and economic bases as they relate to sexual issues must be incorporated in program designs. Emphasis should be placed on developing the skills related to negotiation for safer sex practices and rejection of the double standard that is so pervasive in the lives of these participants and other groups of women. Of critical importance, however, is that empowerment of women be viewed in the context of sociocultural, economic, and political considerations.

REFERENCES

1. Choi K, Coats TJ. Prevention of HIV infection. *AIDS*. 1994;8:1371–1389.
2. Becker MH, Joseph JG. AIDS and behavioral change to reduce risk: a review. *Am J Public Health*. 1988;78:394–410.
3. Flaskerud JH, Rush CE. AIDS and traditional health beliefs and practices of black women. *Nurs Res*. 1989;38:210–215.
4. Flaskerud JH, Nyamathi AM. Black and Latina women's AIDS-related knowledge, attitudes and practices. *Res Nurs Health*. 1989;12:339–346.
5. Jeffery RW. Risk behaviors and health: contrasting individual and population perspective. *Am Psychol*. 1989;44:1194–1202.
6. Jemmott LS, Jemmott JB III. Applying the theory of reasoned action to AIDS risk behavior: condom use among black women. *Nurs Res*. 1991;40:228–233.
7. Ickovics JR, Morrill AC, Bern SE, Walsh U, Rodin J. Limited effects of HIV counseling and testing for women: a prospective study of behavioral and psychological consequences. *JAMA*. 1994;272:443–448.
8. Aggleton P, O'Reilly K, Slutkin G, Davies P. Risking everything? Risk behavior, behavior change, and AIDS. *Science*. 1994;265:341–345.
9. Des Jarlais D, Friedman S, Hopkins W. Risk reduction for the acquired immunodeficiency syndrome among intravenous drug users. *Ann Intern Med*. 1985;103:755–759.
10. Stall R, McKusick L, Wiley J, Coates T, Ostrow D. Alcohol and drug use during sexual activity and compliance with safe sex guidelines for AIDS: the AIDS behavioral research project. *Health Educ Q*. 1986;13:359–371.
11. Grune JPC, Kaplan CD, Adriaans NFP. Needle sharing in the Netherlands: an ethnographic analysis. *Am J Public Health*. 1991;81:1602–1607.
12. DeHovitz JA, Kelly P, Feldman J, et al. Sexually transmitted diseases, sexual behavior and cocaine use in inner-city women. *Am J Epidemiol*. 1994;140:1125–1134.
13. Pivnick A, Jacobson A, Eric K, Doll L, Drucker E. AIDS, HIV infection and illicit drug use within inner-city families and social networks. *Am J Public Health*. 1994;84:271–274.
14. Centers for Disease Control. Update: acquired immunodeficiency syndrome—United States, 1992. *MMWR*. 1993;42(28):547–557.
15. Centers for Disease Control. Additional recommendations to reduce sexual and drug abuse-related transmission of HTLV III/LAV. *MMWR*. 1986;35(10):152–156.
16. Centers for Disease Control. Antibody to human immunodeficiency virus in female prostitutes. *MMWR*. 1987;36(11):157–161.
17. Rosenberg MJ, Weiner JM. Prostitutes and AIDS: a health department priority? *Am J Public Health*. 1988;78:418–423.
18. Fullilove RE, Fullilove MT, Bowser P, Gross SA. Risk of sexually transmitted disease among black adolescent crack users in Oakland and San Francisco, Calif. *Sex Transm Dis*. 1990;263:851–855.
19. Booth RE, Waters JK, Chitwood DD. HIV risk-related sex behaviors among injecting drug users, crack smokers, and injection drug users who smoke crack. *Am J Public Health*. 1993;83:1144–1148.
20. Fullilove MT, Golden E, Fullilove RE, et al. Crack cocaine use and high-risk behaviors among sexually active black adolescents. *J Adolesc Health*. 1993;14:295–300.
21. Edlin BR, Irwin KL, Faruque S, et al. Intersecting epidemics—crack cocaine use and HIV infection among inner-city young adults. *N Engl J Med*. 1994;24:1422–1427.

22. Schilling R, El-Bassel N, Ivanoff A, Gilbert L, Su KH, Saffyer SM. Sexual risk behavior of incarcerated, drug-using women, 1992. *Public Health Rep.* 1994;109:539–547.

23. Leonard MA, Sacks JJ, Franks AL, Sikes K. The prevalence of human immunodeficiency virus, hepatitis B, and syphilis among female prostitutes in Atlanta. *J Med Assoc Ga.* 1988;77:162–167.

24. Guinan ME, Hardy A. Epidemiology of AIDS in women in the United States: 1982–1987. *JAMA.* 1988;257:2039–2042.

25. Melnick SL, Jeffery RW, Burke GL, et al. Changes in sexual behavior by young urban heterosexual adults in response to the AIDS epidemic. *Public Health Rep.* 1993;108:582–588.

26. Day S. Prostitute women and AIDS: anthropology. *AIDS.* 1988;2:421–428.

27. Campbell CA. Prostitution, AIDS, and preventive health behavior. *Soc Sci Med.* 1991;32:1367–1378.

28. Suffet F, Lifshitz M. Women addicts and the threat of AIDS. *Qual Health Res.* 1991;1:51–79.

29. Smeltzer SC, Whipple B. Women and HIV infection. *Image J Nurs Schol.* 1991;23:249–256.

30. Mondanaro J. Strategies for AIDS prevention: motivating health behavior in drug dependent women. *J Psychoactive Drugs.* 1987;19:143–149.

31. Weissman G. Promoting health behavior among women at risk for AIDS. *NIDA Notes.* 1988;(Winter):6–7.

32. Fullilove MT, Fullilove RE, Haynes K, Gross SA. Black women and AIDS prevention: a view towards understanding the gender rules. *J Sex Res.* 1990; 27:47–64.

33. Harris RM, Kavanagh KH, Hetherington SE, Scott DE. Strategies for AIDS prevention. *Clin Nurs Res.* 1992;1:9–24.

34. Spradley JP. *The Ethnographic Interview.* New York, NY: Holt, Rinehart & Winston; 1979.

35. Spradley JP. *Participant Observation.* New York, NY: Holt, Rinehart & Winston; 1980.

36. Leininger M. Evaluation criteria and critique of qualitative research studies. In: Morse J, ed. *Critical Issues in Qualitative Research Methods.* Thousand Oaks, Calif: Sage; 1994.

37. Mondanaro J. *Chemically Dependent Women: Assessment and Treatment.* Lexington, Mass: D. C. Heath; 1989.

CHAPTER 6

Cardiovascular Disease Risk Factors in Anglo and Mexican American Children and Their Mothers

Shelia L. Broyles, PhD

Philip R. Nader, MD

James F. Sallis, PhD

Gail C. Frank-Spohrer, DrPH, RD

Charles C. Berry, PhD

Thomas L. McKenzie, PhD

John P. Elder, PhD, MPH

ALTHOUGH CORONARY heart disease (CHD) has historically been associated with higher-income Anglo Americans, research over the past several years has indicated that this group is no longer a unique risk group. Based on recent findings discussed in the National Heart, Lung, and Blood Institute[1] (NHLBI) Task Force report on cardiovascular diseases, African Americans, Mexican Americans, and Native Americans have higher rates of some CHD than Anglo Americans. In addition, less affluent, less educated groups have higher rates of CHD risk factors and higher rates of CHD. This NHLBI report emphasized the importance of conducting studies to determine the effects of socioeconomic conditions and cultural characteristics on outcomes of risk factor con-

Supported by National Heart, Lung, and Blood Institute Grant HL35109 to Philip R. Nader, MD, and Grant HL39870-08 to Philip R. Nader, MD, and Shelia L. Broyles, PhD.

The authors gratefully acknowledge Thomas Davis, Tricia Hoy, Lawrence McGlynn, Julie Nelson, and Louise Schwartz for their assistance with statistical analyses and Rita Coria for her expert technical and editorial assistance.

Fam Community Health 1996;19(3):57–72
© 1996 Aspen Publishers, Inc.

trol among specific racial and ethnic populations. From a better understanding of variations in risk factors will come more population-specific and effective interventions.

Mexican Americans share high rates of cardiovascular disease (CVD) with other US ethnic groups. CVD mortality rates for Los Angeles County Latinos have been found to be slightly lower than Anglo Americans (ie, non-Hispanic white people) and African Americans but were significantly higher than rates for various Asian ethnic groups.[2] Other studies have found CVD mortality rates for Mexican American men to be lower than Anglo American men, but rates for women were similar.[3–6]

In numerous studies of CVD risk factors in Latino adults[7–14] and children,[15] comparisons were made with Anglo Americans, and similar studies have explored ethnic differences in dietary practices[16–21] and physical activity habits.[22–25] These studies have advanced the understanding of CVD risk in Mexican Americans; however, it is well known that ethnic groups differ on many sociodemographic variables.

Studies of ethnic differences in CVD risk factors and health behaviors must take into consideration the confounds introduced by differences in socioeconomic status (SES), a concept usually measured by variables such as income, education, and occupational prestige. Poverty is known to be an important determinant of many health parameters and has an association with excess mortality that is largely independent of individual behavior.[26] Health status has been found to relate more strongly to income

than to race,[27] and ethnic differences in mortality rates typically disappear or are reduced when SES is controlled.[28] CVD risk factors are strongly associated with SES within some ethnic groups, including Mexican Americans.[9,12,16,29]

It is likely that income strongly influences food selection,[30] which in turn influences nutrient intake and CVD risk. Physical activity has been consistently found to be lower in low-SES populations.[31,32] Several studies have attempted to control for SES differences between ethnic groups, either through systematic subject sampling methods[14,29,33] or various statistical techniques.[10,11,34] At least one study has attempted to identify the component of SES that is most related to health risk.[35] Though these approaches to untangle the effects of ethnicity and SES on health variables have promise, there is no clear consensus on the most appropriate method, and further work in this area is needed.

While most recent multiethnic studies adjust for SES in some way, it is unclear how marital status and family structure are related to the health of parents and children. Marital status has been found to be related to health status in several ethnic groups,[36,37] but other studies have indicated that children from single- or dual-parent families do not differ in health status[38] or in preventive health behaviors when SES is controlled.[39]

The present study examines the relationship between sociodemographic factors, health behaviors, and CVD risk factors in Mexican American and Anglo American families with preschool children. The effects of ethnicity, SES, and marital status are estimated. Through multivariate methods, the relationships of children's physical activity, selected eating behaviors, and physical and physiological characteristics to sociodemographic variables are examined. This study extends previous research by examining multiple risk factors and health behaviors in a biethnic sample of young children and their mothers participating in the Study of Children's Activity and Nutrition (SCAN). SCAN was a longitudinal observational study of Mexican American and Anglo American children who entered the cohort at 4 years of age. The SCAN study was designed to characterize the development of dietary and physical activity behaviors in children, the relationships between these behaviors, and their determinants.

METHODS

Participants

Participants for the Study of Children's Activity and Nutrition were recruited from San Diego County state-funded preschools, children's centers, and Head Start centers. One hundred and eight preschools serving low- to middle-income families were invited to participate, and 63 schools consented. Participating schools were more likely to be public than private [$\chi^2(2, N = 108) = 7.09, P < 0.05$]. However, there were no significant differences between participating and nonparticipating schools on number of children, ethnic distribution, or percentage of single-parent families.

Parents with children enrolled in the 63 consenting schools were invited to participate in the study when they came

to pick up their children. Interested parents were scheduled for a home visit to explain the study and obtain informed consent. Parents or children with a medical condition that limited their dietary or physical activity behavior (eg, diabetes or congenital heart disease) were excluded. Four hundred and six families initially signed consent forms, representing 22% of the children enrolled in the target preschools. Three hundred and fifty-one families (86%) actively participated in two home visits at baseline and thus constituted the cohort. Due to the intrusiveness of the study, it was not possible to compare participating and nonparticipating families.

Family was operationally defined as a household shared by at least one adult and one 4-year-old. Measures were collected on the target child and up to two adult caregivers. The ethnicity, gender, and socioeconomic status of mothers and children are presented in Table 6–1.

As expected, the SES levels of Anglo American and Mexican American families were significantly different, as indicated in Table 6–2. Because one of the primary purposes is to attempt to discriminate the effects of SES and ethnicity, it is important to examine their joint distributions. Most Mexican Americans were concentrated in the lowest SES category. Anglo Americans were more evenly distributed, but by design (ie, school selection) there were few families in the highest SES groups.

Fifty percent of the Anglo American families were headed by two married adults, 10% by two unmarried adults, and 40% by an unmarried or divorced adult. Of the single-parent Anglo American

Table 6–1. Characteristics of mothers and their children at baseline

| | N | | Age | | | |
| | | | Anglo American | | Mexican American | |
Group	Anglo American	Mexican American	M	SD	M	SD
Mothers	146	201	32.2	5.70	30.7	6.12
Children						
Male	82	102*	4.4	0.56	4.4	0.51
Female	67	100	4.3	0.47	4.5	0.48

*One Mexican American child was paired with an Anglo American mother.

families (n = 59), only four were headed by single fathers. Of the 201 Mexican American families, 60% were headed by two married adults, 10% by two unmarried adults, and 30% by a single or divorced female. Because relatively few fathers (n = 93) participated in measurement, data are presented only for participating mothers and children; data from the four unmarried Anglo fathers are not included. It was judged that there was sufficient overlap of distributions in categories 3, 4, and 5 to allow multivariate analyses. Of the 347 mother–child pairs, data from the 329 who were from SES categories 3, 4, and 5 are presented here. There were only 4 subjects in SES category 1 and 15 subjects in category 2,

Table 6–2. Number of SCAN families in each socioeconomic category*

| | Socioeconomic status† | | | | | | | |
Ethnicity of parent	1	2	3	4	5	M	SD	Total
Anglo American†	3	12	46	47	37	3.71	1.01	145
Mexican American	1	3	16	25	155	4.65	0.74	200
Category total (%)	1.2	4.3	18.0	20.9	55.7			345

*Data presented are for participating mothers and their children with complete SES data; data from the four unmarried Anglo fathers are not included. Two families did not complete the demographic questionnaire. SCAN = Study of Children's Activity and Nutrition.
†Based on Hollingshead's[48] two-factor index of socioeconomic status (SES) (1 = high, 5 = low).
‡Ethnic differences in categories 3, 4, and 5 were statistically significant [χ^2 (2, N = 326) = 83.83, $P <$ .0001]; categories 1 and 2 were not tested or used in other analyses.

the highest-income categories. Due to the small cell size, categories 1 and 2 were excluded from these analyses.

Materials and procedures

Assessment of physical activity

Physical activity and eating behaviors of target children were assessed by a direct observation technique called Behaviors of Eating and Activity for Child Health: Evaluation System (BEACHES).[40] BEACHES uses a series of codes to characterize the target child's physical environment (school, home, indoors, or outdoors), social environment (presence of parents, teachers, siblings, or peers), physical activity level (lying down, sitting, standing, walking, or very active), ingestion of food, and interactions relating to physical activity and eating behaviors.[40]

Data were entered as codes into a portable lap-held computer. Home observations began approximately 30 minutes before dinner and were conducted for a total of 60 minutes. School lunch was observed for a maximum of 20 minutes, and school recess was observed for a maximum of 30 minutes. The school recess and lunch observation times varied with individual school schedules.

Energy expenditure was calculated as kilocalories per kilogram body weight per minute (kcal/kg/min) from observed activity.[40] Child energy expenditure was averaged over two home or two school visits.

Parental physical activity was assessed by the Physical Activity Recall (PAR), an interviewer-administered questionnaire, evoking a 7-day recall of weekday and weekend activities.[41] A same-day interobserver reliability of .86 has been reported,[42] and it has been validated in studies with adults.[43] Total energy for physical activity, kcal/kg/day, was determined based on the information provided on the PAR.

Assessment of eating behaviors

A semiquantitative Food Frequency Questionnaire (FFQ)[44–46] was used to assess the parent's typical dietary intake over a 3-month period. FFQ estimates the intake of 62 nutrients based on 116 different foods. Four open-ended questions allow for the inclusion of foods not listed on the questionnaire. Plastic food models were used to increase accuracy of portion size estimates. Total energy intake, mg cholesterol per 1,000 kcal, mg of sodium, percentage of calories from protein and carbohydrates, total fat, and the grams of saturated fat were used to characterize the eating patterns of mothers.

A Food Intake Record (FIR) was completed by the primary caregiver and a trained observer to provide a measure of the child's food and nutrient intake during a 24-hour period. The observer recorded foods the child ate during BEACHES observations both at school and at home. The parent reported foods the child ate at other times of the same days, including breakfast and snacks. Observers were trained in both portion size estimation and interviewing techniques to help parents and other food preparers characterize ingredients and quantities.

The FIR was validated using a 12-hour observation by a trained nutritionist. The average Pearson correlation for 12 key nutrients was .58, with significant differences for protein, cholesterol, and sodium ($P < .05$). The FIR was coded using version 1.3 of the Minnesota Nutrition Data System (NDS) software,[47] which profiles 102 nutrients from a database of over 3,000 foods.

Social and physical environment assessment

A demographic questionnaire was used to obtain information on the following for each available parent: birth date, ethnicity, marital status, number of biological parents living in the home, employment status, occupation, family income, and years of education or highest degree obtained. An SES score was based on Hollingshead's[48] two-factor index. The index is based on years of education and occupational status and ranges from 1 = high SES to 5 = low SES.

Physical and physiological characteristics

Height was measured to the nearest quarter inch using a standard metal measuring tape, and weight was measured with a standard digital electronic scale. Body mass index (BMI) was calculated as kg/m^2.

Measures of triceps and subscapular skinfolds were obtained using calibrated Lange calipers on the right side of the body, perpendicular to the fold of the skin, 1 cm below the raised tissue. Each skinfold measure was repeated until the observer obtained at least two values that differed by 1 mm or less. Reliabilities for the same observer on different days, following training and prior to measurement 1, averaged .94 for triceps and .96 for subscapular sites. Interobserver reliabilities were .92 for triceps and .91 for subscapular sites. The sum of triceps and subscapular skinfolds was used in all analyses.

For both parents and children, resting blood pressures were taken from the right arm (at heart level) at least 5 minutes after the participant was seated. Three pressures with at least 1 minute between readings were taken using random-zero sphygmomanometers. Mean systolic and diastolic blood pressures (fourth or fifth phase for children, fifth phase for adults) were recorded. Test–retest reliabilities for children at home measures were .61 for systolic and .64 for diastolic. Heart rate was recorded twice.

Field observers

Nine of 11 observers were bilingual in Spanish and English. The total training time required for certification of observers prior to the baseline measurement was 103 hours and included classroom instruction with modeling, guided field practice, and rehearsal of home and school visits. Observers were retrained and recertified every 6 months, except for BEACHES skills, on which they were reassessed every 6 weeks.

RESULTS

Association among sociodemographic variables

A chi-square test was conducted to determine if marital status of SCAN mothers was related to ethnic origin. The result was not statistically significant. A chi-square test also failed to demonstrate a statistically significant relationship between marital status of SCAN mothers and SES categories 3, 4, and 5. However, there was a statistically significant difference in SES levels 3, 4, and 5 of Anglo Americans and Mexican Americans, $[\chi^2(2, N = 326) = 83.83, P < .0001]$ (Table 6–2).

Unadjusted differences between ethnic groups

The means and standard deviations for each of the key variables for children are presented in Table 6–3. t Tests were performed to evaluate differences between Anglo Americans and Mexican Americans and between males and females within each ethnicity. Anglo American children had significantly higher energy expenditures at home ($P < .004$) and significantly higher diastolic blood pressure ($P < .03$) than Mexican Americans. Anglo American children had overall higher energy intakes ($P < .0002$) and intake of calories from carbohydrates ($P < .0001$). Mexican Americans had higher intakes of calories from protein ($P < .0001$), calories from saturated fat ($P < .002$), calories from total fat ($P < .0002$), and mg cholesterol per 1,000 kcal ($P < .0001$).

There was one gender difference in the variables tested in Mexican American children; boys had higher systolic blood pressure than girls ($P < .05$). In Anglo American children, boys had significantly higher energy expenditures than girls both at home and recess ($P < .002$ and $P < .02$, respectively), as well as higher en-

ergy intakes ($P < .002$). Anglo American girls had higher total skinfolds than Anglo American boys ($P < .0002$).

The means and standard deviations for each of the key variables for mothers are presented in Table 6–4. Anglo American mothers had higher diastolic blood pressures ($P < .04$), percentages of calories from protein ($P < .04$), total fat ($P < .0001$), and saturated fat ($P < .0001$) than Mexican American mothers. Mexican American mothers had higher energy intakes ($P < .0001$), percentages of calories from carbohydrates ($P < .0001$), mg cholesterol per 1,000 kcal ($P < .03$), and mg sodium ($P < .0001$) than Anglo American mothers.

Regression analyses of sociodemographic and CVD risk variables in children

The relationships of children's physical activity, eating behaviors, and physical and physiological characteristics to demographic factors were examined. Multiple linear regression analyses were performed using SAS PROC GLM (SAS Institute, Inc, Cary, NC). Socioeconomic status, ethnicity, gender, and marital status were used as the independent variables. Dummy variables for the different levels of these factors were constructed using effect coding. Thus, the regression intercept estimates the mean of Anglo American males in SES category 3 whose mothers are married, while the variables "Hispanic," "female," "SES 4," "SES 5," "unmarried with partner," and "unmarried without partner" estimate the increments associated with those characteristics.

Table 6–3. Children's characteristics, by ethnicity and gender

| | Anglo American | | | | | |
| | Male | | | Female | | |
Variable	M	SD	n	M	SD	n
Home energy expenditure (kcal/kg/min)	0.06369	0.0093	74	0.05904	0.0070	60
Recess energy expenditure (kcal/kg/min)	0.0833	0.0129	73	0.0779	0.0124	60
Total skinfold (mm)	17.563	4.782	71	21.706	6.978	59
Body mass index (kg/m^2)	15.837	1.268	65	16.061	2.061	46
Systolic blood pressure (mm/Hg)	95.676	11.231	65	97.673	12.151	48
Diastolic blood pressure (mm/Hg)	60.682	9.100	(65)	62.305	8.884	48
Food intake record						
Energy intake (kcal)	1508.878	318.191	73	1322.534	320.379	60
Protein (% kcal)	15.556	2.746	73	15.217	2.854	60
Carbohydrates (% kcal)	52.903	6.753	73	53.286	6.667	60
Saturated fat (% kcal)	12.959	2.403	73	13.377	2.659	60
Total fat (% kcal)	33.210	5.221	73	33.255	6.018	60
Sodium (mg)	2019.413	654.872	73	1813.371	662.418	60
Cholesterol (per 1,000 kcal)	129.300	76.780	73	136.919	62.158	60

The regression models for children are presented in Table 6–5. Gender was significantly associated with energy expenditure at home ($P < .03$), energy expenditure at recess ($P < .02$), and total skinfold ($P < .001$). Boys had higher energy expenditures, while girls had larger skinfolds.

Anglo American children had higher energy expenditures at home ($P < .02$). Mexican American children had higher intakes of most dietary variables: mg cholesterol per 1,000 kcal ($P < .0001$), intakes of calories from protein ($P < .0001$), intakes of calories from total fat ($P < .02$), and saturated fat ($P < .05$). However, Anglo Americans had higher energy intakes ($P < .007$) and a higher intake of calories from carbohydrates (P < .0001). Lower SES children had higher intakes of calories from total fat (category 4, $P < .003$; category 5, $P <$ .006) than did the middle SES group (category 3). Middle SES children (category 3) had higher intakes of calories from carbohydrates than did category 4 ($P <$ .03) and category 5 ($P < .03$). Marital status of mothers predicted only sodium intake of children: Children of unmarried mothers with partners had significantly higher intakes of sodium than children of married mothers ($P < .05$).

The sociodemographic variables accounted for relatively small amounts of variance in children's CVD risk factors and risk behaviors. The range in adjusted R^2 was .017 to .104 (body mass index and percent of kcal from carbohydrates,

	Mexican American						P value of t test		
								Gender within ethnic group	
Male			Female			Ethnic groups	Anglo American	Mexican American
M	SD	n	M	SD	n			
0.05898	0.0093	99	0.05852	0.0082	97	< .004	< .002	< .72
0.08050	0.0140	99	0.07829	0.0144	96	< .34	< .02	< .29
17.800	6.007	97	18.892	6.553	95	< .13	< .0002	< .23
15.942	1.720	90	15.727	1.970	88	< .69	< .52	< .44
95.475	8.604	89	92.848	8.467	86	< .07	< .37	< .05
59.078	11.707	89	58.395	10.233	86	< .03	< .35	< .69
1276.858	298.829	98	1295.496	366.991	97	< .0002	< .002	< .70
17.064	3.047	98	17.035	2.980	97	< .0001	< .49	< .95
49.290	6.940	98	48.146	7.674	97	< .0001	< .75	< .28
13.924	2.461	98	14.216	2.863	97	< .002	< .35	< .45
34.971	5.073	98	36.264	6.286	97	< .0002	< .97	< .12
1928.076	618.313	98	1948.940	640.446	97	< .87	< .08	< .82
185.361	100.464	98	190.515	93.856	97	< .0001	< .54	< .72

respectively). In the 13 regression models, SES category 5 was significantly different from category 3 in two regressions, SES category 4 was significantly different from category 3 in two regressions, gender was significant in three regressions, ethnicity was significant in seven regressions, and children of unmarried mothers with partners were significantly different from children of married mothers in one regression.

Regression analyses of sociodemographic and CVD risk variables in mothers

The relationships of mothers' physical activity, select eating behaviors, and physical and physiological characteristics were studied with multiple linear regressions of these variables on SES, marital status, and ethnicity. The results are presented in Table 6–6.

Mexican American mothers reported a higher energy intake ($P < .009$), more carbohydrates per 1,000 kcal ($P < .0001$), and more sodium ($P < .005$) than Anglo American mothers. Anglo American mothers reported a higher percentage of calories from total fat ($P < .0001$) and saturated fat ($P < .0001$); and a higher percentage of protein ($P < .04$).

Lower SES (category 5) mothers reported higher energy intakes ($P < .02$) and intake of calories from carbohydrates ($P < .006$) and lower percentage of calories from total fat ($P < .03$) than SES category 3. Category 4 reported

Table 6–4. Mothers' characteristics by ethnicity

Variable	Anglo American			Mexican American			P value of *t* test: Ethnic groups
	M	SD	n	M	SD	n	
Physical activity (kcal/kg/day)	34.449	3.484	129	33.926	3.383	192	< .18
Total skinfold (mm)	45.906	22.348	103	47.873	17.131	178	< .44
Body mass index (kg/m^2)	25.668	6.697	122	26.251	5.256	190	< .42
Systolic blood pressure (mm/Hg)	106.068	12.115	125	103.799	9.838	194	< .09
Diastolic blood pressure (mm/Hg)	67.313	10.475	125	64.903	8.507	194	< .04
Willett Food Frequency Questionnaire[44-46]							
Energy intake (kcal)	2013.753	736.257	129	2342.938	757.957	196	< .0001
Protein (% kcal)	16.112	3.459	129	15.390	2.496	196	< .04
Carbohydrates (% kcal)	48.628	8.051	129	54.516	6.834	196	< .0001
Saturated fat (% kcal)	13.578	2.959	129	11.910	2.483	196	< .0001
Total fat (% kcal)	36.559	6.519	129	32.171	5.205	196	< .0001
Sodium (mg)	1961.784	727.423	129	2301.473	800.098	196	< .0001
Cholesterol (per 1,000 kcal)	147.090	53.040	129	161.788	63.804	196	< .03

Table 6–5. Regression results of sociodemographic variables on CVD risk factors in children*

Dependent variable	Intercept	Mexican American	Female	SES 4	SES 5	Unmarried with partner	Unmarried without partner	R^2	F	P <
Home energy expenditure	0.062	−0.0026	−0.0021	−0.0021	−0.0008	−0.0001	0.0011	.049	2.83	.02
	<.0001	<.02	<.03	<.18	<.55	<.97	<.26			
Recess energy expenditure	0.083	−0.0003	−0.0035	−0.0027	−0.0026	0.0041	0.0018	.034	1.92	.08
	<.0001	<.82	<.02	<.28	<.21	<.10	<.26			
Total skinfold (mm)	18.53	−0.93	2.26	0.031	−0.43	−2.00	0.626	.056	3.14	.006
	<.0001	<.24	<.001	<.97	<.66	<.09	<.40			
Body mass index (kg/m²)	15.80	−0.115	−0.054	−0.010	0.129	−0.345	0.368	.017	0.82	.56
	<.0001	<.63	<.79	<.97	<.66	<.32	<.11			
Systolic BP (mm/Hg)	98.21	−1.11	−0.922	−1.70	−3.11	1.20	0.631	.029	1.43	.21
	<.0001	<.41	<.43	<.41	<.07	<.54	<.63			
Diastolic BP (mm/Hg)	62.32	−1.77	0.141	−1.43	−2.34	0.277	0.649	.023	1.12	.36
	<.0001	<.21	<.90	<.50	<.18	<.89	<.63			
Food intake record										
Energy intake (kcal)	1407.51	−117.16	−71.98	70.59	3.70	47.42	60.79	.060	3.45	.003
	<.0001	<.007	<.06	<.26	<.94	<.45	<.13			
Protein (% kcal)	15.65	1.72	−0.14	−0.258	−0.247	−0.531	0.075	.076	4.43	.0003
	<.0001	<.0001	<.64	<.64	<.59	<.34	<.83			
Carbohydrates (per 1,000 kcal)	54.97	−3.74	−0.46	−3.08	−2.50	0.237	0.138	.104	6.26	.0001
	<.0001	<.0001	<.55	<.03	<.03	<.86	<.87			
Saturated fat (% kcal)	12.61	0.66	0.34	0.665	0.73	0.43	−0.28	.06	2.87	.01
	<.0001	<.05	<.23	<.17	<.08	<.38	<.36			
Total fat (% kcal)	31.18	1.77	0.719	3.14	2.46	0.34	−0.211	.078	4.54	.0002
	<.0001	<.02	<.24	<.003	<.006	<.74	<.75			
Sodium (mg)	1799.32	−17.44	−79.07	118.73	151.34	249.46	118.84	.024	1.37	.23
	<.0001	<.83	<.26	<.32	<.13	<.05	<.12			
Cholesterol (per 1,000 kcal)	116.41	48.01	6.08	17.75	21.85	13.41	−1.90	.099	5.90	.0001
	<.0001	<.0001	<.53	<.28	<.11	<.42	<.85			

Note: Dummy variables were constructed so that the regression intercept estimates the mean of Anglo American males in SES category 3 whose mothers are married, while the variables "Mexican American," "female," "SES 4," "SES 5," "unmarried with partner," and "unmarried without partner" estimate the increments associated with those characteristics. CVD = cardiovascular disease; SES = socioeconomic status; BP = blood pressure.

*Values shown are standardized regression coefficients (Beta) and P values.

Table 6-6. Regression results of sociodemographic variables on CVD risk factors in mothers*

Independent variable	Intercept	Mexican American	SES 4	SES 5	Unmarried with partner	Unmarried without partner	R^2	F	P
Physical activity (kcal/kg/day)	34.10	0.028	1.25	-0.54	0.25	0.46	.038	2.55	.03
	< .0001	< .94	< .06	< .31	< .69	< .26			
Total skinfold (mm)	49.82	2.62	-2.54	-1.98	-8.10	-6.59	.037	2.14	.07
	< .0001	< .32	< .52	< .55	< .04	< .02			
Body mass index (kg/m²)	26.55	0.29	-0.23	0.16	-2.16	-1.63	.025	1.60	.17
	< .0001	< .70	< .83	< .86	< .04	< .02			
Systolic BP (mm/Hg)	105.02	-2.54	4.44	1.87	-0.56	-1.94	.033	2.18	.06
	< .0001	< .08	< .04	< .28	< .78	< .14			
Diastolic BP (mm/Hg)	66.87	-2.09	3.40	0.34	-0.60	-1.31	.035	2.28	.05
	< .0001	< .09	< .06	< .81	< .73	< .25			
Willett Food Frequency Questionnaire[44-46]									
Energy intake (kcal)	1756.37	253.13	284.32	303.94	329.00	81.08	.080	5.57	.0001
	< .0001	< .009	< .05	< .02	< .02	< .37			
Protein (% kcal)	17.05	-0.799	-1.53	-0.605	-0.228	-0.702	.046	3.14	.009
	< .0001	< .04	< .006	< .19	< .67	< .05			
Carbohydrates (per 1,000 kcal)	46.84	4.86	2.60	3.23	-1.04	-0.025	.156	11.86	.0001
	< .0001	< .0001	< .07	< .006	< .44	< .97			
Saturated fat (% kcal)	14.03	-1.43	-0.772	-8.04	0.580	-0.025	.099	7.08	.0001
	< .0001	< .0001	< .15	< .07	< .25	< .97			
Total fat (% kcal)	37.35	-3.56	-1.03	-2.09	1.48	0.272	.142	10.60	.0001
	< .0001	< .0001	< .34	< .03	< .17	< .69			
Sodium (mg)	1889.68	283.18	49.99	138.89	218.18	-43.40	.057	3.90	.002
	< .0001	< .005	< .73	< .26	< .13	< .64			
Cholesterol (% kcal)	154.39	13.61	-18.71	-5.51	4.02	-1.57	.023	1.54	.18
	< .0001	< .08	< .10	< .56	< .72	< .82			

Note: Dummy variables were constructed so that the regression intercept estimates the mean of Anglo American mothers in SES category 3 who are married, while the variables "Mexican American," "SES 4," "SES 5," "Unmarried with Partner," and "Unmarried without Partner," estimate the increments associated with those characteristics. CVD = cardiovascular disease; SES = socioeconomic status; BP = blood pressure.

*Values shown are standardized regression coefficients (Beta) and *P* values.

higher energy intakes ($P < .05$), lower intakes of protein ($P < .006$), and higher systolic blood pressure than category 3 ($P < .04$).

Married mothers had higher total skinfolds than unmarried mothers with partners ($P < .04$) and unmarried mothers without partners ($P < .02$), as well as a higher BMI than unmarried mothers without partners ($P < .03$). However, unmarried mothers with partners reported higher energy intakes ($P < .02$). Unmarried mothers without partners had lower intakes of protein ($P < .05$).

The three sociodemographic variables accounted for small amounts of variance in CVD risk factors and behaviors. The range in adjusted R^2 was .023 to .156 (for cholesterol per 1,000 kcal and percent of calories from carbohydrates, respectively). Of the 12 risk variables studied, marital status category 2 (unmarried with partner) was significantly different from category 1 (married) in two regressions, category 3 (unmarried without partner) was different from category 1 in three regressions, SES category 5 (lowest category) was significantly different from category 3 (middle category) in three regressions, category 4 (low category) was significantly different from category 3 in three regressions, and ethnicity was significant in six regressions.

DISCUSSION

Results of the present study highlight the relationships that exist between sociodemographic variables and CVD risk factors and behaviors. Differences were evident between ethnic, SES, and gender groups for health variables and health behaviors such as physical activity, eating patterns, energy expenditure, and skinfolds.

Determining whether SES or ethnicity is more closely associated with health risk variables is difficult. In the present study, both variables were examined simultaneously in multiple regression analyses. This has the effect of examining ethnic differences while adjusting for SES. The present results support an interpretation that ethnic differences between Mexican American and Anglo American children and mothers exist, even when SES is controlled. Ethnicity and/or SES was significant in 7 of 13 variables for children and 7 of 12 variables for adults. On two variables for children and four variables for mothers, both ethnicity and SES were significant contributors to the model. Thus, the present results confirm the important role of the demographic variables in health studies. However, unlike several previous studies,[27,28] ethnic differences were found even when SES was controlled: In general, Anglo Americans had more favorable risk factor profiles and behaviors. A potential limitation of the present analysis is that the full range of SES was not available, so the statistical control may have been inadequate. Also, the alpha level was somewhat liberal, given the multiple comparisons made.

Although some research has indicated that marital status is related to health status[36] in several ethnic groups,[37] other studies have failed to demonstrate any differences in health status[38] or in preventive health behaviors[39] in children from single- and dual-parent families. The present results indicate that marital status of the mother predicted only one of the dependent variables for the children—intake of sodium. Children of unmarried mothers with partners had significantly higher intakes of sodium than did children of married mothers. Regressions with mothers' data indicated that marital status was significantly correlated with adiposity, energy intake, and protein. Married mothers with partners had larger total skinfolds and BMIs than unmarried mothers with partners and those without partners; unmarried mothers with partners had higher energy intake, and unmarried mothers without partners consumed less protein. Subsequent analyses will examine family aggregation of these and other risk factors and behaviors.

Gender was significantly associated with CVD risk indicators in 3 of the 13 regressions. Preschool boys were found to be more physically active at home and recess and to have smaller total skinfolds than girls. This is a young age at which to find gender differences in physical activity, but this finding supports results of many studies among older children and adolescents.[49]

One of the most striking findings was that four of the most frequently analyzed sociodemographic variables included in epidemiologic studies (gender, ethnicity, SES, and marital status) accounted for a very small portion of the variance across a wide range of physiological, anthropometric, and behavioral variables. The variance accounted for by these variables ranged from 3% to 16% for both children and adults. This leaves a great deal of variance to be explained by genetic and other environmental factors. A limitation of the present study is that the cohort consisted predominantly of low to low-middle SES families. The sample does not represent a normal distribution of income, education, and occupation levels. This restricted range could have led to an underestimation of associations. Our population was also self-selected, which further limits the generalizability of our findings. One other possible limitation is that the "Anglo" group in this study (and others living in the Texas to California border region) is perhaps not representative of white people in the United States in general. The border area population is more likely to acculturate to some extent to the Mexican culture, especially in nutritional patterns.

•   •   •

Based on results from the present study, concerns about the health of children in single-parent homes appear to be unfounded with regard to the variables we measured in preschool children. Ethnicity and SES were related to more risk variables than were gender and mother's marital status.

Continuing to study the relationship of ethnicity and socioeconomic status to the health and well-being of children and adults is well founded. These results demonstrate the need to consider a variety of sociodemographic variables when studying CVD risk factors and behaviors. The inability of the present methods to separate the influence of ethnicity and SES on risk variables highlights the intractability of this problem. Additional methods need to be developed to allow separate estimations of the associations of race and ethnicity and SES with health variables.

REFERENCES

1. U.S. Dept of Health and Human Services, National Institutes of Health, National Heart, Lung, and Blood Institute. *National Heart, Lung, and Blood Institute Report of the Task Force on Research in Epidemiology and Prevention of Cardiovascular Diseases*. Bethesda, Md: USDHHS; August 1994.

2. Frerichs RR, Chapman JM, Maes EF. Mortality due to all causes and to cardiovascular diseases among seven race–ethnic populations in Los Angeles County, 1980. *Int J Epidemiol*. 1984;13:291–298.

3. Becker TM, Wiggins C, Key CR, Samet JM. Ischemic heart disease mortality in Hispanics, American Indians, and non-Hispanic whites in New Mexico, 1958–1982. *Circulation*. 1988;78:302–309.

4. Kautz JA, Bradshaw BS, Fonner E. Trends in cardiovascular mortality in Spanish-surnamed, other white, and black persons in Texas, 1970–1975. *Circulation*. 1981;64:730–735.

5. Stern MP, Gaskill SP. Secular trends in ischemic heart disease and stroke mortality from 1970 to 1976 in Spanish-surnamed and other white individuals in Bexar County, Texas. *Circulation*. 1978;58:537–543.

6. Buechley RW, Key CR, Morris DL, Morton WE, Morgan MV. Altitude and ischemic heart disease in tricultural New Mexico: an example of confounding. *Am J Epidemiol*. 1979;109:663–666.

7. Mitchell BD, Stern MP, Haffner SM, Hazuda HP, Patterson JK. Risk factors for cardiovascular mortality in Mexican Americans and non-Hispanic whites. *Am J Epidemiol*. 1990;131:423–433.

8. Stern MP, Gaskill SP, Allen CR, Garza V, Gonzales JL, Waldrop RH. Cardiovascular risk factors in Mexican-Americans in Laredo, Texas: I. Prevalence of overweight and diabetes and distributions of serum lipids. *Am J Epidemiol*. 1981;113:546–555.

9. Stern MP, Haskell WL, Wood PD, Osann KE, King AB, Farquhar JW. Affluence and cardiovascular risk factors in Mexican-Americans and other whites in three Northern California communities. *J Chron Dis*. 1975;28:623–636.

10. Shea S, Stein AD, Basch CE, et al. Independent associations of educational attainment and ethnicity with behavioral risk factors for cardiovascular disease. *Am J Epidemiol*. 1991;134:567–582.

11. Sorel JE, Ragland DR, Syme SL. Blood pressure in Mexican Americans, whites, and blacks. *Am J Epidemiol*. 1991;134:370–378.

12. Kraus JF, Borhani NO, Franti CE. Socioeconomic status, ethnicity, and risk of coronary heart disease. *Am J Epidemiol*. 1980;111:407–414.

13. Franco LJ, Stern MP, Rosenthal M, Haffner SM, Hazuda HP, Comeaux PJ. Prevalence, detection and control of hypertension in a bi-ethnic community: the San Antonio Heart Study. *Am J Epidemiol*. 1985;121:684–693.

14. Malina RM, Little BB, Stern MP, Gaskill SP, Hazuda HP. Ethnic and social class differences in selected anthropometric characteristics of Mexican-Americans and Anglo adults: the San Antonio Heart Study. *Hum Biol*. 1983;55:867–883.

15. Greaves KA, Puhl J, Baranowski T, Gruben D, Seale D. Ethnic differences in anthropometric characteristics of young children and their parents. *Hum Biol*. 1989;61:459–477.

16. Hazuda HP, Stern MP, Gaskill SP, Haffner SM, Gardner LI. Ethnic differences in health knowledge and behaviors related to the prevention and treatment of coronary heart disease: the San Antonio Heart Study. *Am J Epidemiol*. 1983;117:717–728.

17. Brittin HC, Zinn DW. Meat-buying practices of Caucasians, Mexican-Americans, and Negroes. *J Am Diet Assoc*. 1977;71:623–628.

18. Frank GC, Zive M, Nelson J, Broyles SL, Nader PR. Fat and cholesterol avoidance among Mexican-American and Anglo preschool children and parents. *J Am Diet Assoc*. 1991;91:954–961.

19. Kerr GR, Amante P, Decker M, Callen PW. Ethnic patterns of salt purchase in Houston, Texas. *Am J Epidemiol*. 1982;115:906–916.

20. Burdine JN, Chen MS, Gottlieb NH, Peterson FL, Vacalis TD. The effects of ethnicity, sex, and father's occupation on heart health knowledge and nutrition behavior of school children: the Texas Youth Health Awareness Study. *J Sch Health*. 1984;54:87–90.

21. Murphy SP, Castillo RO, Martorell R, Mendoza FS. An evaluation of food group intakes by Mexican-American children. *J Am Diet Assoc*. 1990;90:388–393.

22. Friis R, Nanjundappa G, Prendergast TJ, Welsh M. Coronary heart disease mortality and risk among Hispanics and non-Hispanics in Orange County, California. *Public Health Rep*. 1981;96:418–422.

23. Sallis JF, Haskell WL, Fortmann SP, Wood PD, Vranizan KM. Moderate-intensity physical activity and cardiovascular risk factors. *Prev Med*. 1986;15:561–568.

24. Roberts RE, Lee ES. Health practices among Mexican Americans: further evidence from the Human Population Laboratory Studies. *Prev Med*. 1980(a);9:675–688.

25. Haffner SM, Stern MP, Hazuda HP, Rosenthal M, Knapp JA. The role of behavioral variables and fat patterning in explaining ethnic differences in serum lipids and lipoproteins. *Am J Epidemiol.* 1986; 123:830–839.

26. Haan M, Kaplan GA, Camacho T. Poverty and health: prospective evidence from the Alameda County Study. *Am J Epidemiol.* 1987;125:989–998.

27. Satariano WA. Race, socioeconomic status, and health: a study of age difference in a depressed area. *Am J Prev Med.* 1986;2:1–5.

28. Keil JE, Sutherland SE, Knapp RG, Tyroler HA. Does equal socioeconomic status in black and white men mean equal risk of mortality? *Am J Public Health.* 1992;82:1133–1136.

29. Stern MP, Rosenthal M, Haffner SP, Hazuda HP, Franco LJ. Sex differences in the effect of sociocultural status on diabetes and cardiovascular risk factors in Mexican Americans: the San Antonio Heart Study. *Am J Epidemiol.* 1984;120:834–851.

30. Popkin BM, Haines PS. Factors affecting food selection: the role of economics. *J Am Diet Assoc.* 1981;79:419–425.

31. Cauley JA, Donfield SM, LaPorte RE, Warhaftig E. Physical activity by socioeconomic status in two population based cohorts. *Med Sci Sports Exerc.* 1991;23:343–352.

32. White CC, Powell KE, Hogelin GC, Gentry EM, Forman MR. The behavioral risk factor surveys: IV. The descriptive epidemiology of exercise. *Am J Prev Med.* 1987;3:304–310.

33. Walter HJ, Hofman A. Socioeconomic status, ethnic origin, and risk factors for coronary heart disease in children. *Am Heart J.* 1987;113:812–818.

34. Winkleby MA, Fortmann SP, Barrett DC. Social class disparities in risk factors for disease: eight-year prevalence patterns by level of education. *Prev Med.* 1990;19:1–12.

35. Winkleby MA, Jatulis DE, Frank E, Fortmann SP. Socioeconomic status and health: how education, income, and occupation contribute to risk factors for cardiovascular disease. *Am J Public Health.* 1992;82:816–820.

36. Moreno CA. Utilization of medical services by single-parent and two-parent families. *J Fam Pract.* 1989;28:194–199.

37. Roberts RE, Lee ES. The health of Mexican-Americans: evidence from the Human Population Laboratory Studies. *Am J Public Health.* 1980(b);70: 375–384.

38. Jennings AJ, Sheldon MG. Review of the health of children in one-parent families. *J Roy Coll Gen Pract.* 1985;35:478–483.

39. Loveland-Cherry CJ. Personal health practices in single-parent and two-parent families. *Fam Relations.* 1986;35:133–139.

40. McKenzie T, Sallis JF, Patterson TL, et al. BEACHES: an observational system for assessing children's eating and physical activity behaviors and associated events. *J Appl Behav Anal.* 1991;24(1): 141–151.

41. Sallis JF, Haskell WL, Wood PD, et al. Physical activity assessment methodology in the Five-City Project. *Am J Epidemiol.* 1985;121:91–106.

42. Gross LD, Sallis JF, Buono MJ, Roby JJ, Morris J. Training and reliability of interviewers using the seven-day physical activity recall. *Res Q Exerc Sport.* 1990;61:321–325.

43. Taylor CB, Coffey T, Berry K, et al. Seven-day activity and self-report compared to a direct measure of physical activity. *Am J Epidemiol.* 1984;120: 818–824.

44. Willett W, Sampson L, Bain C, et al. Vitamin supplement among registered nurses. *Am J Clin Nutr.* 1981;34:1121–1125.

45. Willett W, Sampson L, Stampfer MJ, et al. Reproducibility and validity of a semi-quantitative food frequency questionnaire. *Am J Epidemiol.* 1985; 122:51–65.

46. Willett W, Stampfer MJ, Underwood BA, et al. Validation of a dietary questionnaire with plasma carotenoid and alphacopherol levels. *Am J Clin Nutr.* 1983;38:631–639.

47. Dennis B, Ernst N, Hjortland M, Tillotson JL, Grambsch V. The NHLBI Nutrition Data System. *J Am Diet Assoc.* 1980;77:641.

48. Hollingshead AB. *Two-Factor Index of Social Position.* New Haven, Conn: Yale University Press; 1965.

49. Rowland TW. *Exercise and Children's Health.* Champaign, Ill: Human Kinetics; 1990.

CHAPTER 7

Families Caring for Chronically Ill Children with Tuberous Sclerosis Complex

Marcie Parker, PhD, CFLE

TUBEROUS SCLEROSIS complex (TSC) is a rare and difficult-to-diagnose genetic pediatric neurologic disorder that can affect multiple systems in the body including the brain, kidneys, heart, eyes, and lungs. The initial manifestations may include variable degrees of mental retardation, epileptic seizures, and psychiatric and behavioral problems. In the scientific literature, the acronym TSC is used to distinguish the condition from Tourette syndrome (TS).[1-6] The respondents in this study were TSC parents who acknowledged the existence of TSC in the family and agreed to be interviewed. An unknown number of parents caring for a child with TSC and living in

I dedicate this article to my niece, Scooter, who is a TSC child.

I would also like to thank Carol Bergquist, Dr. Daniel Detzner, Charles Oberg, MD, Dr. Joan Patterson, and Dr. Paul Rosenblatt for their comments on earlier drafts of this article.

Fam Community Health 1996;19(3):73–84
© 1996 Aspen Publishers, Inc.

Minnesota were unwilling to be interviewed.

HISTORY AND BACKGROUND

The first report of this disease was a brief description provided by von Reckinghausen in 1862. In 1880, Bourneville named the disease "tuberous sclerosis of the cerebral circumvolutions" because of the unique cerebral pathologic changes he found in the brain of a 15-year-old mentally handicapped epileptic girl. By the early 1900s, a clinical diagnosis of TSC was possible in patients with a combination of seizures, mental retardation, and adenoma sebaceum, red lesions now more correctly called facial angiofibroma. These three components of the first clinical diagnosis are known as the Vogt triad but it is now known that fewer than one third of all patients with TSC may be diagnosed using this triad.[1]

TSC has long been considered an extremely rare disease; however, estimates of its frequency have risen dramatically in recent years with the recognition of individuals with less severe manifestations of the disorder together with the use of more sophisticated diagnostic studies. While the true incidence of TSC is unknown, its prevalence has recently been estimated to be 1 in 10,000 in the general population and 1 in 6,000 live births. Therefore, there are believed to be anywhere from 25,000 to 40,000 individuals with TSC in the United States and possibly more than 1,000,000 worldwide. TSC occurs in both genders and in all ethnic groups.[1,7]

TSC is a genetic disorder. It is the result of autosomal dominant inheritance; if one parent has the gene for TSC, every child born to that parent has a 50% chance of inheriting the TSC gene. Once TSC occurs, it is transmitted to subsequent generations in the same manner. The individual with TSC has the abnormal TSC gene in one of 22 pairs of chromosomes. In at least 50% to 60% of families, no symptoms or signs of TSC are found in either parent. In these cases, it is believed that TSC may be the result of spontaneous mutation.[1]

Recent empirical and clinical literature[8-10] suggests that chronic conditions are more alike than different in how they affect the psychosocial development of children and their families. Hence, the findings of this study generalize to a broader range of conditions. Families caring for TSC children must cope with controversies surrounding its diagnosis and treatment. TSC is not only difficult to diagnose accurately, but also exceedingly complex to manage because of its unpredictability over time in each individual and because of the variability of its expression from person to person.

Although there are few references to family caregiving for a TSC child in the literature, family members tend to be profoundly affected by caring for a chronically ill child. Successful care of the TSC child must include support for the family.[6,11-26]

METHOD

Subjects

Members of seven families were interviewed in this pilot study for a larger study. The participants in this study were identified through referrals from state and national volunteers of the National Tuberous Sclerosis Association. All volunteers are parents with a TSC child.

Purposive and snowball sampling methods were used to locate as many participants as possible for this study. A representative sample of this population is not possible because some TSC families chose not to identify themselves or participate in conferences, meetings, or support groups. It is not known how many TSC families there are currently in Minnesota. Therefore, it is not known how representative this sample is of TSC families in Minnesota or what proportion of families they represent. In all, seven TSC children were represented in the seven families in this sample. Of these seven children, two were severely affected, four were moderately affected, and one was mildly affected with TSC.

Twelve interviews were conducted (5 married couples [10 interviews] and 2 married women [2 interviews]). These were single (one-time) interviews. No other methodologies were used. Six interviews were done in person, and six were done by telephone because families lived over 100 miles away from the author. The interviews are labeled "Father 1" through "Father 5" and "Mother 1" through "Mother 7." All information about the participants has been changed to protect their privacy. Two married couples were interviewed together (ie, husband and wife together), while the remaining participants were interviewed individually. Each interview lasted from 1 to 3 hours. All participants were white, middle class, well educated, and living in the greater metropolitan area of Minne-

apolis–St. Paul, Minn. All participants ranged in age from 32 to 50 years old. Eight were employed full-time, two were employed part-time, and two were full-time caregivers in the home. All interviews were conducted between January and July 1991. Interviewees are quoted extensively and verbatim in this study.

Additional information for this study, including background on TSC and its effects on family life, was obtained at a 1-day conference on TSC. This meeting was held in Minnesota in October 1992 and sponsored by the National Tuberous Sclerosis Association. In addition, the author conducted an in-depth literature search and consulted with physicians, researchers, and the research literature available through the National Tuberous Sclerosis Association. Respondents were recontacted to discuss tentative conclusions and interpretations, and their feedback was used to refine the themes and conclusions reached in this article.

Procedure

The 12 parents were asked the following questions during the interviews:

1. When did you first think something might be amiss with your child?
2. What was the initial impact of TSC on the family?
3. Describe how, when, and by whom the TSC diagnosis was first made.
4. What has been the ongoing impact of the diagnosis on your family?
5. Describe how your family life or family routine is different due to having a TSC child at home.
6. How have you dealt with case managers, physicians, nurses, school

officials, and teachers and school personnel around the issues of caring for your TSC child?

7. How have you dealt with financial issues around having a TSC child?
8. Please describe your coping and survival strategies while caring for your TSC child.

Themes were developed through an application of the grounded theory approach. The focus of analysis in the grounded theory approach is not merely on collecting or ordering a mass of data but on organizing the many strands of ideas that emerge from analysis of those data.[27] Data analysis using the grounded theory approach consists of the coding process and the constant comparative method of analysis. Fourteen themes emerged using this approach.

RESULTS

The results of these interviews clearly show that most families caring for TSC children are profoundly affected in many areas.

Difficulties in providing care for a TSC child

One mother described her difficulties in deciding how to care for her TSC child as follows:

Peter is extremely physically active and has no common sense at all. He'll run out into the street or bike across the road without looking [in fact, attention deficit disorder and hyperactivity are also symptoms of TSC]. When we have respite care come in, we don't go anywhere but we just relax around the house. Our son is so completely unpredictable that you have to be constantly vigilant and on your guard and never, ever leave him alone. It's a real break for us just to be able to let our guard down and goof around the house.

—Mother 4

Ambiguity in diagnosis and recommended care

Parents bear a heavy day-to-day caregiving burden as they face the ambiguities associated with TSC. TSC is often undiagnosed or misdiagnosed; some families wait years for an accurate diagnosis. When the diagnosis of TSC is first made, families often feel confused, bewildered, angry, and upset. The initial reactions are often denial, minimization of the severity of the disorder, or feelings that the TSC diagnosis simply is not fair. Sometimes TSC is almost symptomless and therefore essentially an invisible chronic illness; friends and relatives find it difficult to believe there is a problem and may be unable to provide much meaningful support to the family.

Families struggle to understand why the disease occurred in their family. Parents wonder if the TSC will improve or get worse, whether siblings will develop it, at what age their TSC child may die, and how much the family should expect from the TSC child. Uncertainty and stress stem from the fact that there is little information available about TSC, and what little information is available is often discrepant. To further complicate matters, TSC affects different children in highly variable and unpredictable ways ranging from almost no problems at all to severe or life-threatening conditions.

Many TSC children have unpredictable, ambiguous health histories. Some experience frequent medical crises and behavioral and developmental problems that can render family life chaotic. Mother 5 reported that her son would throw firewood on the roof or dig up huge patches of lawn if left alone even for 5 minutes. Unpredictability can make family life routines with a TSC child difficult. Parents feel they can never relax and must be constantly on their guard to make certain the TSC child does not harm himself or herself.

Lack of spontaneity in family life

Many parents said that caring for a TSC child prohibits spur-of-the-moment family activities. This would also probably be true for any family caring for a chronically ill family member. One father described this lack of spontaneity as a daily, unrelenting grind. While similar in some ways to caring for any other dependent needing constant care, caring for a TSC child is different in that it does not diminish in intensity or duration. The lack of spontaneity in family life is due both to the unpredictable nature of the disease as well as to the impairment of the child's normal developmental course:

There is no comparison at all between our family life and families in our neighborhood. We never do anything spontaneously. Everything is a major production. If she starts screaming we have to leave, no matter what it is we are doing. She interrupts all our plans, our times out, our dinners, and shopping.

—Mother 7

Chronic grief

Three of the parents in this study described chronic grief. One woman (Mother 4) said the diagnosis of TSC in her child " . . . put me into my own grief." Even though it was good to finally know what the problem was, she was anxious about the forthcoming course of the disease and grieved for the normal life her son might have had.

Having a child with TSC means chronic grieving, chronic sorrow. There's never any closure. There's no end to it. But I can't wear it on my sleeve. I feel intense sorrow, grief, sadness, and fear, and I never talk about it. [This interview was the first occasion where this father discussed his intense feelings.]

—Father 3

The wife of Father 3 said she experienced ongoing ebbing and flowing grief at the TSC in their family. Their child was severely affected. She grieved for the lost opportunity for the family to have a normal second child.

Feelings of guilt

One of the strongest feelings described by some of these parents was guilt. Parents questioned their behavior during pregnancy as a possible cause for the disease in their children—for example, smoking, drinking, falling during pregnancy, or simply passing along a "bad" gene.

Father 5, undiagnosed until 35 years of age when he began to have seizures well after his five children had been born, felt depressed for carrying the disease. He also felt guilty that he was responsible for having given the TSC to two and possibly three of his children, but of course he had no way of knowing he carried the disease at the time. He also felt guilty when he contemplated his own longevity: Will he leave his family alone and unprotected? And even though all family members had only a light expression of the disease, what about the longevity of his own children? Should his children have children? There can also be additional fear and concern expressed by relatives who have started to have children: Will their children have TSC if a relative has it?

Other parents in this study felt guilty when a TSC child had a medical crisis. For example, when a child was hospitalized with a heart attack or stroke, parents were torn between wanting the child to live and wanting the child to die to stop the suffering and the sometimes overwhelming family caregiving burden.

Mother 5 described the death of her son's school friend, who played with matches one day, set fire to his house, and died:

I said to myself, "Well, at least it is over for Chris." But I felt really guilty about feeling that way. It was a very difficult and depressing time for both my husband and me. In fact we couldn't make ourselves go to his funeral. We felt a mixture of relief (that he had died) and guilt (that we shouldn't feel that way). We also looked at our own son with TSC and felt sad that he was still here, still going on, still suffering.

—Mother 5

Health care providers discount parental experiences and input

For many parents, the lack of professional support in their caregiving crisis began early. Most parents claimed that it was immediately apparent to them at birth that there was something different and possibly amiss with their child. Physicians and nurses ignored their input. This lack of support continued when the parent (most often the mother) was left to provide nearly all the care with little or no assistance from health care providers, family members, or friends. A few parents said they experienced understanding and clinical support from health care providers; most parents reported fairly negative experiences. The most common experience reported by parents was that physicians and other health care providers ignored and discounted what they (especially mothers) said about their children's conditions.

While family experiences dealing with health care professionals varied from positive to negative, several parents reported that physicians were generally not helpful. Physicians may not know much about TSC and may misdiagnose or fail to diagnose the disease. Once a diagnosis is made, physicians may send families home with little information, hope, support, or access to home care services, once again leaving them feeling angry, frustrated, and hopeless.

Need for more effective formal professional support

The need for formal professional support for families with TSC children is clear. These parents experienced stress from the child's illness and from having to negotiate the health care system to get needed services. Without help, these stresses can become intolerable.

In rural areas, where specialists and support services are scarce, parents may have an even harder time raising a TSC child. These communities, according to a physician with expertise in TSC family caregiving issues, can barely cope with the health care needs of healthy children, much less the complex care of a TSC child. It is possible that with access to health care providers, medical literature, and family support groups on the Internet, some of this isolation will diminish.

Parents' feelings about support groups

Informal support from extended family, neighbors, and friends to help in caring for a TSC child is critical to reducing family isolation in the community and providing the family with much-needed respite breaks. Even so, the parents interviewed for this study reported extremely ambivalent feelings about joining TSC support groups. Because TSC is quite rare, support groups tended to be small. Those parents who chose to join a support group (and many did not) tended to join groups for retarded or epileptic children. They joined groups to meet more families and to increase the effectiveness of their advocacy efforts to get services, funding, new legislation, and overall visibility for TSC.

One mother explained that joining a support group helped alleviate her feelings of isolation in caring for her TSC child: "It actually helped our whole family to even know that there were other families who had TSC. Until that time, we thought we were the only family in the world with TSC. We felt completely isolated and alone in the world" (Mother 4).

On the other hand, several parents expressed reservations about joining support groups. If, for example, their child was only lightly affected by TSC, they feared seeing TSC children who were more severely affected—what if their child were to become progressively more disabled? Then, too, parents with severely affected children resented seeing families whose children were basically asymptomatic, happy, and healthy. The great variability in the expression of TSC makes each family feel they are coping with a unique disease and makes it difficult for families and support groups to know how to help each other.

A mother whose daughter was severely affected with TSC described her experience in a support group this way:

It has been very frustrating for me to go to support groups because the other TSC kids are okay. I found the support group really depressing. Rita is so severely affected by TSC, and I kept seeing other families and other kids who didn't seem to be very affected at all. It was a real bummer.

—Mother 7

Impact of TSC on family finances

Family finances are clearly important in caring for a TSC child and frequently determine which private services the family will be able to obtain. However, most of the parents in this study mentioned finances only peripherally in their interviews. One father (Father 1) said that all of his daughter's costly medical care was completely covered from birth through Blue Cross/Blue Shield. He has never had difficulty with his insurance denying services or coverage as some other parents apparently experienced with health maintenance organization coverage in other cases.

For one mother, the TSC diagnosis in her 35-year-old husband meant planning for the future, getting a college degree, and preparing for the financial realities of chronic illness:

Twelve years ago when we learned there was TSC in the family and my husband had it, I made a very conscious decision to be financially independent in case he died prematurely. I went back to college and got my nursing degree to help raise the kids. I am worried about the future, a future without Saul, and feel I need to be prepared.

—Mother 7

Impact of caregiving on work life

Maintaining clear boundaries between home and work despite constant anxiety and worry is a challenge for parents caring for a TSC child. For one parent, compartmentalizing his life proved to be an effective coping mechanism:

When you have a critically ill child and go to work, you end up jumping out of your skin every time the phone rings. Is it the hospital? Is it my wife? Is Jake ill? I work in an office with 18 phones; that's a lot of jumping. I have anxiety attacks at work and often panic if my wife doesn't answer the phone right away or if I go home and they're not there. You know, they could be out shopping, but the first thing your mind flits to is the hospital and some life-threatening emergency. In order to keep my sanity, I have had to rigidly compartmentalize my life into my work and my home life. I have two distinct personalities in each place and it takes a lot of energy to keep these two personalities going. I have had to adapt my work to this ongoing crisis.

My wife gave up outside work [engineering] entirely, but I have had to go to work and to keep on working. We know we're having a good day if Jake doesn't go to the hospital. It is very intense for a parent to see his kid die eight or nine times and then be brought back to life by CPR. Whenever he is real sick, my wife and I take shifts and are never relaxed; even when I am off my shift at home I still can't relax because it is always in the back of my mind. It's okay as a parent who is working if you go in to work and say you had one bad night caring for your kid, but it's not okay to have a rough 9 years like I have had.

—Father 3

Impact on marriage

Some parents interviewed worried about the effect on their marriage of caring for a TSC child. Couples tend to put their personal lives and marital relationships on hold to focus intensively on acting as full-time attendants for their sick children. Several parents worried about higher divorce rates for parents with chronically ill children. One mother said,

Having a TSC child is very stressful to a marriage because you basically have to put your relationship and marriage in the background in order to take care of this ongoing medical crisis in your life. You live for your TSC child, and there isn't time for anything else at all.

—Mother 3

Concerns about the TSC child's developmental cycle

Five parents expressed awareness and well-founded concern about their child's developmental progression and their future. Most parents were aware that their TSC child was developing more slowly than other children and might never experience some of the normal stages of development. While the parents expressed concern about missing developmental stages in the children, they also discussed having to cope with normal teenage behaviors such as the drive to separate from the family, find a peer group, become sexually active, and live outside the family. Parents also sought constructive closure to their intense caregiving careers so they would be able to travel and enjoy their marriage. They wanted to feel they could die in peace knowing their special child would be well cared for.

Concerns about the child's behavior as voluntary or involuntary

An additional source of stress for parents is that they often cannot tell which behaviors on the part of their TSC child are voluntary and which are not. Several parents indicated that the TSC child can successfully manipulate the family and family activities by screaming and acting out behaviors:

Now Jake has increasing mobility, intelligence, problem-solving abilities, and greater agility and therefore greater access to all kinds of trouble. We have to pay attention to him all the time and can never leave him alone. He is also going through the normal preadolescent independence surge but without learning the internal controls and self-discipline that go along with it. He has no common sense, no sense of the consequences of his actions. He has little rational ability and bypasses the rules all the time. As parents, we can never be sure how much of this is intentional or not.

—Father 3

Concerns for the future

The mother of three TSC children (she had five children in all) expressed her concerns about the future this way: "My husband and I have a lot of fear about the future. We are afraid our TSC children may become retarded or will have retarded children of their own" (Mother 7).

DISCUSSION

While there is extensive clinical literature regarding the medical treatment protocols for TSC children, there is little research[2-6] regarding the issues that face family caregivers. In particular, there is little to document the specific effects of delivering this care on the family as a whole. This study was conducted to give voice to the experiences of families caring for TSC children. This is perhaps one step toward raising community and health care provider awareness and spurring more effective care and compassionate understanding of these families' caregiving efforts.

These data show that caregiving for a TSC child is different from other kinds of chronic caregiving for several reasons:

- The disease involves highly variable expression from individual to individual, making it difficult to diagnose and treat. In addition, the disease is quite dynamic and presents major ongoing medical and caregiving challenges for families and health care providers as each TSC child ages.
- TSC renders family life more unpredictable than some other chronic

diseases. This unpredictability stems from behavioral problems, physical symptoms, and the unpredictable life course progression of the child.

- TSC parents and family members feel somewhat isolated from other TSC families and sources of mutual help because of the rarity of the disease. Also, some families protect their privacy and choose not to acknowledge publicly the existence of TSC in the family.
- TSC parents feel isolated from the community in general because few people have heard of TSC and simply do not know how to respond to provide effective support.
- TSC families feel isolated from health care providers because few professionals have encountered a case of TSC and fewer still know how to support families even if a correct diagnosis is made.
- TSC families can feel guilty if it has been clearly established by genetic analysis that one parent or one side of the family is responsible for having passed on the chromosome with the defective gene.
- Friends and family may not take TSC seriously if it is very lightly expressed in the child. In these cases, it is a relatively invisible illness.
- One important indication of the limitations of the family and professional support currently available is that these parents were surprised (and then relieved) to learn during the course of this study that some other parents experience the same feelings of hoping their child might

die. For some, this interview was the first time they had ever discussed these taboo feelings.

- Once physicians and nurses have more training in helping families with TSC and more experience with other orphan diseases, a greater sensitivity to family needs may follow together with better diagnoses, fuller explanations, and better assistance in locating community as well as home-based services for these children.

Many TSC families have joined together to advocate for family-centered care (personal communication, C. Shapeland, Family Voices Parental Group, March 1995). Families feel that they know their child better than anyone and that parents need to be completely involved in the options and choices of the child's care. They see the family as the one constant in the child's life. In fact, the family often acts as case manager, coordinator, and communicator across the disjointed health care system. These families are very concerned about health care reform efforts that might limit their choices and options, especially with TSC, which is so variably expressed from individual to individual and over time.

Many aspects of TSC parents' responses are fairly similar to the biopsychosocial concerns of caring for family members with other orphan diseases and rare genetic conditions. In fact, a number of key researchers in this field argue for a noncategorical approach to chronic illness in children, with a focus on the needs of the child and family rather than on disease-specific differences.[8,10]

• • •

Coping with raising a child with TSC often presents an engrossing, intense, ongoing caregiving challenge. This caregiving is accompanied by a periodically chaotic and unpredictable family life, often with frequent medical, emotional, and behavioral crises.

Caregiving difficulties, ambiguity, unpredictability, lack of family spontaneity, chronic grief, guilt, and family isolation may increase or contribute to family stress. In addition, formal and informal support systems generally do not meet the needs of families dealing with this rare, difficult-to-manage disease. Family life tends to revolve around the TSC member and his or her needs. Couples may worry about the quality and duration of their marriage, family finances, and their ability to continue to work.

On the other hand, couples interviewed for this research aggressively sought out information and services that allowed them to take care of their special child. These parents were also clear about what should be done to help them continue to provide this intensive level of caregiving. Some said they need better trained and more sensitive and supportive health care professionals; others wanted a centralized toll-free telephone number to call to more readily locate community-based services. The parents interviewed for this research seemed to be coping with both the challenges presented by caring for a child with TSC and with the other demands of their busy lives.

REFERENCES

1. National Tuberous Sclerosis Association, Inc. *My Child Has Tuberous Sclerosis: A Brochure for Parents.* Chicago, Ill: NTSA; 1994.

2. Hunt A, Stores G. Sleep disorder and epilepsy in children with tuberous sclerosis: a questionnaire-based study. *Dev Med Child Neurol.* 1994;36: 108–115.

3. Hunt A. Development, behaviour and seizures in 300 cases of tuberous sclerosis. *J Intellect Disabil Res.* 1993;37:41–51.

4. Hunt A, Shepherd C. A prevalence study of autism in tuberous sclerosis. *J Autism Dev Disord.* 1993; 23(2):323–339.

5. Hunt A, Dennis J. Psychiatric disorder among children with tuberous sclerosis. *Dev Med Child Neurol.* 1987;29:190–198.

6. Hunt A. Tuberous sclerosis: a survey of 97 cases. *Dev Med Child Neurol.* 1983;25:346–357.

7. Osborne JP, Fryer A, Webb D. Epidemiology of tuberous sclerosis. In: Johnson WG, Gomez MR, eds. *Annals of the New York Academy of Sciences.* New York, NY: New York Academy of Sciences; 1991.

8. Perrin E, Newachek P, Pless I, et al. Issues involved in the definition and classification of chronic health conditions. *Pediatrics.* 1993;91:787–793.

9. Stein R. Growing up with a physical difference. *Children's Health Care.* 1983;12(2):53–61.

10. Stein RE, Jessop DJ. What diagnosis does not tell: the case for a noncategorical approach to chronic illness in childhood. *Soc Sci Med.* 1989;29:769–778.

11. Cherry DB. Stress and coping in families with ill or disabled children: application of a model to pediatric therapy. *Phys Occup Ther Pediatr.* 1989;9(2): 11–32.

12. Barbarin OA. Psychosocial risks and invulnerability: a review of the theoretical and empirical bases of preventive family-focused services for survivors of childhood cancer. *J Psychosoc Oncol.* 1987;5(4): 25–41.

13. Hurtig AL, Koepke D, Park KB. Relation between severity of chronic illness and adjustment in children and adolescents with sickle cell disease. *J Pediatr Psychol.* 1989;14(1):117–132.

14. Shapiro J. Family reactions and coping strategies in response to the physically ill or handicapped child: a review. *Soc Sci Med.* 1983;17(14):913–931.
15. Slaughter D. Care of black children with sickle cell disease: fathers, maternal support, and esteem. *Fam Relations.* 1988;37(3):281–287.
16. Harris SL. The family crisis: diagnosis of a severely disabled child. *Marriage Fam Rev.* 1987;11(1–2):107–118.
17. Dunn-Geier BJ, McGarth PJ, Rourke BP, et al. Adolescent chronic pain: the ability to cope. *Pain.* 1986;26(1):23–32.
18. Pollock GH. Childhood sibling loss: a family tragedy. *Psychiatr Ann.* 1986;16(5):309–314.
19. Chang PN. Psychosocial needs of long-term childhood cancer survivors: a review of literature. *Pediatrician.* 1991;18(1):20–24.
20. Mattsson A, Kim SP. Blood disorders. *Psychiatr Clin North Am.* 1982;5(2):345–356.
21. Asarnow JR, Horton AA. Coping and stress in families of child psychiatric inpatients: parents of children with depressive and schizophrenia spectrum disorders. *Child Psychiatr Hum Dev.* 1990;21(2):145–157.
22. Athreya BH, McCormick MC. Impact of chronic illness on families. *Rheum Dis Clin North Am.* 1987;13(1):123–131.
23. Birenbaum LK. Family coping with childhood cancer. *Hospice J.* 1990;6(3):17–33.
24. Damrosch SP, Perry LA. Self-reported adjustment, chronic sorrow, and coping of parents of children with Down syndrome. *Nurs Res.* 1989;38(1):25–30.
25. Fraley AM. Chronic sorrow: a parental response. *J Pediatr Nurs.* 1990;5(4):273–368.
26. Hymovich DP, Baker CD. The needs, concerns, and coping of parents of children with cystic fibrosis. *J Appl Fam Child Stud.* 1985;34(1):91–97.
27. Strauss AL. *Qualitative Analysis for Social Scientists.* Cambridge, England: Cambridge University Press; 1987.

CHAPTER 8

Dilemmas in Using Respite for Family Caregivers of Frail Elders

Martha Worcester, PhD

Susan Hedrick, PhD

THE PREVALENCE of older adults receiving extensive illness care at home has expanded in recent years due to increased numbers achieving old age, decreased stays in the hospital for acute illness, and sophisticated chronic illness care being delivered in the home.[1] At the same time, fewer persons are available to provide care because of decreases in proportions of younger to older age groups and increased involvement of women in the work force.[2] When compared with noncaregivers in the same age groups, caregivers are more vulnerable to negative influences on health and social life. Documented negative impacts are reduced levels of morale and positive affect; increased physical and mental exhaus-

This research was funded by a National Research Service Award (1 F31 NU05901-01) from the Division of Nursing, Public Health Services, US Dept Health and Human Services; a Health Services Research and Development Field Program training stipend from the US Dept Veterans Affairs; and the Hester McLaws Scholarship Fund, School of Nursing, University of Washington.

Fam Community Health 1997;19(4):31–48
© 1997 Aspen Publishers, Inc.

tion; increased rates of depression; and greater disruption of families' daily routines.[3-6] Caregivers of cognitively impaired adults are more vulnerable to reduction of informal support and stress than caregivers of physically impaired adults.[7-9] Stresses most frequently reported by caregivers include loss of personal time, social isolation, and lack of time to restore needed energy.[10-12]

Respite is the most desired intervention reported by caregivers.[5,10-13] Despite caregivers' expressed need for respite and the growing availability of both in-home and out-of-home respite, caregivers use respite too infrequently and too late in the caregiving trajectory to demonstrate a reduction in health risks.[14,15] Documentation of the effects of respite on caregiver health, institutionalization of the receiver, and the cost of respite programs is necessary, yet research has been limited by the caregivers' infrequent use of respite.[13-15] A few researchers have enumerated difficulties in accessing respite services, but such difficulties have not been the main focus of the research.[13,14,16,17] Given that respite was the most desired service by caregivers, and yet used so sparingly, a closer examination of the issues was needed.

OVERVIEW OF THE STUDY AND METHODS

A qualitative grounded theory approach was used to gain in-depth understanding of the caregiver's point of view.[18] Using symbolic interactionism as the interpretive approach, analysis focused on the caregiver's perceptions of

events and interactions related to considerations about respite use.[19-21] These two questions were addressed: What factors inhibit or facilitate the use of respite by family caregivers? Are different concerns raised about respite care by caregivers of older adults with cognitive impairments than by caregivers of older adults with physical impairments?

For our study we defined the caregiver as any informal unpaid person who lives with the receiver and has primary responsibility for providing the care in the home setting. The receiver was a person who needed the assistance of a caregiver to live in the community. Consistent with other research, respite was inclusive of any situation in which the caregiver left the receiver in the care of another person or agency.[14,22] Respite could take place in any setting with anyone who volunteered (informal helpers) or was paid (formal helpers such as in-home paid help).

Sample selection and description

Theoretic sampling was used to select caregivers of veterans from a large urban ambulatory clinic of a Veterans Affairs Medical Center. Unique to this study's group of caregivers, all had fully reimbursed in-home and out-of-home respite offered as part of the veterans' benefits. Inpatient respite was offered in the nursing home setting for up to 6 weeks per year, and in-home and out-of-home respite was contracted with outside agencies in the veteran's home community.

An equal number of caregivers of persons with chronic cognitive impairments (CCI) and chronic physical impairments

(CPI) were selected. Persons with terminal illnesses were excluded. Criteria were established to ensure that caregivers needed respite and that receivers were easily distinguished between having either a cognitive or a physical impairment. Variation in the types of caregivers was sought to represent the types of kin relationships to the receiver, gender, and race reported in the literature.[1] A screening instrument was administered to ensure that caregivers met the criteria of

- living with the receiver and providing most of the personal care,
- providing care for at least the previous 6 months,
- stating that the care receiver could not be safely left alone,
- caring for a person (receiver) with at least two basic activities of daily living (ADL) deficits (eg, eating, dressing, bathing, toileting, transferring, walking, or continence),[23] and
- stating that receivers had either cognitive or physical impairment.

To strengthen the difference between the two groups, receivers with cognitive impairment needed to be ambulatory without assistance and receivers with physical impairment needed to require assistance with ambulation. Cognitive impairment was determined by the physician diagnosis of dementia and a score of 15 or below on the 30-point Mini-Mental Status Exam.[24] Persons with physical impairment had a score of 28 or higher on the Mini-Mental Status Exam and were not considered cognitively impaired by physicians or caregivers. Caregivers of persons with mixed impairments were excluded from the study.

Thirty participants were obtained (15 CCI and 15 CPI), with only one refusal among persons approached that met the criteria (Tables 8–1 and 8–2). This study's sample was compared with that of the Long-Term Care Survey/Informal Caregivers Study (LTCS).[1] The LTCS sample was a random survey considered representative of characteristics of caregivers of frail elders in the United States. As can be seen in Table 8–1, compared with the LTCS sample of caregivers, caregivers in this study were predominantly wives and had cared for receivers for longer periods of time than the LTCS sample. Receivers in the two samples were similar in age groupings, but this study's sample had proportionately more males and receivers with more ADL deficits than of the LTCS (see Table 8–2). For caregivers to be included in the LTCS, they could reside anywhere in the United States, they did not need to reside with the receiver, and the persons for whom they provided care needed to have only one ADL deficit. This study's criteria resulted in a more restricted sample of caregivers than was obtained in the LTCS sample. Differences also might occur due to the fact that the LTCS sample was obtained 10 years prior to when the current study was done.

Using the Mann-Whitney U-Test to compare the CCI and CPI groups within the study, no significant difference (*p* .05) was found in age, gender, race, marital status, income, relationship to the receiver of care, years of caregiving, and the number of recipient ADL impairments. These findings strengthened the ability to isolate whether CCI or CPI was a differen-

Table 8-1. Study sample of caregiver characteristics compared with Long-Term Care Survey/Informal Caregivers Study (LTCS)

| Characteristic | Study | | LTCS %* |
	n	%	(n = 2,201,000)
Age			
< 45	1	3	21
45–64	9	30	41
65–74	15	50	25
75–84	5	17	(75+)10
Mean age	68		57
Gender			
Male	2	7	28
Female	28	93	72
Ethnicity			
European American	24	80	80
Other	7	20	20
Relationship to receiver			
Husband	1	3	13
Wife	22	73	23
Daughter+	4	17	37
Other	4	13	27
Duration of care			
< 1 yr	1	3	18
1–4 yr	17	57	44
5+ yr	12	40	20
Range	< 1–29		> 1–43

*LTCS percentages[1] include both primary and secondary caregivers, while in the study sample there are only primary caregivers, so the comparisons of percentages are not exact. Percentages are rounded to the nearest percentage point.

tiating factor in caregivers' use of respite. However, because wives caring for husbands were the predominant group in this study, caregivers will be presumed to be wives and receivers husbands unless otherwise noted in the subsequent discussion.

Data collection and analysis

To recruit the sample, clinicians identified potential participants, and caregivers were approached at the clinic and asked to participate. Appointments were made with persons who qualified, and tape-recorded interviews were conducted in the home setting. Ninety interviews were conducted, three with each participant, at 2-month intervals. Face validity of the interview format was established through the literature review and consultation with other researchers of caregiving issues. Information gathered focused on times when caregivers used respite and times when caregivers felt the need for respite but chose not to pursue it. The interview format was pilot tested for caregiver understanding and ability to obtain relevant information. In the first interview the open-ended questions were asked first, followed by administration of short quantitative instruments to obtain demographic information, the amount and type of respite used, and the context of the caregiving situation. In the two subsequent interviews, open-ended questions were directed toward respite that occurred during the time between the interviews. Short quantitative instruments were administered at every visit to measure changes over time on selected variables. Only the portion of the study that related to the qualitative data is reported here.

Data collection and qualitative analysis occurred simultaneously using constant comparative analysis[19] as the vehicle for coding interview data and grouping the responses into meaningful patterns. Interviews usually began with, "Tell me about the last time you left [receiver's name] in the care of others or felt that you wanted to but decided against it." Prompts were then added to assist caregivers in expanding on the situation, such as what was going on at the time, who they considered asking, and which circumstances made it easy or difficult to obtain respite. Sequences of interactions with others and events and conditions before, during, and after each respite episode were explored to gain a contextual picture of respite as it related to other aspects of the caregiver's life. If the

Table 8–2. Study sample of receiver characteristics compared with LTCS[1]

Characteristic	Study (n = 30)	Study %	National %* (n = 1,632,000)
Age			
65–74	12	40	43
75–84	11	37	36
85+	7	23	21
Mean age	77		78
Gender			
Male	28	93	60
Female	2	7	40
ADL deficits*			
0	0	0	7
1–2	2	7	42
3–4	15	50	19
5–6	13	43	32
Mean	4		3

*Activities of daily living limitations in eating, dressing, ambulating, toileting, transferring, and continence.[23]

caregiver used a respite source, she was asked if she would leave the receiver in that situation again and the reasons for or against doing so.

Validity and reliability

The researcher's interpretation of the interviews was validated by presenting coded transcripts at subsequent interviews and asking if the codes captured the caregivers' perceptions of events. This process gained a thicker description of respite issues.[18] Theoretic saturation occurred when no new information was forthcoming.[18] Reliability of the coding process was conducted by constructing clear definitions of themes, selected codes, and the core category.[25,26] Two experts in caregiving research and the researcher then coded six randomly chosen, line-numbered transcripts. Consensus was achieved in the coding process. A total percentage agreement of 80% to 84% over all the codes was obtained and a kappa ranging between .48 to .57. In qualitative research 70% is considered acceptable for total percentage agreement, and figures close to .50 are acceptable for kappa.[27]

RESULTS

Respite use

Consistent with past research, caregivers used very little respite.[14,16] Of the 30 caregivers interviewed, 26 averaged less than 5 hours a week. These times were usually broken into 1-hour segments for activities such as grocery shopping or visiting other ill relatives. The respite was primarily from informal sources (eg, family, friends, church volunteers). Formal sources of respite were used by six of the caregivers. For four, it was a one-time experience because the receiver refused to return. In two of these four instances caregivers took receivers to an adult daycare center, and the receiver clung to the caregiver and she could not get him to let go. Caregivers had to take the receiver back home and did not try again. In other instances receivers attended a respite program for several months and then refused to go and respite was terminated. Further attempts to obtain formal respite were forgone. There was no significant difference (p .05) between the CCI and CPI group in the amount of respite used during the 6 months of the study. All caregivers expressed the need for more respite than they were receiving. The analysis that follows provides an explanation for the phenomenon of caregivers' infrequent use of respite despite their expressed need for more.

Dilemmas in using respite

A grounded theory of the processes caregivers used when considering acquiring respite was developed and named Dilemmas in Using Respite. Significant passages were coded using key words of the participants. Examples included "anticipating needs" of the receiver, "imposing" on helpers, and "watching" how others got along with the receiver. As codes were grouped into more abstract categories, it became apparent that some codes applied to the caregiver's perceptions of interactions between herself and the receiver, between herself and helpers or potential helpers, or between the receiver and helper or potential helpers. By using this categorization of codes, we derived major themes of "knowing," "imposing," and "matching," respectively (Fig 8–1). Conservation, the core category, served as a screen through which all the themes were considered.

Knowing: Caregiver and receiver transactions

Knowing was the caregiver's perception, valuing, and use of shared past and ongoing experiences with the receiver that served as the basis for how she provided care. Caregivers' knowing allowed them to interact in ways that enhanced cooperation in performing daily routines and anticipating the needs of the receiver. The ability to anticipate needs and respond appropriately was considered essential in maintaining the morale of the receiver so he did not feel a burden or incompetent, preventing accidents that might cause more work for the caregiver, and preventing the receiver from making requests or becoming angry or agitated:

> . . . he likes to eat at a certain time and he doesn't want too much milk in his glass or too much food on his plate [because of hand tremors]. He likes a certain bowl for this and that . . . he likes to be home. He does the same things every day, watches the same programs. He wouldn't like me taking him somewhere else to be looked after . . . not for a few hours or half a day . . . he wouldn't

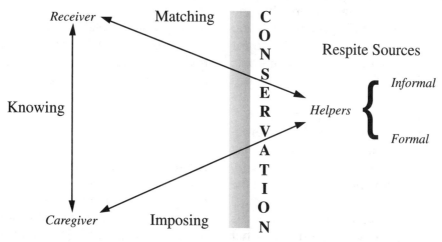

Fig 8–1. Dilemmas in using respite. Caregiver perceptions of transactions (two-way arrows) between persons involved in respite care. *Knowing* the receiver and her own limitations was the theme of caregiver and receiver transactions. *Imposing on* helpers or being imposed upon by those offering respite was the theme of helper and receiver transactions. *Matching* was the theme of trying to make a match between helpers and the receiver so that both would be comfortable when respite was provided. *Conservation* of resources and energy was the screen (or core category) through which all transactions were filtered.

like it. I know that. [CPI, wife of man with severe Parkinson's disease]

. . . he gets up at the same time every morning and I do the same thing. I help him get dressed and I take him in the bathroom. . . . I say, "Here's your comb" and he combs his hair. I'll say, "Drop your pants" and then he knows he should go to the bathroom. Then he's ready for breakfast. Then he'll make the coffee, that's one thing he can still do and it makes him feel good. Then he goes out for a little walk. We've been here a long time so he doesn't get lost. It's the same thing every day. If anything changed it would really mess him up. It's a lot of little steps. If I go anywhere, I go in the morning and take him with me. [CCI, wife of man with Alzheimer's disease]

. . . she has all kinds of strange names for things that aren't even close. I can translate even when it's completely out of context just because I know her. [CCI, daughter of mother with severe Alzheimer's disease]

Part of the knowing was the caregiver's awareness of her own health and abilities, which often precluded being away from home without assistance for herself. Ten caregivers had either chronic or periodic health problems that limited their energy. Respite timing had to accommodate to the caregiver's daily pattern of managing her own health problems. Typical statements were, "I just haven't the strength to be gone very long," and "I don't have energy left in the afternoon, yet that is the time he is most willing to have someone come and be with him." Weighing concerns about her own health needs as well as those of the receiver doubled the factors that needed to be taken into account for any episode of respite.

Caregivers talked about strategies they used with the receiver when they felt the need for respite. Commonly used words were *testing, timing, setting things up, concealing,* and *tricking.* Each is described in turn. *Testing* involved mentioning to the receiver that she wanted to go somewhere and then waiting to see how he reacted. This technique was used frequently with both CCI and CPI groups. If there was an argument about her leaving or the receiver's confusion increased, no respite was obtained. If the receiver reacted positively, she might consider finding a source of respite.

Timing involved considering when to tell the receiver about a respite event and determining the length of time and time of day that was best to leave him. One caregiver told the receiver 2 days in advance of when she intended to be gone and then reminded him several times each day. She had learned if she did, he did not spend hours after she returned asking why she had not taken him with her. Another caregiver reported that she told the receiver just before she left or he repeatedly asked about when she was leaving and became very agitated. These were both caregivers of persons with CCI.

Most often when a caregiver arranged for in-home respite, she would *set things up* so she would be gone for short periods at times when the least care was needed so there would be little disruption in normal routines. Meals and toileting were of special concern. If she had to leave during a meal time, she set everything out just the way the receiver liked it before leaving. If the receiver was embarrassed by others doing his personal care, the caregiver would be sure he went to the bathroom prior to her leaving and tried to return before he might need to use the toilet again. These strategies minimized the resistance of CPI receivers to caregivers' leaving and reduced the possibility of problems when the caregiver returned.

Concealing from the receiver that someone needed to be there in her absence was a common strategy used by half of the caregivers. Most receivers who could communicate well would insist they be left at home alone. In these situations, caregivers timed being away so there would be little interaction between the receiver and the helper. Thus, the receiver was unaware that the caregiver only left when someone else was there. This strategy worked best when the caregiver had others living with her or when family visited and the caregiver left "to do an errand."

For out-of-home respite there was usually more resistance by receivers than to in-home respite. Two caregivers of persons with CCI using adult day care said they had to *trick* the receiver into going. One caregiver told the receiver, "You are going to help care for some people at a senior center." Another caregiver said the receiver thought he was going to work, and she did not correct his misperception. As would be expected, this strategy was not attempted in the CPI group. Because so much was known by caregivers about how to interact with receivers, it was difficult to decide how much helpers needed to know to prevent problems from occurring during respite.

Imposing: Caregiver and helper transaction

Imposing was the caregiver's sense of social boundaries between herself and sources of respite. Imposing was experienced by caregivers as both "imposing on" and "being imposed upon." Caregivers described "imposing on" as asking helpers to do things that were not within helpers' usual routines or roles. Caregivers described "being imposed upon" as helpers interfering with caregiving routines or demanding too much time, energy, or resources.

When caregivers talked about imposing on helpers or potential helpers, they consistently specified which behaviors were expected from different types of helpers (eg, "you just don't ask a neighbor to do that," "that's my job, nobody else's," "only a nurse should be asked to do that"). The circumstances in which caregivers thought about leaving the receiver was "only if absolutely necessary" or "only in an emergency." Most saw respite as a luxury and not a necessity.

Requests for respite from informal helpers were restricted to emergencies, caregiver illness, and important business. Adult children living nearby were considered for respite only if they did not have other obligations (eg, family, jobs). Caregivers explained that adult children already had a full schedule of activities. Relatives already provided other types of assistance such as housework, transportation, and shopping. Friends of caregivers were usually excluded as a respite choice. Caregivers stated, "That's not what friends are for" and "If I want to do something, I want to do it with my friend." Most caregivers had a clear sense of when family members were involved in other tasks. Typical statements included, "If I know it's an inconvenient time for my daughter, I don't even ask" and "They're busy, you can't ask very often."

A consideration in using any informal source of respite, including kin, was whether or not personal care was needed. Bathing, toileting, feeding, and meal preparation were viewed by the caregiver as tasks that were her responsibility and should not be imposed on others. When speaking about personal care, caregivers explained:

> . . . if they [helpers] were hired to do it, but I couldn't ask a friend to come in and do the things I do . . . like wiping his butt. . . . No, I wouldn't ask a friend to give him a bath, I know I wouldn't . . . or take his teeth out, or wash them, and put them back in.

Even among family members, personal care requests were considered an imposition. The caregiver of a man with CPI (obstructive lung disease) had cared for him over 20 years. Many of the family had helped from time to time, but the caregiver stated that the only time family members provided personal care was when he was in a coma at home.

Imposing on formal agencies was expressed as requesting something that was not initially described as part of the service offered. Frequently caregivers found it difficult to talk the receiver into accepting respite or get the receiver from inside the residence to a van that was provided to the respite location. If agency personnel did not anticipate such needs and offer solutions to the prob-

lems, then it was considered imposing to ask for assistance with these difficulties.

Inhibiting influences for caregivers in using both informal and formal helpers were the need for two helpers for a single respite occasion or the necessity of canceling respite arrangements at the last minute. When caregivers could not drive or had health problems that limited their mobility, they needed someone with them as well as someone to be with the receiver when respite occurred. In addition, many times it was necessary to cancel arrangements at the last minute because either the caregiver did not have enough strength to get the receiver ready for respite or because the receiver was "having a bad day." The logistics of fitting several schedules together (usually involving both an informal and formal helper) and the possibility of having to cancel arrangements at the last minute brought on strong feelings of being an imposition on both informal and formal helpers.

Being imposed upon by helpers was described as ways in which helpers made the caregiving experience even more difficult. Informal helpers frequently gave caregivers unsolicited advice. If a potential helper was bossy or nervous, the caregiver simply ignored that person's offer to help or did not mention caregiving problems in order to avert offers of respite. As one caregiver stated, "There is no way I'd have my daughter come. When we go shopping, she tells me what to buy and orders me around all the time. I can't have that when I'm trying to care for him. It just wears me out."

With formal agency respite, participants described in detail the time involved in discovering which agency to access as well as actually achieving a time and type of helper that fit their needs. Initially, caregivers asked for information from informal contacts, which led to several phone calls. Usually months, and in several cases years, passed before a source was used. If too many steps were involved in acquiring respite, the caregiver saw it as too intrusive on the little energy and time she had. Frequent difficulties included needing to make additional calls to arrange transportation; finding papers to see if financial criteria could be met; being interviewed by more than one agency; needing to be available for a helper at times of the day that were difficult for the caregiving routine; and having helpers restricted by the agency in what they were allowed to do for the receiver (eg, volunteers were not allowed to lift or help a person ambulate, chore workers were not allowed to help the receiver to the bathroom, nursing aides were not allowed to give medications). Imposing on and being imposed upon were intricately intertwined as caregivers sought a balance in thinking about whether to use a respite source.

Despite the many barriers to respite, some caregivers developed strategies to facilitate respite. For both informal and formal respite, caregivers reported trying to make it more convenient for helpers by working around helpers' schedules, using respite infrequently, and setting up respite situations so less care was needed for the receiver in the caregivers' absence. With informal helpers, caregivers found ways to reciprocate for the respite to reduce feelings of imposing on helpers. In two instances when friends did provide respite, the friends also were

neighbors caring for a person with a condition similar to the receivers. The friend could, therefore, watch both persons needing care at the same time, and the caregiver could reciprocate. Both caregivers stated, "We try not to take advantage of one another."

Two spouse caregivers took care of the helpers' (daughters') children, and another male caregiver assisted the helper with home repairs. Thus, respite was accepted because reciprocation was possible. However, even when reciprocation was possible, informal helpers rarely offered at regular times that caregivers could count on, and caregivers did not "feel right" about initiating a request. If there was a reason the caregiver wanted respite when it was convenient for her, she felt she should pay for it, even if it was a family member. A typical way that caregivers thought about informal respite was the statement, "It's just that if the opportunity comes at times, why I might take advantage of it, but I don't ask for it. I don't look for it." Informal respite that best met caregivers' needs was that in which family members were in and out of the home, were aware of each others' needs, and worked out a solution that accommodated the needs of both. The ebb and flow of respite occurred more often by chance than design.

Formal agency arrangements were acquired most frequently as a result of the caregiver saying she was tired and a health worker suggesting respite as an option. Formal helpers that facilitated the use of respite asked what difficulties the caregiver might have in using the respite, and then offered solutions for the difficulties. Factors included arranging transportation, gaining the receiver's cooperation, and arranging respite for the best time and place for the caregiver. Caregivers were reluctant to initiate conversations with receivers about inpatient respite. Clinicians who took the initiative to talk with the receiver about the caregiver's need for rest were most effective in facilitating respite.

Matching: Receiver and helper transactions

Matching was the process caregivers used to take into account past and present interactions between potential helpers and receivers. They used that information to judge whether or not leaving the helper with the receiver would be a positive experience for both. Caregivers related how they "noticed" or "watched" what went on between the receiver and others to see how they "got along" and how the physical or social environment affected the interactions. Caregivers took special note of persons who were sensitive to social and emotional needs of the receiver and not just physical needs. Caregivers saw their role as protecting both receivers and those interacting with receivers from harmful, uncomfortable, or degrading experiences. Negative reactions of either the receiver or helper inhibited further consideration of that person as a helper. A receiver's increased agitation when with a helper or negative comments by the receiver about the helper after a respite event were noted by the caregiver. Comments made by potential helpers such as "How can you

stand him? [the receiver]" and nonverbal reactions such as the helper "looking uncomfortable," avoiding looking at the receiver, and talking about the receiver rather than to him were dissuasive. This was a common type of observation:

It was really hard on her [a kin helper]. I mean she didn't actually come out and say it . . . I could just tell. It was difficult for her to see somebody that was very, very strong and independent decline the way she [receiver] has. [CPI, daughter of mother with Alzheimer's disease talking about her mother's sister]

Suggestions that the caregiver should put the receiver in a nursing home or get some help were interpreted by caregivers as meaning the person making the comment did not want to provide respite. Such nonverbal and verbal behaviors caused caregivers to prevent contact between the potential helper and the receiver. Rarely did caregivers describe positive interactions between potential informal helpers and receivers. When they did, these interactions often led to at least one brief episode of respite. A typical example was one in which one caregiver explained:

When I took him [the receiver] out shopping with me last time, my brother was with me. They seemed to enjoy each other even though he [the receiver] can't make much sense when he talks. My brother even took him to the bathroom and they both came out looking like it was no big deal. So I know that they'd get along just fine. [CCI, wife of man with moderate Alzheimer's disease]

This caregiver subsequently asked her brother to stay with the receiver and did not worry about them while she was gone. These types of stories applied to both informal and formal helpers.

Caregivers used several strategies to effect a match. They talked about "keeping their ears open" for persons who had cared for someone similar to the receiver and who verbalized specific knowledge of the difficulties involved; "checking things out" by taking the receiver to a respite setting to see how he responded or calling in-home helpers to see how things were going and questioning the helpers about how things went on returning; and "coaching" by assisting helpers with caring for the receiver several times before actually leaving the helper alone with the receiver. Some times of day were more confusing for the CCI group and more tiring for the CPI group, so caregivers timed interactions with helpers, prompted the helper about types of activities the receiver enjoyed, and assisted arranging the setting to make care less difficult for both the receiver and helper.

Caregivers often expressed the need to have someone of the same gender just come and play a game or talk with the receiver. They were appreciative of out-of-home formal respite settings that met both the social as well as physical needs of receivers. Both receivers with CCI and CPI enjoyed rides and the caregivers explained it took much less energy to get the receiver ready to go for a ride than preparing for someone to come in or the receiver to attend an out-of-home respite setting. Over half of the caregivers said they wished they could ask people to just take the receiver on a ride so they could have some rest. Yet no caregiver asked

anyone to take the receiver for a ride. The one time it occurred, the helper initiated the offer. Caregivers stated they did not feel comfortable making such a request.

Caregivers told detailed stories about both negative and positive experiences of interactions between helpers and receivers. Negative interactions were most common and described with a sense of either sympathy or anger at either the receiver or helper. Positive interactions between receivers and helpers were rare. Caregivers conveyed a sense of surprise and warm appreciation of the helper as though positive interactions were unexpected.

Conservation of resources and energy: The core category

The final core category that bound the themes into a meaningful relationship with one another, "conservation of resources and energy," was derived originally from the phrase "It's just easier not to." Caregivers used that phrase repeatedly when questioned as to the major reason for not using respite even when they were feeling in need of rest or time away. Conservation captured the essence of caregivers' thinking about asking for or accepting offers for respite. They felt a need to maintain a protected environment and not exhaust either their own resources and energy or that of the receivers.

Caregivers were acutely aware of their own and the receiver's limited social and financial resources and physical and emotional energy. Conservation was the central concern in whether or not a particular resource was used. As caregivers talked about the need for time away, they struggled with what needed to be done prior to leaving, what would occur during their absence, and what effect being away would have on receivers. Here are two statements that illustrate the issues well:

I would really like to go out to lunch with my friends but first I have to argue with F [receiver] about needing to go and then call around to see who will stay with him. Then I worry about him and whether he's giving my son [helper] a bad time all the time I'm gone. After I get back I have to put up with him [receiver] asking me a hundred times why I didn't take him with me. It's just not worth it. It's easier just to stay home. [CCI, wife with severe arthritis who was caring for her husband with dementia]

It's that one of the reasons for not asking other people is that it's an added stress. Once this particular routine gets set up, breaking the routine becomes highly stressful because the routine involves so many different tasks. I get even busier if I have to supervise other people besides having to take care of him. [CPI, wife caring for husband with a stroke]

Caregivers talked about the many considerations and interactions with others that were needed regarding care to be given in their absence. They weighed whether money needed to pay for respite care should be used now or saved for "when things got worse." In thinking about helpers, caregivers thought about whom to ask and when, made numerous phone calls to fit schedules together, and arranged the situation so it was least difficult for the helper. The easiest type of respite experiences were those in which helpers were persons who had known the receiver before the disability and continued to assist the receiver in attending

an informal or formal group (eg, church, veteran's club, morning informal coffee at a local restaurant).

Once a routine was established for regular respite and arrangements made, it became less difficult. However, over the 6-month period of the study, only one caregiver had sustained a respite pattern with an informal or formal helper that was over 3 months in duration. Changes in her own health, that of the receiver, and family situations made it necessary to stop using the respite source or alter the way in which respite was used.

Because receivers with CCI had difficulty communicating their needs, caregivers worried a lot even when away. These caregivers frequently called the helper to see how things were going or made sure that they only went places where they could be contacted should anything go wrong. If receivers with either CCI or CPI were having a bad day (eg, increase in physical problems, more confusion), caregivers frequently canceled respite arrangements at the last minute rather than expose themselves to the emotionally draining worry that occurred when they were away.

Conservation was apparent in the ways caregivers evaluated respite and in the decision they made about future use of respite. Difficulties included increased agitation of receivers with CCI and negative verbalizations by receivers with CPI. As one caregiver stated, "It upset him so much the last time he was at day care, that it took me two days to get him straightened around." Increased difficulty in interacting with the receiver caused caregivers to avoid using that source of respite again. In addition, conserving social resources became problematic with informal sources of help. Caregivers recalled experiences when kin offered to stay with the receiver and then, when taken up on the offer, never offered again and subsequently reduced visits and contacts with the caregiver. Such experiences caused caregivers to restrict accepting offers for respite help for fear of further isolation.

Cognitive versus physical impairment as issues

The area of greatest difference for the CCI and CPI group was that of *knowing*. Using the Mann-Whitney U-test we compared numbers of lines coded between the CCI and CPI group. Knowing was the only code with significantly (*p* .001) more lines of data in the CCI group than in the CPI group. It took longer and was obviously more difficult to explain the unique behaviors of persons with cognitive impairment. However, there was no significant difference (*p* .05) in amount of respite used between the two groups.

In the CPI group, 13 of the 15 receivers resisted being left with anyone else. Caregivers had difficulty in bringing up the subject of respite with them. However, receivers with CPI were able to ask for what they needed from helpers. Thus these caregivers expressed less worry about the receiver when they were away. In both CPI and CCI groups, concerns about imposing and matching were similar and there were no significant differences (*p* .05) in the numbers of lines coded for these categories.

DISCUSSION AND IMPLICATIONS FOR REDUCING VULNERABILITY

In-residence family caregivers in this study were predominantly wives that provided 24-hour, time-intensive care to spouses with severe disabilities for an average of 5½ years. Both informal and formal respite providers repeatedly advised caregivers to obtain more respite. However, caregivers reported that persons offering respite did not understand the complexities involved in gaining the cooperation of the receiver, communicating with helpers about what was needed in the absence of the caregiver, or making the respite experience acceptable to both the receiver and helper. Anticipation of what needed to be done prior to the respite experience, concern about what might occur in their absence, and the difficulties that occurred after respite experiences were largely invisible[28] to others. Although there were a few positive respite experiences reported, the process of utilizing respite was overwhelmingly perceived as more stress producing than beneficial.

The theoretic perspective presented here brings caregivers' concerns into a meaningful structure for identifying barriers to respite, particularly among such in-residence caregivers. Practical implications for education of caregivers, informal and formal helpers, and future receivers of care are evident. The *knowing* theme brings to light caregivers' need for assistance in communicating important caregiving routines, best times of day for respite to occur, and how to work with the receiver before and after respite experiences.

The *imposing* theme encompasses important issues for both informal and formal helpers. Caregivers' reluctance to ask for things that are not specifically offered means that helpers must be aware of the types of assistance that must be explicitly offered. Because caregivers frequently need to cancel arrangements for respite at the last minute, helpers need to state their awareness of such a possibility to reduce caregivers' reluctance to set up times for respite. Informal helpers need to reduce caregivers' feelings of being an imposition by finding creative ways for caregivers to reciprocate. To reduce caregivers' perceptions of being imposed on, helpers can reduce unsolicited advice and work with the caregiver to make the respite experience enjoyable.

The *matching* theme emphasizes the importance of selecting a helper who will be compatible with the receiver and creating situations in which the helper and receiver are both comfortable. Caregivers can coach helpers before leaving them alone with the receiver. Negative reactions of receivers can be reduced by selecting helpers who are compatible with the receiver such as same-gender helpers for older men. By arranging varied situations that both receivers and helpers enjoy such as going on rides, caregivers can create positive experiences between helpers and receivers.

The core category of *conservation* brings together the three themes in meaningful relationship to one another. Careful assessment is needed of the caregiver's perception of appropriate types of respite that cause the least amount of disruption and afford the most relief. Awareness of the most common issues can assist nurses and other professionals in educating families about ways to facilitate respite. Currently the caregiver has the added burden of managing helpers as well as the receivers of care. Careful attention to getting to know the receiver and caregiver routines, anticipating situational needs to reduce the caregiver's fears related to imposing, and forming a partnership with the caregiver to match helpers and the receiver are processes that need to be explicated. Ongoing assessment of these factors initially, and as they change over time, can lead to a better meld of informal and formal sources of respite.[29]

Based on the theoretic perspective of Dilemmas in Using Respite, a pamphlet for caregivers and their families was recently published to assist families in identifying their needs and working with a variety of helpers to achieve the optimal amount and type of respite for their situation.[30] Currently respite programs such as adult day care are expanding and are obviously meeting a portion of the need for respite. However, little is written on whether such programs are effective in reducing caregiver vulnerability to factors such as poor morale, physical fatigue, mental exhaustion, depression, family disruption, and social isolation that already have valid measures.[3-6] Several additional outcome measures are needed. First, establishing a standard measure for quantifying both informal and formal respite use is essential to determining the amount and types of respite that best fit individual circumstances. Second, because optimal amounts of respite differ based on the caregiving situation, a measure of effectiveness of respite interventions in clearly reducing rather than increasing the work of caregiving is essential. Enough respite must be obtained for caregivers to experience relief and renewal and to maintain social roles and relationships. Finally, cost effectiveness must be monitored and both informal and formal sources of respite taken into account. Better management of services already available may be an answer, rather than creating more costly new services.

• • •

As the trend continues to provide more difficult care at home for longer periods of time, respite is a critical component in reducing the vulnerability of caregivers to negative effects of caregiving. Maintaining and promoting the health of the caregiver has implications not only for the receiver of care, but for the entire family and formal system because all are involved in the process of caregiving.[31] Respite must be viewed as important and necessary rather than a luxury and must be incorporated early in the caregiving trajectory.

REFERENCES

1. Stone R, Cafferata G, Sangl J. Caregivers of the frail elderly: a national profile. *Gerontologist*. 1987; 27:616–626.
2. Bureau of Census. *Statistical Abstract of the United States 1992*. Washington, DC: US Department of Commerce; 1992.
3. Fengler AP, Goodrich N. Wives of elderly disabled men: the hidden patients. *Gerontologist*. 1979;19: 175–183.
4. Gwyther LP, George LK. Caregivers for dementia patients: complex determinants of well-being and burden. *Gerontologist*. 1986;26:245–247.
5. Snyder B, Keefe K. The unmet needs of family caregivers for frail and disabled adults. *Soc Work Health Care*. 1985;10(3):1–14.
6. Milne C, Sacco C, Cetinski G, Browne G, Roberts J. Correlates of well-being among caregivers of cognitively impaired elders. *Can J Nurs Res*. 1994;26(1):27–39.
7. Birkel R, Jones C. A comparison of the caregiving networks of dependent elderly individuals who are lucid and those who are demented. *Gerontologist*. 1989;29:114–119.
8. Graftstrom M, Winblad B. Family burden in the care of the demented and nondemented elderly—a longitudinal study. *Alzheimer Dis Assoc Disord*. 1995;9(2):78–86.
9. Gatz M, Boyd S, Mellins C. *Mentally and Physically Impaired Elders: Family Consequences*. Presented at the Gerontological Society of America; November 1987; Washington DC.

10. Caserta M, Lund D, Wright S, Redburn D. Caregivers of dementia patients: the utilization of community services. *Gerontologist*. 1987;27:209–214.
11. Clark N, Rakowski W. Family caregivers of older adults: improving helping skills. *Gerontologist*. 1983;23:637–642.
12. Crossman L, London C, Barry C. Older women caring for disabled spouses: a model for supportive services. *Gerontologist*. 1981;21:464–470.
13. Lawton M, Brody E, Saperstein A. A controlled study of respite service for caregivers of Alzheimer's patients. *Gerontologist*. 1989;29:8–16.
14. Theis S, Moss J, Pearson M. Respite for caregivers: an evaluation study. *J Community Health Nurs*. 1994;11(1):31–44.
15. Montgomery R, Borgatta E. *Family Support Project: Final Report to the Administration on Aging*. Seattle, Wash: Institute of Aging/Long-Term Care Center, University of Washington; 1985.
16. Barry G, Zarit S, Rabatin V. Caregiver activity on respite and nonrespite days. *Gerontologist*. 1991; 31:830–835.
17. Miller D, Gulle N, McCue F. The realities of respite for families, clients, and sponsors. *Gerontologist*. 1986;26:467–470.
18. Strauss A. *Qualitative Analysis for Social Scientist*. Melbourne, Australia: Cambridge University Press; 1988.
19. Blumer B. *Symbolic Interactionism: Perspective and Method*. Englewood Cliffs, NJ: Prentice Hall; 1969.

20. Burr WR, Leigh GK, Day RD, Constantine J. *Contemporary Theories about the Family*. New York, NY: New Haven Press; 1979.
21. Denzin NK. *The Research Act: A Theoretical Introduction to Sociological Methods*. 2nd ed. New York, NY: McGraw-Hill; 1978.
22. Montgomery R. Respite services for family caregivers. In: Petersen MD, White D, eds. *Health Care of the Elderly: An Information Source Book*. Newbury Park, Calif: Sage; 1989.
23. Katz S, Ford A, Moskowitz R, Jackson B, Jaffee M. Studies of the aged. The index of ADL: a standardized measure of biological and psychosocial function. *JAMA*. 1963;185:94.
24. Folstein M, Folstein S, McHugh P. Mini-Mental State: a practical method for grading cognitive states of patients for clinicians. *J Psychiatr Res*. 1975;12:189–198.
25. Goodwin L, Goodwin W. Are validity and reliability "relevant" in qualitative evaluation research? *Eval Health Professions*. 1984;7:413–426.
26. LeCompte M, Goetz J. Problems of reliability and validity in ethnographic research. *Rev Educ Res*. 1982;52:31–60.
27. Topf M. Three estimates of interrater reliability for nominal data. *Nurs Res*. 1986;35:253–255.
28. Bowers B. Intergenerational caregiving: adult caregivers and their aging parents. *Adv Nurs Sci*. 1987; 9(2):20–31.
29. Hutchinson RR, Quartyaro EG. High-risk vulnerable populations and volunteers: a model of education and service coordination. *J Community Health Nurs*. 1995;12(2):111–119.
30. Task Force on Aging. *Reclaiming Time: Caregiver Relief and Renewal*. Seattle, Wash: Church Council of Greater Seattle; 1996.
31. Jackson DG, Cleary BL. Health promotion strategies for spousal caregivers of chronically ill elders. *Nurs Pract Forum*. 1995;6(1):10–18.

CHAPTER 9

Access to Health Care: Perspectives of African American Families with Chronically Ill Children

Jane W. Peterson, RN, PhD

Yvonne M. Sterling, RN, DNSc

DeLois P. Weekes, RN, DNS

TODAY THERE IS MUCH discussion about access to health care for vulnerable populations such as children or members of at-risk ethnic groups. Aday stated, "Access implies that people have a place to go and the financial and other means of obtaining care. The way services are organized and the methods that exist to pay for them may not always facilitate either entry or continuity, however."[1(p180)] Families in a pilot study reported in this chapter shared their experiences regarding access to health care.

This chapter focuses on a vulnerable group of African American families who have children with a chronic illness. Families' perspectives of access to health care for asthma are described. Asthma is "the most common chronic illness affecting children in the U.S. . . . The prevalence increased 33% between 1981 and 1988 . . . for all children younger than 18 years of age."[2(p56)] Despite increasing mortality rates among white children, African American children still had a higher preva-

Fam Community Health 1997;19(4):64–77
© 1997 Aspen Publishers, Inc.

lence of asthma in 1988.[3] Betz[4] analyzed ethnic representation in pediatric nursing research and found a lack of diversity among populations studied. In most studies the sample size of African Americans was small and therefore statistically insignificant so that findings are contextualized in the dominant culture.

This chapter discusses African Americans within their own families and communities. The discussion centers around general beliefs and behaviors of the family that affect and are affected by the chronic illness of a child. The intent is to give voice to their viewpoint and advocate inclusion of their perspective as an integral part of a health assessment. This should lead to greater collaboration in the selection of interventions by health care providers and clients. Increased utilization of health care at appropriate primary, secondary, and tertiary levels is more likely with this more collaborative approach leading to positive health outcomes for the population. Advocacy is a strategy for enhancing health care. Families would feel they "had a place to go."[1(p180)]

LITERATURE REVIEW

National and international attention has recently been drawn to the plight of African American children in the United States. The United Nations Development Programme (UNDP) introduced a human development index (HDI) to assess, compare and provide choices on human development in any country. This index "combines indicators of real purchasing power, education and health [which of-

fer] a measure of development much more comprehensive than GNP [gross national product] alone."[5(p10)] According to this index, black (African American) children in the United States are disadvantaged from birth and rank 31st in the world, while the white population in the United States ranks first. One factor that contributes to this disparity, according to Thomas,[6] is lack of access to health services. Davidson and associates,[7] in their study on access to care for 170 asthma patients ages 2 to 17, found that black and Hispanic patients and patients on Medicaid used the emergency room more, without first calling their doctor or clinic, than did white patients. Shields and associates[8] tried a specific education program at a Chicago health maintenance organization (HMO) to reduce this pattern of emergency room utilization among 253 primarily low-income black children with asthma but failed to change their pattern. The researchers attributed this to their failure to target the education program to the specific population and their not increasing knowledge about behavior change while increasing knowledge about asthma.

Evans[9] summarized the lack of access to health care among minority children with asthma. He found the following reasons for problems with access:
- no hospital in the area,
- poor transportation system,
- lack of care for well children while caring for the ill child,
- long clinic and hospital waiting times,
- inconvenient hours of service,
- problems understanding the language, and

- lack of money to pay for service or treatment.

Bosco and associates found that even if access problems were eliminated, in the treatment of childhood asthma "the black urban patient continued to receive less effective therapy with fixed-combination products well after these products had been abandoned in other groups of Medicaid patients."[10(p1,731)] Thus, access to health care might result in different patterns of service and less effective therapy received by this population.

Asthma is a leading cause of disability in people younger than 17 years of age.[10] It "is frequently misdiagnosed or undertreated and causes more hospital admissions, more visits to hospital emergency rooms and more school absences than any other chronic disease in childhood."[11(p1)] Hospitalization, morbidity, and mortality rates have all increased for asthma patients. The population most affected appears to be nonwhite children living in urban areas and the poor.[2,12] Death rates among children 5 to 14 years are 0.7 per 100,000 population for black children and 0.1 per 100,000 for white children.[9] In 1987, black males 5 to 34 years old had a mortality rate five times higher than white patients of both sexes.[12] The prevalence of asthma was 150 times greater for black children than for others during the period 1965 to 1984.[13] A review of hospital admissions for children with status asthmaticus revealed most patients to be young black males.[14] Between 1981 and 1988, the incidence rate for asthma increased more in white than black children, and black children still had a higher prevalence rate in 1988.[3]

What emerges from the literature are high asthma rates for hospitalization, morbidity, and mortality among black children. However, the underlying causes for these findings are not precisely understood. It is not clear whether race or socioeconomic status or an interaction among multiple factors is responsible for the high morbidity and mortality rates.[15,16] It may be that a complex interaction among socioeconomic status, inner-city problems, family adaptive patterns, social support, cultural beliefs, physical environment, and the health care delivery system has unique and combined effects on the vulnerability of black children.[12,17] Newacheck[18] concluded that chronic health problems in children from poor families are not adequately addressed by the existing health care system. He found that these children were more likely than children from nonpoor families to not report chronic illnesses, have a higher risk of severe chronic conditions, experience lack of access to care, be uninsured, and lack a usual source of care. Black children have *differential vulnerability*[1] reflected by their multiple cumulative risk factors, indicating that a disease such as asthma will hurt them more than others.

It appears that black children perceive illness through their cultural lens and are influenced by multiple factors. Health care providers view illness through their professional lens and focus mainly on the disease process and health restoration. A mediator could bridge these two views. Cultural brokering or mediating[19-22] between family and health care provider would help clarify the perspectives of both and the impact of low socioeconomic status and cultural beliefs on a family's access to health care. A cultural broker can "interpret expectations based on beliefs, values and traditions, clarify issues, and provide a common understanding between two groups."[19(p71)] Cultural brokering is an outcome of this study, which asked the question, what are the experiences of black families with a chronically ill child? The ethnographic study design allowed families to share their views as they relate to access to health care services, or "gettin' help" as one mother put it.

METHOD

This study used an ethnographic design. Ethnography "is the work of describing culture"[23(p3)] and makes explicit the meaning of events and actions of the people being studied. Participant observation and interviews were carried out by three African American nurse researchers living in the cities in which the study was conducted. This ensured that the language used by African Americans was faithfully recorded and interpreted within their cultural context. Purposeful sampling was done by obtaining families who had experience with children with asthma and were of African American ethnicity. Families were obtained through outpatient or community health clinics in Seattle, New Orleans, and the San Francisco Bay Area.

Seven families with a child diagnosed with asthma are discussed in this article. Three were from Seattle and two each from the other cities. A total of 11 contacts occurred. Four families were contacted twice and three families only once due to cancelled appointments. Most visits were held in the family's home, with a few in a clinic or an office. The mean age of the children was 11.3 years; the youngest was 5 and the oldest 17. There were four girls and three boys. The seven key informants, all adult women, were the primary caregivers. Six of the caregivers were the mothers (including one foster mother) and one was a paternal grandmother. These women ranged from 31 to 46 years of age, with a mean age of 37. Four women were married and lived with their spouses, while three were single mothers. Two women worked full time, two worked part time, and three were not employed outside the home. One of the women, not employed, had taken what she termed an early "medical retirement" due to her own problems with asthma. Although interviews were conducted mainly with the caregivers, three of the children and one maternal grandmother who was not a primary caregiver participated in the interviews. Each family had a history of asthma. Two of the key informants reported that they had never been responsible for the care of a person with asthma before caring for the child in this study.

All interviews were audiotaped and notes were made. Interview material was transcribed and identifying material removed. Families were referred to by codes, and informants, health care facilities, and health care providers were given pseudonyms to maintain confidentiality. All informants signed consent forms. The researchers met face to face prior to, during, and after data collection to plan, review, and analyze data as a team. Second interviews with four of the families allowed the researcher to validate impressions with the family and receive feedback from them. Families commented on how much they appreciated this and sought to clarify points they thought the researcher misunderstood.

ANALYSIS

All families studied were concerned about the health of their children. Parents or health care providers reported that all children had been diagnosed with asthma by a physician. From the family's perspective, "gettin' help" meant getting the health care they wanted and found acceptable from the health care system. Despite spending time, energy, and family resources the results were not always successful.

The families' perspectives comprised four distinct categories:

1. getting health care that is wanted—three families;
2. getting health care that is unwanted—two families;
3. not getting health care that is wanted—one family; and
4. not getting health care that is unwanted—one family.

Getting health care that is wanted

The three families who were able to get the health care they wanted did so by negotiating with the system, using the system on their own terms, or joining the system.

Case 1

Eddy is a 10-year-old boy who was diagnosed with asthma at 3 months. He lives with his mother, father, and younger sister. Both parents work. However, his mother lost her full-time job and thus her family health benefits due to her many absences from work to care for her son. She now has a part-time job in food services, but no health benefits. This family has been able to negotiate with the health care system to obtain care for Eddy. The mother recounts that when she felt that she was not being heard, and therefore unable to negotiate for health care, she switched health care facilities.

At Mercy Hospital . . . from the time they diagnosed him with the asthma, he's been going every Monday for approximately 4 years, taking two shots, and that's to determine, to try to slow the asthma down. At their determining that his condition looked like it wasn't going to get no better at Mercy Hospital, I switched him to Children's Hospital under the care of Dr. Thomas. Since going to Children's he's improved, he don't go every Monday, he go every 3 months now. The medication has increased, they put him on Provental, and they put him on a steroid tablet at night so he has to take that every night.

This mother considered moving closer to the hospital. "We were constantly going to Mercy, it was like every other day, it was like let's move closer to Mercy, 'cause the child just couldn't make it." The family has strong support from family members and friends who help them decide what actions to take. These people also sanctioned health care decisions.

This is evident when Eddy's mother states, "Until one day a friend of mine told me to contact respiratory. I did. I got the machine for him, it prevented me from having to go to the hospital as much, now I only go to the hospital with him if for some reason that he's having an attack . . . where the machine don't do him no good."

This mother was able to advocate for her child and herself. After losing her health benefits, she applied for a medical card for her son, but was told that he was too old to qualify. She pursued this issue on her son's behalf:

I went through social welfare, through CHAMPUS, they denied it. . . . So one day I was . . . trying to call the clinic and I wound up getting the governor's office. So I spoke to the people at the governor's office. I told them that the child is an asthmatic patient and I was depending on getting the [medical] card for him for his medicine, because I could not afford to pay for his medicine, it's hard. So I went on and talked to somebody in the office and the next month they reinstated his card and I wound up getting his card back for him, that was luck, pure luck.

Thus, this case illustrates how a family obtained the care they wanted by negotiating the system.

Case 2

Derek is a 13-year-old boy diagnosed with asthma at age 3. He lives with his mother who is a secretary at a local university and a younger sister. His older sister is married. His mother's large extended family lives in the area and offers their help when needed. This family uses the health care system on their own terms. For them,

the health care delivery system is only one strategy used to maintain Derek's health. His mother views an active life as an essential part of keeping healthy: "What I have done with him is I've kept him real active in sports, push him real hard about running. . . . I'd say maybe once a year he'll have a chiropractic adjustment, but hardly [have] any problems with Derek."

Her feeling toward doctors is clear when she says, "it's just like doctors aren't all that necessary." Her own sense of control and faith keeps her centered, "it is mind over matter, but it's a matter, . . . my children think more on the lines of they know the Lord will heal them." This belief was talked about in terms of an active belief, one that was incorporated into everyday life, the way they lived, the choices they made. "Faith plays a big part in our life now. . . . There is a lot more peace in my life . . . it's just like I don't allow chaos in my house, you know, no matter what form it comes in."

However, this mother readily takes her child to the hospital when she feels he needs to go. She had certain expectations of the health care system and created ways to have these met.

. . . in terms of interacting with hospitals and clinics . . . they are there when you need them. And there's 2,000 people in emergency [room] or something like that—and I'm going to stay there all day? And I just go to the emergency [room] and tell them something fantastic. "My daughter has a snake on her leg. I want somebody to look at it." And of course when children are having problems with asthma, nobody's going to sit in the waiting room. Because I've never had anybody make me wait in a waiting room for any length of time for my children if they ever have problems with asthma. Never.

This mother often calls a sister who has a master's degree in nursing for advice when she does not understand health care providers' instructions. "And they [doctors] told me, 'Give him this thing tonight and in the morning give him this other.' And then I called [my sister] and she said, 'Well, go on. You give him the medication, the whole thing and call me in an hour or so.' And then I called her back and she said, 'Well how is he doing?' "

With the support of a relative, this mother was able to care for her child successfully through an illness episode. For the most part, Derek goes to his regular clinic appointments by himself. He has an inhaler, and he has medications that he manages on his own. The case exemplifies a family effectively using the system on their own terms.

Case 3

Arthur is 10 years old. He was diagnosed with asthma at 10 months, "since he got here practically," says his paternal grandmother, who is his primary caregiver. He lives with his grandparents. His mother lives in a different part of the state with her husband and children. His father, who is also married and has children, lives in the same city. The strategy this family uses for getting wanted health care is joining the system. Arthur's grandmother became a respiratory therapist. Talking about herself she says, "I don't work as a respiratory therapist now. . . . I had to retire medically from

the post office. . . . See, I worked there for 11 years, and I couldn't take it any more, so then I retired and I was in and out of the hospital all the time, and I just happened to be scanning my hospital bill, and I noticed every time the respiratory therapist came it was $50, right? . . . And I said well, hey, I can do this!"

She worked for a while as a respiratory therapist. She finds that experience "really helpful" in taking care of Arthur. "I have trained Arthur. He can do his own breathing treatments. . . . He knows that when his chest gets tight, what he has to do, and he knows that when there's a cat or something in the house, he knows he shouldn't be there, so he's taking care of himself."

Because of her knowledge, she is able to talk to health care providers using their language:

One particular time we went to the emergency room. He was having a terrible, terrible asthma attack at this particular time, as a matter of fact he wasn't getting any oxygen, OK? . . . What blew me out was I had to tell the doctors, "Look he is not getting any oxygen, you know. He can't breathe. . . ." When I let them know that I know what's going on, they sometimes talk to me a little bit different. Because I do know what's going on, they can tell me certain things in medical terms, so I can really understand it. They don't have to use layman language; they can just say what they have to say, and I'll understand it right away.

Her satisfaction with health care is summarized when she says, "Well, the last clinic visit was a very good clinic visit . . . they determine everything and then they make suggestions. They ask me what do I think, and I tell them what I think. Then they tell me what they think, and then we meet somewhere on common ground, and everything, so it works out pretty well."

Getting health care that is unwanted

Two families expressed concern that the health care they received was not the care they wanted. For one family, health care did not fit what Kleinman[24] called the family's explanatory model of the illness. Explanatory models "offer explanations of sickness and treatment to guide choices among available therapies and therapists and to cast personal and social meaning on the experience of sickness."[24(p105)] The other family felt so indebted to the health care system that they accepted whatever was suggested even when opposed to the suggestions.

Case 4

Ramona, a 17-year-old girl, has an infant son. They live with Ramona's mother and three younger sisters. Ramona and her husband are separated but he comes to the apartment frequently to help with the baby. Ramona was diagnosed with asthma at age 5. Her dislike of the health care system started at the time of diagnosis and persists to the present. Her dissatisfaction with her health care is closely associated with the family's explanatory model of asthma. Ramona's mother describes asthma in the following way: "When I hear asthma, I picture an old man . . . walking down the street with pee stain hat and pee stain pants real dirty and dandruff collar

maybe grease on his pants, maybe a bug or two stuck on it, panhandler with his hand out. This is what asthma reminds me of . . . it is the noise, just the noise. I can handle anything . . . puky old stuff from this old man, but the wheeze. The noise I can't [take]."

Ramona's mother's view of asthma is triggered by the wheezing sound and very much associated with aging.

Even when she was little when she first started wheezing. She was that little old man even then. . . . I didn't see her getting any better, I didn't see any progress whatsoever. The only thing I saw was that she is getting old. And then I saw her heart getting old, her inside parts getting old. So, I figure those are getting old, how could she be getting better? . . . She wouldn't take [her pills] because they would make her heart beat fast. . . . I really did not want her on the pills anyway. Because I felt that if your heart beats . . . twice as fast all the time, that is like speeding up the aging process. I figure her heart is getting really old and by the time she hits 25 or such she'd have a heart attack. This is in the back of my mind, okay? And I figured they just didn't give her good care.

The family's explanatory model also accounted for the fact that Ramona had not grown out of the disease, and to them it did not seem that she was ever going to grow out of it.

The doctor said I should relax and she would grow out of it. I didn't think it was anything permanent. If they had told me it would only last 2 months I could handle that. But years! She may be a teenager, God, I'd be dead. So, this is like sentencing somebody to death row to me, that's torture. They said she could outgrow it anytime, but definitely by the time she is a teenager. . . . I only held onto that [outgrowing asthma] until she was 11 or 12. By that time I knew she was going to have it for life. . . . I didn't see her getting any better. I didn't see any progress whatsoever. The only thing I saw was that she is getting old.

Ramona internalized her mother's explanatory model of asthma. "I feel like an old man. That's how I feel. . . . When you are the oldest child, like me, you have pressure to be doing better than you should be doing. . . . You're suppose to set examples and therefore you can't get sick. . . . Asthma means I am sick. It means you can't be the best you can be because you have a sickness. It means you are different from everybody else. Cause you can't do any of the things they can do. And when I think of asthma, I think of medicine."

Ramona's view of asthma impacts decisions she makes in her life. She feels that she has little control and there is little predictability in what happens to her. This case illustrates the explanatory model of asthma as a condition of the aged who cannot care for themselves and of medication hastening that process.

Case 5

Tameka is 13 years old and was diagnosed with asthma at 5 months. Two of her four siblings have asthma. The children live with their mother and maternal grandmother. The mother's sister and only sibling gave her a car to transport the children to and from the doctor. The overall view of this family toward the health care system is indebtedness for having saved Tameka's life. Because of this they accept most suggestions made by health care providers, even those they do not like. "I love City Hospital. [Tameka] likes

to go to City, but Mercy Hospital is *the* one—before they transferred her to City they [Mercy Hospital staff] really, I think, saved her life; cause my baby had stopped breathing, twice."

Mercy Hospital in many ways has become an extension of the family referred to as Tameka's "second home." Her mother says, "She's been there [to the hospital] so many times and they know her—I feel comfortable when I'm home [and she is in the hospital]. I know they know her and she know them. . . . "

Despite this strong positive feeling for Mercy Hospital, Tameka's mother no longer takes her there. She says, "I don't bring her back to Mercy Hospital. City Hospital doctors get mad. So now I start bringing her to City. . . . Tameka likes City. . . . " This family also puts their trust in God. They are willing to accept whatever happens to them in the belief that God will take care of them.

It bothers me now when she gets sick but I know it's *the* Man up above who's gonna take care of us. He wouldn't have let her been here this long, cause He could have took her when she was small, how sick she was . . . day after day you wonder if she gonna make it this day or if she gonna pass that day and it just help you wondering, keep you praying a lot. The first year of her life was the real hard year of her life.

At first the family refused to consider surgery for Tameka. Her mother prayed, "I ask the Lord that she doesn't have to have the surgery. But if she do, I'll hesitate, stop what I'm doing and put myself in His hands." Tameka's mother's belief that the Lord would do what was right was unshakable. She was willing to live with the consequences no matter how painful for her. She said that doctors did procedures and treatments that she told them she did not want for Tameka. However, she felt there was no use pursuing these differences as she was told that the treatment was to help her daughter. This family passively accepted care given that was not wanted. They felt God was the ultimate decision maker and He would do the right thing; they could live with that.

Not getting health care that is wanted

One family fell into this category. This was a family whose socioeconomic status had decreased. The family felt they were not treated as well as they had been in the past by health care providers.

Case 6

Daria, now 5 years old, was diagnosed with asthma when almost 3. She lives with both parents and an 11-year-old brother. Her father is starting a new business with his brother, and her mother can no longer hold a steady job because "it's no telling when she's gonna go into a asthma attack . . . its back and forth . . . you can't keep somebody who's never at work." Daria's illness adds to the strain on the family finances and in the marital relationship. The family's desire for wanted health care for their daughter is hindered by the family finances.

When we have to get medical [coverage] then it is a big fight. Well, of course I don't feel good when I have to go down to the welfare office for any reason. And then I take that out on him [husband] and he take it out on me cause he's mad cause he doesn't have a job that has medical and we go round and round

like that. . . . I tell him, he can't afford to work there because we need medical. . . . So, it's a real strain when you don't have medical and don't have resources to take care of it. And we're still paying bills from way back. . . . [This last time] I swallowed my pride and went down to the welfare and I, actually I made him [husband] go. . . . I said, "Well, if you can't get a job doing things and get medical, you have to go down there and feel what I feel when I have to go down to the welfare to do this." So he went down there and signed us all up for medical and now we have medical. But it is so hard when you have a fluctuating income.

Balancing the budget is a constant source of strain in this household. They don't eat properly because they prefer to use their money to pay medical bills. As the mother says, "You get to know the doctors and you don't want to cheat anybody of their money." However, they felt their ability to pay affected the health care they received. "I come down here and beg from you guys to get my bills taken care of. And then you go to the doctor and sometimes they don't treat you right, you know, sometimes they look at you kinda like, 'well you know, if you would just get off your behind and take care of your business this wouldn't be' . . . it's rough everywhere you go." The family was also upset because no one told them that a different but equally effective medication was covered by welfare.

Not getting health care that is unwanted

One family fell in this category. They ignored asthma as a disease. Asthma was normalized by referring to the symptoms as common problems of all children—cough, common cold and sneezing. Health care was not sought and not wanted, which preserved the notion that the child was "normal, just like her friends."

Case 7

Nicole is 11 years and 11 months. She was diagnosed with asthma shortly after her 11th birthday. She lives in a foster home in which both parents work and their two children attend school with Nicole. Nicole's foster mother has a large extended family with a familial history of asthma. Other than the initial diagnosis, Nicole has not had health care for her asthma. When asked about the recent move into their new home and how Nicole had managed, she and her mother replied in unison, "Fine." Nicole continued, "I helped unpack the kitchen. That was OK . . . I sneeze. . . ." Her mother interjected, "when I noticed that the painting was bothering her, I just restricted her from that area until it was dry. See, we painted everything in here, she was fine."

Nicole has very limited knowledge about asthma. When asked what asthma means to her, she says, "I haven't even had an asthma attack. I don't know what asthma is like. . . . They say I have asthma because I keep on breathing harder." Her treatment for asthma is an "asthma pump," which she had left at school the day of the interview. Her mother said she had gone camping overnight and had forgotten to taken her pump. She takes no other medication for asthma. On the one hand her mother

tries to manage the asthma; "I told her yesterday to go get her breather. . . . I know she was coughing a lot, I told her to use her inhaler." On the other hand the family leaves it up to Nicole to manage care of her health. However, her focus is not on the day-to-day problems of the asthma symptoms, which have been normalized, but on the potential "asthma attacks." She says, "I don't get it. People with asthma have asthma attacks and I don't have any." Yet Nicole has an unusual fear of having an asthma attack. She says, "If I have an asthma attack . . . they might keep me in the hospital for the rest of my life. . . . I have never been in the hospital." When asked about Children's Hospital she was frankly surprised that there was a hospital exclusively for children and wanted to know if there were lots of children there. "If I be at the hospital until I get to be 21, then will they admit me to a big hospital [hospital for adults]?" she asked. Nicole's model for a hospital was that of a jail with juvenile and adult prisoners and the potential for life sentences. She had no concept of hospital, chronic disease, or treatment regimen.

DISCUSSION AND FINDINGS

All families in this study said they were "dealin' with the asthma." Family reports of access to health care and obtaining the health care they wanted fell into four categories. Each category presents different implications for advocating for an African American family with a child who has asthma. There are also different and quite promising research implications.

Three of the seven families in this pilot study obtained the health care they wanted. These families were able to negotiate with health care providers, had strong support systems that sanctioned their health care requests, used the health care system on their terms, and understood and spoke health care language. This group does not need an advocate to help them access or utilize the health care system. However, a strong partnership model would enhance an already successful health care system for these families.

Two families obtained health care they did not want. One had an explanatory model for asthma that differed from those of the health care providers. For this family, the treatment at times seemed worse than the illness. The expectation that the child would outgrow the disease by a certain age gave them hope. When this did not happen, the family felt that the health care they were getting was "bad," and their unmet expectation was their evidence. The second family in this category felt indebted to the nurses and doctors for saving their child's life but were unable to question health care practices. Faith in God and the belief that "everything will turn out for the best" was another concept that deterred this family from challenging health care practices that they questioned. An advocate can play a useful role in situations such as these. An advocate, somewhat like the mediators[19] or cultural brokers,[22] can help family and health care providers articulate and understand the others' perspective and explanatory model. Advocates can also help the two parties operate in an arena of balanced reciprocity where the family's participation in their health care is rewarded and the health care providers' sensitivity to the family's explanatory model is acknowledged.

The third category included only one family who did not get the health care they wanted. This family's income decreased. They had to "swallow their pride and sign up for welfare." Their perception of themselves diminished, and they reported doctors not treating them as well. An advocate in this situation can help the family assert their right to health care they find acceptable. Specific areas in which this needs to be done are gaining a sense of control over one's own health, knowing the options available, and feeling comfortable making a request. Advocates can also help health care providers understand the effect they have on families with ill children and discuss alternatives so families can make informed health care decisions.

The last category, not getting health care and not wanting health care, contained one family. This family normalized illness symptoms of the child diagnosed with asthma. The mother had experience with and information about asthma but minimized the condition to such an extent that the child had limited opportunity to develop understanding of her illness and its treatment. Treatment regimens for asthma were not followed in this family. This is a family in which an advocate could be of great help making information about asthma relevant to the family and the child in a way that does not directly challenge their beliefs and that fits their lifestyle. Such an advocate would seek opportunities to supplement the family's understanding and their health care activities and help this child to manage her own asthma condition.

Advocates for families who have negative feelings toward the health care system and who do not want health care face an immense challenge. Finding and contacting these families must become a legitimate activity for health care advocates. For families who will not acknowledge their illness, advocates should respond to issues families present. When health care is seen as one factor among multiple complex interrelationships, indirect information on health issues can be provided as other factors are addressed.

Vulnerable populations are those "in a position of being hurt or ignored, as well as being helped, by [others]."[1(p1)] Access to health care is an issue for vulnerable populations. Understanding access from a sociocultural perspective deepens the health care provider's appreciation of these people's vulnerability. In order for African American families to have access to health care, "a place to go,"[1] they need to believe that they have some say in their care. Families in this study describe when they thought they had access to health care and when they thought they did not. The use of an advocate is a strategy that can enhance access. Advocates can make an immense contribution to helping families and health care professionals design collaborative health care interventions to "meet somewhere on common ground . . . so it all works out," as Arthur's mother says.

• • •

Much remains to be learned about African American families and how they understand asthma in their children. Studying explanatory models of health and illness can provide answers to how the chronically ill child is managed and why and when the health care system is accessed. Research on the role of cultural brokers could also provide strategies to enhance access to wanted health care for families. Health researchers need to investigate how to work with vulnerable families who are unwilling or unable to acknowledge their illness. Only when such research is done will more answers be provided about who the key players are in African American families and their participation in health care.

REFERENCES

1. Aday LA. *At Risk in America: The Health and Health Care Needs of Vulnerable Populations.* San Francisco, Calif: Jossey-Bass; 1993.
2. Halfon N, Newacheck PW. Childhood asthma and poverty: differential impact and utilization health services. *Pediatrics.* 1993;91(1):56–61.
3. Weitzman M, Gortmaker SL, Sobol AM, Perrin JM. Recent trends in the prevalence and severity of childhood asthma. *JAMA.* 1992;268(19):2,673–2,677.
4. Betz CL. A culturally biased perspective. *J Pediatr Nurs.* 1992;7:229.
5. United Nations Development Programme. *Human Development Report.* New York, NY: Oxford University Press; 1993.
6. Thomas S. The health of the black community in the twenty-first century: a futuristic perspective. In: Braithwait RL, Taylor SE, eds. *Health Issues in the Black Community.* San Francisco, Calif: Jossey-Bass; 1992.
7. Davidson AE, Klein DE, Settipane GA, Alario AJ. Access to care among children visiting the emergency room with acute exacerbations of asthma. *Ann Allergy.* 1994;72(5):469–473.

8. Shields MC, Griffin KW, McNabb WL. The effect of a patient education program on emergency room use for inner-city children with asthma. *Am J Public Health*. 1990;80(1):36–38.

9. Evans R. Asthma among minority children. *Chest*. 1992;101(6, suppl):368S–371S.

10. Bosco LA, Gerstman BB, Tomita DK. Variations in the use of medication for the treatment of childhood asthma in the Michigan Medicaid population, 1980 to 1986. *Chest*. 1993;104(6):1,727–1,732.

11. Plaut TF. *Children with Asthma: A Manual for Parents*. 2nd ed. Amherst, Mass: Pedipress; 1990.

12. Weiss KB, Gergen PJ, Crain EF. Inner-city asthma. *Chest*. 1992;101(6, suppl):362S–367S.

13. Evans R, Mullally DI, Wilson RW, et al. National trends in the morbidity and mortality of asthma in the US. Prevalence, hospitalization and death from asthma over two decades: 1965–1984. *Chest*. 1987;91(6, suppl):65S–74S.

14. Richards W. Hospitalization of children with status asthmaticus: a review. *Pediatrics*. 1989;84(1):111–118.

15. Gergen PJ, Mullally DI, Evans R. National survey of prevalence of asthma among children in the United States, 1976–1980. *Pediatrics*. 1988;81(1):1–7.

16. Wissow LS, Gittelsohn AM, Szklo M, Starfield B, Mussman M. Poverty, race, and hospitalization for childhood asthma. *Am J Public Health*. 1988; 78(7):777–782.

17. Weitzman M, Gortmaker SL, Sobol AM. Racial, social and environmental risks for childhood asthma. *Am J Dis Children*. 1990;144(11):1,189–1,194.

18. Newacheck PW. Poverty and childhood chronic illness. *Arch Pediatr Adolesc Med*. 1994;148(11):1,143–1,149.

19. LaFargue JP. Mediating between two views of illness. *Topics Clin Nurs*. 1985;7(3):70–77.

20. Leininger MM. *Culture Care Diversity and Universality: A Theory of Nursing*. New York, NY: National League for Nursing Press; 1991.

21. Jackson LE. Understanding, eliciting, and negotiating clients' multicultural beliefs. *Nurse Practitioner*. 1993;18(4):30–43.

22. Jezewski MA. Cultural brokering as a model for advocacy. *Nurs Health Care*. 1993;14(2):78–85.

23. Spradely JP. *Participant Observation*. New York, NY: Holt, Rinehart & Winston; 1980.

24. Kleinman A. *Patients and Healers in the Context of Culture*. Berkeley, Calif: University of California Press; 1980.

CHAPTER 10

The Process of Chore Teaching: Implications for Farm Youth Injury

Pamela Kidd, RN, PhD

Kimberly Townley, PhD

Henry Cole, EdD

Robert McKnight, MPH, ScD

Larry Piercy, MS

ACCORDING TO THE US Census, 1.1 million children less than 14 years of age live on farms.[1] Historically, these children and adolescents have contributed to farm labor in the United States.[2] Among the hazards facing these children are tractors and other machinery, bodies of water, farm animals, agricultural chemicals, confined spaces, flowing grain, and electricity.[3] This figure may be low since it excludes children who work but do not live on farms. Farm work injury rates for children under age 14 are 18 per 1,000 children at risk.[4]

While government regulations have been effective in controlling youth injury in other industries, government safety regulations are viewed as too costly for the small farmer.[5] An amendment passed in 1976 to the Occupational Safety and

This study was supported by the National Institute of Nursing Research, Health Risk Reduction Center for Rural Youth (NIH Grant 1P20NR02979). The authors acknowledge Cassia Herron for her technical assistance with the manuscript.

Fam Community Health 1997;19(4):78–89
© 1997 Aspen Publishers, Inc.

Health Act (OSHA) of 1970 exempted farms with 10 or fewer workers from OSHA regulations.[6] Additionally, under provisions of the US Fair Labor Standards Act (FLSA)[2] minors under 12 years of age (with parental consent) may be employed outside school hours in nonhazardous activities on a farm owned by their parents or another small farm (defined as 10 or fewer employed workers).

Single-family farms continue to decrease in number[7,8] and competitive pressures from agribusiness have created a milieu for exploiting child labor. Farms with annual sales of $10,000 to $100,000 represent 37% of all farms but account for 21% of the total agricultural production in the United States.[9] Expansion is seen as one strategy for increasing farming productivity. But as the farm size increases, so does the risk of injury.[10] The cumulative effect of a high workload, prolonged work hours, fatigue, and anxiety may contribute to injuries in children.

When farm workers' insurance claims were compared with those for children 13 years or younger working in all other industries, farm work accounted for 50% of all severe injury claims, compared with 5% of severe injury claims for food service workers.[11] These findings underscore the importance of understanding parents' views on what are suitable chores for farm youth to perform and what process they use, if any, to teach farm chores if we assume the protection of children from injury ultimately depends on the action of adults.[12]

Epidemiologic studies focusing on childhood farm injuries often yield results that can be used to determine the effectiveness of interventions.[4,10,13] The limi-

tations of these studies, however, relate to their focus on the injury event and not on its precursors. Qualitative research is needed to understand the child's perspective of farm work, the process by which children make safety decisions and learn farm work, and the context in which this work is performed.

The goal of this exploratory study was to gain a clearer understanding of the relationship between chore teaching and farm injuries in children and youth ages 9 to 14 years. Specific aims were to identify parents' perceptions of acceptable chores for children, understand the process used by parents to teach these chores, and explore the relationship between what parents teach about farm safety and the child's perception and application of the knowledge gained.

METHODS

Ten focus groups were conducted in various locations across Kentucky. Groups varied in composition to assess differences in work roles in relation to gender and age. Focus groups are interactive sessions in which participants are gathered to discuss thoughts about a specific topic.[14] Each session was facilitated by a moderator using a semistructured interview guide. Focus groups were used for the following reasons: farming has a rich oral tradition and work practices are verbally taught with psychomotor skill practice, and rural communities tend to interact in oral rather than written forms.[15]

Stories of chore teaching, as well as injury avoidance and occurrence, were elicited. The use of stories was supported by the theory of narrative thinking, a way of knowing and understanding the world through stories heard, stories lived, and stories told.[16] Stories are universal and powerful guides for living and understanding conduct.[17]

RECRUITMENT OF PARTICIPANTS

Seven counties in Kentucky were selected based on their geographic diversity and agricultural production practices. Either the county agricultural extension specialist or county youth agricultural development leader was contacted and asked to invite eight individuals to participate in a focus group on farm safety and health. Both part- and full-time farm families were invited to attend as children are an important labor force in both operations.

After being contacted by the agent or leader, a member of the research team contacted the family by phone to explain the nature and length of the focus group. If the family and child agreed to participate, a package was mailed containing consent forms, assent forms (for children), and a 40-item Farm Information Questionnaire (FIQ). The FIQ was designed to elicit information regarding farm size, production, and the injury or illness history of the family.

The initial discussion questions for both the youth and parent groups were generated by the research team based on the farm stress and injury literature. After the first focus group, discussion areas spontaneously elicited by the participants were framed into moderator questions for future use. These areas included

- ways to make chores and play safer,
- chores children were fearful of completing,
- personal close calls when doing chores, and
- chores parents do not allow the child to complete.

A parallel section of the interview guide was developed to compare what parents said they taught their children about farm safety with what children perceived and applied. For example, the child groups were asked, "Tell me a story about how you learned to work with animals on the farm." The parent groups were asked, "How did you teach your son or daughter to work with animals on the farm?"

Group sessions were audiotaped using a recorder with an external microphone. A research assistant maintained field notes during the session to clarify respondents' comments. Tapes were transcribed verbatim, with names changed to ensure anonymity and protect confidentiality.

DEVELOPMENT OF CODING DICTIONARY

The coding team consisted of the same researchers who conducted the focus groups. Two team members read the first transcript and derived a list of 25 key words, with their definitions based on this first reading. As each additional transcript was coded, the entire team met to discuss areas of controversy or redundancy. Modifications in the dictionary were agreed on by all six members of the research team. The latest edition of the dictionary was used at any given time to code a transcript. The coding dictionary underwent four iterations. The final dictionary contained 70 key words clustered within nine categories: general context, injury or illness, learning, development, play, hazard recognition, safety, chores, and environmental agents.

DATA ANALYSIS

Narrative data were entered into the FYI 3000 qualitative data software program.[18] To eliminate sources of bias, the following measures were taken: Credibility (analogous to internal validity) of findings was examined through the use of iterative groups who had not attended a prior focus group. Kentucky farm injury history data were used to assess transferability (external validity). For example, children frequently mentioned the hazards associated with animal feeding and care. There was support for this hazard since in 1993, 16% of Kentucky farm pediatric injuries were related to animal care.[19] Dependability (reliability) was addressed using the same core questions across groups and comparing field notes with taped interviews. Member checking, the process of clarifying with participants' evolving themes from previous groups, as well as individual comments, was used to enhance objectivity. The moderator presented hypotheses to the participants and the group affirmed or disconfirmed the proposed relationships. The group setting discouraged placing undue emphasis on one participant's comments because areas of disagreement or consensus were sought by the moderator.

Conceptual relationships were identified by examining consequences, causes, conditions, contexts, contingencies, and covariances associated with chore completion (core category).[20] The identified concepts—chore initiation, chore modification, chore limits, and chore progression—were defined using the participant's own words. Data exemplifying each concept were selected across groups. Interrater reliability was assessed using kappa coefficient[21] by randomly selecting 10% of the total number of data bits per transcript and comparing coding. Coefficients ranged from .74 to .87; thus, recoding was not necessary. Matrix analysis was then used to compare groups.[22] Quantitative data that helped to clarify patterns identified narratively were examined and methods for measuring each concept in future research were identified.

RESULTS

A total of 48 farm families, with 63 individuals, participated in the groups (Table 10–1). Two female, two male, and two mixed-gender children focus groups were conducted with 40 participants. These groups were further stratified by age, with 19 participants between the ages of 9 and 11 and 21 between the ages of 12 and 14. Twelve fathers attended the focus groups, seven who had daughters and five who had sons. Eleven mothers also participated, six of whom had sons and five daughters.

Thirty-six of the families completed the FIQ, for a response rate of 75%. Crops were the leading product of gross farm income for 42% of the respondents. Livestock production accounted for the leading product of gross farm income for

Table 10–1. Focus group composition

Composition	Size
Children	
Ages 12 to 14*	5
Ages 9 to 11*	5
Male children	
Ages 12 to 14	8
Ages 9 to 11	7
Female children	
Ages 12 to 14	8
Ages 9 to 11	7
Mothers	
With sons ages 9 to 14	6
With daughters ages 9 to 14	5
Fathers	
With daughters ages 9 to 14	7
With sons ages 9 to 14	5

*Both genders.

58% of the families. Beef cattle were the most frequently produced livestock (71%). For all farms, the leading crops were forage products (79%). The commodity breakdown derived from the FIQ is very similar to the profile of the typical family farm in Kentucky.

Five families (13.8%) had experienced injury events. Injuries were defined as an event that required medical attention or caused the person to lose 1 hour or more from usual work or activities. Six (16.6%) household members were hospitalized from the farm work–related injury event. In one situation, two family members were hospitalized from pesticide exposure. In all cases it was an adult member of the family who was hospitalized.

In terms of high-injury-risk situations, a large percentage used agricultural chemicals (N = 24, 66.6%) and all but one owned tractors. Of the 97 tractors owned by 33 farms, less than one third (30 of 97) were equipped with roll-over protection structures. Eleven parents indicated their child had ridden as a passenger on a farm tractor within the previous 12 months. The average number of days for riding per child was 21.5 days. Thirteen (36.1%) of the parents indicated their child had operated a farm tractor independently during the same time period. Among these child operators, the average number of days of tractor operation was 36. Of the children operating the tractor alone, the mean age was 9.4 years. This finding was supported in the focus groups, with age 10 being cited most frequently as the age at which independent tractor operation begins. The quantitative data from this study are reported in another publication for interested readers.[23]

Parents prohibit their children from performing some farm chores because of their potential for injury. Eighty percent of the requests by children to perform "prohibited" chores were related to machinery. Examples of activities children wish to do but are prohibited by parents are bushhogging, cutting tobacco, and tractor driving.

A total of 212 key words was derived from coding 384 transcript pages, resulting in 982 narrative segments being analyzed. Four categories were derived by collapsing key words based on participants' comments across all groups. These categories were risk, injury, learning, and chores.

An understanding of chore initiation and teaching was derived from analysis of the interview data. Chore initiation is a social process in a farming community, with shared norms and rites of passage. Six concepts—*parental appraisal of child readiness, child interest, safety rules, chore initiation, chore phasing,* and *chore modification*—are central to the teaching of acceptable chores to these children. These concepts are defined next, and sample discourse from the focus groups is provided for contextual understanding.

Parental appraisal of child readiness

The first concept involved the variables examined by parents to determine a child's ability to complete a chore successfully.

Child: I guess when my maturity level was right and I could prove to my parents I could do something, they let me go. I remember one time when I first started driving the tractor, my dad said, "Are you ready?" I said, "Yeah." So he gave me a little test. Drive through two fence posts.

Parental appraisal of child readiness involved the same variables for mothers and fathers, but the weight placed on the variables differed (Table 10–2). For example, fathers placed greater emphasis on the agents used in tasks from the perspective of their complexity as well as economic factors. Use of a complex piece of machinery may result in damage to equipment as well as injury to the child. Mothers focused on injury risk associated with the task.

Child interest

The second concept involved the degree of motivation exhibited by a child to learn a particular task.

Father: You can tell by the interest they show. Whether they wanna go or not. Usually when they can do it, they kinda want to do it, as far as running machinery.

Child: One time when I was six, my dad goes to work every day and he was telling my mom we had just baled a hundred rolls and my dad told my mom not to let me on the tractor to move the bales. When I came home from school, my mom was at a meeting. I got out there and had 25 bales moved when my dad came home.

Moderator: What did he say?

Child: He kinda liked it and then he didn't, because he was kinda mad at me. But then he started telling me, do more stuff.

The child's interest in performing a chore was influenced by both peer and sibling chore completion, as well as a desire to seek parental approval. There were differences among mothers, fathers, and children regarding how chores are selected for teaching (see Table 10–2). Boys and girls did not differ in the factors they considered in selecting which task to learn.

Chore initiation

This concept involves the first step in teaching a chore, where the child observes competent and respected models completing the task. Reinforcement is derived from observing the consequences of a skilled parent's performance, direct praise and feedback by the parent from specific subtasks performed by the child, and direct consequences from performing the task or viewing the consequences of someone else performing the task. Chil-

Table 10–2. Matrix analysis of conditions related to parental appraisal of child readiness

Group	Physical factor	Nonphysical factor	Task selection	Data support
Mothers	Child is of adequate physical size to manage equipment	Child is emotionally mature; husband is not available (eg, working off the farm)	Least lethal tasks are selected for teaching	*Moderator:* "Are there differences in what your father and mother will let you do on the farm?" *Child:* "Yeah, one time we got a new disc mower and my mom didn't want me on it. She went shopping, but she told dad not to let me on it. He let me and when she got back she was real upset cause she thought I could get hurt."
Fathers	Child is of adequate physical size or equipment can be adapted to marginally fit child (eg, step stool)	Child is able to follow directions; inadequate labor supply; potential for decrease in productivity is high (eg, inclement weather)	Least complex tasks are selected for teaching; tasks involving least expensive equipment are selected	*Moderator:* "How old were they when they started to drive the tractor?" *Father:* "When he was big enough to hit the clutch." *Father:* "You put them in the simpler situations. If you force them into complex stuff, they will break things in the machinery."
Children	Are aware that parents assess size; they do not perform a self-assessment	Number of peers who perform the task; number of siblings who perform the task	Tasks most frequently performed by males (equipment operation) are preferred by both genders	*Daughter:* "They always make me feed the animals 'cuz I'm a girl. But I want to drive the tractor." *Son:* "My little brother always wants to do the things I do, but he is too young to run the bush hog [rotary blade machine]." *Son:* "When dad thought I could reach the clutch, he let me drive it."

dren become highly proficient at an early age in a variety of farm chores because instruction is ongoing and extends over a period of years. Most instruction is directed toward the productive completion of chores and not toward safety and health. This does not mean that productive completion of chores requires unsafe behavior. A safe approach to a task may be the most efficient method. Parents do not stress safety specifically in chore initiation. They stress the "right way" to do the task. The right way may or may not be the safest way.

Father: It allows your children to observe you in the working situation. Kids, when they are with you on the farm, they follow you around. I think that is a tremendous learning thing.

Child: I was about 3 or 4, and my dad used to sit me in his lap and I used to drive the tractor down the road when he was doing something. I used to watch him, and I saw him turn the steering wheel and that's what I tried to do.

Gender influences chore initiation if the parent has an economic choice. For example, girls are not encouraged to operate machinery if the farm is financially stable using the available male labor force. If increased productivity is needed for a positive profit margin, girls are taught to operate machinery. This finding is in conflict with other studies where farm families did not distinguish between the work of boys and the work of girls when compared with urban families.[24] The need to maintain productivity has greater influence in parental appraisal of chore initiation than does the child's physical and cognitive development or gender. At times, chores were initiated because the husband or owner and operator was off the farm's premises.

In summary, the need to get the work done with an inadequate labor supply forces parents to allow children to participate in farm work and to be placed in situations that often go against the parents' better judgment.

Safety rules

The fourth concept involves the advice given by parents for the purpose of helping the child avoid injury or illness. Safety rules provide parents with the belief they are helping the child avoid injury while performing a risky chore. These rules are used to explain why limits are placed on a task. However, rules may be more helpful to parents than they are to children. For the participating youth, lessons learned had a greater influence than safety rules on safe chore completion. Lessons learned in this study required instances where people were at risk and experienced negative consequences.

Mother: We have a corn crusher that is really old. And it is dangerous. It has a power take off [PTO] without the shield. Now I know this would not save him [her 9-year-old son] if he got into those flywheels, but you are always saying, "Don't get too close, you're gonna get caught."

Chore phasing

This concept involves the process of learning by progressing from simple to more complex activities. Farm chores were learned in stages and phases beginning with observation and careful supervision of partial task performance and culminating in independent task performance. All participants identified the same sequence. Chore initiation begins with oral instruction. Children then observe models (usually fathers) performing the task. The child gradually performs the task under supervision and progresses to independent performance. The transition between supervised to independent performance may not be anticipated, however, and may be precipitated by need. Children often are fearful of performing some tasks but generally will not express this fear. They value learning traditional male jobs and do not want to be restricted.

Mother: When my son was 2, he started going with his daddy and a lot of it becomes second nature. He sat on the tractor seat so much, he knew how to start it. You tell 'em and show 'em. Probably these children shouldn't even be on tractors at all. But I think under supervision, it can be safe. Raking hay's the first. We break them in on that.

Child: In the beginning, I watched. Then when I was 8, he let me out in first gear with real low throttle and he would ride with me a bit. Then he let me go on my own for a while but he watched me real close. Now I do it on my own.

Chore modification

The last concept refers to improvisation, short cuts, or performance of a chore in a way other than the prescribed safe manner. Children modify chores to complete a task in what they perceive to be a more efficient manner, and this may involve an inaccurate risk appraisal. The child may generalize partial task instruction to a more complex situation not previously encountered. Parents may modify

a chore because of environmental factors such as approaching inclement weather, lack of a skilled labor supply, or labor costs. Unacceptable chores become acceptable in these circumstances. Economic risk frequently outweighs the hazard of having the child perform the chore. Consistent with the findings of previous research, children are economic assets to farm families.[25]

Child: I was going about third gear, going pretty fast, trying to get that manure out. I was trying to get it going a little faster so I could ride four wheelers with my friend. But when I turned, it was wet that day and I turned my steering wheel real hard. The manure spreader pushed, my tractor didn't turn, my wheels just slid sideways and I knocked the whole fence down.

Mother: We have discovered that we may end up in a field with too many vehicles to drive home. You don't have enough drivers. We'll put my 12-year-old son on the tractor and put him between two pick-up trucks and go down the road. Now if it is farther than 10 or 15 minutes, we won't let him do it. That sounds horrid, doesn't it?

Additional results

Parents taught their children the correct way to perform a task as an injury prevention measure. Children listed examples where they performed the task as taught but experienced near injury because of the context in which the learning was transferred. Uneven terrain, wet ground, and groundhog holes were examples given by the children where they had to adjust their performance without prior role modeling to avoid injury.

In farming communities certain expectations may exist for children. In one focus group of mothers, one woman described how their daughter, age 14, was not able to drive and back a tractor when she was enrolled in a high school agriculture class. Other children in the class were able to perform these skills. The mother stated that she and her husband then began teaching the younger 12-year-old sister to operate tractors and other equipment so she could do well when she got to the high school agriculture class.

Parents sell unsafe animals as an injury prevention measure. There are two incentives for selling a difficult animal: it removes a potential injury agent and generates cash. Parents also pay others to apply chemicals for two reasons: First, farm families have become more aware of the personal health risks from chemical exposure. Second, many farmers lack the equipment for large-scale pesticide application. It is less expensive (and safer) for these farmers to contract the application of chemicals than it is to perform the work themselves with smaller, hand-generated sprayers. Yet often they will use marginally safe equipment in a state of disrepair to complete other tasks. The difference between these actions is that equipment repair directly costs without a clear economic benefit being attached to the increased efficiency of the repaired equipment or the indirect decreased injury risk from using repaired equipment:

Father: I bought my father's equipment. There is no shield that covers the PTO. The last time this equipment was used was when I was in high school and that was back in 1977. We will have it worked on when it quits running. You come into money there. You got to wait until you get the money to be able to fix stuff.

DISCUSSION AND INTERPRETATION

In general, little research has been conducted on children's work. A classic study by Straus[26] noted that research is needed to learn the values parents are trying to teach their children through work, the parents' motivations behind asking children to work, and the importance of children's work in preparing them for adult roles. The findings of this study illuminate these issues. The teaching of farm chores to children at an early physical and cognitive age is socially acceptable in farm families. Parents believe this teaching has many benefits in addition to getting the work done. One father said, "I think kids actually begin to have an ownership position in what's going on. They are more responsible. It builds their self-confidence up." However, the teaching of responsibility by assigning chores is not unique to farm families. Urban parents have reported that character building and responsibility are primary reasons for assigning chores.[27]

Certain farm chores are socially acceptable and may serve as a rite of passage (eg, tractor driving). More information on why a chore is acceptable may provide knowledge of how to frame injury prevention in a culturally sensitive manner.

It appears that injury prevention may be economically driven. The relationship between health and economic status of the family farm has been explored.[28] Farms with a higher debt to asset ratio had two times greater injury rates than those with low ratios. A higher debt to asset ratio may force the family to perform chores in a way that increases productivity but may also increase injury risk. Farm children may focus more on preventing damage to equipment and livestock and less on matters of preventing injuries to themselves because they recognize early the economic aspects of farming.

• • •

Although not specifically addressed in the present study, children may influence parental safety behavior through role modeling. For example, children-initiated use of safety belts is associated with subsequent parental use of seat belts.[29] Teaching farm safety principles and the economic ramifications of injury in the school setting through avenues such as vocational agriculture courses may eventually influence farm family safety behavior.

County extension agents and others who work with farm families can help farmers better understand and assess the benefits of injury prevention and the personal costs of injuries in terms of replacement labor, decreased productivity, higher insurance rates, pain, suffering, and permanent disability as well as disrupted family life. When economically framed, safety behavior may become a conscious, logical choice.

Perhaps by helping farm families view injuries in terms of their economic consequences, parents and children will avoid hazards by not taking unsafe short cuts, replacing safety equipment, or repairing unsafe equipment. By framing economic lessons learned from an injury in the form of reality-based stories, injury prevention may be culturally accepted as a priority in chore teaching.

REFERENCES

1. Rivera FP. Fatal and nonfatal farm injuries to children and adolescents in the United States. *Pediatrics.* 1985;76:567–573.
2. Pollack S, Rubenstein H, Landrigan P. Child labor. In: Last J, Wallace R, eds. *Public Health and Preventive Medicine.* Norwalk, Conn: Appleton-Lange; 1994.
3. Wilk VA. Health hazards to children in agriculture. *Am J Indust Med.* 1993;24:283–290.
4. Lee B, Gunderson P, eds. *Childhood Agricultural Injury Prevention: Issues and Interventions from Multiple Perspectives.* Marshfield, Wis: Marshfield Clinic; 1992.
5. Kelsey TW. The agrarian myth and policy responses to farm safety. *Am J Public Health.* 1994; 84:1,171–1,177.
6. Occupational Safety and Health Administration. 29 CFR Part 1928. Field sanitation: final rule. *Federal Register* 52(84):16050–16096; May 1, 1987.
7. Tormoehlen R. Fatal farm accidents occur to Wisconsin children. *Proceedings of the American Society of Agricultural Engineers.* St Joseph, Mo: 1986.
8. Office of Rural Health Policy. *Seventh Annual Report on Rural Health.* Washington, DC: Health Resources and Service Administration, Public Health Service, US Dept of Health and Human Services; 1994.
9. US Bureau of the Census. *Census of Agriculture: Geographical Area Series. U.S. Summary and State Data.* U.S. Government Printing Office, Washington, DC: 1987.

10. Michigan Department of Public Health. *Farm Injury in Michigan*. Lansing, Mich: MDPH; 1989.

11. Heyer NJ, Franklin G, Rivera FP, Parker P, Haug J. Occupational injury among minors doing farm work in Washington State: 1986 to 1989. *Am J Public Health*. 1992;82:557–560.

12. Eichelberger M, Gotchall K, Feely H, Harstad P, Bowman L. Parental attitudes and knowledge of child safety: a national survey. *Am J Dis Child*. 1990;144:714–720.

13. Schenker M, Lopez R, Wintemute G. Farm-related fatalities among children in California, 1980 to 1989. *Am J Public Health*. 1995;85:89–92.

14. Ramirez AG, Sheppard J. Uses of focus groups in health research. *J Primary Health Care*. 1988; (suppl 1):81–90.

15. Weinert C, Long K. The theory and research base for rural nursing practice. In: Bushy A, ed. *Rural Nursing*. Vol 1. Newbury Park, Calif: Sage Publications; 1991.

16. Bruner J. *Acts of Meaning*. Cambridge, Mass: Harvard University Press; 1990.

17. Sarbin TR. *Narrative Psychology: The Storied Nature of Human Conduct*. New York, NY: Praeger; 1986.

18. Software Marketing Associates. *FYI 3000: Data Management and Retrieval System*. Dallas, Tex: SMA; 1991.

19. *Traumatic Farm Injury Surveillance in Kentucky Newsletter*, no. 5. Frankfort, Ky: Department for Health Services, Division of Epidemiology; 1995.

20. Glaser B. *Theoretical Sensitivity*. Mill Valley, Calif: Sociology Press; 1978.

21. Landis J, Koch G. The measurement of observer agreement for categorical data. *Biometrics*. 1977; 33:382–385.

22. Miles M, Huberman A. *Qualitative Data Analysis: An Expanded Sourcebook*. Newbury Park, Calif: Sage Publications; 1994.

23. McKnight R, Piercy L, Townley K, Kidd P, Cole H. Parents' concern for children's farm safety. *Texas J Rural Health*. 1995;14:10–19.

24. White LK, Brinkerhoff DB. The sexual division of labor: evidence from childhood. *Social Forces*. 1981;60:170–181.

25. Light HK, Hertsgaard D, Martin RE. Farm children's work in the family. *Adolescence*. 1985; 20:425–432.

26. Straus MA. Work roles and financial responsibility in the socialization of farm, fringe, and town boys. *Rural Soc*. 1962;27:257–274.

27. White LK. Brinkerhoff DB. Children's work in the family: its significance and meaning. *J Marriage Fam*. 1981;Nov:789–798.

28. Geller J, Ludtke R, Stratton T. Nonfatal farming in North Dakota: a sociological analysis. *J Rural Health*. 1990;6:185–196.

29. Foss R. Sociocultural perspective of child occupant protection. *Pediatrics*. 1987;80:886–893.

CHAPTER 11

Coping with the Cost of Care: An Exploratory Study of Lower Income Minorities in the Rural South

W. Jay Strickland, PhD

David L. Strickland, MA

RECENT HEALTH research has produced extensive minority-nonminority, urban-rural, and poor-nonpoor comparisons of crude health indicators, insurance status, and health service utilization. However, to understand more fully the barriers to health service utilization, it is important to focus on the health status, behaviors, and values of specific underserved populations.[1-3] Consequently, this study examines health service access and coping strategies for lower income minority households in the rural South. Specific research questions include the following: To what extent do these households use health services for acute and chronic con-

Original data were collected by the Center for Rural Health and Research, College of Health and Professional Studies, Georgia Southern University. Funding was received from the Office of Rural Health Policy, Health Resources and Services Administration, PHS grant #HRA-000040-02.

Portions of this article were presented at the 1994 annual meeting of the Georgia Sociological Association and 1994 joint annual conference of the Georgia Association for Primary Health Care and Georgia Rural Health Association.

Fam Community Health 1995;18(2):37–51
© 1995 Aspen Publishers, Inc.

ditions? What are the primary barriers to receiving services for acute and chronic conditions? What coping strategies do these households employ when they cannot afford needed services? In addition, a model of health service utilization is presented, and implications for practitioners are discussed.

BACKGROUND

In studying rural health problems "there is no homogeneous rural America and . . . it is reasonable to expect that health differences among various rural areas and subgroups may be pronounced."[2(pp61,62)] Coincident with the recent "rediscovery of rural health care by policymakers" is an awareness of the need to explore variation within and between underserved populations.[4(p1005)] Just as there is no homogeneous rural America, minority and poor populations do not constitute monolithic classes in terms of health and health needs. Social status variation is relevant for three interrelated reasons:

1. Social status characteristics affect health status.
2. Social status characteristics objectively affect access to health services.
3. Cultural values and norms associated with specific subpopulations affect health behaviors.

Social status and health status

As observed by Williams et al, "Race is only one of several social status categories that can determine one's health. Groups occupying multiple social catego-

ries may have especially poor health status, such as poor black women, since the effects of occupying multiple statuses may lead to cumulative vulnerability that is additive or even multiplicative."[1(p31)] Existing data suggest that lower income black people in the rural South belong to three social status categories that place them at increased risk for poor health—race, socioeconomic status, and rural residence. Although black Americans have recently experienced overall gains in health status, they continue to have poorer health and higher mortality rates than white Americans.[1,5-7] Nationwide, black and poor individuals report higher rates of many chronic conditions—including arthritis, diabetes, anemias, hypertension, and ulcers—than do white and nonpoor individuals.[8] Similarly, 16.7% of rural residents reported that their activity had been limited during the past year because of a chronic condition, while only 12.9% of urban residents made this claim.[8] (Rural residents live outside federally designated metropolitan statistical areas, and urban residents live within these areas.)

Social status and access to services

Health service availability and ability to pay constitute two objective barriers for lower income minority households in the rural South. Although the number of rural physicians across the country has increased during the past 20 years,[9] rural counties in Georgia have half the physicians per capita than do urban counties.[10] The recent demand for primary physicians in urban areas may further increase this disparity.[9] Likewise, the proportion of midlevel practitioners and registered nurses to licensed and vocational nurses is already lowest in the South and shows signs of decreasing further.[9]

Deterrents to practicing in rural areas are formidable and include differential federal funding, community demographics, and provider preference.[9,11–13] At the federal level, "public funding for health care in rural America has consistently lagged behind the U.S. average," with rural areas allocated 42% fewer health service dollars and 50% fewer social service dollars per capita than the national average.[12(p101)] At the community level, rural practitioners are challenged by a limited client base, "aging physical plants, difficulty in hiring and retaining technical staff, lower proportions of private-pay patients, local and regional competition, and perceived (or actual) deficits in quality of care."[14(p88)]

Even when health services are available, ability to pay may be problematic for three reasons. First, rural communities in the South are plagued by persistent poverty and underemployment, and minority households are particularly vulnerable.[15,16] Second, Southern black people are substantially less likely to have health insurance than are Southern white or non-Southern black people.[17] Third, rural poor people are less likely to apply for and less likely to be covered by entitlement programs such as Medicaid and Aid to Families with Dependent Children (AFDC). Compared with 44% of the urban poor, only 36% of the rural poor receive Medicaid.[16]

Cultural values and norms and health behaviors

Green[18] suggested that there are nine distinct subpopulations of black people with different histories, economies, social organizations, and environmental contexts. Each of these "cultural-ecological areas," including the coastal Southeast (South Carolina and eastern Georgia), is characterized by distinct cultures, including values, norms, and behaviors that affect health status. Williams and associates[1] recommended that health researchers focus on these groups to ascertain relative need and impediments to service delivery.

In terms of rural health values, a number of studies[2,19–21] observed that rural people tend to subscribe to the "role performance" model of health. This model assumes that individuals are "healthy" and do not require medical attention as long as they are able to "be productive, to work, and to carry out usual role functions."[2(p59)] Consequently, rural people tend to devalue preventive services and delay seeking care until symptoms are severe.

Other cultural impediments to seeking health services mentioned in the rural health literature include reliance on informal social support networks and distrust of outsiders.[2,20] Whether rural people rely on folk medicine out of preference or necessity,[22] family and friends are often the primary source of medical information for rural women, and confidence in home remedies is often high.[23] Distrust of outsiders may also be exacerbated by the social distance between caregivers and patients when providers are white professionals and patients are both poor and nonwhite.[2,20]

In short, both perception of need and access to health services are influenced by "a complex web of social, cultural, and economic values . . . by persons in different communities."[3(p932)] Patrick and colleagues noted that "people with similar health status do not have similar perceptions nor do they make similar demands for health care because of differences in health beliefs, illness behavior, social networks, willingness or ability to pay for service, and other sociopsychological, economic, and cultural processes."[24(p108)] Assessing health needs of various specific underserved populations is "not simply a matter of relating health status to resource availability and distribution, but also the social, economic, and political environments of individuals and populations."[24(p108)]

RESEARCH DESIGN

Sample

Interview data were collected from a nonprobability sample of 281 lower income minority households from five rural counties in Georgia. Three hundred minority households in rural Georgia were selected through multistage sampling procedures. First, the southern portion of the state was targeted because this region is characterized by lower income and poorer health status indicators than the more industrialized northern region.[25]

Second, Bulloch, Burke, Stewart, Telfair, and Ware counties were selected by the research team through quota sampling. The primary criteria for inclusion

were rural status (no cities with more than 50,000 residents) and a high percentage of minority population. Population ranged from 5,654 to 43,125 for these five counties, and the proportion of black residents ranged from 26.0% to 63.3%. Median black household income ranged from $10,898 to $13,260 and was earned primarily through service occupations, agriculture, manufacturing, and public assistance. The percentage of black residents in poverty ranged from 41.2% to 45.8%, and the percentage of county residents receiving AFDC and Medicaid ranged from 5.8% to 12.8% and 14.5% to 26.9%, respectively.

Third, predominantly lower income black neighborhoods within the county seats were identified by community key informants. Because of the high degree of residential segregation within these communities, it was an effective means of identifying minority households.

Fourth, door-to-door interviews were conducted with knowledgeable members of 300 black households in both subsidized and nonsubsidized housing units. This method of data collection was selected because many lower income households in this region lack telephone service.

Last, households with annual incomes at or below 185% of the federal poverty level were classified "lower income" and retained for analysis. This ceiling was selected because federal guidelines allow states to extend Medicaid benefits to infants and pregnant women with household incomes up to 185% of the poverty level.[26]

The final dataset consisted of 281 households with a mean household size of 2.0 members. The 788 household members included 133 men, 311 women, and 344 children under 18 years of age. Based on federal guidelines, 81.0% of the households were at or below the poverty level. An additional 9.2% were between 101% and 125%, 7.0% were between 126% and 150%, and 2.9% were between 151% and 185% of the federal poverty level.

In terms of health insurance, children under 18 years of age were covered as follows: private insurance only, 19.6%; Medicaid only, 54.8%; and no private or entitlement coverage, 25.6%. Non-elderly adults were covered as follows: private insurance only, 28.2%; Medicaid only, 44.9%; and neither insurance nor Medicaid, 26.9%. Elderly adults 60 years of age and older received benefits as follows: Medicaid only, 4.8%; Medicare only, 36.3%; both Medicaid and Medicare, 31.5%; and no private or entitlement coverage, 27.4%.

Data collection

Household interviews were conducted by trained interviewers and addressed a range of health issues. Variables analyzed in this study included the following: demographic information, treatment history, reasons services were not received, and strategies when households could not afford services. All items were open-ended questions, and interviewers used probes to encourage respondents to elaborate on their responses.

Demographic and insurance status information was collected for each member of the household, and information concerning the remaining variables was obtained for the household as a unit. Content analysis techniques were used to analyze data pertaining to coping strategies.[27] Consequently, conceptual categories of strategies were not imposed on the data but were defined by and generated inductively from the data themselves.

Treatment history

Respondents identified the incidence of acute (nonemergency) illness, chronic conditions, and major medical emergencies within the household during the past year, conditions and episodes for which professional treatment was obtained at least once, and treatment setting. Although additional treatment may have been recommended, one contact with medical professionals was established as a baseline for health service utilization.

Ability to afford services

Respondents were asked whether their household could always afford needed services, and responses were coded yes = 1 and no = 0.

Coping strategies

Respondents were asked to identify what the household did when it could not afford needed health services.

RESULTS

Treatment history

Acute (nonemergency) episodes were most common, at a rate of 38 episodes per 100 individuals per year. Second most common were chronic conditions, including diabetes and hypertension, at a rate of 24 conditions per 100 individuals per year. Major medical emergencies were least common, with 14 episodes per 100 individuals per year.

Professional services were most likely to be used for emergency and chronic conditions (95.6% and 86.9%, respectively), and formal treatment was received for slightly over half (53.8%) of the acute episodes (Table 11–1). As would be expected, the vast majority (84.8%) of major medical emergencies were treated in a hospital setting. Acute and chronic conditions were most frequently treated in a private practice setting (64.5% and 81.3%). Individuals were slightly more likely to receive treatment for acute and chronic conditions in a hospital setting than in a public health setting.

Reasons services were not received

As shown in Table 11–2, the most frequently cited reasons services were not received were lack of need and inability to pay. Preference, lack of provider, lack of time, and poor treatment were cited less frequently.

Perception of need

The most frequently cited reason services were not received was that they were not needed. Respondents felt that services were unnecessary to treat 72.2% of acute illnesses, 45.8% of chronic conditions, and 60.0% of major medical emergencies. Respondents typically explained that acute illnesses were "not bad enough" to warrant professional care. Self-treatment, including home remedies and nonprescription medicine, was often considered adequate for the common cold, influenza, and sinus conditions. In all likelihood, the majority of these conditions did not necessitate professional care. However, the fact that two mothers "did not need" care themselves—but always took their children to the physician with similar symptoms—suggests that

Table 11–1. Medical condition, health service utilization, and treatment setting

| Condition | Episodes treated | Treatment setting | | | |
		Hospital	Clinic	Private practice	Don't know
Acute, nonemergency					
n	162	31	23	98	10
%	53.8	20.4	15.1	64.5	NA
Chronic					
n	161	16	14	130	1
%	86.9	10.0	8.8	81.3	NA
Major emergency					
n	109	89	4	12	4
%	95.6	84.8	3.8	11.4	NA

NA = not applicable.

Table 11–2. Primary reasons health services were not utilized

Condition	Not needed	Could not pay	Did not want	Did not have time	No provider available	Was treated badly
Acute, nonemergency						
n	78	22	6	1	1	0
%	72.2	20.4	5.6	0.9	0.9	0.0
Chronic						
n	11	10	3	0	0	0
%	45.8	41.7	12.5	0.0	0.0	0.0
Major emergency						
n	3	1	0	0	0	1
%	60.0	20.0	0.0	0.0	0.0	20.0

professional treatment may have been appropriate in some of these instances.

Services were more likely to have been received for chronic than acute conditions, and respondents were less likely to claim that services were "not needed." However, the claim that services were not needed for chronic conditions is more suspect. In 4 of the 11 cases, respondents stated that care was not needed for hypertension or diabetes because individuals took the required prescriptions. In an additional six cases, hypertension or diabetes was assumed to be "under control" through diet or self-treatment.

Whether care was needed is also questionable for the emergency conditions. Professional treatment was clearly irrelevant in the case of a young son who was injured and "died immediately." However, the young mother who "had seizures two times when home alone with the infant" was similarly convinced that services were not needed.

Inability to pay

Inability to pay was the second most frequently cited reason services were not received. Respondents felt they could not pay for treatment of 20.4% of acute conditions, 41.7% of chronic conditions, and 20.0% of major emergencies. Over half (56.7%) of the households could not afford needed health services on a regular basis. The percentage of family members covered by Medicaid was significantly associated with household ability to afford needed services ($\chi^2 = 31.37$, $p = .005$). However, ability to afford health services was not significantly associated with the percentage of family members covered by private insurance or household poverty level.

Personal preference

With only one exception, the individuals who "did not want" treatment were elderly, including a 70-year-old woman with an annual income under $5,000 who did not want treatment for hypertension, a 76-year-old man who claimed that his original hypertension medicine made him sick and had not seen a physician in 4 years, and an 83-year-old woman with arthritis who preferred to treat herself. Among those with acute conditions, a 64-year-old domestic "just didn't go" to the physician with two illnesses, as did a 69-year-old woman with a "stubborn temperature of 103°F." The only nonelderly individual who did not desire treatment was a 24-year-old mother who took her children to the physician for acute conditions but preferred to treat herself with over-the-counter medicines.

Other barriers to service utilization

Lack of time, no provider, and rude treatment were each cited once as primary barriers. These instances involved a middle-aged woman who had not yet had time to go to the physician because she supervised her young grandchildren during the day and an individual who could not make an appointment with his physician. In addition, a mother took her school-age daughter to the local emergency department with a 104°F temperature, and after sitting in the waiting room for 4.5 hours and not being seen, they left.

Strategies when households could not afford services

Table 11–3 identifies the range of coping strategies employed when households could not afford needed health services. The unit of analysis for this item was the household, so strategies refer to typical actions of the household as a whole rather than specific individuals within the household. Although eight of the respondents whose households could

not always afford care did not identify coping strategies, 23.2% of the 142 households identified multiple strategies employed on a regular basis.

The 12 specific strategies comprise a typology of 5 broader conceptual categories. In turn, these categories reflect an ordinal-level continuum from greater to less commitment to obtaining professional services, as follows: (1) prioritize care, (2) finance services, (3) ration resources, (4) substitute treatment, and (5) postpone services. The quotations that follow were taken from responses to the question, "What does your family do when they cannot afford needed health care?"

Strategy 1: Prioritize care

If I'm sick, I'll go. But I need to be mighty sick.

If it will pass, let it pass. If it is more serious, pay the doctor instead of the grocery or pay the doctor on time.

Prioritizing health services at the expense of other necessities was the least frequently cited strategy (2.8% of households) and, even when cited, was not the only, most typical, or first response. For example, households often went to the physician only after trying nonprescription medicine (substituting treatment) or if the condition was severe or persistent (rationing resources). The respondents who prioritized services on occasion stated that they employed less assertive strategies first. If these strategies were effective, they did not seek formal treatment.

Table 11–3. Strategies when households cannot afford health services*

Strategy	Item frequency (n = 167)	Percentage of households (n = 142)	Strategy section total (%)	Strategy section rank
Prioritize care				
Purchase services and sacrifice other necessities	4	2.8	2.8	5
Finance services				
Have physician bill for services	33	23.2		
Use free care settings	9	6.3		
Use emergency department and have services billed	6	4.2		
Borrow from friends or relatives	6	4.2		
Have family members pay	5	3.5	41.4	2
Ration resources				
Purchase services for some family members and not others	6	4.2		
Purchase services for some conditions or episodes and not others	6	4.2	8.4	4
Substitute treatment				
Self-treat (eg, nonprescription medicine, home remedies)	23	16.2		
Pray	5	3.5	19.7	3
Postpone services				
Do without health services	60	42.3		
Wait until enough money is available for services	4	2.8	45.1	1

*This table summarizes responses to the question, "What does your family do when they cannot afford needed health care?" Total percentage exceeds 100 because some households employed more than one strategy.

Strategy 2: Finance services

Sometimes we can, sometimes not [afford services]. My family doctor lets us pay by the month, so that helps.

Now I'm not working, our insurance doesn't cover things—we can't afford it. We drive 2 or 3 hours to [a hospital for the indigent outside the county].

We have $65,000 in health care bills [from open heart surgery at a local hospital]. The hospital here sued my wife because she didn't pay, so we don't go back there.

Borrow some money from the finance company or pawn something.

It takes togetherness. My two sisters and I take turns taking care of each other and of my mother. We "part-up." That means we borrow a little money from each relative to make up enough. That's how we survive. Families stick together. Medicaid doesn't pay for it all.

Financing services was the second most frequently cited strategy (41.5% of the households) and typically involved paying physicians on time. Six households used the emergency department because the local hospital was required to treat patients regardless of ability to pay. Likelihood of paying off emergency department bills varied dramatically. Although one woman paid "a little as I go along," another was being sued for defaulting on a $65,000 open heart surgery bill. Using emergency departments was an attractive option when private physicians would not accept payment plans, the medical condition was severe, care was needed outside regular office hours, and the local hospital actually served poor people. At least two of the five county hospitals routinely "shipped" patients without insurance coverage 1 to 3 hours outside the county to a particular hospital that was required to serve the indigent.

Free and sliding-scale services beyond those offered by the county health department were limited and difficult to find. The husband of the woman with the $65,000 hospital bill explained that his only option was to travel 188 miles round-trip to a Florida Veterans Administration hospital every 2 weeks to receive treatment. With almost half (44.6%) of the 281 households participating in the study not owning a car, it is not surprising that 32.8% of the households considered transportation for medical care problematic. A male respondent in his 20s observed that people in his community "can get a friend to drive them to the local hospital, but getting to [a specific hospital that serves the indigent, 35 miles away] is a major problem."

Having friends or family cover medical expenses was not usually a reliable strategy. Respondents typically stated that they "tried" to borrow money or "asked" a relative to help out. Occasionally, a relative assumed full responsibility for outstanding medical costs. An elderly woman could always afford medical care but explained that "my daughter-in-law helps me out—she pays." Caring for family members in turn through "parting up" had been used as a survival strategy by one extended family since the Depression.

Strategy 3: Ration resources

Not always. For my children, I try to take them. For myself, I just deal with it.

I'm supposed to go every 6 weeks. I go every 3 months.

Go to the doctor anyways, but not unless absolutely necessary. I would try medicine from the drug store first.

Rationing resources involved purchasing services for some members of the household and not others, or purchasing services for some conditions or episodes but not others (mentioned by 4.2% of the households each). Rationing by member involved sacrificing care for adults but obtaining services for children, often at any cost. This situation was even more likely to occur when the children were covered by Medicaid but the adults were not. Selecting which conditions to treat was usually based on degree of discomfort. For instance, a woman stated that treatment was needed for her ulcer because it was painful, but hypertension treatment was not needed because it was not giving her any problem.

Strategy 4: Substitute treatment

Just use what I can and keep myself still.

Try to help myself with regular medicine or old leftover prescriptions.

I try to live with it. Once I had a toothache that was so bad, I pulled it myself.

Try home remedies and pray.

Almost one fifth (19.7%) of the households used substitute treatments on a regular basis. This strategy usually involved self-treatment of acute and chronic conditions with home remedies, nonprescription medications, and old leftover prescriptions (16.2% of the households). Reliance on substitute treatments was often the reason respondents considered formal medical services for acute conditions unnecessary. Implicit is the recognition that professional treatment will be sought if self-treatment is not sufficient (rationing). Five of the households mentioned prayer as a coping strategy. Prayer was seen as both a proactive step based on belief in divine healing and an appeal for strength as one suffered.

Strategy 5: Postpone services

Every now and then I get a little piece of money and I go to the doctor, but I can't go much 'cause I haven't the money.

If Medicaid can't pay for it, I suffer.

We [parents] only get care because we have Medicaid, but not all family members are covered. My [adult] son hurt his leg and was in pain, but we could not do anything for him.

Just suffer.

Suffer or die.

Postponement was the most frequently cited strategy (45.1% of the households). Postponement could be short or long term, depending on whether the family was waiting for a monthly check or merely hoping to come up with the money. Postponement was most common when household income was extremely low, friends and relatives did not help with medical costs, physical ailments were not particularly painful, and care was needed for adults rather than children. Respondents were very straightforward and practical about their inability to afford treatment, stating simply that "If we don't have money, we don't go to the doctor." The realization that the logical result was to "suffer," "just suffer," "suffer and keep strong," or "suffer or die" was an inextricable facet of "pragmatic poverty."

DISCUSSION

Utilization patterns

As would be expected by the role performance model of health, individuals were more likely to have received formal treatment for major medical emergencies than for other acute conditions (95.6% versus 53.8%). However, the likelihood of receiving services at least once for chronic conditions was also high (86.9%). The importance of medical treatment—and prescription medication—for chronic conditions was a consistent theme throughout the household interview (Strickland W, Hanson C, unpublished data, 1994).

Individuals were least likely to have been treated in a public health setting. In large part, this finding reflects scarce funding for public health programs and limited availability of private charity programs in the five target counties. During focus group interviews with providers, a health department director explained that the supply of prescription drugs would be exhausted several months into the fiscal year if medicine were distributed on the basis of need (W Strickland, D Strickland, unpublished data, 1994).

Another director explained that the county program was unable to serve all the individuals currently covered by Medicaid, much less all lower income residents. The program was only able to "survive" by refraining from advertising its services and treating only those who found out about the program through the telephone directory, word of mouth, or formal referral.

Public health limitations placed pressure on private physicians, local hospitals, and patients. With an abundance of lower income patients, physicians must contend with Medicaid reimbursement, billing patients, and delinquent—or forfeited—accounts. The use of emergency department resources for acute and chronic conditions is often not appropriate, always costly, and not necessarily going to result in reimbursement. Last, traveling to hospitals outside the county for indigent care is usually difficult and sometimes impossible for patients who lack transportation and are already in distress.

Perception of need

The most common reason services were not received was the perception that they were not needed; the second most common reason was inability to pay. At first glance, the contention that services were not needed appears very straightforward. However, as used by respondents, the phrase reflected several connotations. First, formal treatment was not needed for the common cold, mild influenza, and a number of other nonemergency acute conditions. Medical personnel would concur that these conditions could be appropriately treated with nonprescription medicine at home.

Second, some respondents assumed that hypertension and diabetes were "under control" because they were taking their medication, watching their diet, and felt no distress. These individuals may not have fully understood the importance of monitoring chronic conditions and regulating prescription treatments.

Third, "needed" and "not needed" were economic categories born of extreme poverty. Heads of households tended to classify goods and services as absolutely essential or not essential for the household's survival.[28] For families at and below the federal poverty line, basic shelter, food, and clothing were considered needs. With limited finances, indoor plumbing, heat, and medical services in the absence of a major emergency did not qualify as needs, no matter how desirable they might be.

Pragmatic poverty

Although several respondents expressed anger that physicians received high salaries and that health care was too expensive, the respondents' overriding response to their position was that of "pragmatic poverty." Respondents were realistic about their financial limitations and explained matter-of-factly, "If we don't have money, we don't go to the doctor." Unless the individual was covered by an entitlement program, the household had some extra money, or the condition was severe, services were "not needed."

Pragmatic poverty was more realistic than passive or defeatist. Households actively attempted to provide health care through prioritizing care, financing services, rationing resources, and substituting treatment. Relatively high value was placed on preventive services and treatment for acute and chronic conditions.

With household incomes under the poverty line, coping strategies tended to be relatively ineffective. It is obvious that some services were not received when 45.1% of the households "postponed" services. However, professional care was also not received when individuals substituted treatment and rationed resources. For some individuals, financing was a reliable strategy, but others were dependent on whether friends and family would lend them money or pay for services on a case-by-case basis. Only 2.8% of the households prioritized and then, only on occa-

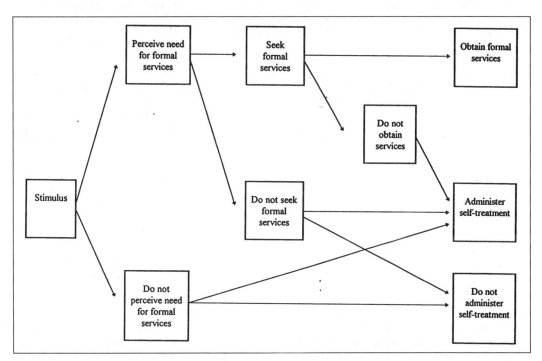

Fig 11–1. Health services utilization model.

sion. This was less a lack of desire than a lack of discretionary money. For families below the poverty level, "we suffer" is often both realistic and unavoidable.

SERVICE UTILIZATION MODEL

The health service utilization model presented in Fig 11–1 was suggested by the data collected for this study. A stimulus, consisting of physical discomfort or health knowledge, suggests that formal medical attention is advised. This stimulus may or may not produce the conviction that services are needed. Those who do not believe that services are needed may or may not initiate self-treatment. Those who believe that services are needed may or may not seek treatment, may or may not obtain treatment, and, if

not, may or may not initiate self-treatment.

•   •   •

At the macro level, insufficient health resources are a primary deterrent to health service utilization. At the microlevel, epitomized by the individual and household, health service utilization is a decision-making process constrained by cultural values, health education, and ability to pay. Although the "more macro-level approach to study[ing] structural and organizational issues in the medical care system"[28(p81)] that has been prominent since the mid-1970s is critical, it is also important to continue focusing on constraints, decision making, and perceived quality of care at the individual and household level, as well as on strategies employed when formal services are not obtained.

REFERENCES

1. Williams D, Lavizzo-Mourey R, Warren R. The concept of race and health status in America. *Public Health Rep.* 1994;109:26–40.
2. Weinert C, Long K. Rural families and health care: refining the knowledge base. In: Unger D, Sussman M, eds. *Families in Community Settings: Interdisciplinary Perspectives.* Binghamton, NY: Haworth; 1990.
3. DeFriese G, Ricketts T. Primary health care in rural areas: an agenda for research. *Health Serv Res.* 1989;23:931–973.
4. Patton L. Setting the rural health services research agenda: the congressional perspective. *Health Serv Res.* 1989;23:1005–1051.
5. Alcena V. Preface. In: Alcena V, ed. *The Status of Health of Blacks in the United States of America.* Dubuque, Iowa: Kendall/Hunt; 1991.
6. Braithwaite R, Lythcott N. Community empowerment as a strategy for health promotion for blacks and other minority populations. *JAMA.* 1989;261: 282–283.
7. Blendon R, Aiken L, Freeman H, Corey C. Access

to medical care for black and white Americans. *JAMA.* 1989;261:278–281.
8. US Department of Health and Human Services, Public Health Service. *Vital and Health Statistics: Current Estimates from the National Health Interview Survey, 1990.* Hyattsville, Md: US Dept of Health and Human Services; 1991. DHHS publication PHS 92-1509.
9. Office of Technology Assessment, US Congress. *Health Care in Rural America.* Washington, DC: Government Printing Office; 1990. Publication OTA-H-34.
10. Ryan R. *Rural Health in Georgia.* Atlanta, Ga: Georgia State Office of Rural Health; 1993.
11. DeLeon P, Wakefield M, Schultz A, Williams J, VandenBos G. Unique opportunities for health care delivery and health services research. *Am Psychol.* 1989;44:1298–1306.
12. National Association of Community Health Centers and the National Rural Health Association. Health care in America: the crisis unfolds. *J Public Health Policy.* 1989;10:99–116.

13. Cordes S. The changing rural environment and the relationship between health services and rural development. *Health Serv Res.* 1989;23:757–784.

14. Bronstein J, Morrisey M. Bypassing rural hospitals for obstetrics care. *J Health Polit Policy Law.* 1991;16(1):87–117.

15. Brown D, Warner M. Persistent low-income nonmetropolitan areas in the United States: some conceptual challenges for development policy. *Policy Studies J.* 1991;19(2):22–41.

16. Rowland D, Lyons B. Triple jeopardy: rural, poor, and uninsured. *Health Serv Res.* 1989;23:975–1004.

17. Korczyk S. *Health Care Needs, Resources, and Access in Rural America.* Alexandria, Va: Analytical Services; 1989.

18. Green V. The black extended family in the United States: some research suggestions. In: Shimkin D, Shimkin E, Frate D, eds. *The Extended Family in Black Societies.* The Hague, The Netherlands: Mouton DeGruyer; 1978.

19. Shannon A. Educators innovative to match changing needs: preparing nurses for rural health care. *Am Nurs.* 1989;23(1):10.

20. Hill C. *Community Health Systems in the Rural American South: Linking People and Policy.* Boulder, Colo: Westview; 1988.

21. Long K, Weinert C. Understanding the health care needs of rural families. *Fam Relations.* 1987;36:450–455.

22. Coward R, Cutler S. Informal and formal health care systems for the rural elderly. *Health Serv Res.* 1989;23:785–806.

23. Bushy A. Rural U.S. women: traditions and transitions affecting health care. *Health Care Women Int.* 1990;11:503–513.

24. Patrick D, Stein J, Porta M, Porter C, Ricketts T. Poverty, health services, and health status in rural America. *Milbank Q.* 1988;66:105–136.

25. Bachtel D, Boatright S, eds. *The Georgia County Guide.* 12th ed. Athens, Ga: University of Georgia; 1993.

26. US Department of Health and Human Services, Health Care Financing Administration. *Medicaid: Characteristics of Medicaid State Programs: Vol. 2. State-by-State Profiles.* Washington, DC: HCFA; 1992. HCFA publication PHS 92-1509.

27. Babbie E. *The Practice of Social Research.* 6th ed. Belmont, Calif: Wadsworth; 1992.

28. Waitzkin H. Information giving in medical care. *J Health Soc Behav.* 1985;26:81–101.

CHAPTER 12

Themes of Stressors for Childbearing Women on the Island of Hawaii

Dyanne D. Affonso, PhD

Linda J. Mayberry, PhD

June Shibuya, PHN

June Kunimoto, PHN

Katherine Young Graham, PhD

Suann Sheptak, MS

S TRESSORS RELATED to individual experiences of pregnancy and postpartum have been described in the literature.[1,2] Several themes have emerged, including distress from physical symptoms, emotional changes, and obstetric events such as fear, pain, and uncertainty during labor and delivery. These themes assist health professionals in understanding women's childbearing experiences because the early literature described stressors in more general terms (eg, change of residence, death, illness, or divorce) without consideration of the unique situation of being pregnant or postpartum.

Although consideration of pregnancy-related stressors is an important factor in prenatal care, an Institute of Medicine report recommends that stress for childbearing women from rural and ethnic minority communities in particular be studied.[3] The current literature on childbearing stressors focuses primarily on urban, middle-class, Anglo American samples. Cultural diversity and rural

Funded by the National Institutes of Health National Center for Nursing Research grant R18 NR02678, 1990–95.

Fam Community Health 1993;16(2):9–19
© 1993 Aspen Publishers, Inc.

lifestyles have not yet been addressed. This chapter describes themes of stressors reported by women living in rural communities known as East Hawaii on the island of Hawaii, specifically those from Filipino, Japanese, Hawaiian, or part-Hawaiian ethnic backgrounds.

THREE ETHNIC GROUPS AS VULNERABLE POPULATIONS FOR LOW-BIRTHWEIGHT INFANTS

Women from Filipino, Japanese, Hawaiian, or part-Hawaiian ethnicities together make a substantial contribution to the overall incidence of low-birthweight (LBW) infants in East Hawaii. Births to Hawaiian, Filipino, and Japanese women represented 67% of the total births from 1987 to 1989 in East Hawaii, but they constituted 77% of all LBW births. Specifically, between 1987 and 1989 the LBW rate was 7.9% for Hawaiian or part-Hawaiian women and 8.3% for both Filipino and Japanese women. The Surgeon General declared that no racial or ethnic groups should have an LBW rate higher than 6% by 1990.[4] Therefore, selection of these three ethnic groups of women for exploration of stressors related to childbearing is timely.

These three ethnic groups of women are viewed as vulnerable populations in the East Hawaii district because of other well-defined risks. For Filipino and Hawaiian women, the median education level is 10th grade with a high percentage of high school dropouts. These two ethnic groups are frequently without insurance options or of low income and are

known as the ethnic gap groups for health care services on the island.

Filipinos are a growing ethnic community in East Hawaii because they were the predominant immigrants who came to work on the sugar cane plantations throughout the 1940s and 1950s. Filipinos preferred to set up camps throughout the district so that they could live in close proximity to their ethnic group and because the camp-style residence provided social and economic supports. They have tended to retain their traditions in language, cooking, and childbearing practices. An additional stressor for Filipino women arises from their difficulties and shyness in speaking English. Limitations with the English language also contribute to their tendency as an ethnic group not to seek standard obstetric care services available in the district. This may increase their vulnerability to unhealthy pregnancy outcomes. Filipinos have a history of a large constituency in the Hawaii labor force or of holding service jobs in the state. However, their socioeconomic status is lower in the district compared to other ethnic groups.

Hawaiians are concentrated in East Hawaii because the district is believed to be the original settlement area of their ancestors from Polynesia. The district contains many Hawaiian heritage artifacts (such as petroglyphs and burial tombs). Modern Hawaiian families have tremendous pride in and commitment to maintaining their Hawaiian traditions and rituals, which are especially visible through a statewide campaign to resurrect Hawaiian healing beliefs and practices. Vulnerabilities for Hawaiian childbearing women emerge from challenges in family life typically related to social unrest, such as domestic violence, economic uncertainties, and perceptions of oppression regarding land rights. Like the Filipinas, they do not seek prenatal care services early and do not have good retention with standard health care services available in the district.

In contrast, Japanese women are typically members of the middle- to upper-class ethnic group in East Hawaii, with many Japanese families being highly educated and holding professional careers. The Japanese were early agricultural settlers in the district and have become prominent land owners or business leaders throughout the years. Vulnerabilities for Japanese women take on a different form, arising from a highly stressed lifestyle in which the dual income necessary to uphold their high socioeconomic status in the district must be maintained. The stressful lifestyle is further complicated by a tendency for Japanese women not to burden others by sharing concerns or feelings or by questioning standard health care that may not be meeting their needs. A noteworthy observation is that Japanese women faithfully keep all their standard obstetric visits with private physicians and yet have LBW rates as high as those of the Filipinas. The LBW rate for Japanese women has been steadily increasing for the past 5 years in the district.

METHODOLOGY TO ELICIT THEMES OF STRESSORS: QUALITATIVE DATA THROUGH FOCUS GROUPS

Themes of stressors have not been previously reported in the literature for ethnic groups of childbearing women living in East Hawaii. It was not appropriate to use quantitative measurements designed for middle-class, urban, and Anglo American childbearing women because of reliability and validity issues. Instead, qualitative data were elicited from groups of women to describe the stressors related to pregnancy experienced by Hawaiians, Filipinas, and Japanese. A pilot survey of approximately 30 women from these ethnic backgrounds living in the district of East Hawaii indicated that women preferred to express themselves through a group format for several reasons. First, storytelling was an acceptable way to share feelings, concerns, and issues because telling stories is a culturally sanctioned mode of communication within these ethnic groups. Also, a group setting was viewed as a safe place to talk about what really bothers these women because there was opportunity for indirect, nonpersonal, and at times humorous expressions from the group as a whole rather than a focus on individuals. Group work also provided emotional and social support to these ethnic women, who are frequently culturally shy about expressing themselves. Through encouragement from other group members, however, the women eventually became active participants over successive group sessions. Based on evaluations obtained from a trial run of group participants, focus group methodology was endorsed by all three ethnic groups of women as a comfortable means for revealing descriptive, qualitative data to help community health care providers design culturally sensitive prenatal care.

Focus group techniques involve obtaining descriptive data through interactions among a group of individuals as opposed to the researcher posing questions and participants responding to a prescribed content.[5] Focus group sessions involve a cognitive approach that uses selected questions and topics that permit an individual to express perceptions of events that are normally held private and not necessarily divulged to health care providers. Important data are revealed through group interactions that would otherwise be difficult to obtain if there was reliance on only individual expression. The emphasis of the focus group is to produce a summary of views on a topic or question through sharing of group members' experiences or stories.

Focus group techniques recommended by Morgan[5] and used in this study were as follows:

1. The session begins with identifying the question or topic in general to be addressed. Three sets of questions were posed to each focus group based on the cognitive adaptation themes of search for meaning, sense of mastery, and self-esteem:
   - What kinds of events or experiences are difficult for a local island woman to handle when she's pregnant?
   - What kinds of feelings do women have during pregnancy or after childbirth that are not easy to deal with?
   - What kinds of events, feelings, or concerns happen within a family that are hard for a pregnant or postpartum woman to deal with?
2. The intent is not to answer the question fully but to obtain an ordered summary of data on the topics discussed by the group.
3. Initially each person offers uninterrupted, autobiographic statements about the topic according to the ground rules that one person speaks at a time, no side conversations are allowed, and latecomers are prohibited from joining the group once it has begun.
4. A table is used to set up a tape recorder; audiotaping is mandatory to produce the transcripts used for content analyses.
5. Discussions are self-managed by participants, although a moderator can be present to guide the process and to prevent individual monopoly (the moderator should maintain a low profile). The moderator may take notes that can be transcribed after the group session.
6. A group consists of 6 to 10 individuals who meet for 1 to 2 hours. A minimum of two meetings is necessary for each group to permit group process beyond initial acquaintances. The site is selected for participant convenience.
7. The data are analyzed by combining elements of an ethnographic summary approach and systematic coding via content analysis.

For the purposes of this study, five groups were constituted. Three female ethnic groups, one for Japanese, one for Filipino, and one for Hawaiian women, were convened. Focus groups were conducted exclusively by ethnicity to provide opportunities for expression of unique cultural beliefs. Also, the women preferred these intimate discussions to occur within their own ethnic identity. A health provider group was convened that consisted of two nurses (one from public health and the other from the obstetric unit at the local hospital), two physicians, a health educator, a social worker, and a nurse educator. The fifth group consisted of local neighborhood women from the three ethnic groups who had previous childbearing experiences and were viewed as leaders in their local communities. Each group was composed of 7 to 10 persons between the ages of 18 and 40 years. All groups met in community settings convenient for the participants, such as a conference room in a supermarket and a member's home. Interestingly, the three groups of ethnic women preferred not to meet in any setting identified with standard health care services offered in the community (ie, a clinic, physician's office, or health department). Each of the five groups, consisting of the same group members, met for three sessions to discuss the three different questions cited as the general topics for the study. Data presented in this article represent a synthesis of group work from a total of 5 focus groups. Each group session lasted for 90 to 120 minutes. None of the groups terminated any session before 1 hour, but all groups stayed within a 2-hour limit.

Overall, the women who participated in the groups responded positively to the interactions that occurred in the sessions. For all groups, the moderator was consistently a public health nurse, who was also the study's project coordinator. A total of 5 focus groups were conducted within a 2-month period. All 5 audiotapes were checked with the written transcripts to screen for errors by another independent group of transcribers. All written transcripts were sent from Hawaii to San Francisco, where they were processed through software for ethnographic coding to produce computerized worksheets for content analyses. The qualitative data were analyzed through several levels of content analysis.

To preserve the Hawaiian style of communicating, local islanders participated as independent raters to identify categories of stressors during the first level of coding. The second level of coding involved raters from San Francisco, who provided another objective review of the original worksheets. The third and fourth levels of content analyses involved merging the codes generated from the Hawaii and San Francisco raters and entering the codes from the ethnographic software to order the qualitative data sets. The final synthesis of stress themes emerged from dialogues among a team that included two local public health nurses, two maternity clinical nurse specialists, and two nurses with doctorates in sociology and psychology.

THEMES OF STRESSORS

Hawaiian women

Three themes were predominant for Hawaiian women. These women were preoccupied with concerns over their body image; overwhelmed by stress and conflict from the relationship with their spouse or mate, who was perceived as dominating or exhibiting "macho" characteristics; and felt conflict over their family's tendency to be overprotective toward females beginning in infancy and extending to adulthood.

Body image concerns were evident by frequent comments related to the following: getting fat and looking ugly, not being able to wear the clothes of one's choice, thinking that one will still be fat after childbirth, being anxious about getting back into prepregnancy-size clothes, and being upset at seeing pretty clothes that one can no longer wear. These concerns are similar to those expressed by samples of women from middle-class, urban backgrounds.[1,2]

What makes this theme of stress an important finding for health professionals is that Hawaiian women typically convey an attitude of indifference about their body image. During standard routine prenatal care services, Hawaiian women are known to joke about their appearance and have been erroneously judged by health professionals as not concerned about their body image. This theme was repeated in every focus group session conducted with Hawaiian women. Possibly some Hawaiian women have acculturated to the modern American lifestyle through endorsement of an anorexia mentality that leads to cognitive distortions for childbearing women. The distorted cognitive paradigm is that fat equals ugly and pregnancy equals fat; therefore, a pregnant woman is fat and ugly. Of particular concern is that Hawaiian women come from an ethnic heritage in which traditional cultural beliefs support the view that big women who look fat are beautiful, gracious in movement, and healthy human beings. This finding about Hawaiian women's concern over body image is important for tailoring pre-

natal care programs to a more culturally sensitive direction while addressing women's concerns and feelings about their bodily changes during gestation. Nurses can work with women to realign their view of a changing body image to be more congruent with Hawaiian cultural beliefs and to become less attached to the American belief that equates fat with ugliness.

Hawaiian women expressed concern and discontent with certain aspects of the relationship with their men. Some Hawaiian women perceived their men as having a need to direct or control them through behavioral commands that are not pleasing or satisfying. For example, men preferred their mates not to go out in public without being accompanied by them and not to be seen by or visit with other men. Women reported how they were made to return home and remove their make-up and jewelry or to change their hairstyle if their mates perceive them as looking too provocative. This finding indicates the need for providers of prenatal care services to work with expectant Hawaiian fathers. Hawaiian women recommended that men attend focus group sessions to express their own concerns. Women wanted men to understand that their desire to look and feel good about their physical appearance throughout pregnancy represents their private struggles in coping with their changing body image.

The family's tendency to overprotect girls and women begins before birth and is reinforced by cultural beliefs and taboos that are viewed as necessary to produce a healthy infant. Hawaiian women expressed being overwhelmed by the advice, counseling, and dictums of their families. For example, a pregnant woman's father may state that if the infant is a girl he is going to select the boy she can date and intends to chaperone her. The pregnant woman will be told not to carry heavy things and not to wear tight jeans or t-shirts that will hurt the infant. Foods the family believes are not good for her are taken away even if the meal has already begun.

Hawaiian cultural taboos were also viewed as repeated reminders that the pregnant woman needs to be protected by her family. Yet women were paradoxically concerned that a lack of adherence to the taboos might result in frightening and detrimental consequences for their infants. Taboos included the following: Do not wear necklaces or leis, or the infant will be born with the cord around the neck; do not perm your hair while you are pregnant, because it will burn the infant and leave a birthmark; do not cut your hair during pregnancy, or you'll be taking away all your good energy.

Women expressed being overwhelmed by these beliefs and taboos during focus group sessions. Women also shared they were confused about what to believe and at times were fearful of the uncertainties associated with failure to comply with the family's need to protect them. Conflicts arose from the women's desire to do what they wanted to take care of themselves against their families' need to protect them from potential dangers. This finding was instrumental in developing a community health nursing prenatal care program that employed cultural healers from each of the three ethnic groups as consultants to guide nurses in assisting

women to reconcile family conflicts. Additional group work that involved pregnant women, their families, the public health nurse, and the ethnic healer was implemented in the innovative community-based prenatal care program. To date, successful outcomes have been reported by positive evaluations of these group sessions from the women, their families, and the healer.

Filipino women

Three themes reported by Filipino women were discomfort in seeking services outside their families and ethnic communities; preoccupation with stress arising from the need to gain social acceptance in the community; and a cognitive style that emphasizes wishful thinking, dreams, and expectations throughout pregnancy that are not congruent with their lived experiences or the realities of their lifestyles.

Pregnant Filipinas in Hawaii generally do not go outside their immediate or extended families or their ethnic group for help. They are a cohesive cultural group that employs elaborate mechanisms to provide resources for social, economic, and environmental supports for each other and their ethnic group as a whole. This attitude permeates their behaviors toward health care. Health professionals frequently experience difficulties locating Filipinas in the community for the purposes of identifying their unique needs, recruiting them into health care services, and monitoring their retention when longitudinal services are necessary. Several factors contribute to these recruitment and retention issues. Filipinas tend to be shy and timid regarding the use of health care services, and they rarely ask questions out of deference to health professionals. In particular, frequent use of medical jargon by health professionals is perceived as intimidating and offensive by Filipinas. Therefore, it is not surprising that Filipinas are often latecomers to prenatal care and are targeted as the ethnic group with no prenatal care.

This is an important finding for health professionals because it has two important implications: (1) The current system of prenatal care is not sensitive to the needs and cultural style of Filipino women, in contrast to the needs and style of Anglo American women, who actively seek and initiate their own entry into health care; and (2) the content available in contemporary prenatal care is designed for middle-class, urban women and uses a medical model of practice that is not relevant to Filipino women. Therefore, it is not surprising that Filipinas do not seek or use available prenatal care services. These two implications are incorporated into the prenatal care program delivered by public health nurses in the district that tailor services to the cultural style of Filipino women.

Filipinos in general are socially conscious people with active social skills. This is most evident in their love of celebrations, parties, and any event that brings a gathering of their cultural groups and communities. A woman's pregnancy and the outcome of a healthy infant typically initiate one of the most festive events in the Filipino community. It is expected that pregnant women are preoccupied with the need to maintain social acceptance in their families and communities. Stress occurs when pregnant women have difficulties fulfilling their social roles and obligations. This can manifest in several ways. A working woman is frequently plagued by fatigue and may lose her desire to engage in the many social events surrounding the family. If a woman becomes pregnant out of wedlock, the shame is not only on her as an individual but also on her family and community. Social obligations are to be fulfilled because the biggest consequence is social ostracism. Ostracism is devastating because the primary sources of support for Filipinos are through their ethnic groups. Ostracism isolates the woman and her family, setting into motion a process similar to social suicide whereby the family dies socially and ethnic identity and community pride dissipate; finally, emotional death can trigger suicidal ideation or the physical act of suicide. Attention to Filipino women's social stress is important because their social livelihood is enmeshed with their sense of well-being and health while they are pregnant. Assessment of social stress is part of the innovative community-based prenatal care services offered to Filipino women in the district.

A finding not described in the literature that profiles Filipinos as an ethnic group living in Hawaii is their active cognitive style and character. Data from focus groups involving Filipino women had a consistent theme of wishes, dreams, and desires concerning what their life will be with the infant and the goodness of their future. A cognitive style unique to pregnant women was theoretically proposed by Rubin[6] and empirically supported by

Affonso and Sheptak.[7] These investigators described only middle-class, urban, Anglo American women, however. This finding is important because it demonstrates that a cognitive style is also relevant to ethnic women from rural settings such as Filipino women living in the East Hawaii district. The future orientation of Filipino women expressed by a belief that things will be good for themselves, their infants, and their families is nurtured by energies that health professionals need to tap during the delivery of health care services. Motivation, positive self-esteem, and a belief that one's life can be better are all energy sources that are essential in teaching women how to take care of themselves during pregnancy. The goal is to place Filipinas on the best pathway toward activating their dreams, desires, and goals.

Japanese women

Four themes were reported by the Japanese women: (1) family-related stress; (2) discomfort in sharing troubling thoughts and feelings because they may burden others; (3) worries about pregnancy and childbirth complications; and (4) tensions, pressures, and anxieties related to maintaining multiple roles and status in the community.

Japanese women in the district are from middle-class backgrounds; therefore, it was predicted that their stresses would have different themes from those of the Hawaiian and Filipino women, who are primarily from another level of socioeconomic status.

There are two predominant themes, both of which are interrelated in their stressful impact. Japanese women are burdened by disagreement with the philosophy of health and life expressed by their families (in-laws included). Frequently they are told that they should embrace traditional philosophy while they are pregnant and during parenting. A common stress is that words are spoken among family members that are frequently misinterpreted and lead to interpersonal tensions. Women repeatedly expressed ambivalence about taking advice from their parents and in-laws and showing deference to these elders while not agreeing with their cultural viewpoints. To magnify the stress, Japanese women have a stoic style that does not allow them to feel comfortable sharing their troublesome thoughts and feelings. Thus they keep their personal stress to themselves and feel that they have no one to tell who will understand their dilemmas. What makes this an important finding is that many Japanese women recommended that focus groups continue to be available for pregnant women because it was a way they felt comfortable sharing such intimate stress and because they trusted the nurses to maintain confidentiality. This recommendation was incorporated into the prenatal care delivered by public health nurses in the district.

Another stressor for Japanese women is worries that something will go wrong during pregnancy and childbirth. Japanese women as a cultural group are one of the most health conscious in the district. They reported several behaviors to affirm this: following careful eating habits, exercising regularly, abstaining from drugs, maintaining distance from people who smoke, faithfully keeping all scheduled obstetrical appointments, paying close attention to physician orders, reading prenatal books, and attending childbirth classes. As an ethnic group in the district, however, their pregnancy outcomes are as poor as those of Filipino women. This demonstrates that the number of prenatal visits through standard obstetric care does not necessarily correlate with favorable pregnancy outcomes. Therefore, concerns about complications among Japanese women are justified, especially because many live far from health care services and require long drives to gain access to emergency care as needed. This theme of stress is important because it affirms the need for women to have several essential components in prenatal care services: basic content about the signs and symptoms of complications, so that they can recognize early changes suggestive of unfavorable fetal status; education about how to monitor their own health status, so that they can be assertive with obstetricians for closer follow-up on subtle changes indicating that something is not right; and commendation for their concern about childbearing complications, so that they feel they are partners with health professionals in detecting early signs of disturbances in maternal and fetal well-being.

Japanese women also expressed a theme of stress related to the maintenance of their status as an ethnic group of considerable socioeconomic stature in the district. Stress arises from their multiple roles of having responsibilities at work; participating in community affairs; upholding stringent commitments to their immediate families, parents, and in-laws; and fulfilling the expectations of their spouses. This theme resembles the stress described by middle-class, urban pregnant women related to fulfilling multiple roles associated with career woman, wife, homemaker, and community volunteer.[1,2] This theme, in combination with the others, gives a picture of Japanese women being under tremendous stress during their childbearing experience. Currently available prenatal care services in the district do not give attention to these psychosocial issues and concerns that plague Japanese women.

IMPLICATIONS FOR COMMUNITY HEALTH CAREGIVERS

It is clear from the analysis of focus group data that each of the ethnic groups from East Hawaii described unique stressors that affect the experience of pregnancy. Hawaiians are concerned about coping with body changes that create conflicts for themselves and in their relationships with significant others, particularly mates and families. Filipino women are faced with family protectiveness issues similar to those of the Hawaiians but identify a greater extended family and ethnic community milieu. Japanese women are torn between traditional family values, social values, and commitments and performing the multiple roles demanded of modern successful women. Both Filipino and Japanese women experience difficulty in dealing with medical care practices, which is based on their reluctance to communicate verbally their specific health problems and needs. Because each group was able to identify significant stressors that can potentially contribute to their vulnerable pregnancy status, it is the responsibility of health care providers to design prenatal care that also addresses stressors on women's lives that are incurred through membership in a particular ethnic group.

Stressors arising from a rural lifestyle coupled with multiple ethnic and cultural belief systems that are often in conflict with the philosophies of available health care systems have yet to be addressed. Current prenatal care continues to be driven on the basis of a medical, biophysical paradigm. Community health caregivers are challenged to work within women's cultural belief and practice sys-

tems that provide resources for them to cope with life circumstances that become complex through pregnancy. The gaps that arise from a lack of understanding of rural and ethnic issues can be bridged by community health caregivers who are sensitive to conducting assessments that yield qualitative data on ethnic women's unique circumstances during pregnancy. Qualitative data, such as those described in this chapter, obtained from focus group techniques provide directions for tailoring prenatal care services that are sensitive to women's ethnic beliefs, styles of communication, and unique lifestyles.

REFERENCES

1. Arizmendi TG, Affonso DD. Stressful events related to pregnancy and postpartum. *J Psychosom Res.* 1987;31:743–756.
2. Affonso D, Mayberry LJ, Sheptak S. Multiparity and stressful events. *J Perinatol.* 1988;8:312–317.
3. Institute of Medicine. *Preventing Low Birthweight.* Washington, DC: Committee To Study the Prevention of Low Birthweight; 1985.
4. Department of Health and Human Services. *The 1990 Health Objectives for the Nation: A Mid-course Review.* Washington, DC: Government Printing Office; 1986.
5. Morgan D. Focus groups as qualitative research. *Methods Series 16.* Newbury Park, Calif: Sage; 1988.
6. Rubin R. Cognitive style in pregnancy. *Am J Nurs.* 1970;70:502–508.
7. Affonso D, Sheptak S. Maternal cognitive themes during pregnancy. *Matern Child Nurs J.* 1989;18:147–166.

Empowering Special Populations

Resiliency and Social Support

Angeline Bushy, PhD, RN, CS

IN RECENT YEARS, health promotion research has focused on factors that contribute to health and maintenance of long-term well-being. These findings have a wide range of implications for professionals working with at-risk and vulnerable groups. More specifically, vulnerability must be balanced against health-enhancing factors that may counteract negative risk factors. The process, as well as the outcome, is termed resilience. In the literature, personal hardiness and support systems are identified as health-enhancing forces. The two are not separate, self-sustaining entities. Rather, these are interfacing catalysts with one enhancing the other to build resilience and decrease the risks that promote vulnerability. Both concepts are examined in subsequent paragraphs along with professional roles that can be used to empower the vulnerable and persons with special health care needs.[1,2]

HARDINESS: PERSONAL RESILIENCE

Hardiness is a concept that is used to describe aspects of resilience in humans and their health sustainment efforts. As a theoretical framework, hardiness refers to the innate factors that keep a person from developing a health problem even with exposure to the risk compared with counterparts who experience adverse effects from it. The concept has historical origins but only recently has the term been applied to health in humans. More precisely, throughout history bold and daring adventurers have been described as hardy. Likewise, reference consistently is made in biology, plant science, and agriculture to sturdy (hardy) breeds of plants and animals having resistance to disease and endurance under hardship.[3-7]

Contemporary use of the concept as psychological resource in humans is consistent with the traditional uses of the term. With respect to humans, hardiness is a constellation of personality characteristics that functions as a (resistance) resource by some who encounter stressful life events and illness. Hardiness is viewed as a potential mediator against risk factors that enables the vulnerable to become empowered. Hardy personality traits also may play a role in some being able to overcome even the most adverse personal, home, and environmental conditions and still having meaningful and rewarding lives. The concept of hardiness consists of three dimensions: challenge, commitment, and control.

Challenge refers to mediating aspects to lifestyle risks and stressful events that contribute to a person perceiving the event as an opportunity for growth. Flexibility and openness help the person to endure and integrate a stress-producing situation into a meaningful and life-enriching event. Consciously, or unconsciously, change is perceived by the hardy individual as a normal aspect of life and an opportunity for personal development. This life perspective often is expressed as "going with the flow" or "seeing the cup as half-full instead of half-empty." In other words, hardy individuals selectively, and effectively, use resources in the environment to deal with unpleasant situations.

Commitment refers to an ability to believe in the personal value of a risk or stress-producing situation. Committed persons have a sense of purpose that allows them to identify with, then find meaning, in untoward events and dynamic personal relationships. On the one hand, even with very high levels of stress, committed people seem to stay healthy. Conversely, those who are alienated often seem apathetic and powerless when confronted with similar situations. The perspective of the latter group promotes vulnerability; subsequently, these individuals seem to manifest more health-related problems.

Perceived *control*, or the lack of it, is another dimension of the concept of hardiness and contributes to vulnerability and health status in humans. The concept, as used in hardiness theory, has origins in social learning theory. Locus of control refers to a person's life experiences and preferences in respect to reward and reinforcement for actions. More specifically, individuals with an external locus view outside forces as a dominant influence in their lives. Thus, these individuals seem to believe that they have little control over what happens to them. Persons with an internal locus of control, on the other hand, believe that life stressors are likely to be the result of individual effort or attribute. When faced with stressors, these individuals tend to rely on personal attributes and resources in their environment to modify the event into a manageable or growth-producing challenge. They seem to have the wherewithal to cope with the seemingly negative situation, regardless of the outcome. Subsequently, this reinforces the sense that they have some degree of control over stress-producing situations and decreasing risk factors.

The interrelationships among challenge, commitment, and control are at the core of hardiness in humans. Essentially, faced with a stressful life event, the hardy person will attempt to change or modify the challenging event (control) into one that is consistent with his or her life purpose (commitment). This frame of reference results in life-learning and personal growth (challenge). Subsequently, the event is perceived as an opportunity that serves to counterbalance and buffer health risks and vulnerability. Instead of negative health outcomes, the hardy person experiences maturation and growth and retains health—however he or she defines that life state.

SOCIAL SUPPORT

Social support can be another counterbalancing force to vulnerability and can mediate health risks. Support comprises formal as well as informal systems. Formal support includes such things as professional services and care rendered in established institutions. Informal support includes the access to, and quality of, the relationship of a person's significant other(s), immediate and extended family, neighbors, and faith community. There is no precise prescription as to who should be included in vulnerable clients' networks as this varies by individual, culture, and community. Essentially, the membership of a social network is defined by the client and his or her family system and this will vary from one cultural group to another.[8–11]

For instance, some cultures have extensive social support networks as is the case for many Native Americans, African American and Latino families. This is evident when a client visits the community health center for preventive care or is hospitalized, accompanied by a large contingency of relatives representing several generations. Some people, however, are not able to identify even one person in their support network. Increasingly, some faith communities are assuming an active role in supporting congregation members as well as outsiders who have no such network. Still, there continues to be a significant proportion of vulnerable persons who can identify only a very small circle of support, or no one at al.[12–13]

PART III: OVERVIEW

Part III, Empowering Special Populations, includes chapters that describe aspects of resiliency and offer empowerment strategies for health professionals caring for at-risk communities. Part III begins with Miser's chapter that speaks to the specializations and clinical judgments of social workers involving acting out female adolescents. This is followed by the Gramling et al's thought-provoking chapter that reconstructs a woman's life experiences with acquired immune deficiency syndrome (AIDS). In the next chapter, Villa, Wallace, Moon, and Lubben present a comparative analysis of chronic disease prevalence among older Korean and non-Hispanic whites. Their findings reinforce that health prevention and promotion interventions should consider the effects of traditional health practices on the management and outcomes of chronic health conditions. Chappell, Dickey, and DeLetter focus on another special population in their chapter, specifically veterans in a community-based residential program. The purpose of their study was to determine whether the use of medication dispensers improved accuracy in medication administration practices in those facilities. In the chapter by Plescia, Watts, Neibacher, and Strelnick the findings of a 10-year longitudinal study with the homeless in New York City is described. The authors entail how their affiliation with a multidisciplinary team located in a community health center provided a reliable and available resource for a particularly vulnerable group having multiple and complex health care needs, the urban homeless.

Gifford and Bettenhausen offer thought-provoking insights regarding obstetricians and gynecologists who accept and those who refuse prenatal care to teenage Medicaid recipients in Chicago. Wing, Crow, and Thompson focus on an especially vulnerable group. They examine the barriers to obtaining care for alcohol-related problems among the Muscogee (Creek) Indians living in rural eastern Oklahoma. The authors explain how cultural views of health contributed to effective health practices and treatment of substance abuse in this minority community. Williams, Lethbridge, and Chambers describe the development of a first-generation inventory tool to assess the health and health promotion behaviors of poor rural women in Alabama. In their chapter, they discuss the special needs of bearing and raising children in single-parent households in rural Alabama. Sullivan, Weinert, and Fulton describe yet another vulnerable rural group in a northern, intermountain state. Their study is of older persons living with cancer in rural and frontier areas and the self-identified health care needs of this vulnerable elderly population. The study identifies coping strategies in the two populations. Part III concludes with a chapter by Cole and Crawford that describes the lifestyle and health risks of a particularly vulnerable minority group, migrant farm workers. The authors describe the lifestyle of these families who are at risk for occupational injuries and communicable diseases. The authors elaborate on a model educational program that can be implemented to empower this often forgotten population through the use of informal support systems.

STRATEGIES AND INTERVENTIONS

Common themes that emerge in Part III include identifying personal and community resources such as hardiness, access to support networks, and the quality of social support systems. The chapters also demonstrate the importance of providing acceptable services that are culturally and linguistically appropriate for the targeted vulnerable population. In respect to the appraisal assessment, this includes the enhancement of mediating resources and development of appropriate interventions for clients using a range of professional roles, specifically advocate, case manager, educator, counselor, partner, and collaborator.[14-16]

Advocate

In the role of advocate, for instance, the professional must be sensitive to the health care needs of a vulnerable group and have a broad knowledge of community resources and how to access them. It includes an ability to communicate in a professional manner and coordinate an array of essential services and providers for the client. Persistence is needed when acting on behalf of those who are vulnerable. Extensive time and patience may be needed to remain in contact and direct the clients who are vulnerable, at risk, or have special health care needs to appropriate resources. Political activism is another dimension of advocacy. In fact, the most significant changes to improve the plight of vulnerable and special needs clients often occur in the policy arena at local, state, national, and even global levels. Advocacy may be in the form of representing consumer interest groups before regulatory bodies and local health commissions, or publicly supporting federal and state initiatives that enhance local services. Advocates' ultimate goal should be to empower clients by helping them to develop the necessary skills to find solutions for their particular concerns.

Case manager

Case management is the process by which services are organized and coordinated to meet a client's particular needs and to use scarce resources effectively. Case managing a particular client often extends over a long period of time, perhaps years. Further, the need for formal and informal services frequently increases in intensity and complexity with client exposure to other risk factors and life situations. The health professional in the role of case manager must ensure that services are not over- or underutilized while reflecting a client's changing needs. Effective case management requires a broad knowledgebase of health and social services as well as sensitivity to clients' accessibility to informal community resources. Case managers have a critical role in preventing the confusion that often arises from clients having contact with multiple persons on the health care team. To function effectively as a case manager, however, the provider must incorporate the advocacy along with the educator and counselor roles when developing, implementing, and evaluating care for clients.

Educator and counselor

Two other important roles of professionals who work with vulnerable clients are educator and counselor. The roles overlap and interface with advocacy and case management strategies. Vulnerable clients experiencing multiple risk factors might be motivated to modify risky lifestyle behaviors if educated about their ultimate impact on health. Education is a cost-effective and noninvasive intervention to inform consumers about pharmaco-therapeutic protocols, health promotion, stress management, developmental changes, and management of chronic health problems. Counseling interventions can be used to provide support with the grief process, adjust to normal life events, and improve communication skills between family members and health professionals. The counselor and educator roles also are important in helping clients to locate and access community resources. Professionals using these role behaviors can work with vulnerable families to help them identify and subsequently ask appropriate questions of agencies and health care providers.

Collaborator and partner

In the educator, counselor, advocate or case manager role, providers are in a position to partner and collaborate with clients and other caregivers to achieve mutually satisfactory health outcomes.

On a broader scale, providers can participate in coalitions of agencies and citizen groups and collaborate with private and community entities to work with vulnerable communities. Further, there may be opportunities to work with other community entities to conduct surveys and publicize information about health promotion services. Essentially, strategies inherent in the advocate, case manager, educator, counselor, and partner roles provide professionals with a repertoire of skills to effect social change as well as meet the special health care needs of vulnerable clients, families, and communities. Finally, the role behaviors are not separate, distinct, or clearly delineated. Rather, each overlaps with all of the others. Professionals working with vulnerable populations or clients with special needs should develop a repertoire of interpersonal skills. Health professionals should be flexible so these skills can be adapted to diverse clients in a variety of situations and environments.

DISCUSSION QUESTIONS

1. Reflect on resiliency and healthiness. Describe individuals that you have encountered or cared for that exhibited these features. Describe their attitudes and behaviors. How do these fit with hardiness theory? How do they describe their support systems?
2. Select a client with special needs. Identify his or her informal support networks. How do these systems impact the individual's health and care?

3. For each of the professional roles described, list three or more strategies that could be used to carry out that function.

4. Analyze each chapter in this part and identify resources that empower clients and contribute to their resiliency.

REFERENCES

1. Sebastian J. Vulnerability and vulnerable populations: an introduction. In: Stanhope M, Lancaster J, eds. *Community Health Nursing*. St. Louis, Mo: Mosby; 1996.

2. Stanhope M, Knollmueller R. *Public Health and Community Health Nurse's Consultant: A Health Promotion Guide*. St. Louis, Mo: Mosby; 1997.

3. Allred K, Smith, T. The hardy personality: cognitive and physiologic responses to evaluation threat. *J Pers Soc Psychol*. 1989;56:257–266.

4. Antonovsky A. *Health, Stress and Coping*. San Francisco, Calif: Josey-Bass; 1979.

5. Bigbee J. The concept of hardiness as applied to rural nursing. In: Bushy A, ed. *Rural Nursing, Vol. I*. Thousand Oaks, Ca: Sage Publications; 1991.

6. Kobasa S, Maddi S, Kahn S. Hardiness and health: a prospective study. *J Pers Soc Psychol*. 1983;42:68–177.

7. Lambert C, Lambert V. Hardiness: its development and relevance to nursing. *Image*. 1987;19:92–95.

8. Cobbs. Social support as a moderator of life stress. *Psychosom Med*. 1976;38;300–314.

9. Roos P, Cohen L. Sex roles & social support as moderators of life stress adjustment. *J Pers Soc Psychol*. 1987;52:576–585.

10. Tilden V. Issues of conceptualization and measurement of social support in the construction of nursing theory. *Res Nurs Health Care*. 1985;8:199–206.

11. Tilden V, Gaylen R. Cost and conflict: the darker side of social support. *West J Nurs Res*. 1987;9:9–18.

12. US Department of Health and Human Services. *Health, United States: 1997*. Hyattsville, Md: Author; 1998.

13. US Department of Health and Human Services. *Healthy People 2010*. (Draft copy). Hyattsville, Md: Author; 1998.

14. Bushy A. Social and cultural factors affecting health care and nursing practice. In: Lancaster J, ed. *Nursing Issues in Leading and Managing Care*. St. Louis, Mo: Mosby; 1998.

15. Bushy A. Cultural and ethnic diversity: cultural competence. In: Hickey J, Ouimette R, Venegoni C, eds. *Advanced Practice Nursing: Changing Roles and Clinical Application*. Philadelphia, Pa: J.B. Lippincott Company; 1999.

16. Bushy A. Vulnerability: an overview. In: Saucier-Lundy K, Jaynes S, Hartman S, eds. *Nursing in the Community: Continuity of Care of Individuals, Families, and Populations*. Sudbury, Mass: Jones & Bartlett Publishers. In press.

CHAPTER 13

Specializations and Clinical Judgments of Social Workers in Cases Involving Acting-Out Female Adolescents

Martha A. Miser, PhD

IN THE MENTAL health literature, acting-out or delinquent behavior is recognized as an associated feature of adolescent depressive disorders.[1-3] These concerns, however, are seldom addressed in the delinquency literature, with a few exceptions.[4] While the data are still limited, several studies show that adolescent depression is often comorbid with other behavioral symptoms, disobedience, anxiety, and oppositional tendencies in particular (Kashani W, Carlson G, Beck N, et al. 1995. Unpublished data.).[5-7] It is not known, however, whether social workers who actually evaluate and treat the acting-out or delinquent behavior recognize the significance of the mental health research for their areas of practice.

Social workers evaluate teenagers who exhibit acting-out or delinquent behavior in such settings as family services, mental health agencies, children and youth services, and criminal justice settings both before and after the problem behavior leads to arrest. As a result, aspects of the behavior that do not conform to the usual criteria of the particular social agency's

Fam Community Health 1996;19(3):1–13
© 1996 Aspen Publishers, Inc.

or social worker's specialization may be overlooked and thereby go untreated.

This biased evaluation is a particular concern with female adolescents. When girls experience depression accompanied by delinquent behavior, alienation from parents, and alcohol or drug abuse, the result is often arrest. In the United States delinquency is defined to include status offenses such as alcohol consumption, truancy, and incorrigibility,[7] which are not crimes for adults. More girls are being arrested for delinquent acts than in previous years, and the juvenile justice system until now has served mostly males.[7,8]

Females continue to experience depression at twice the rate of males.[9] Higher levels of depressive symptoms have been found in girls than in boys, even in children as young as 12 and consistently in 14-year-olds.[10] Because adolescents are seldom self-referred and often come unwillingly to the treatment situation, considerable clinical skill is required to unearth feelings of depression. The study described in this chapter surveyed social workers practicing in four specialization areas—children and youth, criminal justice, families, and mental health—to determine if they differed in their assessments and treatment plans for four delinquent female adolescents. Factors that influence these assessments were also examined.

REVIEW OF THE LITERATURE

Social learning theory

Difficulties in the assessment of juvenile delinquents can be explained by so-cial labeling theory. Social labeling theory posits that any delinquent act, regardless of underlying causes, is a legal construct that carries a label that may influence the clinical judgment of those who must assess and recommend treatment for those so labeled. The abnormal behavior is defined as a law violation. Those who must assess that behavior expect that which is indicated by the label, thereby reinforcing the delinquent behavior.[11,12] Feitts and Hamner,[11] for example, found that the use of the label "delinquent" produced adverse effects on the self-concept, which is believed by some to insulate against delinquency. Bliss[13] found that lower self-concept scores accompany increasingly deviant labels. Schiff[14] also commented on the attribution of a stereotypically defined role to a deviant status. Farrington[15] cautioned that identification of potential offenders should be selective because the nature of the measures could stigmatize those so identified.

Dillon[16] discussed the problems caused by labels in treatment situations. She described the barriers labels can erect between social workers and explained how labels "blur" the worker's ability to see clients as people instead of labels. The labeling effects of delinquent acts, for example, can result in assumptions that all juveniles who commit a certain act have the same psychological characteristics.[17] The consequences of these assumptions can exacerbate the symptomatology, which may include symptoms of depression, especially in females.

Some of the factors, according to the literature, that affect the clinical judgment of social workers are social work specialization, theoretical bias, and various agency and demographic factors.[18] Through constant exposure to a specific range of clients and problems, a clinician's judgment may become desensitized to client stimuli that fall moderately outside that range. This may occur more often in practice settings that serve a restricted range of clients.[19]

The agency's focus also may reflect the theoretical bias of its employees, which may or may not be related to their specializations. In correctional settings, for example, sociology is the dominant social science in the study of delinquency. Treatment thus is focused on the correction of societal conditions that favor delinquency or on remedying the inequities and disadvantages that are said to have created the problem.[20] Individuals with that theoretical leaning, therefore, focus on youth employment programs, vocational training, and other ways to narrow the financial gap that stands between deprived youth and "the good life."[21]

Social workers, on the other hand, also draw from psychology and psychiatry when formulating treatment plans for delinquent adolescents. Behavioral, cognitive behavioral, psychodynamic/psychoanalytic, and existential/humanistic theories of personality are examples of theories commonly taught in schools of social work. The social worker who is limited by the theoretical orientation of one or two theories learned during master of social work (MSW) training or who practices in an agency that subscribes to a particular orientation may limit case planning to certain aspects of the prob-

lem and thereby fail to ask about depression. Wooten talked of the "lopsided concentration upon individual rather than social factors"[22(p319)] that a particular perspective may force on a treatment program or a case plan while ignoring other aspects of a particular problem. If delinquents who are suffering from depression could be identified, the literature of adolescent depression could be used to provide additional treatment alternatives that might be more effective than the more traditional techniques appropriate for other delinquents.

Factors affecting clinical judgment

Agency factors that may affect the clinical judgment of social workers include the source of the agency's support, its source of authority, and its function.[23] In juvenile courts the casework is related to the legal setting. Other agencies provide services to a juvenile court as well as to other clients, as in a private agency that receives large numbers of court referrals. Social workers in juvenile court settings or affiliated agencies may be limited as to what services they can provide because their primary service function is law enforcement and government funding is linked to specific standards and guidelines. One additional agency condition that must be considered in relation to any population of juvenile delinquents is the funneling effect (ie, negative atmosphere) of the juvenile justice system itself.[24]

Other factors that have been found to affect clinical judgments in the treatment of acting-out adolescents include age, parental status, gender, and race of therapists.[25] The year of MSW graduation has been found to influence clinical decision making in regard to adult children of alcoholics.[26]

The literature also addresses the difficulties of assessment in cases of adolescent depression. Most of that depression research has been in hospital settings,[2] but Chiles, Miller, and Cox[24] applied the psychodynamic research findings to a juvenile hall population. Although both the depressed and nondepressed adolescents were acting out in similar ways, observers could be trained in 2 weeks to identify the depressed delinquents. There were more boys in the study but more girls in the depressed group.

It is possible, therefore, that clinical judgments and perceptions of adolescent behavior problems can be affected by a multitude of factors, especially when social workers or social agencies specialize in serving one particular population or case condition. The result may be abridged assessments that result in standardized treatment approaches, which are useful for many purposes but may cause other important problems to be overlooked.

METHOD

Hypotheses

It was hypothesized for purposes of this study that social workers in different practice areas would differ from one another in their perceptions of female delinquents. It also was hypothesized that social workers in different practice areas would vary in their treatment focus and that some would overlook depression in their recommendations for treatment. In addition, it was hypothesized that these differences in assessment would vary in relation to factors such as agency, experience, gender, ethnicity, parental status, and year of MSW training.

Subjects

The sample, drawn in 1990, consisted of 600 members residing throughout the United States randomly selected from the membership directory of the National Association of Social Workers (NASW). From each of four direct practice areas—children and youth, family services, criminal justice, and mental health—150 names were selected. Because the distribution of these groups in the total population is uneven, the sampling method used was disproportional stratified random sampling. This method was deemed appropriate since this study was concerned only with differences between the groups. Disproportionate stratified random sampling ensures each group adequate representation in the sample and reduces sampling error as much as possible by ensuring homogeneity. As a result, a larger percentage (21.4%) of those listed as practitioners in the field of criminal justice were included in the sample, for example, while a smaller percentage (12.3%) of those identified as mental health practitioners were included.

Of 600 questionnaires mailed, 314 responses were received for a response rate of 50.2%. However, only 46.8% (N = 281) of the returned questionnaires yielded data that could be used in this study. There were no significant differences between respondents and nonrespondents with regard to age, sex, and race. There were, however, significant differences between the two groups in year of MSW graduation. Respondents graduated almost 4 years earlier than nonrespondents. Nonrespondents may have answered the questions differently, therefore, if their MSW training had included more or less content related to this study or because they had less experience [$t(436) = 4.33, P < .001$]. This complicates the generalizability of the results.

The sample was predominantly female (74%) and white (87.5%), with a wide distribution of age groups ranging from less than 30 to more than 55 years. The majority were married (60.5%) and had one or more children (64.8%) (Table 13–1). The majority of the respondents had more than 5 years' experience since receiving MSW degrees, though almost one third (30.2%) had less than 5 years' experience (Table 13– 2).

Procedures

A self-administered questionnaire was designed to collect descriptive information about the respondents and their clinical judgments and attitudes. Six case vignettes describing depressed female adolescents were developed to evoke the clinical judgment responses. The use of clinical vignettes provided a common basis for comparisons of the responses and also allowed control of demographic and family structure variables. The vignettes were developed from actual intake infor-

Table 13–1. Demographic profile of respondents

Characteristic	n	%
Gender		
Male	74	26
Female	207	74
Age		
Under 30	30	11.2
31–35	44	16.0
36–40	49	17.4
41–45	50	17.8
46–50	46	16.4
51–55	27	9.6
Over 55	33	12.0
Ethnicity		
White	246	87.5
Black	16	5.7
Asian	4	1.4
Hispanic	6	2.1
Mixed	4	1.4
Other	5	1.8
Marital status		
Never married	63	22.4
Separated	6	2.1
Divorced	34	12.1
Widowed	6	2.1
Married	170	60.5
Number of children		
0	99	35.2
1	50	17.8
2	77	27.4
3 or more	55	19.6

mation gathered when the girls' probation officers applied for agency placement. Each vignette included symptoms of adolescent depression such as somatic complaints, poor school performance, and delinquent behavior that had resulted in arrest. Each vignette also described a single-parent family.

Table 13-2. Number of years since respondents received MSW degrees

Number of years since MSW	n	%
Less than 5	85	30.2
5–10 years	80	28.5
11–20 years	75	26.7
More than 20 years	41	14.6

Drafts of the vignettes first were submitted to a panel of social work reviewers (N = 16) with substantial clinical expertise in practice with adolescents who were depressed or who exhibited other behavior problems. The responses of these experts were used to validate whether the vignettes contained enough information to indicate that inquiry regarding depression was appropriate. The four vignettes selected for use in the questionnaire were those considered most illustrative of adolescent depression by the entire panel of experts, who indicated that depression could be clearly identified by workers who saw such clients regularly, thus validating the content of the vignettes.

A draft of the entire questionnaire next was circulated among colleagues with research expertise (N = 12) to elicit general comments and to determine the length of time required to complete the survey. After a few suggested revisions, the questionnaire was mailed to other colleagues with less research expertise but who had expertise in one of the four practice areas studied to elicit further comments. As a fourth step, a pilot test was conducted on a random subsample of 20 social workers, five from each of the four NASW specializations. The response rate of the subsample was 50% (N = 10). No further changes were made.

Dependent variables

The questionnaire assessed problem perception and treatment/referral plan for the vignette cases, and a scale was then developed to measure clinical judgment.

Problem perception

Problem perception was measured by whether the respondent identified depression as one of the case problems for each vignette. Respondents earned one point for each vignette, for a possible total of four points across all four vignettes.

Treatment/referral

The treatment/referral plan was measured by whether the respondent included depression treatment as part of the treatment plan or made a depression-related referral to another agency. One point was awarded for each vignette, for a possible total of four points for all four vignettes.

Clinical judgment

Clinical judgment was measured using a scale that combined the problem perception and treatment/referral responses, which ranged from a total score of zero to two points for each vignette and zero to eight points for all four vignettes (alpha = .7337). Other responses were solicited in the recognition that they were important adjuncts to treatment but were not measured by this particular study.

Independent variables

Independent variables were social work specialization, theoretical framework, and agency type, as well as several demographic variables.

Social work specialization

The respondents' social work specialization was measured using a simplified version of a scale developed by Levy.[26] The survey form listed the four areas of specialization and asked respondents to identify which areas corresponded with (1) the respondent's own perception of his or her specialization, (2) the types of seminars attended during the past year, and (3) the types of clients comprising the respondent's caseload. A point was awarded in each specialization area a respondent identified in response to the three questions. Respondents who scored two in only one practice area were classified as specialists. Respondents who scored two in more than one area were classified as generalists. Respondents who scored one in one or more areas were classified as nonspecialists.

These questions were developed to assess the degree to which the respondents limited their caseloads to the one area they considered their specialization. Also, the questions were designed to indicate whether respondents were able to draw from resources outside their own areas of specialization to individualize treatment plans.

Theoretical framework

The theoretical framework was measured by a single item asking respondents to select one of five theoretical frameworks: behavioral, cognitive–behavioral, psychodynamic/psychoanalytic, existential/humanistic, or "other." Family systems theory was not included, but some respondents wrote that that theory was their theoretical framework. Respondents were requested to avoid using "eclectic" as a response.

Agency type

Agency type was measured by an item that asked respondents to identify their agency type as public, private nonprofit, private for-profit, or quasi-governmental (private but receives some government funds). Respondents were also asked to identify the type of agency of any secondary employment as well as the types of agencies in which they had previously worked.

Demographic variables

In addition to specialization, theoretical framework, and type of agency, the demographic variables of age, parental status, gender, race, and year of MSW graduation were studied.

RESULTS

According to the specialization scale developed for this study, 25 respondents were specialists in criminal justice, 33 in children and youth, 36 in families, and 85 in mental health. Seventy-seven respondents were classified as generalists, and only four were nonspecialists. The remainder were in some specialization not related to the study, although they had experience in the specialization areas. They therefore were grouped with nonspecialists as "other."

Analysis of variance with eta and contrasts showed significant differences between groups [$F(5, 5) = 3.72$, $P = .003$, eta $= .13$] in problem perception and treatment plans. All of the specialization groups except criminal justice differed significantly from the family specialization group. The children and youth group also differed significantly from the criminal justice group (Table 13–3). Chi-square analysis of the individual vignettes showed significant differences between the six groups on one vignette, which described a female adolescent convicted of a felony [$\chi^2(10) = 18.96$, $P = .04$, $\lambda = .005$]. The highest mean scores were those of the children and youth specialists ($M = 4.18$), the mental health specialists ($M = 3.66$), and the generalist group ($M = 3.69$). The lowest mean score was

that of the family specialists ($M = 2.61$) (Table 13–3).

There were no significant differences in ability to identify depression among respondents based on agency experience, gender, ethnicity, parental status, or MSW graduation year. Theoretical orientation, however, made a significant difference in depression recognition and its treatment for one vignette [$\chi^2(10) = 20.69$, $P = .02$, $\lambda = .004$]: Those with a psychodynamic/psychoanalytic orientation were most sensitive to the depression in the one vignette that described alcoholic family dynamics.

Age also made a significant difference in two vignettes. For the vignette that described an incorrigible female adolescent with school problems, respondents younger than 30 (93%) recognized and treated depression more than other age groups [$\chi^2(12) = 21.21$, $P = .05$]. In a second vignette, respondents younger than 30 (84%) and 41 to 45 (83%) more

Table 13–3. Case perceptions and treatment plans of social workers in each specialization group

Specialization	N	M*	SD	Significant ranges
Criminal justice	25	3.12	1.97	
Children and youth	33	4.18[†]	1.42	$R_2 = 2.93$[‡] $R_1 = 2.79$
Family services	36	2.61	1.59	
Mental health	85	3.66[†]	1.63	$R_4 = 3.10$
Generalists	77	3.69[†]	1.83	$R_5 = 3.16$
Other	25	3.33	1.73	

$F(5, 5) = 3.72$, $P = .003$, eta $= .13$. SD = standard deviation.
*Mean scores on the depression sensitivity scale; possible range, 0–8.
[†]Groups were significantly different at .05 from the family services group.
[‡]Specialists in children and youth significantly different at .05 from criminal justice specialists.

often recognized and planned to treat depression.

DISCUSSION

This study supports the hypothesis that social workers in different specialization groups differ in case perceptions and treatment plans. It also partially supports the hypothesis that the theoretical framework and age of the social worker are factors in the formulation of assessments and treatment plans.

Because social work requires a broad knowledgebase, there was considerable overlapping of specializations and expertise in all of the groups, as indicated by self-reports, type of clientele served, and continuing education classes pursued. Only four respondents were identified as nonspecialists, indicating that most social workers acquire expertise in at least one area.

The specialists in mental health and children and youth and the generalists were most consistent in addressing depression or considering it in relation to the vignette cases. It was expected that mental health specialists would do so, because they were most likely to have exposure to the adolescent depression literature. Generalists also were more consistent in identifying depression, possibly because they are exposed to a broader cross section of clients, which also may be true for children and youth specialists.

It was expected that the groups would differ on the vignette in which the female adolescent was convicted of a felony. The implied seriousness of the labeled offense did not cloud the mental health issues for children and youth specialists and mental health specialists.

It was surprising, however, that family specialists were less sensitive to depression than those in the other groups. They may have focused less on the intrapsychic behavior because they typically see groups instead of individuals, or they may have evaluated the vignettes from the family systems perspective and thereby felt that depression would be alleviated if the family's functioning improved. The criminal justice experts were also less likely to address depression than those in other groups. This is a concern because sometimes an acting-out adolescent is seen only by specialists in criminal justice.

It was expected that theoretical orientation would make a greater difference in problem focus than it actually did. The psychodynamic/psychoanalytic theorists were most sensitive to depression; not surprisingly, behaviorists were least sensitive, which is of concern because most treatment programs for juvenile delinquents are behavioral. While depression can be treated appropriately using behavioral methods, the focus on overt behavior could cloud depression that is hidden by the adolescent's acting out. The only significant difference between theoretical groups occurred with the vignette describing alcoholic family dynamics; perhaps those in other groups considered only alcohol-related factors, currently so in vogue as a practice area, and thus assumed that depression would be addressed as part of a codependency treatment program.

Age made a difference in focus on two individual vignettes. Social workers under age 30 were sensitive to depression in the vignette case describing incorrigible behavior and in the one describing a female adolescent convicted of a felony, a label which may have affected the decisions of others. Social workers between ages 41 and 45 were significantly more sensitive to depression only in the vignette describing incorrigible behavior. Those in the under-30 age group were closer in age to the vignette adolescents and may, therefore, have been able to relate to their underlying feelings. Those in the 41 to 45 age group may have recognized the depressive symptomatology that accompanied the acting out because of personal experience or more social work experience.

Specialization, therefore, is one consideration in understanding practitioners' clinical judgments and attitudes toward adolescent depression. There was such variation in treatment plans for the adolescent girls in the vignettes that it is difficult to assess how any one of these approaches to the problems could be more valid than the others. It is possible that all of the treatment plans would achieve the same results, and most respondents included some consideration of depression for all four, even if in a perfunctory fashion.

The respondents addressed many problems and offered many different kinds of solutions that were not readily apparent from the text of vignettes. It is clear that those familiar with such cases added unwritten material from their own experiences. It may be a problem for social workers, who must assess so many cases, to determine how each case is unique and thereby make accurate assessments.

There are several limitations to this study. It was exploratory and descriptive, and there is systematic bias in group membership. Causality, therefore, cannot be inferred. Other variables not studied may explain the results. Any implications as to direction, therefore, are merely presumptions and should be treated as such.

Another limitation is that the study was based on self-reports. The responses are assumed to be valid, but it is possible they are not. Even though this is a possibility, however, the responses were not unusual, and many respondents went to great lengths to write further explanations related to their decision making.

An additional limitation may be that the nonrespondents would have answered the questions differently from the respondents. There was an adequate response to the survey, however, and respondents and nonrespondents differed very little on demographic variables. Also, the respondents were slightly more experienced than the nonrespondents. Respondents were distributed fairly evenly among the NASW-identified specializations, although those classifications often differed from self-reported specializations as measured by this study. Because social workers provide such a variety of services, it may be difficult to report an actual specialization to NASW.

A further limitation is that the study is based on case vignettes. The vignettes were validated by a panel of experts, however, and the entire instrument was pilot tested. Many respondents enclosed letters with their returned questionnaires accompanied by descriptions of similar cases from their own practices. There are limitations to the use of case vignettes. If the social workers in this survey had been confronted with actual adolescent girls, their responses might have been different from their responses to the vignettes. The written description did not allow the respondents the benefit of nonverbal cues, including body language and facial expression. Also, it was impossible to ask for more information, which, if available, could have resulted in different clinical decisions. On the other hand, these vignettes contained actual information that was provided for four female adolescents at their intake interviews and that was the basis for clinical judgments made at that time.

IMPLICATIONS

This study offers implications for professional social work, social work practice, staff training, and social work education. When juvenile delinquents are evaluated because of behavior perceived as a threat to the community, it is important that assessments be as comprehensive as possible to encompass underlying behavior that interferes with treatment and rehabilitation. Because the presenting problems are so complex, it is possible to become overwhelmed by that complexity and, therefore, to focus only on the behaviors considered most immediate and pressing. Also, juvenile delinquents are labeled when arrested, and the seriousness of the labeled offense can

distort the perceptions of the overall behavior and cause co-occurring behavior to go unobserved. That behavior can worsen, as a result, and continue into adulthood at greater cost to the community. Because social workers often are required to make assessments of such cases very rapidly and within mandated guidelines, it is possible for the importance of other problems to be minimized. In reality, therefore, social workers may narrow their focus to address only the most pressing problems mandated by their agencies.

Social work, however, subscribes to values and principles that consider people in their environments, and it is important that in an effort to achieve a degree of expertise in one area, the tradition of broad assessments is not lost. In spite of the current push toward specialization, moreover, the social work profession continues to perceive problems from the person-in-environment position. Even though most of the participants in this study had acquired expertise in at least one area, their treatment plans included a multitude of strategies and referrals.

This study, therefore, provides reinforcement for the necessity to approach social work education from an ecological viewpoint. It shows that a significant emotional problem can be overlooked and, as a result, go unaddressed and untreated. Since social workers must be trained to address very complex needs of clients, those who educate social workers must assign adequate time to the practice skills needed to perceive cases in their entirety. Because in the assessment process the social worker must understand all the important elements of a problem and the meaning of the problem to the client in that situation, social work education must include consideration of multiple options of treatment so that an appropriate blend may be offered to address the complexities of the problem.

There has been a shift in recent years toward practice concentrations in schools of social work, but it is important that some of the aspects of the so-called generic approach to social work practice be retained. Planning for problem solving is ineffective unless it is based on comprehensive assessments that include inquiry regarding the antecedents of behavior.

Social work education also must provide more content on adolescent depression research both at the graduate level and through continuing education. Such content would help broaden the perspectives of social work students, especially those in criminal justice concentrations, to include sensitivity to underlying causes of behavior and information regarding different types of juvenile delinquency.

Such education would equip social workers in practice with acting-out adolescents with depression and accompanying anxiety, despair, and low self-esteem to direct treatment plans toward rehabilitation instead of punishment and control.

Educators in the field of social work also must include applicable material in all concentrations, regardless of the institution's theoretical framework. Those teaching in mental health concentrations, for example, must teach course material related to families and children as well. Those within a behavioral theoretical framework must stress the importance of inquiry regarding antecedents of the behavior.

In addition, the smaller number of criminal justice specialists who are NASW members points to the need for more social work education directed at this area. The values, knowledge, and methodology of social work have much to offer this field, especially at a time when juvenile delinquency is a major societal concern.

REFERENCES

1. Cantwell D, Baker L. Manifestations of depressive affect in adolescence. *J Youth Adolesc*. 1991;20: 121–133.
2. Carlson G, Cantwell D. Unmasking masked depression in children and adolescents. *Psychiatr Clin North Am*. 1980;2:511–526.
3. Gibbs J. Assessment of depression in urban adolescent females: implications for early intervention strategies. *Am J Soc Psychiatr*. 1986;6:50–56.
4. Quay HC. Patterns of delinquent behavior. In: Quay HC, ed. *Handbook of Juvenile Delinquency*. New York, NY: Wiley; 1987.
5. Compas B, Ey S, Grant K. Taxonomy, assessment, and diagnosis of depression during adolescence. *Psychol Bull*. 1993;114:323–344.
6. Cohen P, Valez C, Garcia M. *The Epidemiology of Childhood Depression*. Presented at the annual meeting of the American Academy of Child Psychiatry; June 1985; San Antonio, Tex.
7. Farrington D. Epidemiology. In: Quay HC, ed. *Handbook of Juvenile Delinquency*. New York, NY: Wiley; 1987.
8. Steffensmeyer D. Assessing the impact of the woman's movement on sex-based differences in the handling of adult criminal defendants. *Crime Delinquency*. 1980;26:344–357.
9. Nolen-Hoeksema S, Girgus J. The emergence of gender differences in depression during adolescence. *Psychol Bull*. 1994;115:424–443.
10. Allgood-Merten B, Lewinsohn P, Hops H. Sex differences and adolescent depression. *J Abnorm Psychol*. 1990;99:55–63.

11. Feitts W, Hamner W. *The Self-Concept and Delinquency*. Nashville, Tenn: Counselor Recordings and Tests; 1969.

12. Jensen G. Delinquency and adolescent self-conceptions: a study of the personal relevance of infraction. *Soc Problems*. 1972;20:84–103.

13. Bliss D. The effects of the juvenile justice system on self-concept. *Criminal Justice Abstracts*. 1977; 10:297–298.

14. Schiff T. *Being Mentally Ill: A Sociological Theory*. New York, NY: Aldine; 1984.

15. Farrington D. Implications of criminal career research for the prevention of offending. *J Adolesc*. 1990;13:93–113.

16. Dillon C. The professional name game. *Soc Casework*. 1969;50:337–340.

17. Quay H. Personality and delinquency. In: Quay HC, ed. *Juvenile Delinquency: Research and Theory*. Princeton, NJ: Van Nostrand; 1965.

18. Kadushin A. *The Social Work Interview*. New York, NY: Columbia University Press; 1990.

19. Bieri J, Atkins A, Briar S, et al, eds. *Clinical and Social Judgment: The Discrimination of Behavioral Information*. New York, NY: Wiley; 1996.

20. Cloward L, Ohlen L. *Delinquency and Opportunity: A Theory of Delinquent Gangs*. Glencoe, Ill: Free Press; 1961.

21. Binder A. An historical and theoretical introduction. In: Quay HC, ed. *Handbook of Juvenile Delinquency*. New York, NY: Wiley; 1987.

22. Wooten B. *Social Science and Social Pathology*. New York, NY: Macmillan; 1959.

23. Perlman H. *Social Casework*. Chicago, Ill: University of Chicago Press; 1957.

24. Chiles R, Miller M, Cox G. Depression in an adolescent delinquent population. *Arch Gen Psychiatr*. 1980;37:1179–1184.

25. Gartner A. Countertransference issues in the psychotherapy of adolescents. *J Child Adolesc Psychother*. 1985;3:187–196.

26. Levy A. Specializations and clinical judgments of social workers in cases of children of alcohol abusers. *Dissertation Abstracts Int*. 1989;49:3158A.

CHAPTER 14

Reconstructing a Woman's Experiences with AIDS

Lou Gramling, PhD

Joyceen S. Boyle, PhD, FAAN

Nancy McCain, DSN

Jimmy Ferrell, PhD

Donna Hodnicki, PhD

Rachel Muller, RN, MSN

WOMEN ARE now one of the fastest growing risk groups for infection with the human immunodeficiency virus (HIV).[1,2] Women have outnumbered men in heterosexual viral exposures in the United States since the epidemic was first recognized in 1981,[3] primarily because HIV is transmitted more effectively from male to female.[4] Women, especially women of color, as well as those living in poverty are at high risk for HIV infection through heterosexual contact and intravenous drug use.[5,6]

Acquired immune deficiency syndrome (AIDS), a result of progressive HIV disease, has become the leading cause of death of women between the ages of 25 and 44 years in several major cities in the United States and is one of the top four causes of death nationwide in this age group.[7,8] This alarming trend

The authors gratefully acknowledge the assistance of Roy DeLamotte, PhD, who provided valuable editorial assistance with the narrative description.

Fam Community Health 1996;19(3):49–56
© 1996 Aspen Publishers, Inc.

continues in spite of efforts to inform the public about prevention of HIV infection.

There is a dawning realization within the medical community that the first manifestation of HIV disease in women often consists of gynecological symptoms such as candida infections, sexually transmitted diseases, and pelvic inflammatory disease.[9] Concurrent with the need for further exploration of the epidemiology and physiological effects of HIV infection in women is the challenge of understanding the contextual life experiences that may be unique to women. This challenge to understand the individual's experience is a mandate to go "beyond head counts to reveal a little of the complex experiences in those heads."[10(p764)]

Larson and Ropka[11] reviewed the AIDS-related nursing literature from 1987 to 1990 and found only a few studies specific to women. No qualitative study was identified in this comprehensive review. However, qualitative methodology is ideally suited for the study of women, as it addresses the context of their lives and the unique personal meaning of illness. This study used a qualitative method of narrative analysis to address these issues.

METHOD

Atkinson[12] discussed a method of narrative analysis in which the researcher "revisits" data to glean insights that may not have emerged during other inductive methods. A narrative analysis requires the researcher to search for story lines, a process that brings about intersubjective understanding through immersion in the story. Listening to women's voices and learning from women's experiences are crucial in reconstructing and understanding the world of those who have HIV disease.

Hall, Stevens, and Meleis[13] suggested that narratives allow for a sharing of power in research, overcoming invisibility and enabling interpretive reflection on experiences. According to Cortazzi,[14] the notion of "voices" is firmly linked to narrative. The term emphasizes the need for consumers of health care to talk about their experiences in their own words. Narratives or "storytelling" from consumers reflect the context of health care, which comes into being as the story is told, explained, or appreciated. The narrative presented conveys meaning that can be translated to other clinical situations.

"Tess's" (a pseudonym) narration began when she was interviewed for a study designed to assess the stressors and coping strategies associated with HIV disease.[15] The study included interviews and observational experiences with 32 males and 4 females attending an infectious disease clinic in a large urban medical center. Tess's interview was tape-recorded in a private setting by one investigator under conditions of informed consent; Tess remained in contact with the researchers until her death. Data analysis from that study yielded three major stages in coping with HIV disease: living with dying, fighting the sickness, and getting worn out. Although the analysis revealed these stages to be true for men and women, it was noted that women's experiences were significantly different from men's and warranted further analysis.

In-depth analysis of women's experiences with HIV disease began with review and coding of the women's interviews (N = 4)[15] and the development of an interview schedule derived from issues previously identified as pertinent to women. Three additional women were recruited to the study and interviewed at this time. Additional data were also collected via participant observation and informal interviews with two women long diagnosed with HIV disease and too ill for in-depth interviews. In total, the sample (N = 9) included women 25 to 40 years of age; four were European Americans and five were African Americans.

The experiences of the nine women were analyzed via a multistep, reflexive process that involved reading and rereading the transcribed interviews, coding, thematic analysis, and dialogue among the team of researchers. Upon reflection on how to best present the experiences of women with HIV disease, it was decided to use one woman's story as illustrative of the experiences of the women in the study. The individual account chosen for this narrative analysis was selected for the richness of the data and the meaning that can be translated to other women with HIV disease and AIDS. Tess was able to reflect on her experiences and share her feelings, insights, and rich descriptions with the investigator.

The narrative analysis revealed Tess's system of knowledge—that is, what she knew, understood, and experienced with respect to AIDS, as well as how she interpreted her life and classified her experiences. Further analysis facilitated a description of Tess's life events and the strategies she used in managing the experiences associated with AIDS. The narrative was constructed by continued review of Tess's interview and the reflected experiences of the researchers. Analysis led to the identification of eight themes and the creation of two story lines: "I Was a Strong, Mean Woman" and "Dying Young."

"I WAS A STRONG, MEAN WOMAN"

Tess was a tall, big-boned woman with dark hair and had weighed 180 pounds before her illness. Even in illness she was quite pretty and usually wore long, dangling turquoise earrings, a cotton shirt, and blue jeans. Her speech and mannerisms were typical of her rural, southern heritage, as was her ability to portray events vividly.

Tess called her childhood "complicated" but said these complications made her stronger. Tess had learned early in her life that it was a tough world and that she had to take care of herself. Displaying mental stamina under the stress of her illness, Tess explained her strengths and "meanness" by describing experiences in her childhood.

I guess I'm that way because I grew up in a bad family. My daddy was a child molester. I never got molested. There was times I thought I would. I slept with a stick. Because of my sister being molested, she has a problem with some things. She jumped on me not long ago 'cause she seen how weak I was. My brother, he's got some kind of a mental problem. I don't know what's wrong with him. He calls me up and harasses me at 3:00 in the morning. See, my family is very complicated. It made me stronger, I think that's what it's done.

According to Tess, the family background influenced her siblings' relationships with her, limiting the amount and kinds of family support, love, and concern that were available to her. In fact, it seemed as if her brother and sister intentionally created problems. Tess spoke about her father but said nothing about her mother, a silence that is puzzling. Although her father died 1 year before the HIV diagnosis, Tess believed her deteriorating condition had been observed by him and possibly contributed to his heart condition and death.

When asked how she coped with her illness, she replied, "I cuss. Actually, I'm a very mean person. Even though I love animals, I'm a mean person. James [her partner and fiancé, also a pseudonym] will tell you that." She looked frail and weak and very ill as she lay on a stretcher during this conversation. When asked about this apparent discrepancy, she explained,

It's a different type [of meanness], it's not being hateful to people. It's not that type of meanness. I'm angry at the world for what we're doing to it. I was like that before I found out I was sick. It's a type of hatefulness, not mean, not like being mean to James' young-'uns. It's like an angry hatefulness.

Tess was very proud of her former physical strength. Before she became weak from AIDS she enjoyed using her strength to fish, handle horses, and ride a motorcycle with James:

Yeah, I was real strong. I could do things most men could do. James is in construction; I've helped him pull heavy loads. I can't do any of that now. I couldn't even hold my horse anymore. I've had to sell my horse because of finances and lack of being able to handle him. I'm just really *deteriorating*. I see myself *deteriorating* every day. I knew it was something serious. I was a really strong person. I was outgoing. I like to fish. I'm at the point now where I can't go fishing by myself, I'm liable to black out.

Tess described her life before AIDS as a way to portray her deteriorating condition and emphasize her losses. So much had changed in her life that she felt powerless and believed she had not coped well with the disease. She could no longer sew or sculpt or paint, activities that had been an integral part of her young adulthood. She had been forced to, as she put it, "let her talents fall":

See, I'm very artistic. I can make things. Just make anything. Things that I see that you can buy, I can make. I do sculptures. We like motorcycles, so we see a lot of biker people. I made halter tops with beads hanging on them, pocketbooks, belts, headbands, just anything you'd want. It's changed. It's killing me to see myself changing like this!

Growing up strong, and developing her talents, defining herself as a strong, mean woman were the story of her life. Then came AIDS.

"DYING YOUNG"

The physicians who treated Tess in the early years of her HIV infection were slow to recognize her symptoms, although they were aware that she had lived with a man with hemophilia:

What's so bad about it is that I went unnoticed for so long and that other people could have really got hurt because of it. And the fellow that gave this to me, he did hurt other people with it. His wife and all, because he didn't know.

For 3 years she had been treated for numerous problems ranging from urinary tract infections to skin problems before she was finally tested for HIV infection. Her repeated attempts to call attention to her potentially positive HIV status were ignored because she was not recognized as being at risk.

I just didn't feel sick but I didn't feel normal either. I couldn't keep up with my friends, didn't want to go out at night, stuff like that. I suspected it for a few years but I knew for sure about 8 months ago. I had made it clear to the doctors that I lived with a hemophiliac and my blood was low then, but they never did test me. When I first come up there to the clinic they said, just looking at me, they said, "You're too healthy to worry about this."

James, her fiancé, always came to the clinic with her. He was a small, bearded man in his 30s, who never said much, just waited for Tess. She was quick to say that James was not the man from whom she caught the virus, rather that he was the man who had stayed by her. There was anger in Tess's voice. Although she was angry about many things, primarily she expressed anger about dying and leaving James. He was the bridge in her life between the happy times and the bad times with AIDS.

Meeting him had been the turning point in her life. He was the man she had always wanted:

Well, for one thing, James's love can fill this room. He supports me 100% on this. Sometimes you go for 3 or 4 weeks and not know what he's thinking or feeling. He's a very quiet person and I'm really insecure about that because I don't know how he really feels about this. He's a good man. If I die, it's upsetting me because I don't want nobody else to have him. I got my opportunity when James came along. He's clean living, he changed my whole life. Now that I've got a man like this, I can't believe he loves me! And now I have to face this. He has sold his motorcycles for me, he went broke trying to keep me in medicine because Social Security won't help me. As many times as I've gotten up to leave, he won't let me go.

Tess was young and wanted what many young women want—a man of her own, a home, and children. Now, at age 25, she was dying of AIDS. In addition to the loss of James, she described an even deeper loss:

My major sadness is the fact that there's babies and children who ain't even going to know what love is about. I'm going to die with this. I can't have any children. That's a big pressure on me now. You don't know how bad you want them until you can't have them.

James's two teenage children lived with them, but that did not seem to replace babies of her own. Tess said the children considered her a hypochondriac because she was frequently ill, and they did not know the nature or seriousness of her health problems. They were not told because Tess feared repercussions on the children if anyone found out she had AIDS.

She described her condition as "deteriorating." She suffered from chronic pulmonary and renal infections, mouth ulcers, and herpes virus blisters. During one conversation, Tess touched a fever blister on her lip and it began to bleed. She dabbed it with a tissue and said,

There were about 2 months I couldn't eat at all or stand up straight because of this AIDS. Everything I would eat would throw spasms through my back. I even thought it was my heart when it first started. It started in my ears, actually, and moved down into my chest. I was so sick that I couldn't go to the grocery store. But the AZT [zidovudine] has changed all that. I haven't had too much trouble with side effects other than my low blood count. I guess because my blood is so bad, that my fever blisters won't heal. This one just pours blood. I still have trouble eating. I can't eat unless the food is fresh fruits. Without the right money, I can't just walk into the grocery store and buy just for me. There's other people in the house that have to eat.

Tess believed that worrying about her medical bills made her many physical problems worse. She and James had no health insurance coverage because James was self-employed. Furthermore, because of her illness Tess could no longer work and help pay her medical bills:

The hospital has been sending me bills and harassing me on the phone. I tell them that I'll start paying the bills as soon as I get some money. They send me information saying that I agreed to pay them and send me envelopes to send my payments in and I can't pay them. I don't think my doctors realize they [hospital billing staff] are harassing me.

Tess had been advised to apply for Social Security benefits. The paperwork and repeated telephone conversations necessary to master that bureaucracy would have been a challenge for anyone but proved especially difficult for a woman dying of AIDS in the late 1980s. She had tried to tell those she had spoken with in the social system that she was too sick to work, but no one seemed to understand that she was dying of AIDS:

I can't decide which is most stressful. The number 1 stress is seeing myself in a coffin, and the number 2 is what Social Security has put me through. Without any kind of help, I don't have any money. Nobody's going to hire me as weak as I am. Social Security just refuses to believe I'm sick.

EPILOGUE

Not long after her interview, James pushed Tess in a wheelchair into the clinic for the last time. She was not scheduled for an appointment that day but because she was so sick, she had called and was told to come into the clinic. She was seen fairly soon by a physician, who decided that she should be admitted to the hospital. Someone helped her from the examining room and left her sitting on a stool in the hallway. James stood by her side.

Tess was so short of breath that all she could say was "I am really sick" when asked how she felt. The clinic nurse said they were waiting for a hospital bed to become available for Tess; meanwhile, she had to wait in the hall so the next clinic patient could be seen in the examination room. Space in the busy clinic was limited. Examination rooms were used for physicians to see patients, not for patients who had to wait for an available hospital bed. Tess was gasping for air. Nurses and assistants hurried by her. Finally, she was taken to a hospital room. Within days, Tess was dead.

DISCUSSION

Loss is the thread running through both stories. Tess told about her former self ("I *was* a strong, mean woman") as a way to contrast who she was against who she became after AIDS. The first story was told as a way to delineate her losses as she detailed her former self. The second story continues the theme of loss as she begins to lose her life.

Kalish[16] described several losses accompanying the dying process: loss of experience, people, control and competence, the capacity to complete projects, and the body. Three of those key losses are especially pertinent in Tess's story: people, the ability to complete projects, and the body. Tess grieved the anticipated loss of James, the man of her dreams, as well as the real loss of her artistic abilities. Long before she knew she had AIDS, Tess experienced the loss of her body as she had known it to be.

Anticipatory grief includes coping with multiple losses in the past, present, and future. Losses of the dying person occur over the dying trajectory[17] as the illness robs the individual of former strength and abilities. This series of losses demands coping strategies that may be especially difficult when the person lacks prior experience with the dying process. Young adults such as Tess may be particularly vulnerable because of limited experience with death and dying.

"The major losses associated with AIDS pervade every facet of a person's life."[18(p14)] Tess's losses were many and profound; they were both experienced and projected. These real and feared losses include occupational and economic status and privacy and autonomy, as well as the more profound losses of self-esteem related to the stigma of AIDS and of support networks, friendships, and loved ones. People with AIDS must also confront an unrelenting loss of vigor and energy along with progressive losses of functioning and self-control. Finally, the dying person must contemplate the ultimate loss of self, including the loss of hopes, dreams, and future.[17,18] As Humphrey noted, the existential issue of being a nonperson is "almost impossible to comprehend, and yet must be confronted when one is facing imminent death."[19(p67)]

Of the adaptational tasks for the dying person identified by Kalish,[20] coping with the loss of loved ones and self seemed to be Tess's priority issues during the time of this study. Tess openly grieved her loss of youth and vigor, her "strong, mean" self, and lamented her daily deterioration. When speaking of her artistic talent, Tess clearly acknowledged her grief over the loss of her former self by proclaiming, "It's killing me to see myself changing like this!" Her pain related to loss of her relationship with James was palpable, and she declared her "major sadness" was in not having a future with children of her own. In final testimony to the inherent difficulty in comprehending one's nonbeing, Tess avowed that her "number 1 stress" was seeing herself in a coffin.

• • •

This narrative portrays one woman's experience with AIDS. Yet it provides an opportunity to understand the progression of HIV disease not from a pathological perspective, but from an experiential viewpoint. Tess's experience with AIDS and the health care system is not unique. Her life circumstances and encounters within the health care environment created a personal narrative that is potentially shared by other women.

Losses associated with AIDS are similar to those experienced in other terminal illnesses but with some distinct differences. Women who have difficulties in obtaining a diagnosis of HIV disease undergo unexplained losses in health status while searching for a cause of their illness. Losses associated with AIDS generally occur over time, as do the associated health changes. Tess's losses were compounded by her youth and her anguish from the existential loss of self. The strength and "meanness" that embodied her resilience and enhanced her survival failed her when confronted with the complexity of the health care system and the devastation of HIV disease.

REFERENCES

1. Rose MA. Health concerns of women with HIV/ AIDS. J Assoc Nurses AIDS Care. 1993;4(3):39–45.
2. Smeltzer SC. Women and AIDS: sociopolitical issues. Nurs Outlook. 1992;30(4):152–156.
3. Centers for Disease Control. Projections of the number of persons diagnosed with AIDS and the number of immunosuppressed HIV-infected persons—United States, 1992–1994. MMWR. 1992; 41(RR-18):1–29.
4. Guinan ME. HIV, heterosexual transmission, and women. JAMA. 1992;268:520–521.
5. Campbell CA. Women and AIDS. Soc Sci Med. 1990;30:407–415.
6. Fletcher SH. AIDS and women: an international perspective. Health Care Women Int. 1990;11: 33–42.
7. Centers for Disease Control. Increased HIV/AIDS mortality among residents aged 25–44 years—Baltimore, Maryland, 1987–1989. MMWR. 1992;41: 708–709, 715.
8. Centers for Disease Control. Update: mortality attributable to HIV infection among persons aged 25–44—United States, 1991 and 1992. MMWR. 1993;42:869–872.
9. Smeltzer SC, Whipple B. Women and HIV infection. Image J Nurs Schol. 1991;23:249–256.
10. Viney LL, Bousfield L. Narrative analysis: a method of psychosocial research for AIDS-affected people. Soc Sci Med. 1991;32:757–765.
11. Larson E, Ropka ME. An update on nursing research and HIV infection. Image J Nurs Schol. 1991;23:4–12.
12. Atkinson P. The ethnography of a medical setting: reading, writing, and rhetoric. Qualitat Health Res. 1992;2:451–474.
13. Hall JM, Stevens PE, Meleis AI. Marginalization: a guiding concept for valuing diversity in nursing knowledge. ANS. 1994;16(4):23–41.
14. Cortazzi M. Narrative Analysis. Washington, DC: Falmer Press; 1993.
15. McCain NL, Gramling LF. Living with dying: coping with HIV disease. Issues Ment Health Nurs. 1992; 13:271–284.
16. Kalish RA. Death, Grief, and Caring Relationships. Monterey, Calif: Brooks/Cole; 1981.
17. Rando TA. A comprehensive analysis of anticipatory grief: perspectives, processes, promises, and problems. In: Rando TA, ed. Loss and Anticipatory Grief. Lexington, Mass: Lexington Books; 1986.
18. Teguis A, Ahmed PI. Living with AIDS: an overview. In: Ahmed PI, ed. Living and Dying with AIDS. New York, NY: Plenum Press; 1992.
19. Humphrey MA. Effects of anticipatory grief for the patient, family member, and caregiver. In: Rando TA, ed. Loss and Anticipatory Grief. Lexington, Mass: Lexington Books; 1986.
20. Kalish RA. The onset of the dying process. Omega. 1970;1:57–69.

CHAPTER 15

A Comparative Analysis of Chronic Disease Prevalence among Older Koreans and Non-Hispanic Whites

Valentine M. Villa, PhD

Steven P. Wallace, PhD

Ailee Moon, PhD

James E. Lubben, MPH, DSW

THE LINK BETWEEN LOW socio-economic status and poor health among the elderly has been well documented.[1] Poverty, low income, and low education levels have been found to be related to poor self-rated health and functioning, and major diseases such as cardiovascular disease, diabetes, cancer, and hypertension (V.M. Villa, S.P. Wallace, A. Moon, J.E. Lubben, unpublished data, 1995).[2-6] The reasons given for the consistent association between low socioeconomic status and poor health include poor access to health care, stresses associated with poverty, substandard and debilitating working conditions associated with low-paying jobs, an absence of resources for dealing with stress, and prevalence of health risk behaviors associated with poor health.[7] Many argue that while the importance of the link between socioeconomic status and health has been recognized in the litera-

This research was supported by Grant RO1-AG11182 from the National Institute on Aging.

Fam Community Health 1997;20(2):1–12
© 1997 Aspen Publishers, Inc.

ture, it is not adequately reflected in gerontologic research, nor is the relevance of the relationship between socioeconomic status and health for health promotion and disease prevention programs.[1,5,8] According to Williams,[6] an understanding of how one's socioeconomic status affects one's health is "critical" to research on health status, and for health programs aimed at improving health outcomes.

Studies exploring the relationship between socioeconomic status and poor health among ethnic minority elderly, in particular, find that health gaps between minorities and non-Hispanic whites narrow when socioeconomic status is held constant (V.M. Villa, E.M. Crimmins, unpublished data, 1993).[7,9] These findings lend support to the argument that health differences between minority and non-minority populations are due in part to socioeconomic differentials, rather than solely to genetic or biological factors related to race or ethnicity. Most studies in this area, however, have focused on black vs white and Hispanic vs white differences in health and have not included Asian-American elders. The absence of Asians from studies exploring the relationship between socioeconomic status and health, according to Takeuchi and Young,[10] is due in part to the prevailing image that all Asian-Americans have high income levels. Closer examination of poverty levels among Asian-Americans finds that of the 17 Asian American groups, 14 have poverty levels above the US average, which is 9.6%.[10] Indeed, Chen[11] reports that poverty rates among elderly Asians range from 7% for Japa-nese to 45% for Vietnamese. According to Takeuchi and Young,[10] myths about financial and educational attainment, as well as viewing the Asian population as a homogeneous group has led policy makers to erroneously conclude that Asians are not at risk for health problems, and to underestimate the health problems of specific Asian populations.

Examination of the health status of the elderly Asian population, in particular the link between socioeconomic status and health status, is warranted in light of the evidence regarding poverty levels found among Asian elders as well as the current and expected dramatic increase in the size of the Asian elderly population.[12-14] Toward this end, this chapter will assess the self-reported prevalence of chronic disease among a sample of older Koreans and non-Hispanic whites living in Los Angeles County. The purpose is threefold:

1. to assess if there are differences in disease between the two populations;
2. to ascertain if these differences persist once socioeconomic status and other social and sociodemographic variables are held constant; and
3. to generate recommendations regarding possible areas of intervention for disease prevention.

BACKGROUND

The Asian population is currently the fastest growing minority population in the United States,[15] doubling in size between 1980 and 1990.[16] There are

7,273,662 Asians in the United States and whereas the total US population grew by 10% between 1980 and 1990, the Asian population grew by 108%. The population age 65 and older is the fastest growing age group in the Asian population, and is expected to represent 10.3% of the Asian population by the end of the century.[17] Within the Asian population, demographic data indicate that the Korean population has increased by 130% since 1980, with the largest increases occurring and expected to continue to occur among the population over age 65.[16,18]

Despite the rapid growth in the Korean elderly population, little is known about the health status of this population. According to Markides and Black[8] as of yet systematic data on the health status (ie, functioning and disability) of *any* of the ethnic subgroups that constitute the Asian population is lacking. The bulk of what is known about the health status of Asian elders is based for the most part on scattered studies of older Chinese, Filipinos, and Japanese.[7] Mortality data indicate that there are no significant differences in mortality between these populations and whites.[8] According to Liu and Yu[19] mortality data have been used "judiciously" to make inferences about the health of Asian populations but they are "woefully" inadequate, and exclude politically impotent and invisible minorities within the Asian population such as Koreans. The few studies that have focused on morbidity indicate that older Asian Americans are disadvantaged for high blood pressure, cardiovascular disease, diabetes, coronary heart disease,

and suicide.[19-21] Extrapolation of the results of these data to older Koreans or other Asian subgroups is unwise given the cultural, socioeconomic status, and demographic diversity of Asians.[12,22]

The limited data on the health status of older Koreans indicate that poor eyesight, diminished hearing, high blood pressure, digestive disorders, and diabetes are among the population's major health problems.[23,24] A recent investigation by the authors utilizing the same data as used in the current analysis found that the sociodemographic indicators of ethnicity, age, education, and morbidity are related to poor self-rated health and difficulty in some areas of functioning among older Koreans (personal data). This finding is consistent with research conducted on other minority populations that demonstrates that low socioeconomic status and lack of social support, as well as advanced age and being female, are related to poor health and decreases in "well-being" in old age, and help explain differences in health that are observed between minority populations and non-Hispanic whites.[1,25-29] Absent from these analyses, however, is an examination of whether these same determinants are related to morbidity, specifically the prevalence of chronic conditions among Asian elders. An analysis of morbidity and the factors related to morbidity is necessary if health researchers are to gain insight into the health status of older Koreans and ultimately design more effective disease prevention programs.

Therefore, in the following analysis a logistic regression analysis was performed to test the effect of socioeconomic status, other sociodemographic indicators, and social isolation on chronic disease among older Koreans and non-Hispanic whites. The investigators were interested in whether differences in disease prevalence exist between older Koreans and non-Hispanic whites, after socioeconomic status, other sociodemographic variables, and social isolation were held constant. These are the specific hypotheses of this study:

- Korean elders will have higher prevalence of disease than non-Hispanic whites.
- Differences in disease prevalence among older Koreans and non-Hispanic whites will be related to socioeconomic indicators and social isolation.

These hypotheses are based on the data presented above regarding the impact that socioeconomic status, sociodemographic indicators, and social support have on the health status of the older population, as well as data that reveal that 16% of the older Korean population are in poverty, and that many are experiencing a decrease in status within the family and witnessing a decline in filial piety, both of which have been found to be related to poor health and difficulty in functioning among other minority populations.[18,23,30]

DATA AND METHODS

Data for this analysis come from a self-weighting multistage sample of older Koreans and non-Hispanic whites residing in Los Angeles County in 1993. Respondents were chosen using a three-stage probability sampling method in selection of census tracts blocks and households. The Korean population was drawn from households in 130 randomly sampled blocks in the 25 census tracts of Los Angeles County, where Koreans comprise 15% or more of the population. The non-Hispanic white population was selected from households in 60 randomly sampled blocks in 861 census tracts of Los Angeles County, where the non-Hispanic white population exceeds any other racial ethnic group (ie, Asian, African American, and Hispanic). The response rate was 74% for the Korean sample and 76% for the non-Hispanic white sample. A total of 223 Koreans and 201 non-Hispanic whites participated in the study. Participants range in age from 65 to 97.

A questionnaire was administered in person to study participants by trained interviewers. In addition to health status items, the questionnaire also contains items that measure the level of social support, socioeconomic status, and other sociodemographic indicators. The questionnaire was translated into Korean using a back translation method. The Korean version was reviewed by two focus groups, five bilingual health and service agency workers in Koreatown, Los Angeles, and six Korean elders to ensure that the questionnaire was congruent with written Korean language usage and easy to understand. All interviews with Korean elders were conducted in Korean. To increase data reliability, cards displaying multiple response categories provided visual cues. While Koreans in this study are only representative of Koreans that live in neighborhoods with substantial proportions of older Koreans, the decreased representativeness of the sample is balanced by the improved data quality obtained by face-to-face interviews, as well as random house selection made possible by this sampling.

These chronic diseases are included in the analysis: osteoporosis, heart disease, arthritis, stroke, diabetes, hypertension, chronic lung disease, chronic kidney disease, chronic liver disease, and cancer. In the survey respondents are asked to indicate whether or not they have ever had the specified disease.

Two indicators of socioeconomic status are included in the analysis: income and education. Income reflects the combined income of respondents and their spouses. Data on income were collapsed into three categories. The official 1993 poverty level was used as a guide in constructing the income categories. Category 1 includes respondents with incomes below the poverty level (<$8,500). Category 2 includes respondents with incomes that fall between poverty and up to 200% of the poverty level ($8,500–$17,000). Category 3 includes all individuals above 200% of the poverty level (>$17,000). Other sociodemographic indicators included in this analysis are ethnicity, age, and gender. Ethnicity is constructed as a dummy variable, such that 1 = Korean and 0 = non-Hispanic white. Age is a continuous variable covering the range from 65 to 97. Gender is coded as a dummy variable, 1 = female, 0 = male.

Social isolation is measured using the Lubben Social Network Scale (LSNS).[31] The LSNS is a refinement of the Berkman-Syme Social Network Index (BSNI).[32] That is, the LSNS was modified specifically for use with the elderly population. The LSNS is an equally weighted sum of 10 aspects of an elderly person's social network. It examines the size of a person's active network, the size of the intimate network, confidant relationships, and frequency of contact. Possible scores range from 0 to 50. Low scores on the LSNS indicate weaker social networks. A score of 25 or lower is indicative of a respondent being "at risk" of isolation.[25] For the purpose of this analysis we created a dummy variable for risk of isolation where scores of 0 to 25 on the LSNS are at "risk of isolation," and scores greater than 25 are "not at risk of isolation."

A descriptive analysis of the independent variables, and the prevalence of disease among the sample, is presented. Next, a logistic regression analysis is performed.

RESULTS

The results of the descriptive analysis indicate that the older non-Hispanic white population is significantly more educated than the Korean population, and a significantly higher percent of older Koreans report low income levels (Table 15–1). Older non-Hispanic whites are significantly older than the Korean population. No other sociodemographic differences were found. Additionally, there were no differences between the two populations for risk of social isolation.

The disease prevalence pattern is more favorable for non-Hispanic whites in some diseases, and more favorable for

Table 15-1. Sociodemographic and social isolation indicators of older Koreans and non-Hispanic whites

	Korean (%)	Non-Hispanic white (%)	Chi-square
Age, yr			
65–74	63	46	15.83*
75–84	33	42	
> 85	4	12	
Female	59	64	1.14
Education, yrs			
< 10	56	11	102.15†
10–12	29	41	
> 13	15	48	
Income, $			131.74‡
< 8,500	22	62	
8,500–17,000	26	35	
> 17,000	52	3	
At risk of isolation	10	11	.2772

* $p < .05$
† $p < .01$
‡ $p < .001$

Koreans in others. Koreans reported a higher prevalence of diabetes and kidney disease, while non-Hispanic whites reported a higher prevalence of cancer, stroke, and osteoporosis (Table 15–2). There were no significant differences between the two populations for the prevalence of heart disease, arthritis, hypertension, chronic lung disease, and chronic liver disease. Arthritis and hypertension are the two most common chronic conditions in both groups.

Results of the logistic regression analysis indicate that the non-Hispanic white disadvantage for stroke and cancer remains significant even when controlling for socioeconomic status, sociodemographic variables, and social isolation (Table 15–3). Specifically, older whites are more likely to report having had a stroke and more likely to report having cancer than older Koreans. The Korean disadvantage for kidney disease remains significant, such that older Koreans are two times more likely to report having chronic kidney disease when all categories of variables are held constant. The older Korean disadvantage relative to non-Hispanic whites for diabetes does not remain significant when socioeconomic status, sociodemographic indicators, and risk of isolation are held constant; still Koreans are twice as likely to report having diabetes.

DISCUSSION

Support for the hypotheses was not found; older Koreans in this study were not disadvantaged relative to whites for the majority of diseases. Further, the results reveal that socioeconomic status, sociodemographic, and social isolation controls do not eliminate ethnic differences in disease in any substantial way. Therefore, the differences between Koreans and non-Hispanic whites are not simply a function of different demographic distributions. Because of their lower income levels and low education level it was expected that the Korean sample would be in worse health than the non-Hispanic white sample. An important question, then, for further discussion is, Why do Koreans who have significantly lower education and income levels do better than non-Hispanic whites on the majority of the disease indicators?

One explanation may be that the Korean sample are all immigrants; moreover, they are recent immigrants. The mean number of years in the United States for the Korean sample is 11. The mean age at migration is 62 years old, with 60% of Koreans in the study immigrating to the United States at age 60 or above. The finding that Koreans are not disadvantaged relative to non-Hispanic whites for most disease indicators despite their low socioeconomic status, coupled with the fact that they are all immigrants, lends credence to the "selective migration" perspective. The selective migration perspective proposes that it is the healthier members of a population who immigrate because they are better able to withstand the immigration process than less healthy members of a population.[33] Therefore, immigrants are generally "healthier" than the native born population.[8]

Table 15–2. Disease prevalence among older Koreans and non-Hispanic whites

% Reporting disease	Korean	Non-Hispanic white	Chi-square
Osteoporosis	3	10	8.23*
Heart disease	28	25	.62
Arthritis	45	47	.25
Diabetes	20	11	5.99*
Hypertension	40	45	1.03
Chronic lung disease	9	7	.58
Chronic liver disease	4	1.5	2.49
Chronic kidney disease	6	2.5	3.55†
Cancer	3	13	16.99‡
Stroke	4	11	8.70*

*$p < .01$
†$p < .05$
‡$p < .001$

Table 15–3. Regression of disease on selected sociodemographic and social support variables*

	Osteoporosis	Arthritis	Stroke	Diabetes	Chronic kidney disease	Cancer
Korean	−.4733	.0949	−1.651[†]	.6302	1.385[†]	−1.258[†]
	(.6229)	(1.100)	(.1918)	(1.878)	(2.504)	(.2841)
Age	−.0045	.0131	.0136	−.0068	−.0073	.0198
	(.9955)	(1.013)	(1.014)	(.9932)	(.9927)	(1.020)
Female	2.819[‡]	.7725[‡]	−1.320[‡]	−.2829	−.6371	.3512
	(16.76)	(2.165)	(.2672)	(.7536)	(.5288)	(1.421)
Income	.3162	.0583	−.2486	.0366	−.4069	.1475
	(1.372)	(1.060)	(.7799)	(1.037)	(.6657)	(1.159)
Education	.0392	−.0130	−.0713	−.0137	−.0469	.0182
	(1.040)	(.9871)	(.9312)	(.9864)	(.9542)	(1.018)
Social isolation	−.8339	−.3153	1.1334[†]	−.2575	−.5739	−.3621
	(.4344)	(1.060)	(3.107)	(.7730)	(.5633)	(.6962)

*Odds ratios in parentheses.
[†]$p < .05$
[‡]$p < .01$

While socioeconomic status and other controls did not eliminate disease differences between the populations, there are prevalence rates for certain diseases that merit discussion. Diabetes and chronic kidney disease are the two disease conditions where a Korean disadvantage is observed. While the Korean disadvantage for diabetes relative to non-Hispanic whites is no longer significant after controlling for the socioeconomic status, sociodemographic, and social isolation variables, it does remain positive and close to twice the ratio of the cross tab. The findings relative to diabetes suggest that preventive interventions are warranted among the Korean elderly population. Diabetes is a chronic condition that

carries with it negative consequences for quality of life and mortality if not properly controlled. Diabetes-related complications include end-stage renal disease, blindness, and lower extremity amputations.[34] Obesity, poor diet, and a sedentary lifestyle are related to adult onset diabetes,[34] therefore areas of intervention for older Koreans at minimum should include attention to proper diet, and adequate levels of exercise.

While there are no differences with regard to arthritis and hypertension between the populations, both Koreans and non-Hispanic whites have high rates for both diseases. These health problems, relative to Koreans, may not have been severe enough to dissuade immigration, still they are progressive conditions that can lead to serious limitations in functioning and debilitation later on. Therefore, health promotion that emphasizes the impact that proper diet and exercise can have in slowing the disease process, managing pain, and increasing mobility and functioning is warranted. For example, the prevalence of hypertension among Korean elders may be explained in part by the use of "chaut," a pickled fish brine high in salt that is regularly used in a traditional Korean diet as a marinade. Health promotion efforts, therefore, targeted to this population should educate older Koreans on the potential hazard this food may pose for their health, relative to hypertension. Furthermore, because the Korean population is an immigrant population targeted intervention efforts should be made that are language and culturally appropriate (ie, brochures and outreach efforts should be in Korean). Diet suggestions should call for foods that are "healthy" but that are also consistent with a Korean, rather than Western, diet (ie, suggest vegetables and fruits that are traditionally eaten in Korean culture). For example, "kim-chee," a cabbage-like vegetable, is high in vitamins and is a staple of the Korean diet. While it is a healthful food, it is traditionally prepared with great quantities of salt and spice. Appropriate diet intervention could aim at suggestions regarding alternative methods for preparing kim-chee that require less salt.

Further exploration of areas of intervention for disease prevention among Koreans should explore the role of health practices in determining disease and disease differences between older Koreans and non-Hispanic whites. Studies on other populations have found that smoking, poor diet, and lack of exercise are related to morbidity.[35,36] An analysis by the authors using these data found some differences in health practices between these two populations (ie, older Korean males smoke more than non-Hispanic white males and older Korean women are less active than non-Hispanic white women).[37] Further, analyses utilizing these data should examine whether or not health practices predict disease prevalence among this population. In this regard, both practices that are health debilitating as well as health promoting should be examined. For example, the prevalence of cancer and stroke is relatively small for older Koreans. Therefore, a follow-up analysis should not only examine those health behaviors that are related to diabetes prevalence among Koreans, but also those practices that "insulate" them from cancer and stroke. Examination of the way that minority populations maintain their health in spite of environmental or structural barriers (ie, discrimination, poverty, poor living conditions) is necessary for designing more effective disease prevention and health promotion programs.

In designing health programs for minority or immigrant populations, researchers should consider cultural factors (ie, acculturation level, language ability, cultural practices and cultural beliefs) that may impact prevention and health promotion efforts. Among this population of Korean elders, all are foreign born and the majority immigrated to the United States at older ages. Prevention and treatment of chronic conditions, therefore, cannot occur within the context of standard procedures. Further analysis should explore health values and beliefs about disease prevention, as well as what motivates older Koreans to seek preventive medical treatment, or to participate in health promotion programs.[38]

• • •

In conclusion, the pattern of chronic diseases and socioeconomic status reported by older Koreans presents a complex picture. Older Koreans have much lower education and income levels than non-Hispanic whites, leading us to expect increased rates of chronic diseases associated with low income. Yet both the simple rates as well as the rates after adjusting for sociodemographic variables show that older Koreans have a generally similar pattern of chronic illnesses. The only conditions that older Koreans are more likely to report are kidney disease and diabetes, but they are less likely to report stroke and cancer. The lack of relationship between socioeconomic status and these conditions is probably influenced by the selective migration that often occurs, with healthier persons migrating. The recent immigrant nature of

most older Koreans could therefore be a major cause of their positive chronic condition profile in comparison to non-Hispanic whites. Yet the prevalence of chronic diseases among older non-Hispanic whites is not ideal, and both groups would benefit from increased attention to hypertension control and the symptomatic treatment of arthritis.

The very factor that may benefit older Koreans—their recent immigration—also then becomes a complicating factor since they remain much more "Korean" than "American" in their health behaviors, values, and expectations. Addressing the health needs of this community thus requires additional work to design screening programs and interventions that fit a Korean way of life. The need to tailor both the targeting of needs and interventions makes it obvious that there is no single Asian formula that can work for the diversity of older Asians. The third-generation Japanese-American, the Filipino World War II veteran who has been in the United States for 40 years, and the recently arrived older Korean will each have very different needs in addition to different cultures and experiences. In order to provide adequate health services to all Americans, health researchers must incorporate knowledge of the great diversity of Americans into our health services.

REFERENCES

1. Mutchler JE, Burr JA. Racial differences in health and health care service utilization in later life: the effect of socioeconomic status. *J Health Social Behav.* 1992;32:342–356.
2. Antonovsky A. Social class, life expectancy and overall mortality. *Milbank Mem Fund Q.* 1967;45:31–73.
3. Syme SL, Berkman LF. Social class susceptibility and sickness. In: Conrad P, Kern R, eds. *The Sociology of Health and Illness: Critical Perspectives.* New York: St. Martin's; 1981.
4. Feinstein JS. The relationship between socioeconomic status and health. *Milbank Q.* 1993;71: 279–322.

5. Kaplan GA, Haan MN, Syme SL, Minkler M, Windeby M. Socioeconomic status and health. In: Amler RW, Dull HB, eds. *Closing the Gap: The Burden of Unnecessary Illness.* New York, NY: Oxford University Press; 1987.

6. Williams DR. Socioeconomic differentials in health: a review and redirection. *Social Psychol Q.* 1990; 53:81–99.

7. Markides K, Mindel CH. *Aging and Ethnicity.* Newbury Park, Calif: Sage Publications; 1987.

8. Markides K, Black SA. Race, ethnicity, and aging: the impact of inequality. In: Binstock RH, George LK, eds. *Handbook of Aging and the Social Sciences.* 4th ed. San Diego, Calif: Academic Press; 1994.

9. Jackson JJ. Social determinants of the health of aging black populations in the United States. In: Jackson JJ, ed. *The Black American Elderly.* New York, NY: Springer; 1988.

10. Takeuchi DT, Young KNJ. Overview of Asian and Pacific Islander Americans. In: Zane NWS, Takeuchi DT, Young, KNJ, eds. *Confronting Critical Health Issues of Asian and Pacific Islander Americans.* Newbury Park, Calif: Sage Publications; 1994.

11. Chen Y. Improving the economic security of minority persons as they enter older age. *Minority Elders—Five Goals Towards Building a Public Policy Base,* ed 2. Washington, DC: The Gerontological Society of America; 1994.

12. Angel JL, Hogan DP. Demography of minority populations. In: *Minority Elders.* Washington, DC: The Gerontological Society of America; 1994.

13. Berkanovic E, Lubben JE, Kitano HL, Chi I. The physical, mental, and social health status of older Chinese: a cross-national study. *J Aging Social Policy.* 1994;6(3):73–87.

14. Wykle M, Kaskel B. Increasing the longevity of minority older adults through improved health status. In: *Minority Elders.* Washington, DC: The Gerontological Society of America; 1994.

15. Browne C, Broderick A. Asian and Pacific Island elders: issues for social work practice and education. *Social Work.* 1994;39(3):252–259.

16. US Bureau of the Census. *Poverty in the United States: Current Population Survey Reports. 1990.* Series P-60. No.175, Table 3. Washington, DC: Government Printing Office; 1990.

17. Ong P. *California's Asian Population, Past Trends and Projections for the Year 2000.* R892 Los Angeles, Calif: Graduate School of Architecture and Urban Planning and Asian American Studies Center, University of California, Los Angeles; 1989.

18. Yamamoto J, Rhee S, Chang D. Psychiatric disorders among elderly Koreans in the United States. *Community Mental Health J.* 1994;30(1):17–27.

19. Liu WT, Yu E. Asian/Pacific American elderly: mortality differentials, health status, and use of health services. *J Appl Gerontol.* 1985;4(1):35–64.

20. Polednak AP. *Racial and Ethnic Differences in Disease.* New York, NY: Oxford University Press; 1989.

21. Morioka-Douglas N, Yeo G. *Aging and Health: Asian/Pacific Island American Elders.* Stanford, CA: Stanford Geriatric Education Center; 1990.

22. Antonucci TC, Cantor MH. Strengthening the family support system for older minority persons. In: *Minority Elders.* Washington, DC: The Gerontological Society of America; 1994.

23. Furuto SM, Biswas R, Chung DK, Murase K, Ross-Sheril L. *Social Work Practice With Asian Americans.* Newbury Park, Calif: Sage Publications; 1992.

24. Lee JA, Yeo G, Gallagher-Thompson D. Cardiovascular disease risk factors and attitudes towards prevention among Korean-American elders. *J Cross-Cultural Gerontol.* 1993;8:17–33.

25. Rubinstein RL, Lubben JE, Mintzer JE. Social isolation and social support: an applied perspective. *J Appl Gerontol.* 1994;13(1):58–72.

26. House J, Kessler R, Herzog A, Mero R, Kinney A, Breslow M. Social stratification, age, and health. In: Schaie K, Blazer D, House J, eds. *Aging, Health Behaviors and Health Outcomes.* Hillsdale, NJ: Lawrence Erlbaum Associates; 1992.

27. Mor-Barak ME, Miller LS, Syme LS. Social networks, life events, and health of the poor, frail elderly: a longitudinal study of the buffering versus the direct effect. *Fam Community Health.* 1991; 14(2):1–13.

28. Verbrugge L. Gender, aging, and health. In: Markides K, ed. *Aging and Health, Perspectives on Gender, Race, Ethnicity, and Class.* Newbury Park, Calif: Sage Publications; 1989.

29. Syme S, Berkman L. Social class, susceptibility, and sickness. *J Epidemiol.* 1976;104(1):1–8.

30. Choi WG. Korean-American elderly in New York. *Joong ang iibo,* p. 4, July 1978.

31. Lubben JE. Assessing social networks among elderly populations. *Fam Community Health.* 1988; 11(3):42–52.

32. Berkman LF, Syme SL. Social networks, host resistance, and mortality: a nine-year follow-up study of Alameda County residents. *Am J Epidemiol.* 1979;109:186–204.

33. Gardner R. Mortality. In: Zane NWS, Takeuchi DT, Young KNJ, eds. *Confronting Critical Health Is-*

sues of Asian and Pacific Islander Americans. Newbury Park, Calif: Sage Publications; 1994.

34. US Public Health Service. *Healthy People 2000: National Health Promotion and Disease Prevention Objectives.* Washington, DC: Government Printing Office; 1991.

35. James SA, Keenan NL, Browning S. Socioeconomic status, health behaviors, and health status among blacks. In: Schaie KW, Blazer D, House JS, eds. *Aging, Health Behaviors, and Health Outcomes.* Hillsdale, NJ: Lawrence Erlbaum Associates; 1992.

36. Kaplan GA. Health and aging in the Alamada County Study. In: Schaie KW, Blazer D, House JS, eds. *Aging, Health Behaviors, and Health Outcomes.* Hillsdale, NJ: Lawrence Erlbaum Associates; 1992.

37. Wallace SP, Villa VM, Moon A, Lubben JE. Health practices of Korean elderly people: national health promotion priorities and minority community needs. *Fam Community Health.* 1996;19 (2):29–42.

38. Kiyak HA, Hooyman NR. Minority and socioeconomic status: impact on quality of life in aging. In: Abeles RP, Gift HC, Ory MG. eds. *Aging and Quality of Life.* New York, NY: Springer; 1994.

CHAPTER 16

The Use of Medication Dispensers in Residential Care Homes

Hazel W. Chappell, MSN, RN

Connie Dickey, MSN, RN

Mary DeLetter, PhD, RN

IN AN ERA IN WHICH HEALTH care is moving out of the hospital and into the community, a variety of settings are used to provide various levels of health care. In the US Department of Veterans Affairs (VA) system, the residential care program is a community-based program in which veterans are provided with community-based assisted living. These veterans are often older, have multiple chronic physical illnesses, and frequently have mental health disorders that prohibit them from living independently. Thus, they require at least a minimal level of supervision in day-to-day living. These veterans are particularly vulnerable because they have no family or significant others to offer such care; thus, they are placed in residential care homes.

As is common in the general population, veterans with chronic illnesses typically maintain their optimal levels of health through the use of one or more

Funding for this study was received from Apex Medical, Inc., Sioux Falls, South Dakota.

Fam Community Health 1997;20(2):48–57
© 1997 Aspen Publishers, Inc.

medications. The significantly cognitively or physically impaired individuals require administration of their medications to be supervised or performed by others. Traditionally, caregivers in residential care situations have administered medications from individual bottles. However, the accuracy with which this is done is extremely difficult to monitor. It is often assumed that the caregivers can accurately provide medication supervision, yet they have less education and training than home health aides, who typically are restricted by law from filling medication dispensers for their clients. The purpose of this study was to determine whether the use of medication dispensers by caregivers of veterans in residential care homes would improve medication administration accuracy.

This study was conducted within an existing residential care program at a VA Medical Center. A residential care home is a state-licensed and VA-approved private home in which the owner provides board and care at a set rate for veterans requiring minimal supervision and assistance with activities of daily living. The term *resident* refers to a veteran who lives in a residential care home. The individuals who provide board and care for groups of one to six residents are referred to as "caregivers." The caregivers have minimal training (4 hours per year at their local VA Medical Center) and are provided with a reference guidebook for day-to-day referral. Caregivers are paid monthly according to the complexity of care required by their residents. Unlike many other board and care homes, these residential care homes are visited annu-

ally by an inspection team, consisting of a master's prepared community health nurse, licensed social worker, registered dietitian, and a safety engineer. In addition, the social workers visit on a monthly basis to evaluate the residents' ongoing living situation.

One of the major responsibilities of these caregivers is medication administration for their residents. Our goal with this study was to determine whether the use of medication dispensers by caregivers of veterans in residential care homes would improve medication administration accuracy.

REVIEW OF LITERATURE

Most of the literature regarding medication administration has focused on strategies for decreasing medication errors and improving medication compliance in two situations: medication delivery by trained health care providers and self-administration by community-dwelling patients. Little attention has been given to medication delivery by caregivers in other community or residential care settings.

Conn and associates[1] found that for older adults, medication adherence was inversely correlated with medication regimen complexity. However, they suggested that complexity involves more than just the number of medications or the number of pills prescribed. They observed that the most commonly reported reason for not taking medications correctly was forgetfulness. Gravely and Oseasohn[2] found that ethnicity and number of daily prescribed pills were two predictors of noncompliance in an elderly self-medication veteran population.

The two most common interventions for increasing compliance or decreasing administration errors are educational programs and specialized delivery systems. Various types of educational programs have been effective for high-risk patient groups such as the elderly or chronically mentally ill.[3] Hawe and Higgins[4] demonstrated the effect of a group-based educational program for previously noncompliant elders who required four or more medications. A significantly higher percentage of the educational group were compliant compared with the control group. Cargill[5] demonstrated the effectiveness of educational programs combined with follow-up phone calls from nurses for elderly patients from a general medicine clinic. Those patients who received both the educational sessions and the follow-up phone calls were more compliant than the patients who received either no intervention or the educational program alone. Whyte[6] provided written medication cards to 24 elderly subjects discharged from a medicine ward. When compared with a control group of 24 elders, those receiving the medication cards made fewer errors and had greater medication knowledge, as well as a more favorable attitude. The only report of a medication administration strategy in congregate housing was that of Joyner and associates.[7] They described the benefits of a medication-monitoring service provided by a clinical pharmacist to geriatric patients in two congregate housing facilities for 18 months. The investigators reported a

96% mean compliance rate, but the study lacked scientific design and the report provided little supportive data.

Other investigators evaluated various medication administration systems for reducing medication errors and improving compliance. Bazire[8] demonstrated that the use of a one-week medication dispenser increased compliance of psychiatric patients with anxiety or unstable moods. However, its use was not effective for patients with cognitive dysfunction. Similarly, Wong[9] evaluated a commercially prepared calendar mealtime blister-pack for elderly veterans with a controlled crossover design. Noncompliance decreased significantly with use of this device. Those patients who lived alone and administered all their own medications demonstrated an even greater compliance with the blister-pack than with the standard medication bottles. Other variables such as age, mental status, frequency of medication administration, and number of doses prescribed did not influence the compliance rates. Murray and colleagues[10] also demonstrated that reducing the number of doses per day and providing patients with a "unit of use" dispensing system was effective. Medication compliance was higher for those subjects who used the special dispensing system twice daily than for two other groups: those who had no change in dosing or packaging and those who used twice-daily dosing with standard medication bottles.

Although various patient reminder systems have been used for many years, these systems do not necessarily improve accuracy in administration.[11] Limited information exists on the efficacy of strategies for both improving compliance and reducing error rate. In our own residential care program, we were looking for a means of increasing medication administration accuracy for caregivers supervising small groups of residents.

METHODS

A two-group experimental posttest only design was used. The caregivers were randomly assigned to groups. The control group of caregivers used the traditional prescription bottle method of administering medications on a daily schedule, depending on memory to determine whether medications had been given and completing a medication record at the end of each day. The experimental group of caregivers were given one medication dispenser for each resident, and administered the medications from this prefilled dispenser rather than the medication bottles. This group also kept a written record of medication administration.

Sample

Subjects for this study were female caregivers who housed male veteran residents in their homes. The subjects were recruited from the residential care program of a single medical center in which 37 caregivers supervise 130 veteran residents. Of these, 27 caregivers supervising 78 residents completed the study. Of the 10 caregivers who were not included, 6 had already participated in a similar pilot program, 2 refused participation, and 2 began the study but withdrew prior to completion.

The variables that determined each caregiver's medication administration workload are listed in Table 16–1. No differences were found between the control and experimental caregiver groups on the number of pills or the number of prescriptions administered per day. However, caregivers in the control group had significantly more residents per home than those in the experimental group (3.5 ± 2.0 and 2.3 ± 0.8, respectively, $t_{27} = 2.17$, $p = .03$).

Table 16–1. Variables affecting caregivers' medication administration workload

Variable	Mean ± SD	Range
Mean age of residents (yr)	66 ± 11	39–85
Mean number of residents per caregiver home	2.9 ± 1.6	1–8
Mean length of resident's stay per home (yr)	7.5 ± 7.6	1–31
Mean number of prescriptions administered by a caregiver per day	7.1 ± 5.3	1–23
Mean number of pills administered by a caregiver per day	16 ± 15	2–66
Mean number of prescriptions administered by a caregiver per resident per day	2.6 ± 1.6	1–7

Measures

Outcome variables were measured weekly for 3 weeks and included a count of medication duplications, omissions, and total errors in administration. Weekly pill counts were made with a KLX automatic tablet counter (Kirby Lester, Stanford, CT) for weekly pill counts. All unopened prescription bottles available in the household were included in the count. All regularly scheduled prescription oral medications administered to residents by caregivers were included in the study. Liquid, external, aerosol, as-needed, and over-the-counter medications were excluded.

Based on the weekly pill counts, total medication errors were broken into two major categories: medication omissions and medication duplications. Caregivers were given the opportunity to explain any omissions or duplications that were knowingly committed, such as a pill that was dropped down the drain or a change in the prescription. Only reported errors were included in the dataset. Precise recordings of the expected and actual pill counts were made.

Procedure

Prior to recruitment, all caregivers in the residential care program were included in an introductory group class on the use of medication dispensers. Next, the caregivers were assigned to one of eight locality zones for randomization to treatment groups. The locality zones were created to avoid protocol contamination, since many of the caregivers

were related, lived in close proximity to each other, or had already established informal communication networks. Written informed consent was obtained from each participating caregiver.

The control group (13 caregivers supervising 46 residents) continued to dispense medications from prescription bottles. Data from these caregivers were obtained on a weekly basis by reviewing self-reported medication records and counting the pills remaining in the residents' prescription bottles. This group of caregivers was fully aware that their medication administration practices were being monitored. Rapport was established through assurance that pill counts would be used to improve medication administration techniques, and not for punitive reasons.

The experimental group (14 caregivers supervising 32 residents) used 7-day medication dispensers for 4 weeks. Prior to the start of the data collection, the caregivers received specific instructions on how to fill each dispenser for each resident using his prescribed regime. Data from this group were collected by examining the medication dispenser, reviewing the medication records, and counting the pills remaining in the medication bottles. The caregivers received follow-up instructions and guidance for each weekly refill of dispensers.

Caregivers in both groups agreed to maintain written documentation of doses knowingly and appropriately missed or duplicated (eg, one caregiver reported dropping a pill in the drain). These doses were not included in the error data but were used to correct the actual pill counts. All caregivers were encouraged to maintain their usual routine, and were assured of no punitive actions as a result of the weekly pill counts. All data were collected in the caregiver's homes. Both groups received the same attention with regard to weekly visits, education, and pill counts.

RESULTS

The frequency of duplicated and omitted doses of prescribed oral medications was monitored over the 3-week period of the study (Table 16–2). The total number of errors made by the 13 control caregivers for their 46 residents was 149, compared with only 30 by the 14 experimental caregivers for their 32 residents. This difference was significant (t_{76} = 2.22; p = .03). The difference in the number of duplication errors was not significant between groups. However, the difference in omission errors was significant (Table 16–3). The control group caregivers committed 113 omissions compared with only 21 from the experimental group caregivers (t_{76} = 2.22; p = .03). Additionally, it was observed that during the 3-week protocol, the number

of medication errors per week decreased for the caregivers using the medication dispensers, but increased for the control group caregivers (Fig 16–1).

In addition to examining the number of errors made by caregivers, the authors evaluated the proportion of residents who encountered medication errors. In the control group homes, errors were made on 33 of the 46, or 72% of the residents. In contrast, only 13 of the 32, or 41% of the residents in the experimental group homes, were subjected to medication errors. Using a chi-square analysis, the difference was significant [$\chi^2(1) = 7.55$; $p < .01$].

The investigators were concerned about the finding that the control group caregivers had significantly more residents per home than the experimental group caregivers. Thus, an analysis of covariance was used to determine whether the number of errors was attributable to the use of the medication dispenser, independent of the number of medications administered and the number of residents in each caregiver's home. Controlling for these two variables, the analysis showed that the number of medications administered per resi-

Table 16–2. Number of medication errors by 27 caregivers in residential care homes

Time	Control group (n = 13)			Experimental group (n = 14)		
	Duplications	Omissions	Total	Duplications	Omissions	Total
Week 1	11	19	30	9	12	21
Week 2	18	24	42	0	5	5
Week 3	7	70	77	0	4	4
Total	36	113	149	9	21	30

Table 16–3. Mean medication errors per patient in residential care homes

	Control group mean (*n* = 46)	Experimental group mean (*n* = 32)	*t*	*p*
Duplications	.78	.28	1.21	ns
Omissions	2.46	.66	1.87	.06*
Total	3.23	.94	2.22	.03†

*$p < .10$
†$p < .05$

dent per day did not affect the total number of errors. However, the number of residents per caregiver significantly affected the error rate (Table 16–4).

It is important, however, to note that the individual caregiver who made the most medication errors had only three residents in her home. This particular caregiver created 22 out of 149 (15%) of the total errors, all of which were due to untimely reordering of a single resident's prescription. This was a common prob-

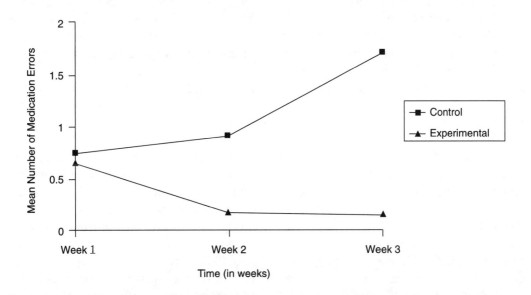

Fig 16–1. Mean number of medication errors per week.

Table 16–4. Analysis of covariance for number of medications per resident and number of residents per caregiver*

Source	df	F	p
Overall model	3	6.7	.0005†
Total number of medications per resident	1	.22	ns
Total number of residents per caregiver	1	19.73	.0001†

ns = not significant.

*There were 27 caregivers administering 191 prescribed medications to 78 residents.
†$p = .0001$

lem in the control group, and accounted for the high frequency of omission errors throughout the 3-week protocol.

A small survey was conducted with the 14 experimental group caregivers to determine if they generally liked the 7-day medication dispensers. Twelve of the caregivers responded to this survey. The majority (75%) reported that the medication dispensers were easier and less time consuming than the traditional method of using each prescription bottle for each dose of medication. All but one caregiver said it was more convenient, and most (67%) perceived less chance of making an error when using the dispensers.

DISCUSSION

Medication is often the major therapeutic intervention for controlling symptom severity associated with chronic illnesses. Given this, the correct administration of medications is crucial. In many home situations, informal caregivers are responsible for the care of only one family member and may be able to administer medications without difficulty. Similarly,

in institutional settings, trained health care providers have fairly sophisticated systems for efficient and accurate medication administration. However, in the residential care program described here, minimally trained caregivers are responsible for administering several prescription medications to several patients each day. Without a systematic administration method, the risk of medication errors is high. Using multiday medication dispensers may be a practical way of improving accuracy of medication administration by nonprofessionally trained caregivers.

In the study, the number of medication errors and the proportion of affected residents were significantly greater for the caregivers using the traditional bottle dispensing method than for the caregivers using the 7-day medication dispenser. Both omissions and duplications occurred less frequently when the medication dispenser was used. In both groups, duplications occurred less often than omissions, and caregivers often could offer no explanations for them. However, the most common reason for omissions was running out of medications before a refilled prescription was available. At the time of this study each outpatient was required to renew prescriptions on a monthly basis. This could be conducted via mail; but when doing so, it required several days for the transaction to be completed. Because the caregivers often did not remember to routinely order medications, but waited until their current supply was nearly depleted, many omission errors occurred.

It is important to emphasize that the number of residents per home was a confounding variable that clearly influenced the medication error rates. However, it also is important to understand that this was not necessarily the root of all errors. In an anecdotal evaluation, the authors found that the caregiver with the greatest number of errors (accounting for 15% of all errors in the control group) had a relatively small resident group size (three residents in the home). As described above, the problem that led to her high frequency of errors was her failure to recognize the need for ordering a prescription refill in a timely manner. This problem was nearly eliminated for the caregivers using the medication dispensers, who indicated that the advance filling of the dispensers alerted them to the need for a prescription refill in a more timely manner.

Although the Hawthorn effect was a concern with this study, it did not appear to have a profound effect on the outcomes. Both groups of caregivers were visited weekly during the protocol, thus, they encountered more frequent one-on-one interaction with the practitioners than is typical in the residential care program.

Pill counts were conducted for all VA residents at both control group and experimental group homes. When errors were found, the investigators discussed them with the caregivers, trying to understand the nature of the error and prevent such future occurrences. Finally, although the method of administration was different between groups, the investigators spent time with caregivers in each group educating them about medication administration efficiency and accuracy. Thus, it was not surprising that the error rate decreased for the experimental group caregivers, but it was surprising that the error rate actually increased for the control group caregivers (Table 16–2).

As expected, the caregivers in the medication dispenser group improved medication administration with education and experience. All caregivers became independent with the dispenser by the fourth week. This is consistent with two previous investigations that also demonstrated that compliance significantly improved with education.[4,5] In the current study, the caregivers who used the medication dispensers expressed overall satisfaction and preference for this method of administration.

This study demonstrated that use of the 7-day medication dispensers was beneficial. The major difference in error rates was not simply an outcome of the intervention, but was confounded by the number of residents per home. Still, we observed that the medication dispensers prompted caregivers to order prescription refills in a timely manner whereas this remained a significant problem for the caregivers using the traditional bottle method. Thus, the control group caregivers had significant omission errors that potentially could have profound impact on individual resident's health.

• • •

Although the use of sophisticated medication administration systems is common in institutional settings, and the use of daily or weekly medication dispensers is common for self-administration, such methods have not been integrated into residential care programs. We believe that minimally trained caregivers of multiple residents need a systematic means for administering medications in an accurate and efficient manner.

REFERENCES

1. Conn VS, Taylor SG, Kelly S. Medication regimen complexity and adherence among older adults. *Image.* 1991;23:231–235.
2. Gravely EA, Oseasohn CS. *Res Nurs Health.* 1991;14:51–58.
3. Smith GR, Knice-Ambinder M. Promoting medication compliance in clients with chronic mental illness. *Holistic Nurs Pract.* 1989;4:70-77.
4. Hawe P, Higgins G. Can medication education improve the drug compliance of the elderly? Evaluation of an in-hospital program. *Patient Educ Counsel.* 1990;16:151–160.
5. Cargill JM. Medication compliance in elderly people: influencing variables and interventions. *J Adv Nurs.* 1992;17:422–426.
6. Whyte LA. Medication cards for elderly people: a study. *Nurs Standard.* 1994;8(48):25–28.
7. Joyner JL, Fikrat HT, Catania PN. Evaluation of a medication-monitoring service for geriatric patients in a congregate housing facility. *Am J Hosp Pharmacol.* 1983;40:1509–1512.
8. Bazire S. An assessment of the "Dosett" compliance aid in psychiatric patients. *Br J Pharmaceut Pract.* 1984:316–320.
9. Wong N. Evaluation of a novel medication aid, the calendar blister-pak, and its effect on drug compliance in a geriatric outpatient clinic. *J Am Geriatr Soc.* 1987;35:21–26.
10. Murray MD, Bird JA, Manatunga AK, Darnell J. Medication compliance in elderly outpatients using twice-daily dosing and unit-of-use packaging. *Ann Pharmacother.* 1993;27:616–621.
11. Simpkins CV, Wenzloff NJ. Evaluation of a computerized reminder system in the enhancement of patient medication refill compliance. *Drug Intell Clin Pharmacy.* 1986;20:799–802.

CHAPTER 17

A Multidisciplinary Health Care Outreach Team to the Homeless: The 10-Year Experience of the Montefiore Care for the Homeless Team

Marcus Plescia, MD, MPH

G. Robert Watts, MPH, MS

Susan Neibacher, MSW

Hal Strelnick, MD

O VER THE LAST TWO decades homelessness has become an increasingly pervasive and seemingly intractable problem in the United States. The causes of homelessness are multiple and have been discussed extensively.[1–5] Voluntary and civic initiatives to address this problem have included providing shelter, food, legal representation, education, counseling, and social services. Health care has become an additional focus because of the higher prevalence of acute and chronic diseases and of mental

The authors would like to acknowledge the work of the following individuals: Edsel O'Connor, CNS; Deborah Barrow, ANP; Eileen O'Connor, FNP; Monica Gayle, FNP; Imogene Evans, BSW; Ken Thompson, MD; and Andrea Fox, MD. It is their dedication and commitment to serving the homeless that has made the Montefiore Care for the Homeless program a success.

Fam Community Health 1997;20(2):58–69
© 1997 Aspen Publishers, Inc.

health and substance abuse problems affecting the homeless population.[2,4–6]

Studies in cities across the United States document inadequate access to health care for the homeless population. Barriers to health care affect homeless families and poor families with homes differently; homeless families have greater problems of access to health care.[7,8] These problems derive from a lack of insurance, lack of a regular primary care provider, and other barriers such as transportation and length of wait to see a care provider. Among homeless adults problems of access are similar.[9] Existing sources of care, mostly hospital emergency rooms, provide fragmented care.

Over the last decade a wide variety of models for providing primary care health services to the homeless population have been created.[10,11] Services may be provided through the use of mobile clinics, permanent facilities built near shelters, and site visits with temporary clinics set up in the facility. Primary care providers may be salaried or voluntary. They include shelter-based nurses, nurse practitioners, physician assistants, and primary care physicians.

This chapter describes the history, philosophy, and interdisciplinary practice of the Care for the Homeless team at Montefiore Medical Center in the Bronx. The team provides regular health care to homeless people at the sites where they live, eat, or congregate. Care is provided regardless of insurance coverage, and free medications and transportation for referrals are often available. Affiliation with a community health center allows the team to mainstream patients in need

of more extensive care into a health care system that remains available to the patient regardless of relocation. Because providers work predominantly with the homeless, the providers are familiar with the unique problems of this needy population.

HISTORY

The National Health Care for the Homeless program was initiated in 1984 by the Robert Wood Johnson Foundation and Pew Charitable Trusts, together with the US Conference of Mayors. As a requirement to obtain funding from this initiative, municipalities had to form partnerships with private advocacy and voluntary organizations serving the homeless; thus, the New York City Coalition for Health Care for the Homeless was formed. Representatives from approximately 25 public and private agencies serving the homeless with diverse roles and ideologies joined the coalition.

Funding was awarded to the New York City Coalition in 1985 to implement its proposed project along with 18 other municipalities. In 1987 a permanent funding stream for these programs was established through the Stewart B. McKinney Homeless Assistance Act (Section 340 of the US Public Health Act). Monies now come from these sources, Ryan White Title IIIb Early Intervention for HIV, Ryan White Titles I and II; the NYC Department of Homeless Services; Medicaid; Comic Relief; and other private philanthropies. In 1993, the administrative component of Care for the Homeless projects became an autonomous body with its own board of directors and administrative staff. Of the initially subcontracted teams, the Montefiore and Bedford Stuyvesant teams remain in operation today.

At the inception of the program, arrangements were made to allow the subcontracted Care for the Homeless teams to use their own addresses for their patients and, thus, receive their Medicaid cards. An expedited application process was also developed and implemented that allows the team social workers to enter data directly into the Medicaid computer system, avoiding the necessity of patients traveling to Medicaid's central office in Manhattan to make their applications.

DESCRIPTION

The Montefiore Care for the Homeless team reaches out to homeless persons in Bronx soup kitchens, transitional housing, and private and public shelters. The project serves homeless people mostly in the South Bronx, a congressional district with a national reputation for its poverty and recent history of urban deterioration.

The team provides integrated medical, social, and mental health services with three principal goals:
1. to care for the immediate needs that prompted the person to approach the team;
2. to build a trusting relationship that will lead the person to turn for help with other problems; and
3. to then mainstream the person into established services such as drug treatment programs, mental health clinics, or community health cen-

ters that have the resources to deal with chronic problems.

Activities are coordinated and supervised by the psychiatric nurse specialist who acts as project director and leads the clinical team. A family physician serves as medical coordinator and supervisor of clinical care.

Since its founding in 1986 the team has provided site visits at least once a week at a number of permanent facilities. To be eligible for services a site must supply the minimum of a sink, a bathroom, and a private area or open space that can be enclosed with screens. In addition, permanent staff at the site are expected to cooperate with the team by making clients aware of the team's services and schedule, ensuring availability of a safe and clean clinical work area, and providing follow-up on treatment plans and referral appointments. On several occasions services have been terminated due to inadequate facilities or lack of cooperation. At this time the team serves six sites: three transitional family shelters, one women's shelter, and two church soup kitchens.

The team provides outreach and care at each site and coordinates more complicated care with available resources. The goal is to introduce clients to a reliable system of care that will remain available to them. Each nurse practitioner has a one-half day clinical session at the Montefiore Family Health Center (FHC) where patients can be seen in a more intensive medical environment. The practice philosophy of the FHC is community-oriented primary care.[12] Access to diagnostic services and consultation with other health professionals are readily available in this setting. Patients needing specialized care are generally seen at the FHC and their evaluation and referral is coordinated by a primary care clinician. Round-trip transportation is arranged for specialty referrals, and a team member will at times accompany the client to the appointment if help is needed negotiating the system.

The homeless team is also a training site for medical residents at the Montefiore Residency Program in Social Medicine, medical students at Albert Einstein College of Medicine and visiting students from other institutions, first- and second-year medical students from the Robert Wood Johnson School of Medicine, and nurse practitioner students from New York University. These electives are pursued by health professionals interested in working with the homeless. Residents and students participate in daily team activities and function in all roles at the health care sites. An emphasis is placed on conveying an understanding of both the medical and social implications of homelessness, and on sensitive and appropriate forms of health care delivery for this population.

PROGRAM EVALUATION

All patient encounters at homeless team sites are recorded on a standard precoded encounter form by a team member. Information is collected on age, sex, ethnicity, diagnoses, interventions, follow-up services and referrals, and third-party reimbursement coverage. Data are compiled at the project administrative office and semiannual reports are prepared that summarize the experience and trends of each team. These data are used to identify areas for improvement in services offered, to monitor the demographics of the populations served, and to track the range of diagnoses identified.

Staffing

In 1992 the Montefiore Care for the Homeless program averaged 1.42 full-time equivalent (FTE) nurse practitioners, 0.27 FTE physician, and one FTE clinical psychiatric nurse specialist. The team expanded to its present size in 1993 to comprise three FTE nurse practitioners in addition to the clinical psychiatric nurse and physician. Additional nurse practitioner staffing was necessary for the team to accept responsibilities for family care at an additional family shelter. The team also has two FTE medical assistants, one FTE health educator, and one FTE outreach worker. The team is ethnically diverse. The four full-time clinicians are all African-American females, as are one medical assistant, the social worker, and the outreach worker. The remaining medical assistant and the health educator are Hispanic females. The physician is a white male.

The majority of documented care is provided by nurse practitioners. In 1995 66% of patients were seen by nurse practitioners compared with 5% by a physician. In addition, 5% of encounters were with the clinical psychiatric nurse, 11% were with the social worker, and 13% were with the health educator. Of the medical encounters 93% were done by a nurse practitioner.

Service delivery and demographics

After an increase in capacity in 1993 the team has seen a steady number of patients at shelter sites throughout the South Bronx (Table 17–1). The majority of patient encounters have been at Kingsbridge, a women's shelter, and at Jackson and Powers family shelters. Love Gospel and POTS, both soup kitchens, remain relatively consistent, and these two sites have been served since the team's inception.

Table 17–2 classifies the patient population by age, sex, and ethnicity. The team has been progressively serving a larger proportion of women than men. In 1993 and 1994 almost two-thirds of patient encounters were with women. The team also provides the majority of services to persons under 35 years of age. Most clients were categorized as African American. Hispanics are the second largest group.

Continuity of care and common diagnoses

Many of the patient encounters, roughly 40%, are single visits. An almost equal percentage of patients return for a total of two to four visits per year. Over the last 4 years, 15% to 20% of patients had greater than 5 visits per year.

An audit of care for patients with human immunodeficiency virus (HIV) was performed on all Care for the Homeless teams by a private consultant during April and May 1993.[13] This revealed that the Montefiore team provided continuous care to 77% of HIV patients seen. On average HIV patients had 10.7 visits per chart, and the team saw 236 patients with HIV during this 2-month period.

Table 17–3 outlines the most common types of problems encountered among the homeless served by the Montefiore team. Well child and adult care are the most frequently documented. The leading medical diagnoses are upper respiratory infections, delayed immunizations, and chemical dependence.

Referrals

During the 1992 to 1995 period from 13% to 21% of patient encounters resulted in a referral outside the team

Table 17–1. Number of encounters at service sites over a 4-year period

Sites	1995	1994	1993	1992
Love Gospel Assembly	662	1,116	891	812
Kingsbridge Women's Shelter	3,229	2,253	2,782	1,569
Part of the Solution	302	478	159	296
Thorpe Family Residence	525	507	337	361
Powers Family Shelter	98	1,020	1,817	1,650
Jackson Family Shelter	1,854	1,774	795	
Family Health Center	335	492	373	293
Total	7,005	7,640	7,154	4,981

Table 17–2. Patient demographics

Demographics	1995 n (%)	1994 n (%)	1993 n (%)	1992 n (%)
Men	603 (0.3)	1017 (0.33)	887 (0.31)	798 (0.35)
Women	1396 (0.7)	2036 (0.67)	2053 (0.69)	1471 (0.65)
African American	1183 (0.59)	1764 (0.57)	1416 (0.58)	1331 (0.59)
Hispanic	530 (0.26)	872 (0.29)	824 (0.28)	671 (0.3)
White	131 (0.07)	172 (0.06)	191 (0.07)	173 (0.07)
Other	155 (0.08)	244 (0.08)	209 (0.07)	94 (0.04)
< 20 yr old	369 (0.18)	834 (0.29)	763 (0.26)	530 (0.23)
20–34 yr old	690 (0.35)	1045 (0.34)	1113 (0.38)	902 (0.4)
35–44 yr old	524 (0.26)	693 (0.23)	686 (0.28)	518 (0.23)
> 45 yr old	416 (0.21)	481 (0.14)	378 (0.13)	319 (0.14)

(Table 17–4). Many referrals are to community health centers. Approximately 200 visits (20% of those referred) each year are to the team's health center affiliate, where patients continue to be cared for by the nurse practitioner. Most prenatal patients at the family shelters are referred to nearby facilities that are closer than the health center affiliate. Heavy referral patterns are seen for substance abuse programs, social services, and mental health centers.

DISCUSSION

General characteristics

The data presented show staffing patterns, productivity, demographics, continuity, diagnoses, and referrals during the latter half of the team's first decade of existence. These data are limited to a discrete segment of the homeless population, coding and collection have not been rigorous, and there are no data on patient outcomes. Nonetheless, certain aspects of the data reflect the team's experience and can be instructive for other programs designed to serve the homeless.

Over the last 10 years the team has served a significant number of homeless individuals in a variety of settings. As the team has expanded, the number of patient encounters has almost doubled. The authors believe that the team serves a particularly isolated and transitory homeless population in the soup kitchen sites, and it is for this reason these services are continued despite limited space and resources, and decreased productivity. The majority of patient encounters occur in three family shelters. With the recent increase over the last decade in family homelessness this seems an important emphasis. Homeless families are generally less transitory than single adults, allowing better follow-up of acute prob-

Table 17–3. Common diagnoses

Diagnosis	1995 *n* (%)	1994 *n* (%)	1993 *n* (%)	1992 *n* (%)
Well adult/child	392 (0.2)	503 (0.17)	488 (0.17)	272 (0.12)
Delayed immunizations	276 (0.14)	337 (0.11)	193 (0.07)	95 (0.04)
Chemical dependence	232 (0.14)	296 (0.13)	301 (0.14)	307 (0.18)
Upper respiratory infection	291 (0.18)	540 (0.18)	438 (0.15)	154 (0.11)
Asthma	141 (0.07)	153 (0.05)	168 (0.06)	117 (0.05)
Rashes	140 (0.07)	184 (0.06)	106 (0.04)	106 (0.05)
Otitis	99 (0.05)	129 (0.04)	146 (0.05)	60 (0.03)
Depressive reaction	64 (0.04)	52 (0.02)	37 (0.02)	28 (0.02)
Anxiety	47 (0.03)	46 (0.02)	47 (0.02)	41 (0.02)
AIDS	119 (0.07)	141 (0.06)	147 (0.06)	51 (0.03)
Sexually transmitted disease	79 (0.05)	127 (0.06)	145 (0.06)	114 (0.06)
Pregnancy	53 (0.04)	115 (0.08)	98 (0.07)	73 (0.06)
Anemia	64 (0.03)	166 (0.05)	46 (0.02)	25 (0.01)
Hypertension	86 (0.04)	71 (0.02)	69 (0.02)	53 (0.02)
HIV positive	69 (0.04)	66 (0.03)	80 (0.03)	19 (0.01)

lems and easier tracking within the shelter system. Recent debate over welfare reform reveals a degree of political sensitivity concerning children living in poverty, and a likely mandate to continue Medicaid coverage for them. Unfortunately the same is not true for single adults.

Most of the clients served by the team are of African American or Hispanic ethnicity. This is consistent with the Bronx, which comprises mostly ethnic minorities, and with national demographics showing a greater prevalence of homelessness among minority groups. Data on age show a relatively young population, which likely reflects the team's work with a large maternal and child health population in the family shelters. Finally,

the team has been seeing a larger proportion of women than men. This is not reflective of the gender composition of the homeless population in New York City, or of the other Care for the Homeless teams. As mentioned above, the majority of services in the Bronx are to homeless families. These families are generally headed by a single woman. Nonetheless, poor use of health services by males is a common problem in the health care system. The all-female staffing pattern of the team (except for the 0.3 FTE supervising physician) may also be an additional barrier.

The 14% to 35% of patients making greater than 5 visits per year reflects the continuity population. Given the team's emphasis on providing access to care, the data on continuity are disappointing. Unfortunately, little continuity data are available in the literature on the experience of programs providing health care to homeless persons. Furthermore, such data are highly dependent on the demographic nature and local resources available to the particular homeless population that is being targeted. Lack of more continuity reflects the chaotic lives of the homeless and the competing priorities of more basic needs such as food, emotional support, and shelter.

Engaging clients with HIV to participate in continuous care is a special concern. In 1995 a case manager and substance abuse counselor were hired by the parent organization, Care for the Homeless. They have collaborated with team members to address the needs of HIV-positive clients. Committing these extra resources and personnel has enabled the program to increase continuity of services to this population.

Common diagnoses

The rates of common diagnoses were relatively stable over the 1992 to 1995 period. For example, the diagnosed asthma rate remained between 5% and 7%, and the rate for pharyngitis ranged from 3% to 4%. The change over time in the rates of some conditions is a function of changes in sites. Delayed immunizations increased from 4% to 14% as the team delivered greater services at family residences. Of particular note is the increase in HIV/AIDS from 3% to 7% over the 4-year period. This occurred despite a relative decrease in the rates of services by the team to soup kitchens, which are generally used by the most transient and at-risk patients. These data support

Table 17–4. Team referral patterns

Referrals	1995 n (%)	1994 n (%)	1993 n (%)	1992 n (%)
Family Health Center	104 (0.12)	183 (0.18)	169 (0.15)	256 (0.22)
Medical emergency room	41 (0.05)	39 (0.04)	56 (0.05)	41 (0.04)
Psychiatric emergency room	2 (0)	2 (0.02)	3 (0)	5 (0)
Drug and alcohol treatment	51 (0.06)	75 (0.07)	110 (0.1)	78 (0.07)
Mental health center	68 (0.08)	54 (0.05)	62 (0.05)	57 (0.05)
Dental care	33 (0.04)	4 (0.04)	42 (0.04)	15 (0.01)
Prenatal care	23 (0.03)	35 (0.03)	33 (0.03)	42 (0.04)
Social services	104 (0.12)	211 (0.21)	232 (0.2)	224 (0.21)
Other	476 (0.53)	405 (0.4)	442 (0.38)	325 (0.31)
Total referrals	902	1008	1149	1043
Total patient encounters	7020	7640	7154	4982
% of encounters referred	13	13	16	21

present concerns about homelessness as a specific risk factor for HIV.

Review of the gross data from encounter forms reveals that the majority of the team's services are for social issues. These data are not represented in Table 17–4 because our data cannot differentiate redundancies (a single visit that may document many social problems). Furthermore, documentation for this category may have declined because emphasis has been placed on documenting other more discrete and reimbursable diagnoses for financial and program accountability reasons.

Because of the magnitude of social problems among the homeless, the team works closely with staff and volunteers at the shelter sites. On-site services allow close follow-up with families and individuals and a close working relationship with shelter staff members. The provider has a sense of the patients' daily lives and problems and is able to communicate easily with shelter staff and act as a patient advocate within the social services system. Shelter and soup kitchen staff are often the main source of dependable social support for the population they serve. They have been helpful in team efforts to provide follow-up care, coordinate outside services, hospitalize patients, and facilitate their discharge planning.

The role of the nurse practitioner

A study by Doblin et al[14] on homeless teams funded by the McKinney Act reports that health care for the homeless services vary widely in the degree to which they utilize the full training and scope of care that a nurse practitioner can provide. In many settings nurse practitioners are used predominantly as ancillary staff and not as an alternative to physicians. The role of nurse practitioners in working with homeless and underserved populations is particularly important given the recruitment difficulties reported by many programs. More than half of McKinney Fund recipients had difficulty recruiting physician providers; 80% of clinics employ a nurse practitioner or other midlevel provider.

The most methodologically strenuous evidence on the effectiveness and safety of nurse practitioners comes from the 1974 Burlington randomized trial on health outcomes of patients.[15] The results showed that nurse practitioners were able to effectively manage 67% of their patient visits without physician consultation. This issue has attracted recent interest in a thought-provoking article by Mundinger[16] on nurse practitioner-physician collaboration, which suggests nurse practitioners are more effective than primary care physicians and easier to recruit. This has incited considerable editorial comment and debate.[17]

The Montefiore team has a favorable experience effectively utilizing the skills of nurse practitioners. Although the data reveal that most of the clients have multiple health and social problems, most of the encounters do not result in a referral outside the team. The patient's needs are generally addressed within the multidisciplinary team and the nurse practitioners refer only for emergent care or specialty services. Nurse practitioners provided the majority of medical care and less than 15% of patients seen were referred elsewhere for medically related problems. Often referrals were to the community health center, where the nurse practitioners may continue to provide care for their patients. The nurse practitioners also provide a significant amount of preventive care as mentioned above. This includes patient education and basic public health interventions and reflects the strong preventive component of nurse practitioner training, which is valuable in a needy population whose health maintenance may be overlooked because of the number of acute and chronic problems that must be addressed.

The Montefiore program's success with appropriate utilization of nurse practitioners may stem from the institution's and family practice physicians' commitment to midlevel practitioners. The nurse practitioners on the team have readily available consultations with the supervising physician and other physicians at the FHC. The physician supervisor is available by telephone or pager whenever the nurse practitioners are in the field. The nurse practitioners' weekly role within the health center allows consultation with other family practitioners, obstetrician-gynecologists, and a range of other providers.

Team building

The frustration and emotional toil of working with an extremely needy and marginalized population can result in significant professional disenchantment and attrition. The Montefiore team has maintained remarkable stability over the years because of its success with provider retention. The clinical psychiatric nurse has been with the team since its inception. Our senior nurse practitioner has a 5-year tenure as did her predecessor. Our social worker has been with the team for 7 years and our outreach worker for 6 years. Much of this success might be attributed to the significant emphasis placed on team building and multidisciplinary cooperation. The team has a central office space separate from the shelter facilities in the department of ambulatory care. Team meetings are held weekly to address administrative business, case management, frustrations in the field, and clinical topics. Finally, Montefiore provides a supportive environment for nurse practitioners with a favorable work contract and opportunity for professional advancement.

Recent developments

While this chapter focuses on one of the five contracted health and social service teams, the parent organization is committed to diversifying its services to better meet the needs of homeless people. Care for the Homeless has recently been awarded a contract by the city to manage the Kingsbridge Women's Assessment Center and hopes to become more involved in using its experience to effect public policy.

Care for the Homeless and other homeless providers have been concerned with the unsuitability of managed care for itinerant people. Unfortunately, these concerns have been verified by experience. The Montefiore team has found that many patients have been enrolled in managed care plans without fully understanding what they are or the ramifications of enrollment. Since many plans in New York City operate in only part of the city, many patients are effectively without coverage when they are transferred from one shelter to another. They are surprised when they cannot find a provider or use a community health center. Regardless of benefits, patients are seen by the Montefiore team, but care is still compromised. For example, prescriptions that the practitioner writes cannot be filled by the patient if the practitioner is not a participant in their managed care plan. The declining portion of reimbursable visits that the team provides is a financial drain on the program and threatens future services. In the future, managed care programs must be required to make point-of-access exceptions for homeless persons in order for them to be able to obtain accessible care. Alternatively, as with many mental health programs across the country, the home-less Medicaid population must be carved out of Medicaid managed care and financed separately.

• • •

This multidisciplinary team demonstrates a model in which nurse practitioners serve a population with special needs. The program's affiliation with a well-established, academically oriented community health center provides readily available physician consultation and has contributed stability and continuity. Onsite services allow close working relationships with shelter staff in addressing the social problems of the homeless and case management has been a useful recent resource. Medicaid managed care has introduced considerable difficulties in providing services to this population. While these factors play a vital role, the most important component of the program's success is the strong team development and the commitment of the individual providers to a population with which it can be challenging and rewarding to work.

REFERENCES

1. Bassuk E. Why does family homelessness occur? A case control study. *Am J Public Health.* 1988; 78:783–788.
2. Brickner PW, ed. *Under the Safety Net: The Health and Social Welfare of the Homeless in the United States.* New York, NY: United Hospital Fund; 1990.
3. Institute of Medicine. *Homelessness, Health and Human Needs.* Washington, DC: National Academy Press; 1988.
4. Hibbs JR, Benner L, Klugman L, Spitzer R, Macchia I, Mellinger A, Fife D. Mortality in a cohort of homeless adults in Philadelphia. *N Engl J Med.* 1994;331:304–309.
5. Neibacher S. *Homeless People and Health Care: An Unrelenting Challenge.* New York, NY: United Hospital Fund; 1990.
6. US Conference of Mayors. *A Status Report on Homeless Families in America's Cities: A 29-City Survey.* Washington, DC: US Conference of Mayors; 1987.
7. Wood D, Valdez B. Barriers to medical care for homeless families compared with housed poor families. *Am J Dis Child.* 1991;145:1,109–1,115.
8. Bassuk E, Ruban L, Laurent A. Characteristics of sheltered homeless families. *Am J Public Health.* 1986;76:1,097–1,101.

9. Breakey WR, Fischer PJ, Kramer H, Nestadt G, Romanoski AJ, Ross A, Royall R, Stein O. Health and mental health problems of homeless men and women in Baltimore. *JAMA*. 1989;262:1,352–1,357.

10. Brickner PW, McAdam J, Torres R, Vick W, Congren B, Dettano T, et al. Providing health services for the homeless: A stitch in time. *Bull NY Acad Med*. 1993;70(3):146–170.

11. Fournier A, Perez-Stable A, Greer P. Lessons from a clinic for the homeless: The Camillus health concern. *JAMA*. 1993;270:2,721–2,724.

12. Strelnick H, Younge R. Another kind of Bronx cheer: community oriented primary care at the Montefiore Family Health Center. *Health/PAC Bull*. 1992;22(3):19–23.

13. Dollar M. *HIV Chart Audit, April–May 1993*. New York, NY: New York City Care for the Homeless Program; 1993.

14. Doblin B, Gelberg L, Freeman H. Patient care and professional staffing patterns in McKinney Act clinics providing primary care to the homeless. *JAMA*. 1992;267:698–701.

15. Spitzer WO, Sackett DL, Sibley JC. The Burlington randomized trial of the nurse practitioner. *N Engl J Med*. 1974;290:251–256.

16. Mundinger MO. Advanced practice nursing—good medicine for physicians? *N Engl J Med*. 1994; 330:211–214

17. Nurse practitioners in primary care. *N Engl J Med*. 1994;334:1,537–1,540. Correspondence.

CHAPTER 18

Physicians' Receptiveness to Teen Medicaid Recipients Seeking Office-Based Prenatal Care

Blair D. Gifford, PhD

Kenneth L. Bettenhausen, PhD

EXISTING MODELS OF PHYSICIAN participation in Medicaid have been developed exclusively through the use of physician surveys or Medicaid claims records and usually focus on the availability of prenatal care.[1] These studies generally find that physician participation in Medicaid is dependent on their competition for paying patients.[2] That is, physicians expand the Medicaid portions of their practices in response to declines in private patient income or insurance, or increases in Medicaid fees or coverage. Their acceptance of Medicaid patients is reduced as private market conditions become more favorable.

The value of physician surveys, however, is limited because physicians may be reluctant to report an unwillingness to accept Medicaid patients. Likewise, utilization studies, which use claims data, often do not differentiate between those physicians who have an occa-

Fam Community Health 1997;20(2):70–79
© 1997 Aspen Publishers, Inc.

sional Medicaid claim and those for whom Medicaid patients comprise a sizable percentage of their practice. Thus, both types of studies tend to overstate physicians' participation in Medicaid.[3] Also, they typically only account for the economic factors in physicians' decisions to accept Medicaid patients. In an attempt to get a complete and more realistic view of physician participation in Medicaid, the research presented in this chapter takes an alternative tact. It considers participation through the perspective of first-time teen prenatal care patients attempting to gain appointment information from obstetricians-gynecologists' (ob/gyn) offices.

The chapter also presents and empirically tests an alternative model, the physicians' receptiveness model, that considers physicians' willingness to accept new teen prenatal patients who are Medicaid recipients. This model considers the extent to which physicians look for ways to reduce the costs associated with treating Medicaid patients in an attempt to lessen the gap between Medicaid reimbursement and private pay levels. Further, this model considers whether there are practice characteristics, such as appointment availability, waiting time, and receptionists' helpfulness, that may lessen the incentives for Medicaid patients to seek care at a particular physician's office. In effect, these cost containment and limited accessibility management practices may profoundly affect the accessibility of health care for Medicaid patients. Identifying such practice characteristics will enhance our understanding of why some physicians accept Medicaid patients while others do not.

PHYSICIANS' RECEPTIVENESS MODEL AND RESEARCH HYPOTHESES

Considerable research on physicians' participation in Medicaid has considered the availability of office-based prenatal care to pregnant teens who are Medicaid recipients.[1,4-7] This population has been the focus of research attention due to its heightened health concerns. For example, teens have higher rates of infant death and diseases and physical complications during pregnancy.[8] Also, miscarriages, stillbirths, and low birthweight infants are twice as common among teens than adult women.[9] As such, most teen-oriented programs, like those for high-risk women generally, adopt a more intensive approach than is typically offered as part of conventional maternity care. These comprehensive systems entail nutritional, educational, and psychosocial support and counseling and have been shown to result in improved pregnancy outcomes.[10,11] Of course, the usefulness of these programs is limited if teens do not have access to a prenatal care provider.

Participation models concentrate on the economic trade-off for physicians between private pay and Medicaid patients.[2] However, these models do not appear to explain the highly unequal distribution of Medicaid patients across physicians. For example, a study found that 62% of 958 primary care physicians had 1% or less Medicaid recipients in their patient populations. Alternatively, another study found that a very small proportion of physicians in Illinois provide a majority of Medicaid care.[12] Of 24,000 physicians in the state, only 240 physicians (1% of total) accounted for 41% of all Medicaid bills in Illinois in 1993. These research results indicate that Medicaid patient care is more than an economic substitution process. That is, physicians appear to manage their practices to attract certain patient types and these patient recruitment practices are reflected in different patterns of physicians' participation in Medicaid.

Physicians' receptiveness model

This research considers the extent to which participation in Medicaid is based on physicians' management of patient care practices. It is argued that by differentially managing the care of Medicaid and private pay patients, physicians are in a better position to overcome lower reimbursement levels for providing care for Medicaid recipients. Two dimensions of this model are introduced and empirically tested. The cost-containment dimension considers cost saving practice management strategies and the limited access dimension considers practice setting characteristics that might be used to dissuade Medicaid patients' usage.

Cost-containment dimension

It is argued that physicians who accept Medicaid patients will have higher incentives to manage their practice costs in a more efficient and economical manner to compensate for the gap between private pay and Medicaid reimbursement rates. Since this gap is especially large in urban areas, one might expect cost-containment practices for Medicaid patients to be especially pronounced in an urban area. Seeking Medicaid patients is the condition that is often depicted in the high patient volume "Medicaid mills" that are found in urban areas. In such practice settings, a physician may serve up to 60 and 70 Medicaid patients in a day, limiting patient visits to an average of 4 or 5 minutes.[12] This suggests that the care given at these physicians' offices will be oriented toward cost-containment practices.

A number of cost-containment practices are possible. First, less costly health professionals, such as nurses or physician assistants, could handle an increasing percentage of patient care time. Second, physicians could decrease the amount of time spent with each patient, thus increasing the volume of patients seen. Third, physicians may attempt to increase revenues by administering a higher number of prenatal care tests, for which physicians are separately reimbursed, in an attempt to make up for lower Medicaid patient revenues. These three research hypotheses posit that ob/gyns who accept Medicaid patients exhibit more extensive cost-containment efforts:

1. Participation in Medicaid will be higher for ob/gyns who limit the duration of a patient's first prenatal care appointment.
2. Participation in Medicaid will be higher for ob/gyns who substitute their presence at the first prenatal care appointment with less expensive health care professionals.
3. Participation in Medicaid will be higher for ob/gyns who administer a higher number of tests in a patient's first prenatal care appointment.

Limited access dimension

A second provider strategy is simply to continue serving paying patients and limit or deny services to Medicaid patients. In such a practice setting, physicians may attempt to limit the attractiveness of their practice to new Medicaid patients. For example, the physician may try to limit access by not having appointment times available to Medicaid recipients for a week or two. Research has consistently shown that inaccessibility of office-based care severely limits Medicaid recipients' ability or willingness to obtain prenatal care.[13]

Prenatal care use is also influenced by the attitudes and styles of providers. For example, poor communication about procedures, failure to answer questions, and hurried and otherwise depersonalized care results in reduced utilization of health care services.[13] Limited and difficult communication toward a prospective teen patient seeking a prenatal appointment may lead to an unfortunate mix of hostility, passivity, and evasiveness on the part of the client, often leading her to look for care elsewhere.[11,14] This can be seen in a physician receptionist's willingness to help first-time prenatal patients make appointments. Since first-time pregnant patients often seek information, receptionists play a key role in projecting an image of receptiveness. These two additional research hypotheses reflect ways ob/gyns can limit access to care for Medicaid participants:

4. Participation in Medicaid will be lower for ob/gyns who have longer wait times for prenatal care appointments.

5. Participation in Medicaid will be lower for ob/gyns whose office receptionists are less helpful to information-seeking prenatal care patients.

DATA AND METHODS

For this study the researchers surveyed 221 Chicago-area physicians who self-report as obstetricians-gynecologists on the American Medical Association's Physician Master File. The Master File, updated in 1993, lists the entire US physician population, including members and non-members of the AMA. Of 671 ob/gyns, 431 had offices in Chicago; the remainder (240) had offices in Chicago's suburbs. The Master File had office phone numbers for 215 Chicago physicians (49.9%) and 139 suburban physicians (57.9%). Of these, many phone numbers were incorrect. The final sample (221, 32.9% of the total) contained 136 physicians from Chicago and 85 physicians from Chicago's suburbs. Other Master File variables included in this research were physicians' medical school location (ie, foreign or US), gender, and medical school graduation date. The medical school graduation date was used to determine a "years in practice" variable.

Two white female graduate students in their mid-20s each posed as the sister of a pregnant teen in order to gain information for this study. These interviewers called obstetricians' offices during normal working hours and generally encountered the office receptionist. The interviewers explained that they were attempting to gain information about the care provided in a first prenatal care appointment to help their "sister" determine where to seek care. There was no attempt to make an appointment. It was necessary to have interviewers pose as an older sister because it was thought that the kinds of information being sought may have been perceived as being too sophisticated to be credibly sought by a teen.

Phone interviewers asked a number of questions including appointment availability and the length of the first prenatal care appointment. Interviewers also scored each interviewee in terms of "helpfulness" in providing asked-for information. A helpfulness indicator is particularly pertinent for considering whether teens seek prenatal care.[11] A helpfulness protocol was determined through pretesting on obstetricians in another city. Interinterviewer reliability was enhanced through common interviewing technique education. The tests-administered variable was an aggregate of whether a patient would receive a complete blood count, urinalysis, pelvic examination, and a pap smear test in the first office visit.

After gathering the required information, interviewers asked whether the physician would see a new patient who is Medicaid eligible. Responses to this question were used to divide physicians who accepted teen Medicaid patients at their offices from those who did not. A few interviewees (less than 2% of the total) qualified negative responses by stating the physicians would see a Medicaid patient at a clinic. These responses were coded as having the physicians unavailable to see a Medicaid patient (at the physician's office).

A bivariate analysis of physicians' responses was conducted to determine the extent to which the answers of Medicaid-accepting physicians' differ from non-Medicaid-accepting physicians. Finally, the feasibility of the physicians receptiveness model is considered through significance testing using logistic regression. Dummy coding was used for categorical variables. However, dummy coding was not used when a categorical variable represented discrete locations on an underlying, continuous distribution.

RESULTS

Ob/gyns' participation in Medicaid

Overall, 81 of 221 physicians (36.7%) accepted new Medicaid patients for prenatal care (Table 18–1). Participation rates varied widely between ob/gyns with offices in Chicago (44.1%) and the suburbs (24.7%). The overall physician participation rate of this research is lower than previous studies and appears to be in line with downward trends in the rate of physician participation in Medicaid and participation by obstetricians and gynecologists.[4,5] Table 18–1 also shows that physicians who accept new Medicaid patients are likely to be foreign.

Table 18–2 illustrates the extent to which physicians' receptiveness variables differ between ob/gyns who participate or do not participate in Medicaid. Table 18–3 reports the results of the logistic regression. As shown in Table 18–3, obstetricians who are based in Chicago and are foreign medical graduates (Table 18–3) are significantly related (both at $p < .01$) to accepting teen prenatal patients

Table 18–1. Practice characteristics of the obstetricians and gynecologists who accept new Medicaid patients

	N	% Accepting new Medicaid patients
Total	221	36.7
Office location		
Chicago	136	44.1
Suburbs	85	24.7
Gender		
Male	158	25.9
Female	63	30.0
Country of medical education		
US	134	28.6
Foreign	87	58.0
Years in practice (mean = 22.6, SD = 10.7)		
< 10	25	20.0
10–19	73	28.8
20–29	64	54.7
30	59	33.9

who are Medicaid recipients. These results are consistent with previous physician participation research.[7]

Physicians' receptiveness model

Our analyses indicate considerable support for both dimensions of the physicians' receptiveness model: cost containment at first appointment and limited access. Hypotheses 1–3 consider whether participating ob/gyns are more actively pursuing cost containment in patient care. As shown in Table 18–3, hypothesis 1, which tests whether physicians who participate in Medicaid have shorter appointment times for their patients than those who do not participate, is supported ($p < .025$). Also, hypothesis 3,

use of more prenatal tests, was supported ($p < .025$). However, our results do not support hypothesis 2 (use of lower-cost health care professionals).

Hypotheses 4 and 5 consider whether ob/gyns might limit access to their care. It is suggested that rather than directly denying care to a Medicaid recipient, some physicians might attempt to avoid Medicaid patients by being less accessible. Table 18–2 indicates that prenatal care patients are somewhat more likely to get an appointment within the week with participating physicians (hypothesis 4), but this variable was not a significant predictor in the logistic regression analysis (Table 18–3). Also, Table 18–2 shows that Medicaid-participating physicians' offices are more likely to be helpful in as-

Table 18–2. Physicians' receptiveness model: practice characteristics of the obstetricians and gynecologists who accept new Medicaid patients

	N	% Accepting new Medicaid patients
Cost Containment (at 1st appointment)		
Physician involvement		
No physician	8	25.0
Physician present	213	37.1
Appointment duration		
< 20 min	21	61.9
20–45 min	123	41.5
> 45 min	77	22.1
Test administered (mean = 3.2, SD = 1.2)		
No answer	2	50.0
1	16	31.3
2	43	30.2
3	61	39.3
4	68	38.2
5	31	38.7
Limited Access		
Appointment availability		
< 6 days	102	50.0
6–12 days	63	27.0
> 12 days	56	23.2
Receptionist helpfulness		
Difficult	24	4.2
Adequate	83	27.7
Very helpful	114	50.0

sisting prenatal care patients who are seeking appointment information (hypothesis 5) and that over 95% of the receptionists who were "difficult" toward inquiring patients worked for physicians who would not accept new Medicaid patients. These findings are further supported in Table 18–3, which shows that the "receptionist helpfulness" variable is highly significant ($p < .01$) in relation to an ob/gyn's Medicaid participation.

DISCUSSION

Overall, 36.7% of ob/gyns accepted new teen Medicaid patients for prenatal care. This finding is of particular interest because this is the first study that measures participation via Medicaid patients' interest in making their first prenatal care appointment. It is argued that the design of this survey more accurately reflects the barriers that a pregnant Medicaid-eligible patient encounters when seeking office-based prenatal care. Research results also indicate the strength of adding a physicians' receptiveness model to the traditional dual-market model to understand physician participation in Medicaid. One dimension of the physicians' receptiveness model is the notion of the degree to which physicians' cost-containment practices account for whether they participate in Medicaid or not. Analysis indicates that ob/gyns who participate in Medicaid may attempt to compensate for lower revenues per patient by seeing more patients and, to a lesser extent, administering more tests. Further research needs to consider whether other cost-containment measures are more prevalent in the practices of Medicaid-participating physicians and whether such cost-containment practices are prevalent among other physicians' specialties and in other rural and urban locations. Also, research should consider whether similar cost-containment strategies are becoming more prevalent with the growth of Medicaid health maintenance organizations (HMOs). This situation is suggested by research on Medicaid HMO physician enrollees in New York City.[15]

A second dimension of the physicians' receptiveness model considers how physicians may limit their accessibility to Medicaid patients. Analysis shows that

Table 18–3. Physicians' receptiveness model: logistic regression of obstetricians' and gynecologists' participation and nonparticipation in Medicaid

Variable	Coefficient (SE)
Intercept	−4.348* (1.832)
Physician characteristics	
Office location	1.297† (.439)
Country of medical education	1.405† (.458)
Years in practice	−.003 (.021)
Gender	.118 (.460)
Cost containment (at 1st appointment)	
Physician involvement	.253 (1.228)
Appointment duration	−.864* (.330)
Tests administered	.381* (.164)
Limited access	
Appointment availability	−.938 (.238)
Receptionist helpfulness	1.142† (.377)
Log likelihood	−90.38
Number of cases	221
Degrees of freedom	9

*$p = .025$
†$p = .01$

participating ob/gyns are more likely to have appointment availability within the week. This may be because participating ob/gyns have shorter appointment times and, presumably, have the ability to see a higher volume of patients. Alternatively, it may indicate that physicians with busier practices may be less inclined to accept Medicaid patients. Another salient finding is that non-Medicaid-participating ob/gyns are much more likely to have receptionists who are not helpful to patients with questions. This finding begins to capture the extent to which patients' feelings toward the physician offices' receptivity are indicative of whether a physician is willing to accept new Medicaid patients or not. This finding points to the need to consider the extent to which attitudinal and organizational barriers may be compounding the problems of the accessibility of office-based physician care to Medicaid prenatal patients. For example, previous research indicates that ob/gyns perceive Medicaid patients to be more litigious and higher risk.[5]

The presented research indicates that physician participation in Medicaid is guided by both economic and social concerns. That is, physicians appear to manage their practices to attract certain patient types, and these patient recruitment practices are reflected in differing patterns of physicians' participation in Medicaid. To expand on this finding, further research might consider whether physicians may be willing to accept some, but not all, Medicaid prenatal patients; that is, whether there may be a "tipping point" at which a physician's practice loses its identity as a private practice and becomes a Medicaid practice. Research might also consider whether physicians' offices discriminate against certain types of teen Medicaid recipients (eg, minorities). Interviewers in the presented research were articulate, white adults. It is conceivable that the overall participation rate of this study (ie, 36.7%) would be even lower for teens and, in particular, minority teens who attempt to gain prenatal care appointment information.

• • •

Readers should be aware of potential shortcomings with this research. First, appointment information is given before the interviewees know that the potential patient is a Medicaid recipient. Subsequent research could consider whether receptionists may respond differently to patients who identify themselves as Medicaid recipients at the beginning of appointment inquiries. Second, this study focuses on Medicaid-eligible teens and the type of prenatal care they can obtain from obstetricians. It is not clear whether these results may be generalizable to other Medicaid patient populations or physician specialties. Third, it is unclear from this research the extent to which some ob/gyns may accept new Medicaid prenatal patients in an institutional setting such as hospital outpatient departments, public health clinics, and community health centers. Fourth, there was no attempt to compare answers for pregnant teens on Medicaid with a control group of insured patients. Despite these limitations, however, this research provides a first step toward helping researchers build a stronger and more holistic model of physician participation in Medicaid. Ultimately, this should lead to a better understanding of how to combat the problems of access for the country's most needy populations.

REFERENCES

1. Lewis-Idema D. *Monitoring Medicaid Provider Participation and Access to Care.* Washington DC: Center for Policy Research, National Governors Association; 1992.

2. Sloan FA, Cromwell J, Mitchell JB. *Private Physicians and Public Programs.* Lexington, Mass: D.C. Heath; 1978.

3. Physician Payment Review Commission. *Annual Report to the Congress 1993.* Washington DC: PPRC; 1993.

4. Mitchell JB, Schurman R. Access to private obstetrics/gynecology services under Medicaid. *Medical Care.* 1984;22(11):1,026–1,037.

5. American College of Obstetricians and Gynecologists. Ob/gyn services for indigent women. *Report of the Committee on Health Care for Underserved Women.* Washington, DC: ACOG; 1988.

6. Yudkowsky BK, Cartland DC, Flint SS. Pediatrician participation in Medicaid: 1978 to 1989. *Pediatrics.* 1990;18:567–577.

7. Perloff JD, Kletke PR, Fossett JW. Which physicians limit their Medicaid participation, and why. *Health Services Res.* 1995;30(1):7–26.

8. Makinson C. The health consequences of teenage fertility. *Family Planning Perspective.* 1985;17:132–139.

9. Morris L, Warren C, Aral S. Measuring adolescent sexual behaviors and related health outcomes. *Pub Health Rep.* 1993;108:31–36.

10. Buescher PA, Smith C, Holliday JL, Levine RH. Sources of prenatal care and infant birth weight: the case of a North Carolina county. *Am J Obstet Gynecol.* 1987;156:204–210.

11. Stevens-Simon C, Fullar S, McAnarney ER. Tangible differences between adolescent-oriented and adult-oriented prenatal care. *J Adolesc Health.* 1992;13:298–302.

12. Brodt B, Possley M, Jones T. Medicaid: system in chaos. *Chicago Tribune.* 1993; Oct 31–Nov 9.

13. Institute of Medicine. *Prenatal Care, Reaching Mothers, Reaching Infants.* Washington, DC: National Academy Press; 1988.

14. Ross C, Duff R. Returning to the doctor: the effect of client characteristics, type of practice, and experience with care. *J Health Social Behavior.* 1982; 23:119–131.

15. Green M, Kohn J, Lee CG. *Managed Confusion: How HMO Marketing Materials Are Tricking the Elderly and the Poor.* New York, NY: Office of the Public Advocate; 1995.

CHAPTER 19

An Ethnonursing Study of Muscogee (Creek) Indians and Effective Health Care Practices for Treating Alcohol Abuse

Donna Marie Wing, EdD, RN

Shelly S. Crow, MS, RN

Timmy Thompson

ALONG THE HIGHWAYS and country dirt roads of Muscogee (Creek) Nation in eastern Oklahoma, life appears to be wooded and serene, with much foliage and a peaceful atmosphere. However, when one views the small crosses on the curves and intersections across the Nation, one realizes that on that site a life was lost, most likely due to an alcohol-related accident.

In 1830, under the Indian Removal Act, five major Indian tribes were banished from their homes in Alabama, Georgia, and Florida into Indian territory in eastern Oklahoma. These tribes became known as the Five Civilized Tribes of Oklahoma (sometimes called the "Five Major Tribes" or the "Five Tribes"). The

This study was funded by grants from the Oklahoma Center for the Advancement of Science and Technology (OCAST) #HR3-044, Sigma Theta Tau International, Sigma Theta Tau Beta Delta Chapter, and the Oklahoma Nurses Foundation. The authors thank Dr Joan Haase, University of Arizona, and Dr Kathleen Knafl, University of Illinois at Chicago, for their consultation on this research.

Fam Community Health 1995;18(2):52–64
© 1995 Aspen Publishers, Inc.

Muscogee tribe, later given the white name "Creek," settled in a region that today comprises nine counties in northeastern and central eastern Oklahoma.

By the time the Muscogee (Creek) settled in Oklahoma, they were experiencing problems related to excessive alcohol use. These problems were of recent origin, for the tribe had no cultural ties with alcohol prior to the European migration to North America. Rum was first introduced in the 16th century as a gift of friendship; later, it was considered a valued trade commodity.[1] With the introduction of alcohol, the peace and harmony that had existed within the tribe for so long were destroyed.[2] The Muscogee (Creek) constitution, enacted on March 15, 1824, contained a provision for protecting people who were intoxicated while committing a crime. Drunkenness became such a serious problem for both the Muscogee (Creek) community and the dominant culture that the US government decreed the Indian Intercourse Act of 1832, which prohibited the sale of alcohol to Indians.[3]

Between 1832 and 1953 the Muscogee (Creek) experienced a period of prohibition enforced mostly by the dominant culture, who perceived Indians as unable to handle alcohol. The Muscogee (Creek) Council authorized the Lighthorse Brigade (tribal law and order patrol) to "search, find and spill" intoxicants.[3(p181)] However, bootlegging and illicit whiskey trade flourished. By the time prohibition was rescinded in 1953, alcohol abuse was already an issue for the Muscogee (Creek), resulting in multiple health, economic, and family problems.[1,2]

Prohibition is still practiced at the various ceremonial grounds where the traditional people do not permit drinking and intoxication. However, even though there are currently tribal criminal codes that address public intoxication as a criminal offense, the laws do not designate penalties for the offense.[4] According to the current Lighthorse Chief, there were 19 arrests between October 1993 and July 1994 for alcohol-related problems. Only one case was referred for treatment.

Reliable data concerning drinking patterns among American Indians are scarce.[5] The authors found few statistical reports regarding the incidence and prevalence of alcohol-related problems among the Muscogee (Creek), with no mention of cultural and social dimensions of drinking. This scarcity is due, in part, to the challenge of collecting data from tribes such as the Muscogee (Creek) whose members do not live on reservations. Correspondence with the Muscogee (Creek) Tribal Court indicated that many alcohol-related cases are presented as child abuse or domestic violence problems and therefore are not enumerated as alcohol-related incidents.

An alcoholism needs assessment of the Five Major Tribes was conducted in 1982 by the Eastern Oklahoma Planning Board with funds from the Indian Health Service. It found that 51 of 100 Indians who sought mental health services had alcohol-related problems, and 75% of all cases of the social services department at the Indian Health Resource Center were alcohol related.[6] Even though this study provided an indication of the extent of alcohol-related problems among eastern

Oklahoma Indians, it was limited in studying only those who accessed the Indian Health Service.

For those who have sought help for alcohol abuse, treatment has often been unsuccessful.[7,8] Reasons for poor response of Muscogee (Creek) people to treatment may be found in the programs designed by and for the dominant culture. LaFromboise[9] applied the term "cultural genocide" to underscore the ramifications of using Western-oriented treatment approaches instead of traditional healing rituals of American Indians. Several researchers[7,10–12] studying tribes other than the Muscogee (Creek) found that recovery from alcohol abuse was most effective when traditional and cultural healing practices were implemented. However, even when traditional Indian healing practices are used, there is often the expectation that all tribes and all tribal members will respond identically to any given situation.[5]

Nurses and other health care professionals are challenged by multidimensional beliefs about health and illness that exist among American Indians, as well as diverse cultural customs, definitions of drinking, and perceptions of effective health care practices for alcohol abuse and alcoholism. These definitions and perceptions are at the heart of this study, because the culture of a group influences the labels that the group places on behavior.[13] It is therefore imperative to understand individual and social perspectives of drinking practices, alcohol abuse, and traditional health care practices among American Indians so that health care can be meaningful and culturally sensitive.

To unearth the perspectives of the Muscogee (Creek) people, the authors asked two questions:

1. What are the barriers to seeking and obtaining care for alcoholism and alcohol-related problems among the Muscogee (Creek) Indians?
2. What is the Muscogee (Creek) culturally based view of health, as well as the events, phenomena, and influencers that are perceived to contribute to effective health practices in the care of alcohol abuse?

THEORETIC FRAMEWORK

Leininger's[14] theory of cultural care diversity and universality provided the theoretic framework for this study. The theory gives structure to the process of learning the cultural and social structural dimensions that influence health and health care. These dimensions include technologic factors, religious and philosophic factors, kinship and social factors, cultural values and lifeways, political and legal factors, economic factors, and educational factors. Following this framework, nursing care is an integration and balancing of cultural care or folk practices with professional nursing and health care systems. The ultimate goal of nursing and other health care professionals is to provide care that is culturally meaningful and sensitive, yet effective in responding to the needs of community members.

By using Leininger's[14] theory, the authors were able to learn the beliefs, values, meanings, and influencers of alcohol abuse and health care that each indi-

vidual perceived as important. Ethnonursing, the research method, provided a
natural link between the research questions and the theoretic framework. The
cultural and social structural dimensions
gave direction for collecting and organizing data to be considered in studying the
meaning and impact of alcohol use and
abuse at the individual and cultural levels.

METHOD

Ethnonursing is a naturalistic discovery
process for eliciting primarily emic data.
The method allows for the description
and explication of individual meanings
and interpretations in relation to nursing
phenomena.[14] Because the phenomena
in this study were effective health care
practices and barriers to seeking care for
alcohol abuse, the participants' world-
view and perceptions of alcohol, health,
and health care were the focus of data
collection.

Domain of inquiry

The population of the Muscogee
(Creek) Nation is approximately 36,000,
with 25,000 living in a 9-county catchment area. Except for Tulsa, all counties
are predominantly rural. The domain of
inquiry was the Muscogee (Creek) community, including both urban and rural
residents. After obtaining the support
and consent of the Muscogee (Creek)
Health Board and the Chief's Office, the
authors initiated this research study.

Although legitimate entry was provided by the Muscogee (Creek) administration, their jurisdiction over the cer-

emonial grounds is limited. The grounds
are the "towns" or communities within
the tribe. In the Muscogee (Creek) tribe
there are 14 grounds, each led by a
micco, or chief. Grounds members practice traditional religion and curative practices, with the *heleshaya*, or medicine
man, as the healer. Because the chief's
position is government imposed, many
traditionalists do not recognize the authority of the chief; they are bound to the
cultural lifeways and laws of their
grounds.

The primary author was invited to five
of the grounds to observe traditional rituals and to experience the ceremonies
from an emic perspective. The *heleshaya* from one ground eventually became the research assistant and third author. Consequently, the primary author
was able to appreciate the wide continuum of health care beliefs and practices among the Muscogee (Creek)
people.

Participants

Three hundred and ninety members of
the Muscogee (Creek) community were
interviewed (231 men and 159 women).
Twenty-two of the men and 10 of the
women were either health care professionals or tribal leaders. Thirty-eight of
the participants admitted to being alcoholic. Ages ranged from 17 to 90 years.
Approximately half the participants practiced traditional healing practices, while
the other half used Western-oriented
treatment facilities and practitioners. All
nine counties of the Muscogee (Creek)
Nation were represented.

Data collection

A strength of this study was the orchestration of the insider-outsider roles. The researchers complemented each other. The primary author was an outsider who lacked previous knowledge of health care practices of the Muscogee (Creek) people. She was able to observe and examine cultural practices that were habitual to the other authors. The second author, being Second Chief, provided insightful interpretations for practices questioned by the primary author. The third author, being a *heleshaya* and fluent in the Muscogee (Creek) tongue, provided translation and access to the traditional community.

The authors spent 3 years in the field as observers-participants. Data collection methods included interview, observation-participation-reflection, and archival investigation. Tribal meetings, social events, churches, dances, ceremonial events, schools, hospitals, clinics, and alcoholism recovery support meetings served as data collection sites.

To select participants, the authors approached community members, tribal leaders, medicine men, and health care professionals; explained the purpose of the research; and requested an interview. Many of the participants introduced the authors to others who likewise consented to being interviewed. The authors monitored the participants' backgrounds to ascertain that the Muscogee (Creek) community was adequately represented across gender, age, geographic location, and orientation (traditional or modern).

Each author used an interview guide that contained questions about perceptions of effective health care practices and barriers to seeking care for alcohol-related problems. However, a strict interview format was not followed because it is the Muscogee (Creek) practice to tell stories and to speak in a manner that transcends time and topic restrictions. For example, the primary author was interviewing a woman and her son at one of the ceremonial grounds. The woman asked a friend and her family to join the discussion. Over a 3-hour period, 15 different friends and family members entered and exited the conversation. The questions in the guide were asked and answered, but they evolved out of the conversation.

In observation-participation-reflection, the primary author first observed the activities of the community, then participated in activities, and finally reflected on the cultural contexts of the experiences.[14] This technique allowed her to perceive the environment from the participants' point of view (emic), which is the essence of the research questions. Interview data were substantiated with observations. For example, when participants told the primary author about family adaptation to alcohol abuse, she then observed the interactions of family members in treatment centers.

Archival investigation involved the review of documents, statistics, literature, newspaper articles, and any written material that illustrated the sociocultural impact of drinking on the Muscogee (Creek) people. Archival investigation provided the dominant culture's interpretation of data (etic).

Both interview and field note data were documented in a field notebook.

Three kinds of notes were recorded: (1) observational and interview notes of what the authors saw or heard, (2) interpretive notes of the observations and interviews within Leininger's[14] framework and the research questions, and (3) procedural notes of avenues to pursue or questions to answer.[15,16]

Data analysis

Data collection and analysis occurred simultaneously using Leininger's[17] ethnonursing phases of qualitative data analysis. The analytic process had four phases. In the first phase the authors focused on emic data. Cultural lifeways were analyzed, as well as the contextual meanings and interpretations of alcohol use and abuse. During the second phase, the authors identified descriptors and codes using both emic and etic data. The emphasis was on meaning-in-context, denoting that the data were discernible and relevant within certain situations, settings, and life experiences.[17] Some initial codes were "passivity," "reserved comportment," and "harmony with nature."

In the third phase, pattern and contextual analysis, all incidences within a given code were compared and common properties were identified. The authors composed their own words that explained the relationships between the codes derived from the narratives and observations. Codes were clustered to form categories. For example, "reserved comportment" and "passivity" were two of the codes that formed the category "humility."

The final phase of analysis involved synthesis of thinking and theoretic configuration. The authors developed major research findings, formulated themes, and made recommendations for advancing nursing and health care practice.

FINDINGS

The two research questions are discussed jointly because the five emerging themes provided insight into the Muscogee (Creek) world view of wellness, effective health care practices, and barriers to seeking alcoholism treatment. Although approximately half the participants practiced traditional ways and half practiced Western-oriented health care, these themes generally spanned both groups.

Theme 1

Theme 1 holds that wellness and spirituality are inseparable. *Wellness* is harmony of the body, mind, and spirit; *illness* is disharmony in one or more areas. Drinking encourages disharmony.

To the Muscogee (Creek), humans are threefold—body, mind, and spirit. The mind is the link between the body, or physical world, and the spirit. While the mind and body are ephemeral, the spirit is eternal. It existed before coming into the body and continues to exist after the body dies. To maintain wellness, one must have harmony in all three areas.

The concepts of spirituality and harmony were prevalent among both traditional and nontraditional Muscogee (Creeks). Groundspeople and church members stressed harmony as the major component of wellness. Nearly all participants emphasized the human relationship with the Creator, God, or higher power. A Muscogee (Creek) alcoholism counselor made the following statement:

You need to recognize Indian spirituality. You have to go into each situation knowing they have a belief in the Creator. Every Indian does. Unlike with whites, where one wonders, "Does he or she have a belief in the Creator?" with Creeks you know they do. One time a drunk Creek man came to me. His behavior was intolerable. I said to him, "Stop that. Creator doesn't like that." The behavior stopped. Many white people do not know how to talk with Indians when they are drunk.

Nontraditional Muscogee (Creeks) perceived drinking as a serious threat to spirituality, as obstructing one's relationship with God. Church members prayed that individuals afflicted with alcoholism would be relieved of temptation and spiritual weakness. They viewed drinking and alcohol abuse as ultimately individual choices, thereby underscoring individual responsibility.

Traditional people held a somewhat different perception. While they believed that alcoholism was caused by a lack of spirituality, it was a "third party" or "evildoer" who was responsible for the affliction. A person who was jealous or resentful of another would ask the evildoer to place alcoholism on the victim. Because a truly spiritual person would have taken medicine for protection against evil, the afflicted one was not spiritually healthy. However, the person could restore health by taking medicine. A medicine man explained this concept further:

A barrier is placed by the third party. It is both a physical and a mental barrier. It is placed so that something bad will happen to the person, but the person may start believing that it can't be removed. White doctors' medicine don't work. The barrier is there and the white doctor doesn't know that. The medicine man has to remove the barrier.

Muscogee (Creek) resistance to seeking help from the dominant culture is due, in part, to the separation of healing and spirituality among white practitioners, as well as the lack of knowledge of how to treat someone suffering from the work of the evildoer. Many participants said that white medicine overlooks the holistic approach that is essential to healing.

Theme 2

Theme 2 holds that the admission of alcohol abuse causes much embarrassment and shame, which obstruct the seeking of help. Embarrassment and shame were the most frequent responses when asked why the Muscogee (Creek) did not seek care for alcohol-related problems. The two words were used interchangeably by participants, indicating no discernible difference in their meanings. To the Muscogee (Creek), the alcohol problem does not exist until it is admitted. Therefore, the embarrassment is not with the actions committed while drinking, for these are often blamed on someone else, but with the admission of alcoholism. A 50-year-old woman explained this view as follows: "The Creeks are a proud people. Admitting a problem with alcohol is shameful. Therefore, it is denied or taken lightly. There is embarrassment to oneself, family, and clan to admit alcoholism."

This conclusion may appear antithetical to the earlier discussion about spirituality among the traditional people. It is at first difficult to understand why someone would be embarrassed by admitting alcoholism in the traditional domain where the third party, not the individual, is at fault. Further investigation revealed that the alcoholic person was perceived as having lost touch with the spiritual world and was existing only in the physical and mental. A 38-year-old man emphasized this perception: "We use the medicine wheel. There are four components to each of us: physical, spiritual, mental, and emotional. Illness [alcoholism] affects all parts, and you have lost your relationship with the spiritual component."

Because a spiritual person does not abuse alcohol, and an alcoholic is perceived as having lost spirituality, admitting alcoholism is tantamount to admitting spiritual loss. There is embarrassment in admitting alcoholism but greater embarrassment in admitting loss of spirituality. Therefore, a traditional Muscogee (Creek) person is usually unwilling to admit a problem with alcohol.

Theme 3

Theme 3 states that the strength and cohesiveness of the family, especially in the presence of illness, can be detrimental as well as supportive. At a Western-oriented inpatient treatment facility, the primary author observed a 41-year-old male Muscogee (Creek) patient refuse to attend a group session because his parents were visiting. Because it is disrespectful to ask one's parents to leave, the patient waited until they had departed before attending the group. The staff identified the patient as "noncompliant" and referred to his close relationship with his parents as "emotionally dependent for a man of his age."

The Muscogee (Creek) values of parental obedience, familial respect, and authority of the extended family (relatives, clan, community) differ from the dominant culture's emphasis on the nuclear family. The extended family has as large a role in child rearing as do the parents. The concept of nuclear family does not exist. One participant drew an analogy between the Indian concept of family and sharks' teeth: "When a shark loses a tooth, another grows to replace it. In our family, when one member is lost, another person replaces that one. The family is always whole."

Children are expected to maintain close relationships with parents, even into adulthood. Families, in return, have a responsibility to care for their members. However, in a modern society of countless stressors, young people often turn to alcohol or drugs because they believe their parents' ways cannot help. Once the person is addicted, the family turns its attention to helping. In the face of alcoholism, the family's commitment is unequivocal. A 44-year-old woman gave this account:

When my mother found out that I was using heroin, she confronted me about it. She then gave me a box of clean needles and told me to protect myself. She asked me if I was talking to the Creator. There were nights when my brothers came in drunk at 3:00 AM. We served them coffee and gave them cold towels. We loved them.

But here lies a contradiction of helping the afflicted person and promoting the illness. Many within the tribe explained that the Muscogee (Creek) value of protecting the family was not always in the best interest of the children. A medicine man agreed with this interpretation: "Many times the parents encourage the drinking. Lifestyles have become accustomed to alcohol in the home. On a weekend a man might go out drinking and the woman goes to her mother's house. The children get used to being with the grandparents." A 50-year-old woman supported this point: "The parental role of protecting their alcoholic children by taking care of their grandchildren has caused many people not to look for help."

The strength of the family can also incapacitate the family. The authors observed family members passively refusing to confront a family member. Children are protected by grandparents until the age of 7 or 8. Then they start mimicking the alcoholic behavior seen in parents. The grandparents are often too frail to deal with the problem, so they continue to love and protect the children, facilitating the drinking behavior. A Muscogee (Creek) nurse related the following: "I have done elderly home visits. Just about everyone was living with a young person who was abusing alcohol. Many of the grandparents are angry and resentful, but they are too weak to do anything about it."

Theme 4

Theme 4 states that the Muscogee (Creek) people are discriminating in whom they trust. Developing trust and intimacy with strangers requires time and experience. Participants acknowledged that they do not easily trust non-Indians because of the history of white oppression. Traditional people spoke of their distrust of "our own progressives," people who have abandoned traditional ties to embrace the lifeways of the dominant culture. Intimate information, then, is selectively shared with those who are trusted not to misuse it.

Recovering alcoholics who had received Western-oriented inpatient treatment said that practitioners encouraged them to discuss their personal and family history of alcohol use. They were assigned to group therapy where intimate information was expected to be shared immediately. The common response was for the person to withhold details or to share partially correct or even incorrect information in an attempt to protect individual or family integrity.

In a Western-oriented treatment center, the primary author observed situations where Indian patients were designated "resistant" or "unwilling to work the program" because they refused to speak during group sessions. When an Indian does talk, it may appear that he or she is discussing someone else or a hypothetical situation when he or she is indeed sharing intimate information. The following statement by a 40-year-old man elucidates this point: "Storytelling is important to us. White people want direct responses. A Creek may tell a story about someone else that expresses how he's feeling. We often speak in the third person and with symbols."

Participants offered recommendations regarding the type of care they believed would be effective in treating alcoholism. One-to-one meetings in conventional places such as homes, community centers, churches, and schools were suggested. Almost all of the participants agreed with a social worker who said, "Trust is an issue. Many Indians do not trust anyone who is not identifiably Indian." They argued that the most effective practitioners share a cultural affiliation with their patients.

Theme 5

Theme 5 holds that the practice of humility is a Muscogee (Creek) spiritual value as well as a cultural lifeway that hinders Western-oriented alcoholism treatment. The Muscogee (Creek) people, especially those who are traditional, do not openly exult in personal triumphs and often underrate their accomplishments. At the grounds, it is typical for a person to look down while speaking and to permit others, especially elders and guests, to speak first. Status is associated with individual character rather than career, socioeconomic level, or education.

Humility is a cultural lifeway and a spiritual value. A good person is humble. Whether Christian or traditional, the Muscogee (Creek) believe that no person is to be considered superior to another. Traditionalists also believe that if one boasts and is not humble, others may harbor resentment and encourage the intervention of the evildoer. One is therefore unpretentious about accomplishments and possessions. Several people spoke of medicine men who lost their powers and leaders who lost their influence because they were boastful.

Participants who were treated in a Western-oriented treatment facility said that they were expected to be assertive, to give "I" messages, and to directly state what they wanted. They indicated that this value conflict presented a barrier to their participating in and benefiting from treatment.

IMPLICATIONS FOR TRANSCULTURAL HEALTH CARE

Leininger's[14] theory of cultural care diversity and universality provides structure for planning culturally sensitive care through health care preservation, accommodation, and repatterning. *Health care preservation* is understanding and respecting a cultural health care practice and espousing that practice as an essential aspect of care. *Health care accommodation* is the integration of traditional ways with modern ways to optimize the patient's level of health. *Health care repatterning* is the modification of traditional ways that may have become ineffective in sustaining health. Based on Leininger's framework and the five emerging themes, the authors identified implications for transcultural health care professionals caring for Muscogee (Creek) clients suffering from alcohol abuse.

Health care preservation

It is important for health care professionals to appreciate that Muscogee (Creek) spirituality and healing cannot be separated. A holistic approach to care where the Creator prevails in every circumstance is fundamental. With traditional people, health care professionals must be sensitive to the third party, for most traditional people will hesitate to discuss the evildoer with someone who is not of the medicine culture. When the appropriate situation arises, the health care professional can question the patient about third-party involvement while remaining nonjudgmental. If the patient believes that the alcohol problem was caused by an outsider influence, the health care professional may suggest that the *heleshaya* be contacted.

It is important for health care professionals to realize that admission of alcoholism may be extremely demanding for a Muscogee (Creek) person. To say, "My name is _____, and I am an alcoholic," as is done in Alcoholics Anonymous (AA) meetings, is difficult for a Muscogee (Creek) person to do in front of an audience. It is advantageous to arrange private, one-to-one meetings as opposed to group counseling to deal openly with personal issues.

The Muscogee (Creek) relationship with elders and the extended family is often a difficult concept for the dominant culture to grasp. These close familial bonds represent a healthy cultural value that helps the individual and the community sustain their sense of completeness and security. The mother's family is very important to the circle of life. One's whole existence in the universe is through the mother, her clan, and her extended family. Because it is a matriarchal system, a maternal uncle is more important in the guidance of life than is the father. Health care professionals must understand that the client's

uncle may play a significant role in recovery.

Health care professionals should not expect family issues to be discussed impersonally and quickly, and they should understand that the Muscogee (Creek) share a lot about themselves through storytelling. When telling a story about another person or family, a patient may use a metaphor. Health care professionals should not attempt to interpret these stories back to the patient, but should be aware of the message that the patient is communicating. It is also important to understand that when obtaining a family history, often only the mother's family will be discussed.

Open-ended questions are helpful because they encourage storytelling. Too much information should not be expected too soon. Walk-in clinic visits and drop-in home visits are ways of getting around the frustration of missed appointments. Familiar sites such as homes, community centers, churches, and schools are effective locations for providing care.

Health care accommodation

An effective approach to caring for many nontraditional Muscogee (Creek) is to harmonize modern treatment ways with traditional ways. Expressive (art) therapy, music, and dance are symbolic and metaphorical ways to encourage communication and understanding.

The authors observed the integration of AA practices with traditional ways. For example, the 12 Steps of AA have been discussed in relation to the medicine wheel. Some treatment centers and communities offer Indian-only AA meetings where storytelling is practiced and a spiritual bond is present. Several treatment facilities offer a sweat lodge for those desiring it.

In accommodating, health care professionals must be careful to instill harmony and balance between the traditional way and the modern way, not to mold a Muscogee (Creek) tradition to fit a modern treatment approach. It is important to assess at the level of blending of traditional and modern a particular patient's needs, because some traditionalists avoid modern treatment, and some Muscogee (Creek) divorce themselves from traditional ways.

Health care repatterning

The authors observed two practices that need to be modified if the Muscogee (Creek) people are going to overcome alcohol-related problems. These practices are a crisis orientation and families' refusal to confront the alcohol problem.

Health care professionals have a definite role in transforming a crisis-oriented community into one where prevention prevails. Many participants said that low self-esteem as children and youths led them to drink. Building self-esteem is an integral aspect of alcoholism prevention. Whereas education programs can be offered in schools, churches, and community centers, development of self-esteem must be inspired in the family and community. Participants said that promoting self-esteem is best accomplished by Muscogee (Creek) and other Indian role models who can instill a sense of pride in the young.

Family reeducation is a sensitive area and one that is difficult to confront. The extended family concept must be preserved, and family acceptance of the alcoholic is not to be discouraged. The challenge facing health care professionals is how to use family strength and cohesiveness to discourage alcohol use and encourage some form of treatment whether traditional, modern, or a combination.

The structured family programs offered in treatment centers are often too rigid and overwhelming for the family. An effective intervention is to say to the family, "We need your help," followed by incremental and specific directions. For example, the health care professional can tell the family that it is not helpful to keep alcohol in the home. It is important to recognize the impact the family can have on recovery and to use this resource to its fullest.

•   •   •

This study revealed some important ethnonursing implications for caring for members of the Muscogee (Creek) community suffering from the effects of alcohol abuse. The authors anticipate that this knowledge will promote a culturally based understanding of the Muscogee (Creek) views of health and thereby help alleviate some of the individual and social suffering caused by alcohol abuse.

REFERENCES

1. US Dept of Health and Human Services. *IHS Alcoholism/Substance Abuse Prevention Initiative: Background, Plenary Session, and Action Plan.* Washington, DC: Government Printing Office; 1986.

2. Weibel-Orlando JC, Weisner T, Long J. Urban and rural drinking patterns: implications for intervention and policy development. *Subst Alcohol Actions Misuse.* 1984;5:45–56.

3. Debo A. *The Road to Disappearance.* Norman, Okla: University of Oklahoma Press; 1941.

4. *An Ordinance of the Muscogee (Creek) Nation Adopting the Muscogee (Creek) Nation Criminal Code*, NCA 92-14.

5. Beauvais F, LaBoueff SL. Drug and alcohol abuse intervention in American Indian communities. *Int J Addict.* 1985;20:139–171.

6. US Congress, Senate Select Committee on Indian Affairs. *Indian Juvenile Alcoholism and Eligibility for BIA Schools: Hearing Before the Select Committee on Indian Affairs.* 99th Congress, 1st session, S1298. Washington, DC: Government Printing Office; 1985.

7. Lange BK. Ethnographic interview: an occupational therapy needs assessment tool for American Indian and Alaska Native alcoholics. *Occup Ther Ment Health.* 1988;8(2):61–80.

8. Stratton R. Relationship between prevalence and alcohol problems and socioeconomic conditions among Oklahoma Native Americans. *Curr Alcohol.* 1981;8:315–325.

9. LaFromboise T. American Indian mental health policy. *Am Psychol.* 1988;43:388–397.

10. Herring RD. The American Native family: dissolution by coercion. *J Multicultural Counsel Dev.* 1989;17:4–13.

11. Walker RD, Kivlahan DR. Definitions, models, and methods in research in sociocultural factors in American Indian alcohol use. *Subst Alcohol Actions Misuse.* 1984;5:9–19.

12. Westermeyer J, Neider J. Cultural affiliation among American Indian alcoholics: correlations and change over a ten year period. *J Operational Psychiatry.* 1985;16:17–23.

13. Flaskerud JH. Perceptions of problematic behavior by Appalachians, mental health professionals, and lay non-Appalachians. *Nurs Res.* 1979;29:140–149.

14. Leininger MM, ed. *Culture Care Diversity and Universality: A Theory of Nursing.* New York, NY: National League of Nursing; 1991.

15. Wing DM. Involuntary chemical addiction treatment: EAP implications for occupational health nurses. *AAOHN J.* 1991;39:466–473.

16. Yin RK. *Case Study Research: Design and Methods.* Beverly Hills, Calif: Sage; 1984.

17. Leininger MM. Ethnomethods: the philosophic and epistemic bases to explicate transcultural nursing knowledge. *J Transcultural Nurs.* 1990;1(2):40–51.

CHAPTER 20

Development of a Health Promotion Inventory for Poor Rural Women

Roma D. Williams, PhD, CRNP

Dona J. Lethbridge, PhD, RN

William V. Chambers, PhD

LIFE FOR LOW-INCOME southern women in rural areas of the United States is sometimes described as bleak, isolated, and lacking resources.[1] These women have a greater risk of suffering illness or premature death than their more affluent, urban counterparts.[2] They have little access to health care. Services are usually limited to crisis care. Health promotion services are virtually nonexistent. These women often live in conditions of dire economic hardship that result in psychosocial stress.[3] Difficult living conditions may jeopardize their perceptions of their own health and use of disease prevention and health promotion behaviors. Describing these perceptions

Funding for the first study in this program of research was received from US Dept Health and Human Services, Agency for Health Care Policy and Research (Grant no. RO3 HS08018-02). Portions of this article were presented at the First Biennial International Nursing Conference, University of Iceland, Reykjavik, Iceland, 1995. The authors acknowledge Regina M. Barrett for her contributions to this project.

Fam Community Health 1997;20(2):13–23

is important in the development of a theory on rural health.

This chapter describes the development of a first-generation inventory tool to assess the health and health promotion behaviors of poor, rural women in Alabama. This research is part of a larger goal to increase the disease prevention and health promotion behaviors used by various groups of poor rural women in the southern United States. Studies of health protection and promotion behaviors have primarily dealt with the middle class; therefore, approaches and measurements must be tested for relevance to the lives of low-income, rural individuals. While there are many definitions of health promotion, this research uses the World Health Organization (WHO) definition that describes health promotion as a process of enabling people to increase control over and to improve their health.[4]

DEMOGRAPHIC AND HEALTH DIFFERENCES

The United States is a multicultural nation with some regions that reflect conditions often found in developing countries despite the fact that much of the nation is industrialized. While the cost of living may be lower in rural than urban areas, additional expenses such as the need for reliable care are unavoidable.[5] Rural households are particularly vulnerable to environmental-related events such as natural disasters, weather conditions, or economic conditions.[5] Pockets of poverty exist in many rural communities, with a greater percentage of poverty affecting rural minorities in the South.[6] Many rural southerners do not have basic services

such as running water, electricity, or indoor plumbing.[7,8] Yet, very poor rural southern families do not identify these deficits as needs; instead, they report needs as shelter, food, and clothing.[8]

As in developing countries, these individuals also have shorter life expectancies.[9] Thus, being low-income, rural, and southern is linked to a shorter life expectancy and poorer health status. Based on an analysis of sociodemographic correlates of mortalities, Rogers[10] concluded that increased standards of living and improved lifestyles, including better housing, nutrition, and health care, could reduce the disparities in health status that exist in America.

Southern United States

Most of the poorest counties in the United States are in the southern rural regions. In fact, rural poverty is concentrated in the South and includes 55% of all US rural poor. In 1990, 95% of all rural African Americans lived in the South, and of these 97% were considered poor and rural.[11] Rural poverty is related to the demographics of the population; a disproportionate number of individuals are economically marginal by virtue of age, education, or disability. The more educated, healthier, and younger rural people have moved to cities to find work. Although more rural women are entering the paid work force, they are employed in low-skilled and low-waged occupations, and there is less opportunity for advancement or full-time work with benefits. Lack of educational opportunities and child care also make it difficult for rural women to seek higher-level employment. In the South, rural African American women are in the lowest paying and least desirable jobs.[12]

Rural women as compared with urban women have higher rates of many chronic conditions, with the greatest differences seen in the incidence of arthritis, back disorders, bursitis, and hearing and visual impairments.[2] The greatest concern of poor rural women 50 years of age and over is cancer in general and specifically breast cancer.[13] Poverty and cancer represent a double jeopardy. There is a disproportionate number of cancer deaths among poor Americans. African Americans have the highest cancer incidence and mortality rates of any population group in the United States.[14]

For women living in the South, access to health care is often difficult. Some of the poorest counties of Alabama, for instance, have only three physicians for populations of over 15,000.[15] In fact, the rural South leads the nation with the largest number of Health Professional Shortage Areas (HPSAs), and the most underserved populations.[16] The health of rural populations is further threatened by hospital closings.[17] Indeed, rural areas are the most underserved in terms of health care services. Women are especially vulnerable, because many of them lack support in bearing and raising children in single-parent households and care for elders.[18] Unfortunately, government-funded programs (eg, health insurance, food stamps) are based on state incomes and only the poorest have access to this support. This means that many individuals who are at or just below the poverty line do not qualify for programs such as Medicaid, which

would increase their financial access to health care. The proportion of low-income people without any type of public or private health insurance, is greater in rural areas.[19,20] Medicaid is related to state welfare eligibility, which may be less beneficent in rural states. In Alabama, for instance, monthly income eligibility for Medicaid is 10.6% of the federal poverty level compared with 14.5 percent nationwide.[21] The magnitude of Alabama's poverty is reflected in the number of pregnant women and children who receive Medicaid. Forty-five percent of all births in Alabama are covered by the Sixth Omnibus Budget Reconciliation Act (SOBRA). In 1987 this act extended Medicaid coverage for pregnancy-related services to women with incomes up to 100% of the federal poverty level at the option of each state. In addition, nearly half (48%) of Alabama's children age 5 and under hold a Medicaid card (Mike Murphy, Director, Financial Planning and Analysis, Alabama Medicaid Agency; personal communication; October 24, 1995).

Alabama

Alabama is one of the least developed states in the country, with 8 of the nation's 100 poorest counties, and is 41st in per capita income.[11] Of the 67 counties in Alabama, all but 7 are designated as HPSAs and at least a portion of every county is considered medically underserved (Alabama State Health Planning and Development, personal communication, February 1995).

Infants and children, pregnant women, and older adults with chronic illness are particularly vulnerable due to lack of access to health care. Alabama is second in the United States in infant mortality with 67.2 infant deaths per 1,000 live births in 1993 to mothers who had received no prenatal care.[22] In Alabama, the infant mortality rate among African Americans is almost twice that of the nation.[23] Other alarming statistics related to the health of Alabama women and their families include a rate of heterosexual acquired immunodeficiency syndrome (AIDS) transmission that is one of the highest in the country; high rates of stroke and heart attacks as a result of untreated hypertension, diabetes, and poor dietary habits; and a lack of health education.[24]

PROGRAM OF STUDY

This study argues that women living in rural low-income conditions, due to their unique living situations and relative isolation from the dominant US culture, represent a subculture of the United States, and that their particular situations will especially influence their health perceptions and behaviors. The study described here includes both African and European American low-income rural women in Alabama. There are many similarities in the living situations of low-income, rural African and European American women, including cultural and language similarities. Two studies, for instance, have shown that myths, beliefs, and language related to women's issues, such as menstrual health and childbearing, are very similar for the two groups.[25,26] This work focuses on the issues of poverty and poor living conditions that impact the lives of

rural women, both African and European American, in Alabama. Blane[27] notes a positive correlation between income, education, and social class and health status. In addition, fewer investigations are focusing on race as a variable. Muir[28] reviews the historical definitions of race and points out their inadequacies in modern society, casting doubt on race as an important difference among human beings.

Instruments to measure health and related concepts have generally been developed for the dominant US middle-class and are usually oriented to such beliefs as cause and effect, personal autonomy and control, and self-actualization.[29,30] This research believes it is important that participants' beliefs be reported in their own language. In cross-cultural study, the term *etic* is used to denote a theory that is assumed to be comparative and cross-cultural, whereas *emic* is relevant to one culture exclusively.[31] An instrument to measure behavior may be *etic*, assumed to represent absolute or universal criteria, or *emic*, developed after in-depth study and relevant to the internal characteristics of a culture.[32,33] Dana[34] referred to the term *pseudoetic* to describe the use of the middle-class Anglo-American culture as the standard for comparison with other groups. For an instrument measuring health promotion to be an accurate reflection of behaviors, it should be general enough to be applicable to a wide social strata or else designed for and solely used for a specific well-described group under study. Thus, this work was ultimately aimed at an instrument that was emic and reflected the broad low-income culture of rural Alabama women, including both African and European American women.

DEFINITIONS

In this study, the terms *rural* and *low-income* are defined as follows: The US Bureau of the Census defines *rural* as "Geographic areas sparsely populated, with population densities of less than 2,500 per square mile, or those areas that are outside incorporated and Census-designated metropolitan places or are the rural areas of extended cities."[11] In fact, rural counties in Alabama are more likely to have population densities of 14 to 60 people per square mile. The Census definition for *low-income* includes women with household incomes at or below the US poverty level (adjusted for family size). In 1992, the weighted average poverty threshold placed a family of four at an annual income level of $13,359.[11] This figure is updated yearly by the US Bureau of the Census, and thus is likely to change with subsequent studies.

STUDY SITES AND PARTICIPANTS

Study participants were low-income, African American and European American women from two medically underserved rural counties in Alabama. No attempt was made to match participants from the two study sites. One site, in western Alabama, is 80.6% African American.[15] The second site, in northern Alabama and contiguous with the Appalachian populations of Tennessee, Virginia, and West Virginia,[15] is 93.5% European American (Table 20–1).[15,35]

Participants were women who were indigenous to the communities, consistent with Spradley's criteria that participants should be those individuals who are thoroughly involved in the culture under study.[36] These women were recommended for participation by community leaders and early study participants. We sought black and white low-income women living in rural settings who were age 19 or over and of varying marital and childbearing and educational and occu-

Table 20–1. Alabama health data*

	Population density per square mile	Per capita income	Infant death rate (number/rate per 1,000 live births)	% Low-weight births
United States	74.2	$20,800	116,973/9.9	7.0
Alabama	83.8	$17,129	2,180/11.7	8.4
Western Alabama	15.7	$11,422	13/24.3	10.3
Northern Alabama	44.3	$16,125	12/6.2	8.7

*Source: Information abstracted from Auburn University at Montgomery, *Alabama Health Data Sheet*, Alabama Diversified Health Services, Inc., Montgomery, Ala, September 1992, and *Alabama Population Data Sheet*, Center for Demographic and Cultural Research, November 1995.

pational status. Theoretic sampling was used wherein subjects were selected who, as indigenous members of the subculture, would provide data that would extend or test the developing description of health and health promotion.[37]

METHODOLOGY AND RESULTS

First, an ethnographic study of poor rural women from both sites described above was done using seven focus groups and seven individual interviews. These were aimed at eliciting views about the meaning of health, as well as health promotion and maintenance behaviors, barriers and facilitators. In addition, women were asked questions regarding conventional health behaviors identified in the literature, such as those from the Alameda study and *Healthy People 2000*.[38,39] For example, women were asked their beliefs about the need for exercise and ways, if any, that they themselves exercise. This enabled the identification of their personal behaviors in specific areas as well as the barriers and facilitators to health promotion.

Forty-nine women participated. Of these, 52% of the women were African American and 43% were married. Thirty percent of the women completed junior high, and 41.3% had a high school education. Four percent of participants reported that they had no formal education, and 13% reported that they had completed elementary school. The mean age was 48 years with a range of 18 to 86. Income and living standards were indirectly assessed by asking women to answer a question about their household finances. Forty-six percent of women responded that they barely made ends meet; 13% reported that they did not have enough money to pay bills; and 34.8% indicated they had enough money to pay bills with a little left over each month.

Data were analyzed using constant comparative analysis, a methodology in which participants' emic utterances are used in their original form to provide the basis for the development of higher-level concepts.[37] Each transcript was read in its entirety to get a sense of the whole. Individual units in the form of topics or themes from each transcript were identified and coded, whenever possible using the participants' own words. Similar codes were clustered and given an initial category label. Data collection and analysis took place in concert, and as additional data were analyzed, comparisons resulted in changing codes and categories. Through ongoing analysis, the concrete language of the codes was transformed into more conceptual terms.[40] After analysis of the total data set, larger themes that encompass the categories were identified and described. Data were organized using MARTIN, a computer program that facilitates qualitative data analysis.[41]

Investigators and data collectors met together weekly and bimonthly. Two of the data collectors were members of the community and served as key informants during data analysis.[42]

The qualitative analysis revealed a central descriptive process these women used: "being able to do for oneself and one's family." The major themes—"rural wisdom," "our own and others' needs," and "health habits"—had various subthemes[1]:

- Rural wisdom
  - Being right with God
    - Having a feeling of inner peace
    - Living right
  - Knowing the old ways
    - Remembering family traditions
    - The natural way of doing things
  - Staying healthy in the country
    - Being safe and quiet and clean
- Our own and others' needs
  - Women's obligations
    - Taking care of others when they need it
    - Teaching the children
  - Knowing what you can and can't do
  - Reasons I can't be healthy
    - No money
    - Not using formal health care
- Health habits
  - Rest and sleep
  - Eating healthy
    - Breakfast every day
    - Low salt, low fat, no or low alcohol
  - Exercise
    - Caring for children
    - Walk some

Next qualitative findings were used to design a health promotion behaviors inventory. In order to develop the list of items, health promotion behaviors were identified, using content analysis of the qualitative interviews as described above.[43] A list of behaviors was formulated using the words of the informants. The resulting list of items (117) was then scrutinized for behaviors known to be health promoting that may not have been represented. Items were presented so that participants could respond to them as characteristic or not on a Likert-like scale. Items were presented in simple language since low-income, rural southern adults have been found to have mean reading levels of from third to fifth grade.[44] Prior to administration the items on the inventory were analyzed for reading level using the Flesch-Kincaid (Grammatik Computer Program) and SMOG[45] Readability Formulas and found to be between third- and fourth-grade reading levels. Once the instrument was formulated, clarity was evaluated by asking rural, low-income women to note items that were unclear or that seemed "useless" (to assess meaningfulness). Items were revised as necessary and then administered to an initial sample of 61 low-income, rural women. These participants were selected from communities that were similar to the ones used during qualitative data collection and that were located in the same regions of the state as the original participants.

The instrument was tested through verbal administration to women during interviews by trained research assistants (unpublished data). Unlike other studies of this type, telephone interviews cannot be used since approximately 33% of households do not have telephones in the poorer, rural parts of the state (Western Alabama Rural Health Consortium, personal communication, October 1993). In order to expedite data collection, women were sought in settings where they congregated such as churches and other non-health-care settings.

For initial testing of reliability, items were subjected to inter-item and item-total correlations. Items that appeared redundant through inter-item correlation or had item-total correlations of less than .30 were discarded, in preparation for further testing. Sixty-six items were discarded because of poor item-total correlations. This resulted in a total of 51 items (see Exhibit 20–1). Since the instrument is newly developed, a conservative item correlation was used to retain items at this juncture of instrument development.[46] The resulting alpha is .92.

It should be noted that a limitation of this study is that self-report is the mode of data collection. Kirscht[47] has noted that in the study of health promotion behaviors this method is prone to faulty recall and intentional distortion, possibly due to social desirability issues or the fear of recrimination from caregivers. Data collectors were carefully trained to provide an atmosphere of comfort that would encourage study participants to speak frankly. Since data collectors were not from surrounding health clinics the possible fear of recrimination was further reduced.

FUTURE RESEARCH AND RECOMMENDATIONS

Additional testing of the instrument with a larger sample is planned for the next phase of the research program. It is important to have a psychometric mechanism to measure health promotion behaviors that is efficient and useful for both research and clinical settings. Culturally appropriate tools are needed that measure the baseline health promotion

Exhibit 20–1 Sample Items from the Health Promotion Inventory for Rural Southern Women

Rural wisdom
When I think I am sick, I go to God in prayer before I go to a doctor or nurse.
I think the old ways of healing sickness are best.
I think in the country you have a chance to relax more than if you live in the city.
The natural way of growing food is best.
Our own and others' needs
I think it is my duty to try to help the sick.
I think health is being able to do for yourself.
I need to stay healthy to take care of the older people in my family.
You only need to go to the doctor if you find something.
Health habits
I think a woman should have a time for rest sometime each day.
I eat breakfast every day.
My diet is low in salt.
I keep a check on my blood pressure regularly.

behaviors and postintervention behaviors of this population.

It is difficult for many researchers and health care providers to believe that individuals live in conditions similar to those of the direst poverty of developing countries. These individuals often live in geographically isolated areas. They are generally not seen by the health care system and may be virtually invisible. Providers must use ingenuity in finding these individuals and designing health care interventions that are feasible and culturally acceptable. These are some possible interventions suggested by the qualitative data used to develop this health promotion inventory:

- Health professionals should engage layworkers who are familiar with the communities, yet also conversant with the professional community— the "marginal" workers used in ethnographic studies and health care delivery in rural areas. In the case of extreme poverty, it is the local people who can help educate health care professionals of their existence and locations.
- Providers in such industrialized countries as the United States should read the international literature, especially journals that address the needs of those living in dire poverty. Often many problems such as epidemics, serious malnutrition, exposure to the elements, and living with a total lack of health care are similar, and similar interventions may be warranted.
- Introduction of technology and telecommunication systems into rural regions, where many pockets of extreme poverty are located, would be an ideal way to support the health care practitioners in these areas. Since impoverished individuals often have extremely acute and urgent conditions, access to specialty advice is imperative for the rural practitioner.
- Providers must acknowledge that individuals living in such conditions are often fiercely self-reliant. This cultural characteristic, existing in areas where health care support is negligible to nonexistent, can be seen as an asset for these people. Interventions must address the independence of the people and acknowledge the importance of the informal support system that is so important to those living in isolated rural regions.
- Finally, it is still a question as to what form health promotion activities might take for individuals living in rural poverty. If health promotion is truly viewed as what professionals term "secondary interventions" (ie, taking prescribed medications or complying with prescribed behaviors), as the early stages of this program of study suggest, then that should be the focus of research and clinical practice, aimed at promoting health in these populations, rather than working to increase knowledge of and compliance with preventive practices.

• • •

This program of research is exploring regional differences in rural health. Describing how women with limited means perceive their health, health promotion, and health protection is an important first step in elaborating on rural theory and research base, as suggested by Weinert and Long.[48] For low-income women living in the rural South, health care needs are great. Rural counties in the South tend to be predominantly African or European American, yet both groups often are equally impoverished. It is unlikely that this region will ever have adequate health care support, and it is imperative that rural dwellers be self-sufficient, yet have available to them a culturally relevant, accessible, and appropriate health care delivery system that fits within the context of their lives. In order to promote health and prevent disease in these women, researchers and providers must work together to develop strategies that are culturally sensitive and that recognize the constraints in these women's lives.

REFERENCES

1. Williams RD, Lethbridge DJ. Health promotion behaviors for women in Third World areas of industrialized countries. Presented at the First Biennial International Nursing Conference, University of Iceland; Reykjavik, Iceland; 1995.

2. US Dept Health and Human Services. *Action Plan for Women's Health*. Washington, DC: US Government Printing Office; 1991. DHHS publication No. (PHS) 91-50214.

3. Dietz M. Stressors and coping mechanisms of older rural women. In Bushy A, ed. *Rural Nursing*. Newbury Park, Calif: Sage Publications; 1991.

4. World Health Organization. The Ottawa Charter for Health Promotion. *Health Promotion*. 1986; 1:iii–v.

5. Bigbee JL. *Stressful Life Events Among Women: A Rural-Urban Comparison*. University of Wyoming, School of Nursing. 1985. PhD dissertation.

6. Sherman A. *Falling by the Wayside: Children in Rural America*. Washington, DC: Children's Defense Fund; 1992.

7. Lewis S, Messner R, McDowell W. An unchanging culture. *J Gerontol Nurs*. 1985;11:(8):20–26.

8. Strickland WJ, Strickland DL. Coping with the cost of care: an exploratory study of lower income minorities in the rural South. *Fam Community Health*. 1995;18(2):37–51.

9. Schultz TP. Mortality decline in the low-income world: causes and consequences. *Am Econ Rev*. 1993;83:337–342.

10. Rogers RG. Living and dying in the USA: sociodemographic determinants of death among blacks and whites. *Demography*. 1992; 29(2):287–303.

11. US Bureau of the Census. *Statistical Abstract of the United States*. 112th ed. Washington, DC: US Government Printing Office; 1992.

12. Smith BE. North Carolina: Who benefits from economic development. *Voices of the Rural South*.

Lexington, Ky: Southeast Women's Employment; 1986.

13. Freeman HP, Wasfie TJ. Cancer of the breast in poor Black women. *Cancer*. 1989;63:2,562–2,569.

14. American Cancer Society. *Cancer Facts and Figures*. Atlanta, Ga: ACS; 1995.

15. Alabama Family Practice Rural Health Board. *The Road to Rural Health*. AFPRHB; 1991.

16. Kolimaga JT, Konrad TR, Ricketts TC. Does subsidizing rural community health centers hurt private practice physicians? *J Health Care Poor Underserved*. 1994;5(2):124–141.

17. Johnson LW. Saving rural health care: strategies and solutions. *J Health Care Poor Underserved*. 1994;5(2):76–82.

18. Thomas D, Williams RD. Women's health. In: Swanson J, Albrecht M, eds. *Community Health Nursing: Promoting the Health of Aggregates*. Philadelphia, Penn: Saunders; 1993.

19. Sulvetta MB, Swartz K. *The Uninsured and Uncompensated Care*. Washington, DC: National Health Policy Forum, George Washington University; 1986.

20. Tavani C. Report on a seminar on financing and service delivery issues in caring for the medically underserved. *Public Health Rep*. 1991;106(1):19–26.

21. Levit KR, Lazenby HC, Cowan CA, et al. State health expenditure accounts: building blocks for state health spending analysis. *Health Care Financing Rev*. 1995;17:201–254.

22. Alabama Department of Public Health. *Alabama Vital Events*. Montgomery, Ala: ADPH; 1993.

23. Alabama Dept of Public Health. *Healthy Alabama 2000: Health Promotion and Disease Prevention Objectives for the Year 2000*. Montgomery, Ala: Alabama Dept of Public Health; 1991.

24. Raczynski J. Alabama: a risk portrait in black and white. *UAB Magazine.* 1995; Spring:16–17.

25. Scott CS. The relationship between beliefs about the menstrual cycle and choice of fertility methods within five ethnic groups. *Internat J Gynecol Obst.* 1975;13:105–109.

26. Snow LF, Johnson SM. Modern day menstrual folklore. *JAMA.* 1977;237:2,736–2,739.

27. Blane D. Social determinants of health—socioeconomic status, social class, and ethnicity. *Am J Public Health.* 1995;85(7):903–904. Editorial.

28. Muir DE. Race: the mythic root of racism. *Sociological Inquiry.* 1993;63:3,339–3,350.

29. Sampson EE. The decentralization of identity: toward a revised concept of personal and social order. *Am Psychologist.* 1985;40:1,203–1,211.

30. Spindler GD, Spindler L. Anthropologists view American culture. *Annu Rev Anthropol.* 1983; 12:49–78.

31. Denzin NK. *Interpretive Interactionism.* Newbury Park, Calif: Sage Publications; 1989.

32. Trimble JE, Lonner WJ, Boucher JD. Stalking the wily emic: alternatives to cross-cultural measurement. In: Irvine SH, Berry JW, eds. *Human Assessment and Cultural Factors.* New York, NY: Plenum; 1983.

33. Van de Vijver FRJ, Poortinga YH. Cross-cultural generalization and universality. *J Cross-Cultural Psychol.* 1982;13:387–408.

34. Dana RH. Culturally diverse groups and MMPI interpretation. *Prof Psychol Res Pract.* 1988;19(5): 490–495.

35. Auburn University. *Alabama Health Data Sheet.* Montgomery, Ala: Alabama Diversified Health Services, Inc; 1992.

36. Spradley JP. *The Ethnographic Interview.* New York, NY: Holt, Rinehart, & Winston; 1979.

37. Glaser BG, Strauss AL. *Discovery of Grounded Theory: Strategies for Qualitative Research.* Chicago, Ill: Aldine Publishing; 1967.

38. Berkman LF, Breslow L. *Health and Ways of Living.* Oxford, UK: Oxford University Press; 1983.

39. US Department of Health and Human Services. *Healthy People 2000.* Washington, DC: US Government Printing Office; 1990. DDHS Publication No. (PHS) 91-50212.

40. Miles MB, Huberman AM. *Qualitative Data Analysis: A Source Book of New Methods.* Beverly Hills, Calif: Sage Publications; 1984.

41. Diekelmann NL, Lam S, Schuster R. *MARTIN: User Manual.* School of Nursing, University of Wisconsin-Madison; 1991.

42. Lynam JJ, Anderson JM. Generating knowledge for nursing practice: methodological issues in studying immigrant women. In: Chinn PL, ed. *Nursing Research Methodology: Issues and Implementation.* Gaithersburg, Md: Aspen Publishers; 1986.

43. Krippendorff K. *Content Analysis: An Introduction to Its Methodology.* Beverly Hills, Calif: Sage Publications; 1980.

44. Jackson RT, Davis TC, Bairnsfather LE, George RB, Crouch MA, Gault H. Patient reading ability: An overlooked problem in health care. *Southern Med J.* 1991;84(10):1,172–1,175.

45. McLaughlin HG. SMOG-grading: A new readability formula. *J Reading.* 1969;12:641–646.

46. Nunnelly JC. *Psychometric Theory.* 2nd ed. New York, NY: McGraw-Hill; 1978.

47. Kirscht JP. Preventive health behavior: a review of research issues. *Health Psychol.* 1983;2:277–301.

48. Weinert C, Long K. The theory and research base of rural nursing practice. In: Bushy A, ed. *Rural Nursing.* Newbury Park, Calif: Sage; 1991.

CHAPTER 21

Living with Cancer: Self-Identified Needs of Rural Dwellers

Therese Sullivan, PhD, RN

Clarann Weinert, SC, PhD, RN, FAAN

Rodney D. Fulton, MS, MEd

S TORIES OF those living with cancer are full of testimony to the fact that managing cancer in the home involves a series of events made even more challenging for those living in rural parts of the nation. Although many research projects have sampled urban or suburban populations to establish cancer management models, the Montana Family Cancer Project (MFCP), funded by the National Cancer Institute, has surveyed individuals managing cancer in rural and frontier areas. Two participants speak clearly to the challenges of living with cancer in rural America. One 43-year-old woman with cancer said, " . . . Cancer is, for rural people, a very lonely experience, and as prevalent as the disease is, not many people can understand the emotional toll it takes." Another 57-year-old chose the following words: "Cancer is a very hard disease to live with, it affected

Funded by the National Institutes of Health National Cancer Institute grant 5R01CA46330. Unless otherwise attributed, all quotations in this article are excerpts from survey responses collected under this grant, entitled "Home Care of Rural Cancer Patients in Montana."

Fam Community Health 1993;16(2):41–49
© 1993 Aspen Publishers, Inc.

my way of thinking and my heart goes out to others who have it. There is so much that can be done and such a long way to go."

Health care for vulnerable populations in rural areas is one of the most pressing needs in the field recently targeted for study. The majority of residents in rural areas are under age 17 or over age 65 and are considered high-risk aggregates who are particularly subject to chronic illness and disability.[1] Health problems in rural areas are intensified by several major factors that complicate the delivery of effective health care. These factors include geographic isolation; distance from health care and lack of transportation; poverty; lack of health care providers; health policy inequities; and rural values, beliefs, and lifestyles.[2–5]

Rural Montana families experiencing cancer face these same obstacles to obtaining quality health care. Montana is the fourth largest state in the United States and ranks 44th in population density and 48th in resident population per square mile. There are just two metropolitan statistical areas: One comprises 113,000 residents and the other 78,000.[6] Access to cancer treatment is limited because there are only four centers in the state. For many, this involves travel of up to 500 miles for diagnosis, treatment, and follow-up care. Others seek treatment in other states, which usually involves even more extensive travel and expense.

Earlier stages of research and beginning theory development into health needs of this rural subgroup have revealed a number of concepts that are important in understanding how health and health care needs are perceived by these individuals. Health is viewed in relation to the ability to function and work. Self-reliance and self-help are identified as significant coping strategies. In addition, family and close friends are relied upon for support more frequently than formal health care agencies and care providers.[7,8]

Little research has been conducted that explores the needs of families managing cancer who are living in sparsely settled regions. From whom do these individuals find assistance, and what are the costs to the individuals and to the family unit of dealing with the demands of cancer?

THE MFCP

The MFCP assesses family; informal and formal caregiving; the needs associated with managing and treating cancer; and the impact of the illness on individuals, dyads, and the family system. The informal network and the formal health care system are examined to determine how they interact with the patient-caregiver dyad and what effect they have on assisting the dyad with issues related to home care and management of the demands of the illness. The study specifically focuses on those living in sparsely populated areas of Montana or Wyoming.

The research discussed here was based on the larger study; this article presents the self-identified needs and concerns of persons with cancer and their caregivers. Information selected by the participants as important may assist community health care workers in planning holistic health care interventions for vulnerable populations residing in rural areas.

Families who volunteered to participate in the MFCP were interviewed by phone and completed mail questionnaires. The 420 families who participated represented residents of 47 of the 56 counties in Montana and 6 northern Wyoming counties. Approximately two thirds of the families lived in small towns, in rural areas near small towns, or in more isolated areas. A large portion of the households comprised two people, with 91% of the care providers being the spouse of the person with cancer. Persons with cancer 65 years of age or older constituted 41% of the sample, with another 35% being in the 50- to 64-year age group. The remaining 24% were under 50 years of age. Virtually the same age pattern applied to the caregivers: 37% were 65 years or older, 37% were in the 50- to 64-year age group, and 24% were under 50 years of age. At the time of the study almost half the patients were in treatment and were traveling an average of 140 miles for treatments, with those in the more isolated areas traveling more than 200 miles round trip. For appointments with the oncologist, those in the rural areas traveled an average of 214 miles, and those in isolated areas traveled an average of 296 miles round trip.

As participants joined the study, they were interviewed by phone to obtain information related to individual and family characteristics and details about the disease itself, such as the type of cancer, length of time since diagnosis, and extent of care needs. After the telephone interview, individuals with cancer and their caregivers were sent in-depth written questionnaires. These questionnaires contained scales that measured the physical and psychologic status of the person with cancer, the needs associated with managing the cancer, and the impact of the illness on the family.

A large subsample of 290 respondents, 166 with cancer and 124 care providers, gave written feedback to the open-ended question at the end of the questionnaire, which asked, "What have we not asked you about living with cancer that we should have asked?" The responses to this question from both the persons with cancer and the care providers were transcribed verbatim and entered into the software program Ethnograph for analysis.[9] By means of content analysis, major themes or categories were identified, and the data were coded on the basis of their similarity of meaning.

FINDINGS

The findings are presented quantitatively in terms of frequencies and percentages and qualitatively in categories for explanatory and illustrative purposes. Use of the participants' own words from their narratives provides special access to their perspectives and captures their interpretation of living with cancer in a rural setting. Table 21–1 displays the categories of needs and the frequency with which these categories were identified by both the persons with cancer and their care providers. The categories of coping, knowledge, support, interpersonal relationships, effects of treatment, life view, reactions to diagnosis, attitudes, diagno-

Table 21-1. Self-identified needs

Needs/concerns	Total group (N=290)		Person with cancer (N=166)		Caregiver (N=124)	
	Frequency	Percent	Frequency	Percent	Frequency	Percent
Coping	49	17	26	9	23	8
Coping with change	10	3	4	2	6	2
Knowledge	26	9	18	6	8	3
Support	19	7	11	5	8	2
Spiritual support	11	4	5	2	6	2
Group support	11	4	7	2	4	2
Interpersonal relationships	18	6	11	4	7	2
Effects of treatment	15	5	12	4	3	1
Life view	12	4	9	3	3	1
Reactions to diagnosis	9	3	5	1.5	4	1.5
Diagnosis	7	2	5	1.5	2	0.5
Attitude	7	2	4	1	3	1
Feelings	5	2	5	2	0	0
Problems	5	2	4	1.5	1	0.5
Depression	4	1	4	1	0	0
Fear	4	1	4	1	0	0
Loneliness	4	1	3	1	1	0

sis, feelings, problems, depression, fear, and loneliness were identified.

COPING

The main challenge expressed by persons with cancer and their care providers in this rural study was coping with the many demands and stresses that resulted from the illness and its contingencies. Coping with the changes resulting from the diagnosis itself was a major area of concern. The other categories specifically identified as creating needs and concerns related to coping were finances, fear of recurrence, uncertainty, death, family and children, treatment, travel, discrimination, lifestyle changes, home health needs, and spiritual concerns.

A 46-year-old man provided a pertinent narrative of a family experience that exemplifies the obstacles encountered in rural areas. He expressed his concerns and frustrations in obtaining care for his son, who had died of cancer a few years ago, and in caring for his wife, who was currently experiencing cancer:

Your questions on transportation do not bring out the difficulties that transportation can be for rural Montanans. Doctors are few and far between, but cancer is not a question of going to the nearest doctor. It is a matter of special care at a few centers in the state . . . we had to travel 220 miles every time we had an appointment with a doctor.

For the wife's cancer treatment, they decided to go to one of the cities with a cancer treatment center, where they could stay with the wife's parents for the immediate postoperative period. He continued regarding follow-up care:

Round trip from where we live to Missoula is 520 miles. We made numerous trips . . . through the fall and winter. This travel had to be done around my work schedule. It would have been best for treatments to take place on Saturday, but no treatment was available on the weekend and no exceptions could be made even though we were driving 520 miles. As the weather got worse, crossing the divide became more difficult.

His needs regarding these obstacles were specifically described in the following manner:

The families of cancer patients and cancer patients in a state as rural as Montana need special facilities close to larger medical centers where they can stay inexpensively for periods of time to be available to support the cancer patients during the most difficult and scary part of their treatment. Some flexibility on the part of the health care providers for people who are traveling long distances would also be helpful.

His account of attempting to provide terminal care to his 2½-year-old son was vivid:

He was extremely disabled and needed constant nursing care. Rural Montana provides almost no organized care for such a situation. It was only through our acquaintance with a very giving nurse who lives in the area that we were able to do it at all. We called her for advice at all hours of the day and night, and she came and stayed with Bobby some nights when my wife was too exhausted to care for him and when I had to work the night shift. I feel that having our son at home was the right thing to do for him. He needed to be in a familiar environment even though his sensory perceptions were now impaired. He needed to be in the environment that he was used to. But the obstacles were great! We found no organized help. Most people would not have it. Something needs to be done to help rural Montanans when they need to care for cancer patients.

He also identified the need for support groups as a major concern:

Support groups are few and far between in rural Montana. . . . My wife and I tried to make contact with the Compassionate Friends organization and even tried to get a chapter going, but the distances overwhelmed us. While in Missoula, my wife was contacted by support groups in Missoula for women who have experienced breast cancer, but as soon as we came home . . . all support ceased. Cancer is lonely in rural Montana. Support groups need to be extended to cancer patients who live in rural areas.

This broad spectrum of self-perceived needs includes all the multiple dimensions of the illness experience requiring assistance from community health care providers.

KNOWLEDGE

Information needed to manage the problems faced by those with cancer and their care providers was the second most frequently expressed area of concern, as exemplified by the statement of a 60-year-old woman with cancer:

. . . I do feel that doctors should explain more to family members what the cancer patient's emotions can be, so that family members can perhaps have a little more understanding of the patient's feelings. There are feelings of despair, hopelessness, fear, and anxiety, which require a lot of love and understanding.

The other areas of informational needs specified were related to coping, finances, interpersonal relationships, treatments and side effects, types of cancer, hair loss, alternative treatments, feelings, support groups, and depression. These findings indicate the need for a holistic assessment of each individual's and family's informational needs and learning styles so that appropriate educational materials and delivery systems can be utilized.

SUPPORT

The needs identified for assistance to cope with the demands of living with cancer in a rural setting were in several different categories, as typically expressed by a 66-year-old man providing care for his wife:

We were not prepared financially for this catastrophe that hit us in retirement years. . . . When we could not afford the medicines or supplies needed we went to Family Services, who helped us for a limited time for which we are grateful. Also a family who lost their son assisted us in transportation. No self-help group ever contacted us. We live out of the city where we had to go for medical attention and thought we might get more help, but this has been devastating to us.

Group and spiritual support were the most frequently mentioned categories of inadequate support. The various types of assistance were reported as being required throughout all phases of treatment, but particularly when the patients returned to their home communities. As a 53-year-old woman with cancer stated, " . . . there was no one who came to my family to help them cope with the stress. . . . The nurses talked to me in the hospital, but after I got home we were on our own."

These findings indicate that the various needs identified as related to support are felt to be lacking primarily in the rural communities. The kind and form of support requested and required must be considered carefully in light of previous research findings indicating that self-reliance and self-help are strong values of rural residents.

Interpersonal relationships

Disruptions and problems in relationships represented another category of self-identified needs. The narratives described concerns in relating to and interacting with health care professionals, spouses, children, friends, acquaintances, and coworkers. Ineffective communication skills appeared to be a major reason for the difficulties described.

An example of concerns expressed in this category that are of special significance to health care workers in rural areas was given by a 28-year-old woman with cancer: "Relationships with doctors and nurses in trying to get them to understand that a patient has more needs than medical. The right to live a quality life, not just live."

Recognizing the necessity of effective and satisfying relationships and interactions to those living with cancer, these findings indicate the need for community health care providers to utilize a holistic framework in their practice. This is espe-

cially important when one is working with rural populations because previous studies have discovered that family and close friends are relied upon for support more frequently than formal health care providers and that self-help and self-reliance are important values.

This approach to the provision of health care to rural-based people within the context of rural culture and lifestyle is vital to the desired outcome of effectively assisting the person with cancer and his or her family with issues related to home care and the management of the demands of the illness.

Effects of treatment

Although a number of advanced and successful forms of cancer treatment are available, many adverse reactions must be endured. Some of the patients with cancer as well as their care providers described needs related to the effects of treatment. Most of the side effects identified were related to chemotherapy and included loss of hair, diarrhea, nausea and vomiting, weakness, loss of weight, and numbness in the arms.

Although home health care is increasingly needed and is experiencing growth within the health care delivery system, few such services are available in rural areas. As a result, rural family members caring for cancer patients must assume responsibilities with limited assistance from health care professionals. The difficulties of this experience are represented in a poignant narrative by a 40-year-old man caring for his mother:

My mother took one treatment of chemo-therapy and experienced extreme pain and I now believe was in and out of shock. We were not warned to watch for this severe effect. As a result she fell and had a minor fracture of her lower leg. I feel this was a result of incompetence/indifference of the medical "professionals" involved. Also availability of medical help in an emergency situation—particularly late at night—was grossly inadequate in our situation.

Life view

Concerns and needs resulting from the challenges presented by a diagnosis viewed as life threatening were also shared. A few patients and care providers stated that they needed assistance in adjusting to this existential crisis, where their central beliefs regarding life's priorities and meanings were questioned.

These data suggest the need for community health care workers to allow and encourage the open expression of these feelings. This requires unusual patience, sensitivity, and understanding, especially in light of rural theory findings that self-help and self-reliance are highly valued by rural dwellers.

Additional themes

The narratives also described the often long and difficult journey that only begins with the diagnosis of cancer. The other themes presented by the respondents regarding living with cancer were related to the diagnosis, reactions to the diagnosis, attitudes, feelings, problems, depression, fear, and loneliness. These themes were described usually in terms of the psycho-logic responses associated with the uncertainty of the outcome of the illness.

IMPLICATIONS FOR COMMUNITY HEALTH CARE PROVIDERS

The themes presented from the perspectives of this vulnerable population of persons living with cancer and their care providers relating to their needs and concerns of managing the disease in a rural area have important implications for community health care providers. Hearing from them in their own words should advance health care professionals' understanding and increase their awareness, leading to more effective, sensitive, and informed practice.

The respondents varied in a number of ways, as did their concerns, depending on the stage of the illness. Some of the themes were shared by many but varied in intensity. Others were experienced by fewer people. Nevertheless, the concerns are important in the sense that they were prominent in the subjective experience of those for whom they existed.

The wide array of self-identified needs indicates the necessity of using a holistic approach to identify the health needs of rural residents and to determine ways to improve their access to care within the context of the rural environment and culture. The wellness model of health care, which views individuals and aggregates who assume responsibility for their own health holistically from a biopsychosocial viewpoint, provides a basis for such an approach.[9] This health-oriented, comprehensive framework will enhance the integrity of the individual and the family as they move toward their highest potential and the optimum level of functioning that is realistic to attain.

The interventions must be designed jointly by the community health care workers and the client and family. Following this holistic framework and taking into consideration rural values, lifestyles, and environment will generate interventions that are realistic and acceptable.

With regard to access to care in rural areas, exploration and planning of the use of technology for networking are exciting possibilities. The use of 24-hour telephone access and computer networks with the major medical centers can serve as a system for delivering health care. These mechanisms can provide 24-hour-a-day information, decision assistance, communication, and support. This would involve meaningful discharge planning with the oncology team and the community health care workers utilizing the formal and informal services available.

•   •   •

In summary, these narrative descriptions provide community health care workers with unique access to the experiences of persons with cancer and their care providers in a rural setting. Moreover, they provide insights not only into the realities of cancer management but also into the manner in which the participants understand and view their experiences. Community health care workers and all involved in the development of public policy for health care delivery in rural areas should be aware of the self-identified needs and concerns of cancer patients and their care providers. Also, the subcultural values that affect help-seeking patterns must be acknowledged. For health care services to be effective, they must be acceptable and available and must accurately address the needs of individuals and families who are attempting to maintain a quality lifestyle while living with cancer.

REFERENCES

1. National League for Nursing. *Public Policy Bulletin.* New York, NY: NLN; May/June 1991.

2. Hanson C. Care of the client in rural settings. In: Clark MJ, ed. *Nursing in the Community.* Norwalk, CT: Appleton & Lange; 1991.

3. Bushy A. Rural determinants in family health: considerations for community nurses. *Fam Community Health.* 1990;12:29–38.

4. Weinert C, Long K. Understanding the health care needs of rural families. *Fam Relat.* 1987;36:450–455.

5. Davis D, Henderson M, Boothe A, et al. An interactive perspective on health beliefs and practices of rural elders. *J Gerontol Nurs.* 1991;17:11–13.

6. *Statistical Abstracts of the United States 1991.* Washington, DC: United States Department of Commerce; 1991.

7. Weinert C, Long K. Rural families and health care: refining the knowledge base. *Marriage Fam Rev.* 1990;15:57–75.

8. Long K, Weinert C. Rural nursing: developing the theory base. *Sch Inq Nurs Pract.* 1989;3:113–127.

9. Dossey B, Keegan L, Guzeeth C, Kalkmeier L. *Holistic Nursing.* Gaithersburg, MD: Aspen; 1988.

CHAPTER 22

Implementation and Evaluation of the Health Resource Program for Migrant Women in the Americus, Georgia Area

Angela Cole, BSN, RN

Lynda H. Crawford, MN, RN

APPROXIMATELY 3 to 5 million individuals engage in migratory farm labor throughout the United States.[1,2] *Migrants* are defined as the mobile farm worker population that travels throughout the United States harvesting crops. Because of the migrants' long work hours, nomadic life-style, impoverished social status, and other barriers, accessibility to health care is severely limited. The purpose of this chapter is to acquaint the reader with the unique health problems of migrant workers related to their lifestyle and to describe one nursing approach to address these multiple, complex needs.

Migrant workers travel along three main interstate routes within the United States (see Figure 22–1). The eastern route (or stream) originates in Florida and extends up the east coast. The midwestern stream, the largest in numbers of migrants, begins in Texas and

Source: Angeline Bushy and Lynda H. Crawford, Rural Nursing Kit, pp. 364–374, copyright © 1991 by Sage Publications, Inc. Reprinted by permission of Sage Publications, Inc.

reaches upward into the midwestern states. The western stream also starts in Texas but moves up the West Coast. Due to the unpredictable nature of farmwork, the three streams are not clearly delineated; weather conditions and employment opportunities affect movement patterns.

Remaining in an area for only 6 to 8 weeks, migrants work in the fields 6 days a week from sunrise to sunset. All members of the family are involved in the work process, including preschool and school-age children. Because children are viewed as income producers, an estimated 80% of them quit school at an early age.[3]

Migrants travel together as "crews" or groups, each having its own "crew leader" (also called "crew chief" in many areas). The crew leader is usually male and is the liaison between the workers and the farmer. The farmer frequently pays the crew leader directly for migrant earnings, and the crew leader in turn pays the workers. An unscrupulous crew chief could, therefore, keep workers constantly in debt. Entry into the camps is contingent upon approval of both farmer and crew leader. Crew leaders often formulate their crews at the beginning of the season and transport them throughout the stream. Occasionally crew leaders and their crews remain unchanged year after year. It is not uncommon for an entire crew to comprise one family of aunts, uncles, cousins, siblings, and their offspring traveling together.

While working in the fields, migrant workers frequently are not provided with sanitation facilities or fresh drinking water, and fields may be located in isolated areas on the outskirts of rural communities.[4,5] An Occupational Safety and Health Act (OSHA) law implemented in May and June of 1987 required field sanitation and fresh drinking water to be placed at each 1 mile of field on farms employing 11 or more farm workers.[6] That law, however, was amended in August of 1989 to state that only farms with 11 or more workers together in a 1-mile stretch of field would be required to provide water and field sanitation. Large corporate farms can now simply space the workers and legally avoid the regulations.

At the end of the working day, migrants return to dilapidated and overcrowded barracks, trailers, buses, or sheds[5]: 90% of all migrant homes have no sink and 95% of all homes have no sanitation facilities.[3] One example of housing conditions common among migrant camps was a camp in Alabama where workers lived in a converted chicken house. The upper portion of the wall had been removed for ventilation, hence flying insects and birds had easy access. The floors were dirt, and a single low-watt light bulb provided the only lighting. Sanitation facilities consisted of two portable toilets located some distance away from the building. The farmer who had renovated the facility had failed to remove stacks of nail-ridden, termite-infested lumber from inside the chicken house, making a dangerous playground for the approximately 12 children who lived there for a time. The only water for the approximately 60 people living in this chicken house was provided through two sinks in the common living area. Beyond the common area were individual apartments divided by plyboard walls. Although a few apartments had mattresses, most did not and their inhabitants slept on the floor. Because the workers were harvesting potatoes, potato baskets conveniently served as the only furniture. Families cooked their meals on hot plates.

If a migrant child survives his or her initial entrance into the world, education becomes secondary as employment becomes primary. Children have difficulty attending school because of the itinerant movement of the family and complete, on the average, only 7 years of education.[3] Placing the child in the proper grade is virtually impossible because age and expected status do not always correlate.

HEALTH STATUS

Clearly the lifestyles and environments of these workers influence their health status. Delivered into a group of nomadic, impoverished harvesters, the migrant child stands a 2.5 times greater chance of never surviving infancy than a normal child.[3] Among migrant workers the death rate from tuberculosis and other communicable diseases is 25 times greater than among the general population.[5] Heat stress occurs nearly 2 times as often as in other high-risk industries and about 4 times as often as in the general population.[7] Urinary tract infections are more common in migrant women, with prevalence rates 3 to 10 times higher than in the general population.[7] The risk to migrant workers for parasitic diseases is about 16 times greater than in the general population, and diarrhea occurs 10 times more frequently.[7] Parasitic rates among US migrant farm workers range from 20% to 78%, whereas parasitic rates among the general population register around 3%.[5,7] These rates are comparable to those found in developing countries; Feacham,[8] for example, found the prevalence of parasitism among children in rural Guatemala to be 26%. The incidence of malnutrition among migrants is higher than in any other subpopulation in the United States.[5] In a 1986 survey of 65 migrant health centers, it was found that 57% of the pregnant migrant women surveyed received poor prenatal care.[9] In addition 37% of those surveyed underutilized the government food stamp program.[9]

Migrant workers are at much greater risk for pesticide poisoning than the general population. Agrichemicals are commonly used in the United States. Pesticide exposure usually occurs during application and at initial reentry into the field. Many migrant camps are located within large open fields or on the fringes of fields. Hence overhead spraying endangers not only those at work in the fields but also those in the camp. Poor sanitation facilities and poor water supplies enhance the absorption and spread of agrichemical residues.

There is a significantly higher rate of miscarriage among citrus-picking women and significantly higher rates of muscle weakness during the spraying season.[5,7] Other symptoms of pesticide exposure commonly observed are conjunctivitis, excessive thirst, excessive sweating, and excitability.[7] Skin diseases occur frequently among farm workers and can be very severe.[4] Symptoms include rashes, welts, excoriated arms and underarms, swelling of the face, and tremendous itching over the entire body.[4] The California Department of Industrial Relations found that agricultural workers constitute only 3% of the state labor force yet suffer more than 13% of the occupational skin diseases.[7]

Silhouetted against the skyline of health and prosperity in the United States, migrant workers cast a shadow of illness and poverty that parallels that of the developing world. As with many in the developing countries, migrant workers' accessibility to health care is severely limited. Their long work hours, nomadic lifestyle, and impoverished social status create barriers to existing health care services. Migrant camps are usually located in isolated, rural areas some distance away from health care facilities, adding distance and lack of transportation to problems of accessibility. Language and cultural barriers present more of a challenge than many communities are willing or able to address. In many areas resentment of community members and health care providers toward migrant workers prevents the provision of quality health care. Continuous environmental hazards both in the workplace and in the camps help keep migrant workers from achieving a state of wellness. When illnesses or injuries occur in the field, farm workers do not want to lose time from work to seek health care, often working until the health problem becomes too debilitating for them to continue. Often county health departments or public emergency rooms are used to handle emergencies,

but a story recounted by Coles[10] illustrates problems encountered by the migrants seeking health care: When a pregnant migrant woman in labor sought help at a nearby hospital, the nurse on duty told her that she could not be admitted because she was not under the care of a physician and could not make a deposit toward payment of the hospital bill. The woman left and had her child in the camp.

HEALTH RESOURCE PROGRAM

To address the multiple, complex health needs of these people, the Migrant Camp Health Aide Program was developed by the Midwest Migrant Health Office and has been successful in Nebraska, Ohio, and other states.[11] The program was designed to train selected "leaders" within each migrant camp to do peer training. Topics covered in the program included hygiene and the spread of disease; preventive health information; family planning information; the causes and effects of the most common migrant illnesses; the need for sanitary drinking water and toilets; the basics of prenatal care; nutritional counseling; pesticide poisoning facts and treatment; and the existence, location, and costs of available health care and human services in a given area. Migrant women trained in this manner are able to provide on-site care, decreasing the amount of time lost from work and reducing complications due to inattention to health problems.

A similar program was implemented in Americus, Georgia, in July 1988, where a migrant community of approximately

1,000 have lived at any given time. In the first group, nine migrant, Hispanic women, each representing a different migrant camp, were selected to participate in the pilot program. Then in 1989, six women participated in the program. Each of the 15 participants was bilingual, was married, had children, and had completed less than 10 years of formal education. The program sought not only to increase the health education of the women but also to empower them as individuals.

Selection of the participants was conducted by Sisters at the local Catholic Church. The church in Americus is noted for its involvement with the farm worker population through Spanish mass, distribution of food and clothing, English classes, and transportation to medical facilities, and it funded the program. The Sisters had routinely entered the camps, so credibility and trust were already established with the farmer and migrant crew leader. Prior to the initiation of the program, the Sisters entered the camps and asked the camp members to select women to be trained as their health resource person (HRP). The women selected were perceived by others in the camps as leaders. It was desirable for the participants to be English speaking because the HRP would be expected to interact with local health care providers.

For the women to participate in classes without loss of family income, each woman was paid a salary of $4.25 per hour for class time plus 21¢ per mile for travel. Transportation was provided by the church when needed. Eight 2-hour classes were conducted over 4 days at the local Catholic Church, and lunch was provided by the congregation.

Health topics covered in the classes included hygiene and the spread of disease, preventive health information, family planning information, the causes and effects of the most common migrant illnesses, the need for sanitary drinking water and toilets, the basics of prenatal care, nutritional counseling, and pesticide poisoning facts and treatment. The existence, location, and costs of available health care and human services in the Americus area were discussed as well as the information helpful to have available when contacting health care providers. Also covered were well-child care and basic first aid for bleeding, cuts, scrapes, small wounds, snakebites, heat exhaustion and heat stroke, poisoning, and skin problems. The curriculum was developed in part from the *Camp Health Aide Manual*[11] and *Where There Is No Doctor*[12] and also from the needs expressed by the women themselves. Each participant was given a copy of the book *Where There Is No Doctor* (in either English or Spanish), a first aid manual, a bag containing first aid and baby supplies, and a certificate of completion at the end of the course.

It was hoped that the women trained in this program would be able to provide care, reducing both time lost from work and complications due to inattention to health problems. To determine the impact of the program, follow-up interviews were conducted to obtain information about the personal experiences of the participants as well as demographic information. Completion of the course was not contingent upon participation in the follow-up research. Each interview was taped with the consent of the participant and was conducted at the convenience of the women.

RESULTS

Each interview lasted approximately 2 hours, although most participants requested additional interviews throughout the summer. All of the participants agreed to be interviewed. Several very distinct themes emerged through interview data analysis.

The central theme of the participants' responses was that the program presented an opportunity for them to learn. One woman responded, "I went through sixth grade. I wished that I had been able to attend school and really done something . . . what little school we had wasn't enough. And now we're eager to learn, you know." Another responded,

I passed the seventh [grade], but, they had to take me out, my parents, cause I had to go to work.... My dad wanted us to finish school, but we couldn't, 'cause we had to work. There were only three of us [kids]. The smaller one [of the kids] was 10, or 9, something like that.

All of the class members showed interest in attending more Health Aide classes. One member stated, "I wouldn't mind going again and again and again [to the classes], just as long as I learn more."

Each woman reported experiencing a sense of accomplishment and worth, and one woman even commented that it was

the first time she had known anyone to take the time to teach migrant workers. Another participant experienced a similar surge of self-confidence and pride. For the first time in her life, she felt she had the ability to pursue her high school diploma. Her ability to learn the content taught in the Health Resource classes proved to her that she could accomplish a goal.

Each participant described increased opportunities for socialization and friendships with others. Although migrant women have very few social contacts outside their immediate family, the women in the program bonded strongly, lingering after each class to ask questions and socialize with each other. They maintained contact with each other throughout the summer. In response to the question: "What was the one thing that meant the most to you about the classes?" one woman said, "Getting to know y'all. I enjoyed that. You know . . . I don't have much time to go out and visit friends or be with people close to my age, and I really enjoyed that."

In addition to increased socialization, the women felt that for the first time they had knowledge to share with others. One woman responded to the question concerning family interest in the classes by relating the following:

My husband sat up until 1 in the morning. To bed, we go to sleep about 9:30 or 10, that's usually . . . and I finished washing dishes, and he said, "juss leave everything there" . . . just so he could ask questions, and . . . we'd keep on talking, I'd be so sleepy . . . until 1 in the morning . . . what else do you do? . . . And the more I would tell him, the more he wanted to know . . . and the next day, he'd go tell his boss that, and the guy that worked with him out in the fields what I was doing and they were really happy for me.

One participant responded to the question "What did you enjoy most about the classes?"

Well, the teaching and the asking us questions. It helped us a lot.... And I enjoyed learning too.... My mom said it would be better [to go to the classes] 'cause staying at home you don't learn much, and if you go where they teach you, you get to learn. She says now that if my dad would have let us finish school, that we wouldn't have to be working in the fields, and so, now, she knows that it's important for us to learn.

This participant's response is enlightening both about the migrant culture and about the Health Resource program. Within the migrant lifestyle, men are dominant. Even though the women work in the fields, give birth to and care for the children, and assume the duties of caring for the home, the men make the decisions regarding the family. This is reflected in a participant's response as she remembers that her father would not "let her" finish school. As indicated earlier in the chapter, all hands are needed in the fields to increase the family's income. Hence education is not usually a primary concern.

As part of the evaluation process for the program, the women were asked to identify issues that were not covered in the classes but should have been. They all agreed that alcoholism and family violence were topics that needed to be addressed in future sessions. They also validated that certain subjects were more applicable and helpful than others. For example, one interviewee said of the pesticide issue "It's really bad, 'cause when they're spraying, the people are right there. They're spraying on this end, and the people are standing there."

CONCLUSION

The Migrant Camp Health Aide Program was successful not only in relating health knowledge but also in empowering those who participated. As one class member commented, "I see things differently than I did a few weeks ago, a month ago.... [The program] just made me look at things in a different way."

Migrants remain an underserved subpopulation within the United States. The Health Resource program is a cost-effective, community-based program that increases accessibility to health care by training migrants to convey health knowledge to other migrants. The women trained to be HRPs carry their skills with them as they travel throughout the stream, and graduates of the program have referred other women to the classes. Lay health worker programs play an integral role in raising the health status of migrant farm workers within this country, and nursing can be the driving force behind this initiative.

REFERENCES

1. Chellis R, Seagle J, Seagle B. *Congregate Housing for Older People: A Solution for the 1980s.* Lexington, Mass: Lexington; 1982.

2. Colorado Migrant Council. *The Farmworker in the United States: A Profile.* Wheat Ridge, Colo: Colorado Migrant Council; 1980.

3. Dement E. *Out of Sight, Out of Mind: An Update on Migrant Farmworker Issues in Today's Agricultural Labor Market.* Paper presented to the National Governor's Association: March 1985; Washington, DC.

4. Bureau of National Affairs. OSHA preamble to final field sanitation standard [52 FR 16050, May 1, 1987]. *Occup Saf Health Rep.* 1987;16(48): 1362–1407.

5. Tidwell et al. *Outreach Health Services to Migrants: The Reality, the Dream.* Unpublished manuscript, developed in conjunction with the Office of Migrant Health.

6. Occupational Safety and Health Administration. 29 CFR Part 1928. Field sanitation; final rule. *Federal Register.* 1987;52(84):16050–16096.

7. Gangarosa E. *Epidemiological Analysis of Data Presented in Evidence in the Rulemaking Record (Docket No. H-308) in Connection with Field Sanitation (Document* No. 29 DFP 1928.110); 1994.

8. Feachem E. *Sanitation and Disease: Health Aspects Excreta and Wastewater Management.* New York: Wiley;1983.

9. Select Committee on Hunger, U.S. House of Representatives. *Document (Y4.H89:99-22), 87.5618.* Washington, DC: Government Printing Office; 1986.

10. Coles R. *Migrants, Sharecroppers, Mountaineers.* Boston: Little, Brown; 1971.

11. National Migrant Worker Council, Inc. *Camp Health Aide Manual.* Detroit: Midwest Migrant Health Information Office; 1987.

12. Werner D. *Where There is No Doctor.* Palo Alto, Calif: Hesperian Foundation; 1977.

Population-Based and Community-Focused Approaches to Vulnerability and Disadvantage

Partnership Models

Juliann G. Sebastian, PhD, RN, CS

HISTORY OF COLLABORATION AND PARTNERSHIP

Collaboration and partnership are central to the activities of many health organizations in this first part of the twenty-first century.[1] While not new phenomena, these interagency processes are the focus of more attention and more deliberate goal-setting than ever before. As more communities move toward establishing integrated delivery systems with varying levels of formality and different types of ownership and organizational structures, it has become more important to understand the nature of effective collaboration. Interorganizational processes may be competitive or cooperative, but the current focus is on better understanding cooperative relationships.[2] Porter-O'Grady et al[1] argue that partnerships at all levels will be required for organizations to be effective in the future. From the perspective of special populations, interorganizational partnerships seem to be an optimal approach to providing the comprehensive health and human ser-

305

vices that are often needed. With the health disparities that exist between special populations and the United States population as a whole, and the need for comprehensive, culturally and linguistically competent care for these groups, collaboration across multiple organizations will become increasingly necessary. This part will provide an historical and theoretical context for community partnership models and provide a context for the chapters to follow.

Collaboration between community-based organizations is rooted in work begun in the 1960s between agencies serving the severely mentally ill. Following the passage of Kennedy's Community Mental Health Centers Act (CMHC) in 1963, planned deinstitutionalization of severely mentally ill adults from state mental hospitals accelerated.[3] At the same time, community-based agencies developed using funding made possible by the CMHC Act to provide services necessary to help maintain severely mentally ill adults in the community. It became necessary for these health and human service agencies to coordinate their services, develop smooth referral patterns, and participate in joint planning to avoid duplication of services. Throughout the 1970s and 1980s, concern grew for effective system integration as policy makers, professionals, and consumers addressed problems associated with service fragmentation.

Just as the CMHC Act stimulated interorganizational coordination within mental health, the Tax Equity and Fiscal Responsibility Act (TEFRA) of 1982 had the long-term impact of developing the need for greater coordination among community-based health care agencies.[4] With its focus on reducing costs of hospitalization for Medicare beneficiaries, the TEFRA legislation resulted in development of the prospective payment system to reduce lengths of hospital stays. As more individuals were discharged earlier and families assumed increased responsibility for rehabilitative care, reliance on community-based health agencies grew. Managed care accelerated the trend toward more community-based care and toward coordination within integrated systems of care delivery. Questions about the most effective ways to integrate systems, under what circumstances, and the goals to be achieved by integration have not yet been fully answered. For example, in a study of interorganizational systems serving the severely mentally ill in four cities, Provan and Milward[5] found that centralized interorganizational coordination by a single lead agency was associated with the best client outcomes. It was also found that internal consistency of integrative processes, in this case referral flows and case coordination, was related to the effectiveness of client outcomes.[6]

A body of literature has developed around the concept of system integration. The chapters in this section exemplify advances in the science of systemwide collaboration and partnership. In addition to mental health services, the literature on partnership, collaboration, and integration grew out of business, where concerns exist about the most effective strategies for mergers and acquisitions. Collaboration with communities is central to the field of community development. In the health care industry as a whole, policy makers, payers, investors, health professionals, and consumers need to understand the differential impacts of horizontal and vertical integration on health service quality, cost, and access.

Just as occurred in mental health years earlier, stakeholders in these processes are focusing on ways to provide a more seamless health care experience for consumers in today's health care marketplace, which is heavily influenced by managed care cost reduction strategies. These strategies not only favor moving care out of costly acute care facilities, but also moving care into the least costly and most effective home and community-based environment. It is not always clear how to achieve the combined goals of cost reduction and quality enhancement within a framework of collaboration and partnership. For example, vertical integration, in which a single organization owns all services necessary for a full continuum of care, may have advantages related to organizational efficiency and the ability to better ensure coordination, but disadvantages related to limitations in choice and alternatives for care. As the boundaries between care providers and care recipients fade with an increasing emphasis on self-care and family care, consumers also are insisting on greater participation in designing health systems most responsive to their needs.

FORMS OF COLLABORATION AND PARTNERSHIP

Two major types of collaboration will be described in this part. First, collabora-tion at the organizational level will be explored from the perspectives of the motivations, structures, processes, and outcomes involved. Second, collaboration between providers and clients will be examined in terms of the blurring of roles that is occurring as more care is provided in the community and in terms of the impact on designing models of health services for special populations.

Models of interorganizational collaboration and partnership can develop within organizations, linking departments and units of care, or outside of organizations, creating interorganizational linkages.[1] The linkages may be administrative, financial, or clinical.[7] Administrative links take place in the form of joint programs, shared clinical records, or service subcontracting agreements. Financial links establish smooth funding flows and billing procedures across organizations. Linkages also may be clinical, occurring at the point of service, as when clinicians consult or make referrals on behalf of clients. Mental health has a long tradition of bringing families and clients into this clinical linkage by involving them in interdisciplinay care planning sessions.

In their study of 11 integrated delivery systems, Shortell and his colleagues[7] concluded that although systems of effective administrative and fiscal integration have been developed, clinical integration is still relatively underdeveloped. Not only is it unclear what forms of clinical integration will be the most effective for different populations, it also is not entirely clear what constitutes clinical integration. The current trend toward an expanded definition of health recognizes the critical role that precursors to health play and suggests that clinical integration includes linkages across both health and human service agencies. Increasingly, programs serving special populations are establishing partnerships that more comprehensively serve the health and social service needs of these groups. A definition of health that includes social and economic precursors to health indicates then that integrative links across health and social service agencies are clinical linkages.

Theoretical and empirical understanding of interorganizational cooperation has developed out of the organizational theory literature and is grounded in issues of exchange of resources, costs and benefits of cooperation, and values supporting cooperation. Interorganizational cooperation can occur between individual pairs of organizations, specialized clusters of organizations coordinated by a single agency, or large networks of organizations each of which possesses some level of interdependence.[8] The complexity of relationships and processes increases as the number of partners grows. Decision-making autonomy is reduced as well, making partnerships attractive only when organizations perceive the benefits of these relationships to be greater than the costs.[9,10]

Polivka's[11] model of interorganizational collaboration incorporates issues related to the costs of reduced decision-making autonomy and increased complexity. Her model focuses on not only understanding how and why these relationships function as they do in health care, but also how to make interorganizational collaboration work more effectively for vulnerable populations. Polivka recommends analysis of environmental, situational, and task characteristics that influence the actual exchange of resources across organizations. Examples of relevant environmental factors include socioeconomic variables, while situational variables include levels of consensus, trust, and agreement. Aspects of work tasks that influence interorganizational relationships include task complexity and uncertainty. Successful negotiation of interorganizational relationships is important for many special population groups because so often members of these groups need services from many different health and human service organizations.[12,13] Although evidence exists that some groups may be more effectively served by a single agency providing comprehensive services,[5] many communities do not have access to single health organizations that provide both health and social services. Thus, negotiating successful partnerships and collaborative models becomes critical to fully and appropriately serving special populations.

Levels of collaboration may vary across organizations, ranging from limited to moderate to strong cooperative relationships.[14] Early work by Thompson[15] explicated three levels of task interdependence that determine the level and nature of exchanges necessary between organizational units. Thompson argued that task interdependence could be pooled, sequential, or reciprocal. Pooled interdependence reflects a situation in which the outputs of all units are important for other units, but do not actually become part of the input of other units. Sequential interdependence, on the other hand, occurs when the output of one organization or unit becomes the input for another. Reciprocal interdependence occurs when outputs of both units become inputs of the other. In health care, referral flows can occur either sequentially or reciprocally. Reciprocal interdependence indicates a much higher degree of mutual dependence on work processes across organizational or unit boundaries. Care coordination across organizations exemplifies pooled interdependence.

Collaboration may occur between organizations within the same sector of the economy, resulting in collaboration among potential competitors, or collaboration across sectors, resulting in more symbiotic forms of collaboration.[14] Because organizations in different sectors are not competing for identical resources, interorganizational collaboration may be easier to achieve. What this suggests for health and human service agencies serving members of special population groups is that it is likely easier and more appropriate to develop relationships such as referral flows and case coordination between agencies that provide different, yet complementary, services. On the other hand, exchange of information may occur more smoothly between organizations that provide similar services or serve populations with certain similarities. The relationships that are developing between the public health system and providers of personal health services illustrate one systemwide,

complementary type of collaborative relationship.

Members of the Committee on Medicine and Public Health, initially established by the American Medical Association and the American Public Health Association, determined that collaboration between medicine and public health is essential to develop the capacity to make substantial improvements in health outcomes.[16] Several trends seem to be driving the move toward greater collaboration between these two sectors within health care. First, more complex patient populations, most notably Medicaid beneficiaries, are receiving services through managed care arrangements with private providers. Members of these special populations often require "wraparound" services that integrate health, transportation, child care, translation, and other social services.[16] Because the full scope of these services is not often available within a single agency, creative new forms of interorganizational collaboration are needed. Second, clinical services that had previously been provided primarily within public health are now also being provided in private health care organizations. Health promotion and illness prevention services are increasingly provided by managed care organizations in order to keep their populations of enrollees as healthy as possible. In essence, private health care providers are finding it necessary to adopt a population-based perspective to their practices because of the incentives inherent in managed care. With the underlying economic structure of managed care placing providers at risk for the cost of illness care, providers are finding it critical to understand the patterns of health and illness in the populations for which they provide care, and for those who could become enrollees in the future. Shifts in financing streams, economic and performance pressures, and trends toward increasing market consolidation all support greater collaboration between the personal and public health care sectors.[16]

Collaboration in providing services to special populations should involve partnerships between providers and consumers. This approach is more likely to recognize and build on the strengths of a community and to incorporate culturally appropriate care strategies for needs defined by community members themselves. The ASSETS model of community planning is one model that incorporates community members as equal partners in planning customized strategies for meeting a wide range of community-defined needs and capitalizing on the special strengths within local communities.[17-19] Another model for community-based planning partnerships is the Healthy Cities movement, which is based on a decentralized approach to planning for healthier local communities.[20-22] Both the ASSETS model and the Healthy Cities initiative build on the perspectives of those who will be affected by decisions about the nature, structure, and functioning of health services. In this way, both models blur the roles between those who are planning care and those who are recipients of care.

PART IV: OVERVIEW

In this part, the first chapter by Aday describes a community-oriented policy approach to providing care for vulnerable populations. Aday argues for policy-level interventions to have the greatest impact on improving health outcomes for special populations. Provan details a large, four-city study of service implementation networks for severely mentally ill adults and offers conclusions regarding the structure of integration related to the best outcomes for this population. Finally, Strickland and Strickland describe the nature and impact of provider-patient partnerships with lower-income, rural Southern black clients.

SUMMARY

Partnerships of all types are becoming increasingly common in health care, including those that span sectors, organizational boundaries, boundaries within organizations, and traditional provider-client roles. Understanding the most effective structures and processes in these collaborative forms is key to developing fresh and original approaches to improving health of special populations and reducing health disparities between these groups and American society as a whole.

DISCUSSION QUESTIONS

1. Identify a community-based partnership that serves a special population group in your area. Interview several key stakeholders in the partnership to determine who is involved; how the partnership functions; and its clinical, organi-

zational, and fiscal outcomes. Discuss with the key stakeholders their views on the advantages and disadvantages of community-based partnerships from the perspectives of their organizations and clients.

2. Conduct a needs assessment of one special population group in your community and determine whether their health needs are being adequately met. If not, what services and organizational arrangements would you recommend to best meet those needs? How would you work with consumers to validate your perceptions and jointly design responsive health services?

3. Analyze how local political, economic, and cultural factors influence the nature of community-based partnerships most likely to be effective in your area. What roles do you think health professionals should assume at the policy level to facilitate the development and delivery of the most appropriate and acceptable services for special population groups?

REFERENCES

1. Porter-O'Grady T, Hawkins MA, Parker, ML. *Whole-Systems Shared Governance: Architecture for Integration*. Gaithersburg, Md: Aspen Publishers; 1997.
2. Sebastian JG. *Resource, Efficiency, and Institutional Pressures and the Structure of Cooperative, Interorganizational Relationships in a Mental Health Service Delivery Network*. Unpublished dissertation. Lexington, Ky: University of Kentucky; 1994.
3. Mechanic D, Rochefort DA. Deinstitutionalization: an appraisal of reform. *New Dir Ment Health Serv.* 1990;43:5–18.
4. Sebastian JG. Vulnerability and vulnerable populations. In: Stanhope M, Lancaster J, eds. *Community Health Nursing: Promoting Health of Individuals, Aggregates, and Communities*. St. Louis: Mosby; 1996.
5. Provan KG, Milward HB. A preliminary theory of interorganizational network effectiveness: a comparative study of four community mental health systems. *Adm Sci Q.* 1995;40:1–33.
6. Provan KG, Sebastian JG. Networks within networks: service link overlap, organizational cliques, and client outcomes in community mental health. *Acad Manage J.* 1998;41(4):453–463.
7. Shortell SM, Gillies RR, Anderson DA, Erickson KM, Mitchell JB. *Remaking Health Care in America: Building Organized Delivery Systems*. San Francisco: Jossey-Bass; 1996.
8. Provan KG. The federation as an interorganizational linkage network. *Acad Manage Rev.* 1983;8(1):79–89.
9. Provan KG. Interorganizational cooperation and decision making autonomy in a consortium multihospital system. *Acad Manage Rev.* 1984;9(3):494–504.
10. Pfeffer J, Salancik G. *The External Control Organizations: A Resource Dependence Perspective*. New York: Harper & Row; 1978.
11. Polivka BJ. A conceptual model for community interagency collaboration. *Image: J Nurs Schol.* 1995;27(2):110–115.
12. Aday LA. *At Risk in America: The Health and Health Care Needs of Vulnerable Populations in the United States*. San Francisco: Jossey-Bass; 1993.
13. Flaskerud JH, Winslow BJ. Conceptualizing vulnerable populations' health-related research. *Nurs Res.* 1998;47(2):69–78.
14. Alter C, Hage J. *Organizations Working Together*. Newbury Park, Calif: Sage; 1993.
15. Thompson, JD. *Organizations in Action*. New York: McGraw-Hill; 1967.
16. Lasker RD, The Committee on Medicine & Public Health. *Medicine & Public Health: The Power of*

Collaboration. New York: The New York Academy of Medicine; 1997.

17. Kretzmann JP, McKnight JL. *Building Communities from the Inside Out: A Path toward Finding and Mobilizing a Community's Assets*. Evanston, Ill: Northwestern University; 1993.

18. McKnight JL. Two tools for well-being: health systems and communities. *Am J Prev Med.* 1994;10(3, suppl):23–25.

19. McKnight JL. *The Careless Society: Community and Its Counterfeits*. New York: Basic Books; 1995.

20. Flynn BC, Dennis LI. Health promotion through Healthy Cities. In: Stanhope M, Lancaster J, eds. *Community Health Nursing: Promoting Health of Aggregates, Families, and Individuals*. 4th ed. St. Louis: Mosby-Yearbook, Inc; 1996.

21. Flynn BC. Healthy cities: toward worldwide health promotion. *Annu Rev Public Health.* 1996;17:299–309.

22. Flynn BC. Partnerships in healthy cities and communities: a social commitment for advanced practice nurses. *Adv Pract N Q.* 1997;2(4):1–6.

CHAPTER 23

Vulnerable Populations: A Community-Oriented Perspective

Lu Ann Aday, PhD

VULNERABLE POPULATIONS are at risk of poor physical, psychological, or social health.[1] Health can be measured along a continuum of seriousness with good health, defined by the World Health Organization (WHO) as a "state of complete *physical*, *mental*, and *social* well-being,"[2(p1)] being at the positive end of the continuum and death, as the total absence of health, defined by population-specific mortality (death) rates, at the negative end.

Vulnerable populations may be identified based on those for whom the risk of poor physical, psychological, or social health is or is quite likely to become a reality:

- *physical*: high-risk mothers and infants, chronically ill and disabled individuals, persons with acquired immunodeficiency syndrome (AIDS);
- *mental*: mentally ill and disabled persons, alcohol or substance abusers, suicide- or homicide-prone individuals; and

Fam Community Health 1997;19(4):1–18
© 1997 Aspen Publishers, Inc.

- *social*: abusing families, homeless people, and immigrants and refugees.

There is, of course, overlap among these groups, and the boundaries should be viewed as diffuse rather than distinct. Poor health along one dimension (physical) is quite likely to be compounded by poor health along others (psychological or social). Health needs are greatest for those who have problems along more than one of these dimensions.

Underlying this concept of vulnerability is the epidemiologic notion of risk, in the sense that there is a probability that a person will become ill over a given period of time. Based on this conceptualization, everyone is potentially vulnerable. There is always a nonzero chance or probability that individuals will experience some form of physical or mental illness or a sense of social isolation or lack of support in the course of their lives.

Some groups and individuals are more at risk than others, however. The relative or differential risks for different groups will vary as a function of the material and nonmaterial resources associated with their demographic and related social-structural characteristics (age, sex, race or ethnicity); the nature of the ties between and among them (family members, friends, neighbors); and the schools, jobs, incomes, and housing that characterize the neighborhoods in which they live. The corresponding rewards and resources associated with these individual and social arrangements include social status (prestige and power); social capital (social support); and human capital (productive potential).[1] Effective approaches to mitigating vulnerability to poor health must broaden the design of health policy to address these social and economic contexts and correlates of risk.

Market (private), governmental (public), and community-oriented (voluntary) approaches are broad definitions of the principal models for health and health care policy development. With the dramatic evolution and expansion of managed care, market-oriented solutions have come to dominate both public and private sector health care reform. Concerns have been raised, however, about the potential impact of these market-driven transformations on access for vulnerable populations that have traditionally been less likely to be served by profit-centered systems of care, on financially strapped public and safety net providers placed in a position of competing for medically indigent patients who have coverage (Medicaid clients) to facilitate financing services for those who do not (the uninsured), as well as on where the locus of responsibility for the health of populations or communities will come to reside in a landscape dominated by discrete and competing medical care providers.

On the other hand, ample evidence testifies to the failures of public initiatives to realize promised access, cost, and quality objectives as well. Many providers' doors remain closed to eligible individuals covered by Medicaid. The expenditures under this and the Medicare program challenge the limits of the general and specific revenues available to finance them. Epidemics of tuberculosis, human immunodeficiency virus (HIV) or AIDS, syphilis, and preventable morbidity and mortality continue to ravage communities plagued by persistent social, economic, and health care disadvantage and disinvestment.

This chapter presents a critical review of the defining principles of a community-oriented perspective on health and health care policy; applies these principles in illuminating both the limits and possibilities of market- and government-driven reforms in addressing the needs of vulnerable populations; and illustrates the implications of a community-oriented perspective for reshaping national and local health policy design. It is intended to surface new approaches to shaping health policy from the point of view of the populations and communities affected by public and private policy prescriptions.

CONTRASTING POLICY PERSPECTIVES

Contemporary social critics such as German philosopher Habermas[3,4] have argued that the rational, technical, and instrumental underpinnings of the institutions that dominate modern life, such as the economy and the state, fail to acknowledge the intimate, affective, and interactive "life worlds" of family and community, for example, in which individuals most immediately lodge and find meaning. Habermas[3,4] suggested that people's life worlds have, in fact, become "colonized" (or dominated and constrained) by these bureaucratic rational systems, with the attendant consequences of a sense of disempowerment and corollary cynicism toward the public policy sphere. Similarly, US social scientists Bellah and colleagues,[5] McKnight,[6] and Putnam[7] cited the severing of the ties that have traditionally held individuals and communities to-gether, due to the dominance of the individualistic-oriented normative ethic or disruptive and destructive bureaucratic intrusions into community life.

Social philosophers Sandel and associates[8] and sociologist Etzioni[9] have contributed to the emergence of communitarianism as a school of thought and social movement that has as its central focus the revivification of a sense of the community norms and context that shape human action and organization. Feminist, minority, and other critics of communitarianism have, however, cited its tendency, either overtly or implicitly, to suppress differences and marginalize those who do not represent or reflect the views of the dominant majority.[10,11] These insightful critiques provide a foundation for distilling the defining principles of market, government, and community-centered approaches to formulating policy choices, and how elements of each may limit or influence the other (Table 23–1).

Government perspective

Values implicitly or explicitly underlying public solutions to social and health policy problems include those of beneficence and the public good. The concept of beneficence is rooted in the utilitarian normative tradition "to do good," or at least "to do no harm."[12] In medical ethics this translates into the duty to seek to provide benefits and to balance the likely positive and adverse outcomes of medical decision making. At the public policy level beneficence refers to promoting the overall public good or welfare in weighing the costs and consequences of policy choices. The principal means available to

Table 23–1. Major dimensions of government, community, and market policy perspectives

Dimension	Government	Community	Market
Values	Beneficence Dependence Public good	Reciprocity Interdependence Mutual benefit	Autonomy Independence Private interests
Resources	Power	Trust	Money
Means	Control	Communication	Competition
Ends	Accountability	Empowerment	Profitability
Organizations	Public institutions	Voluntary organizations	Private corporations
Individuals	Clients	Citizens	Consumers

Examples	Public hospitals
	Public health
	Community-oriented
	   primary care
		Nongovernmental organiza-
		   tions, community-based
		   organizations
			Health maintenance
			   organizations
			Preferred provider
			   organizations
			Fee-for-service providers

federal, state, and local government entities in carrying out their charges are the power of the constitutional, legislative, and regulatory foundations for their authority and the consequent control of how and for what purposes tax-based revenues are committed and expended. Large-scale publicly supported bureaucracies emerge to execute and administer these mandates and to ensure accountability to the legislative entities and ultimately to the public on which their representative authority rests.

A corollary outcome of the commitment to beneficence, however, is that it may often place those to whom the benefits are conferred in the position of deference to or dependency upon the agents or agencies charged with conferring. In the medical care decision-making arena this surfaces as paternalism on the part of providers and in the social policy arena in the mandated dependency and corollary disempowerment of clients receiving tax-supported benefits and services.

Market perspective

The market model has its foundations in the theories of supply and demand and the requisite conditions for autonomous and informed consumers to engage in transactions with suppliers of products and services, based on prices and preferences, to satisfy their private interests. Dominant values that undergird these transactions are those of autonomy—from the Greek *autos* (self) and *nomos* (rule)—and independence.[12] In the microcosm of medical practice these norms persuade patients to be proactive and knowledgeable participants in choosing among alternative courses of therapy, and in the macrocosm of the medical care marketplace, to be prudent and informed purchasers of health care services. The exchange of dollars is the principal dynamic fueling this market-oriented system of allocation, with the twin aims of ensuring the profitability of providers and satisfying the preferences of consumers through the medium of market competition.

What the market perspective on health care may fail to reveal, however, is that the "medical care market" is, in fact, a distorted rather than a pure expression of this allocational ideal: public and private third-party insurers lead both consumers and purchasers to confront very different prices than would be the case in their absence; "patients" feel less secure and informed in making choices about their health care provider or treatments based on plan report cards or patient utilities than they might as "consumers" devouring *Consumer Reports* on the merits of goods and services less essentially defining of their well-being; and some players (the uninsured or those with preexisting conditions) may not be invited to play the economic board game if they have few or no chits to put on the table or are anticipated to command too much of the other players' resources.[13]

Community perspective

A community perspective on the normative underpinnings for the transactions between and among individuals and the contexts in which they occur highlights the notions of reciprocity, interdependence, and mutual benefits. This point of view sees individuals as essentially connected through the roles, statuses, and relationships that govern their social interaction and discourse, as well as through the cultural and environmental underpinnings that give shape and meaning to these exchanges. Trust is the major resource upon which these transactions rely, and authentic and open communication is the means through which they are sustained. A sense of personal and collective empowerment around affective (relational) or instrumental (rational) aims is the principal legacy of these exchanges, and the benefits that accrue are not just to oneself but self-consciously to others as well.

The communicative and collaborative ideals manifest in this perspective are, however, more often honored in the breach. Intergroup power differentials and turf wars are quite likely to govern who is included and who excluded from the effective "community" of decision makers. The normative visions of reciprocity, interdependence, and mutual benefit are de facto obscured by the collectively derived barriers erected in defining "us" versus "them" in debating what is best for "us."[3-11]

The characterization and thereby the implicit "character" of individuals and groups are rooted in the origins of the terms defining of their roles in these respective systems—that of client, consumer, and citizen. The essences of meaning of these designations ironically mirror their normative and practical limits as well. The notion of client (akin to the Latin *clinare*, "to lean"—a person that is under the protection of another: dependent) surfaces the de facto disempowerment of those whom helping institutions may seek to serve with nonetheless benevolent intent. Consumers (from the Latin *com + sumere*, "to take up"—one that consumes, especially one that utilizes economic goods) are clearly those who "take," but it is less transparent what they "give." The designation of citizen (alteration of the Old French *citeien*, from *cité*, "city"—an inhabitant of a city or town, especially one entitled to the rights and privileges of a *freeman*), historically and contemporarily excludes certain categories or groups from the arena of privilege on the basis of gender, national origin, or race.[14]

POLICY PERSPECTIVE

The policy perspective presented here is intended to illuminate how the principles defining each of these approaches may compete with or bound those underlying the other and demonstrate how the muting of principles defining of a community-oriented perspective, such as reciprocity, interdependence, mutual benefit, trust, communication, and empowerment, may be useful in analyzing and interpreting the failures of previous market, government, and community approaches to health policy and program design for vulnerable populations.

This perspective provides guidance for addressing a series of questions in contrasting the roles that market-, government-, and community-oriented norms play in shaping policy decisions that directly or indirectly influence the health of individuals and populations.

These questions include
- Who is left out? who is included? and who is rewarded? in exploring the role of public and private investments and disinvestments in groups and communities with different social status (power), social capital (social ties), and human capital (productive potential) (Fig 23–1);
- What programs are needed? in delineating the array of medical and nonmedical services required to ameliorate the correlates and consequences of health risks (Fig 23–2); and
- How should policies be reshaped? in identifying the principles and examples manifest in a more community-oriented health policy framework (Fig 23–3).

Social status: Who is left out?

Age, race, and gender are fundamentally defining of historical and contemporary social and political power differentials between and among groups.[11] The role and influence of children and the elderly, minorities, and women within the social, economic, and public policy-making spheres have been constrained and contained either overtly through constitutional or legislative interpretation or intent or covertly through social norms that sanction the "power over" these groups on the part of corresponding others—working-age adults, whites, and men. These same groups—children and the elderly, minorities, and women—or combinations thereof (elderly minority women) are also often the *most* vulnerable in our society.

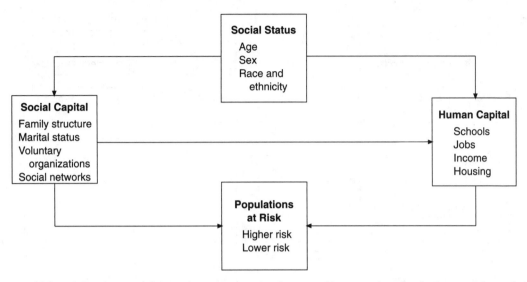

Fig 23–1. Predictors of populations at risk. *Source:* Reprinted with permission from LA Aday, *At Risk in America: The Health and Health Care Needs of Vulnerable Populations in the United States*, p. 7, © 1993, Jossey-Bass/Pfeiffer.

Government

Governmental initiatives, particularly at the federal level, have attempted to redress the social and political differentials for these groups through rights enforcement–oriented judicial rulings, affirmative action legislation, and supportive categoric social insurance and welfare eligibility. Many of these assurances are, how-ever, eroding in a political climate in which the dominant players are concerned that the rights and benefits granted these groups may have come seriously to infringe upon their own.

Market

A market-oriented perspective on these social categorizations has most often turned to whether they designate groups

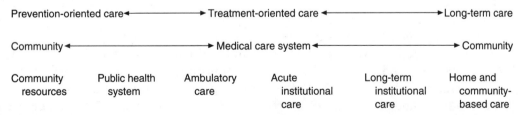

Fig 23–2. Continuum of care for vulnerable populations. *Source:* Reprinted with permission from LA Aday, *At Risk in America: The Health and Health Care Needs of Vulnerable Populations in the United States,* p. 117, © 1993, Jossey-Bass/Pfeiffer.

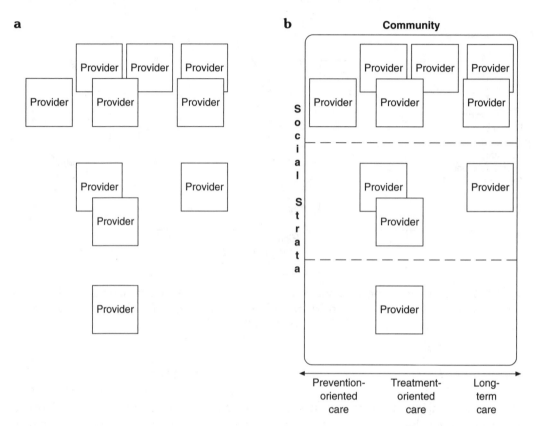

Fig 23–3. (a) A provider-oriented perspective to health care policy. **(b)** A community-oriented perspective.

to whom marketing or demarketing efforts should be directed. There is evidence, for example, that industry interests that have a potentially major role in "marketing" health risks (such as the tobacco and alcoholic beverage industries) view the niches occupied by these groups (adolescents, women, and minorities) as the ones they may most want to penetrate.[15] On the other hand, for profit-oriented entities interested in marketing health care, the most vulnerable among these groups may be those whom they are least likely to desire to attract.[1]

Community

Community-oriented counterweights to the limitations of governmental and corporate strategies to advance these groups' interests have been manifest in major social movements (in the instance of minorities and women) or identity group politics (around children or the elderly, for example). The interdependency of interests across groups or over time is acknowledged in weighing the effects of intergenerational or intergroup inequities and dependency (reflected in the ratio of those drawing upon versus paying into social insurance and benefits systems now and in the future), as well as the recognition, rather than the suppression, of the "politics of difference" in accommodating and attending to the growing importance of diverse cultures within US society.[11]

Efforts to invite and involve traditionally disenfranchised or disempowered groups in developing programs and services may be found at a variety of levels. Examples include organized and vocal advocacy groups for women, minorities, children, and the elderly; the convening of focus groups of affected populations or their representation on advisory boards to influence program and funding priorities; and expanded community-based sites of practice and cultural sensitivity training in enhancing the technical and social competencies of providers in serving racially and ethnically diverse populations.[1,16,17] Differential vulnerability to poor health and its consequences as a function of age, gender, or race have deep social, cultural, and historical roots that are not likely to be easily nor substantially mitigated. These activities represent selected examples of efforts to address disparities that can be ensured to persist or deepen in the absence of policies and initiatives that acknowledge their fundamental existence and impact on the health of individuals and groups.

Social capital: Who is included?

University of Chicago sociologist James Coleman has provided an enriched understanding of the structure and function of the ties that bind individuals to others through elaborating the theoretical and empirical underpinnings of the concept of social capital.[18] Social capital is a resource that resides most directly in the quantity and quality of interpersonal ties and interaction between people. It emerges in the crucible of communication, thrives under conditions of trust, and dissipates in the absence of either. Social capital reflects the investments that individuals make in others and acknowledges that the pay-off or returns may in fact be equal or greater for others than for themselves. Those for whom the ties that bind are the weakest—elderly individuals living alone; female heads of families; persons who are single, separated, divorced, or widowed; or homeless or refugee populations, for example—are also among the most vulnerable and, perversely, most in need of the ties that define these groups by their absence.

Government

Governmental and bureaucratic policies may in fact be either blind to or distrustful of the ties that generate reservoirs of social capital. What might be viewed to be well-intentioned social programs such as welfare or public housing have, for example, required that individuals be stripped of other defining familial or community connections as a condition for the receipt of "benefits." Urban renewal has often overtly or implicitly mandated the removal of offending populations (homeless or ethnic subgroups) without the attendant attention to where they might subsequently put down roots. Those who informally render care are suspect because it is difficult to ensure accountability in the ways one might of those who formally deliver services.[1]

Market

In the market-oriented perspective, social capital parallels the concept of externalities—the positive benefits or consequences for others, in this case, that might result from transactions on the part of individuals acting primarily out of their own interests. The provision of full childhood immunization coverage under a given health care plan may be good business in terms of reducing the occurrence of infectious diseases among enrolled dependents. The fact that it also reduces the incidence of these diseases in general in the community is a positive but incidental consequence.

Community

The generation of social capital is directly supported by the principles most centrally defining of a community perspective: reciprocity, interdependence, mutual benefit, trust, communication, and empowerment (Table 23–1). Its utility in shaping health policy related to vulnerable populations is that it provides a new and powerful set of lenses for scrutinizing the likely outcomes of policies for either dissipating or developing the fragile ties that might exist to support them. A community perspective compels that those affected by decisions be invited to be full participants and partners in defining how their collective interests might be served. It recognizes that trust cannot be legislated or compelled, but must develop

and grow in the context of authentic acts and communication; that empowerment is not a consequence of "organizing communities," but of "communities organizing"; and that externalities do, deceptively enough, surface as internalities, if their consequences are consciously or unconsciously ignored.

Specific approaches to identifying and addressing the needs of vulnerable populations have, in particular, been influenced by this perspective.[6,19] These include a shift from focusing on community deficits to assets, that is, in seeking to inventory the array of formal and informal resources and networks in an at-risk community that may exist to address identified needs. This perspective also acknowledges that these needs and the solutions for addressing them must be identified by the affected communities themselves and that they may differ from those defined by "expert" outside consultants or planners. The commitments and empowerment that result when community members come to own and shepherd this process also serve to generate social capital, including informal networks, as well as more formal community-based organizations, for addressing an array of community-identified problems.

Human capital: Who is rewarded?

Human capital refers to the educational and training investments required to produce a skilled and productive work force.[20,21] It has also been more broadly applied to the array of social and economic investments (schools, jobs, income, and housing) needed to ensure and enhance human productive potential.[1] Coleman[18] has argued that social capital may in fact be an essential ingredient for fostering human capital investments in individuals, families, and communities: the advantages of good schools and jobs and decent incomes and housing do not come to those who are disempowered and silent. Another perspective is that the globalization of the economy and its attendant flexibility for investing in or discarding workers or relocating to other economically more favorable climates offer few opportunities for localities to leverage desired human capital benefits. However, those to whom these benefits are least available are also likely to be most vulnerable to the health risks associated with poor education, poverty, unemployment, and substandard housing.

Government

State and local governments have been a major source of public investments in human capital through the support of public primary and secondary education. The foundations for financing these commitments rest, however, on increasingly shaky ground with stagnating economies and corresponding eroding tax bases in many states and localities, taxpayer revolts over what appear to be ever increasing payments to public coffers for steadily diminishing benefits, and charges of gross and widening inequities between resource-rich and resource-poor districts in what they can afford to provide.[22]

Market

Market-oriented economic development initiatives have, on the other hand, been criticized for the growth-, rather than community- and jobs-oriented, thrust of these efforts. The consequence, equity planners in particular argue, is that the generous tax break incentives provided to investors, the shareholder rather than community orientation of the developers, and the service rather than skills focus of many of the jobs that are ostensibly created have resulted in a net loss, rather than gain, in terms of community and human capital benefits.[23-25]

Community

An effective approach to ensuring the health of communities, and particularly the most vulnerable members of it, cannot proceed disembodied or disengaged from the activities in other sectors directly and indirectly supportive of human capital investments (education, housing, and business, as well as government). Community-oriented health policy must then seek to envision both the horizontal (intersectoral) linkages within a community as well as the vertical (national and international) connectors external to it that can profoundly affect the prospects for enhancing human productive potential and thereby directly and indirectly the health of its citizenry.

SYSTEM: WHAT PROGRAMS ARE NEEDED?

The multidimensional social and economic origins and complex medical and nonmedical consequences of the health and health care needs of vulnerable populations are best addressed by a long-term, prevention-oriented continuum of programs and services (Fig 23–2).[1] The programs and services that might comprise such a continuum include primary prevention–oriented community resource development and public health programs; treatment-oriented care delivered primarily through the medical care and related professional service delivery systems; and long-term care institutional and community-based programs and services. The organization and integration (more often lack of integration) of these programs do not typically acknowledge the emergence and evolution of vulnerability over the life course of individuals, as well as its essential roots in the communities from which people emerge and to which they return after being treated by the formal professional service delivery systems. Specific examples of programs and policies supportive of this more community-oriented continuum of care are highlighted in the discussion that follows.

HOW SHOULD POLICIES BE RESHAPED?

Health care reform is proceeding at a rapid-fire pace at the state and local levels through the widespread adoption of managed care in both the private and public health care sectors. The number of privately insured individuals enrolled in these arrangements continues to grow, as does the proliferation of federal waiver requests submitted by states to expand managed care under the Medicaid program.[26]

This market-oriented approach to health care reform focuses on the management of and competition between discrete providers of services. It is manifest in the proliferation and consolidation of provider networks into integrated systems of delivering and financing medical care that impose varying constraints on providers' fees and consumers' utilization of services (Fig 23–3a). Applying community-oriented lenses to these developments would seek to illuminate the resultant distribution of and linkages between providers along a continuum of prevention-oriented, treatment-oriented, and long-term care (Fig 23–3b).

A community-oriented health policy to address the health and health care needs of vulnerable populations acknowledges the essential social origins and consequences of poor physical, psychological, and social functioning and the array of community-based, nonmedical social and community support services required to ameliorate both the risk and consequences of vulnerability. It also considers the distribution of programs and services across social and economic strata (defined by social status, social capital, or human capital resource differences) within the community. To begin to attend to the dimensions and scope of the problem of vulnerability to poor health in the United States, policy makers must come to envision a sense of community and the normative compass and context it provides.

A broader set of goals and objectives is required to more fully capture the scope and impact of a community-oriented approach to health policy. It seeks to surface and address the overt and covert attitudes and practices, reinforced by both local and larger institutions (such as business, the media, governmental entities, and special interests), that constrain the regard, power, and opportunities accorded different age, gender, and racial or ethnic social status groups.

It simultaneously acknowledges, draws upon, invests in, and generates the essential and important nonmaterial social capital resource by inviting, listening to, and maximizing the participation, involvement, and empowerment of individuals and groups within the community in defining priorities and developing resources to address them.

It seeks to enlarge the human capital assets and investments (such as jobs, schools, housing, and other resources) that undergird and enrich the immediate and long-term productive potential of those who live, work, and raise and care for their families in those neighborhoods.

It envisions a blueprint and a team of architects—from the public and private sectors and affected communities—to undertake the design of a comprehensive, integrated, prevention-oriented continuum or system of programs and services accessible to all members of the community.

It embraces a comprehensive definition of health and well-being and embodies a restive normative judgment of outcomes, motivated by assessments of the extent to which the health of the community as a whole, not just individual patients or clients within it, can be improved.

This more community-oriented perspective is manifest in a number of existing and emergent program and policy options that offer the potential for addressing the health and health care needs of vulnerable populations, each of which may have their dominant roots in either governmental, market-driven, or community-based initiatives.

Government

At the federal level, community and migrant health, as well as community mental health, centers represent important governmental commitments to serving particularly vulnerable and at-risk populations. The most successful of those efforts have in fact been ones that have undertaken broad prevention-oriented public and community health initiatives (in housing, nutrition, sanitation, and environmental safety, for example) in addition to core primary and preventive medical care services delivery functions.[27] At the state and local levels, tax-supported safety net providers and public health departments have been the principal governmental entities charged with promoting and protecting the health of the most vulnerable. Cutbacks in the tax bases and sources of support for these programs, as well as the rapid transformations of their form and functions in the context of the market-driven managed care environment, pose significant threats to their sustained organizational and financial viability. On the other hand, these changes also pose important questions regarding what the defining roles of these and related entities might be in this transformed medical care environment. Phil Lee,[28] the Assistant Secretary for the US Department of Health and Human Services, has, for example, called for the reinvention of public health to focus more on core community health rather than medical care delivery functions in a reformed health care system. The role of public health and community providers might then come to lie in providing leadership or assisting in conceptualizing and designing a multisectoral continuum of programs and services to address the health risks and consequences for the most vulnerable.

The major national and international governmental entities involved in promoting public health research, program development, and practice—the Centers for Disease Control and Prevention (CDC) and the WHO, among others—have developed models and resources that might be employed by public health agencies and practitioners toward this end. The WHO has, for example, encouraged the promulgation of the Healthy Cities Model for eliciting and inspiring interest across the array of diverse sectors within a community toward promoting the health of community residents.[29] The WHO, as well as the CDC Model Standards and Planned Approach to Community Health (PATCH) programs, and the National Association of County Health Officials' APEX-PH (Assessment Protocol for Excellence in Public Health) models, also provide technical assistance and resources to communities in identifying their needs as well as the capacities within those communities for addressing them.[30,31] The future promise and success of governmental initiatives in promoting the health and well-being of vulnerable populations may then lie in developing programs *with*, rather than simply *for*, them.

Market

A central concern with the increasing dominance of the medical care environment by for-profit managed care entities is that the most vulnerable (especially those who have or are most likely to have the poorest health) are also most likely to be the ones these plans are most likely to seek to exclude. The failure of universal health insurance reform, the diminished availability of employment-based coverage to many workers and their dependents, and the portent of a federal divestiture of the Medicaid program also raise serious concerns about the growing number of Americans without any form of private or public insurance coverage, many of whom may be placed at substantial risk of providers' doors being closed to them. Nonetheless, managed care–dominated reforms continue to transform the coverage and services provided the employed and their dependents as well as Medicaid- and Medicare-eligible individuals. The question then becomes what possibilities might exist for shaping them to serve the needs of the most vulnerable.

Interestingly, health services researchers and consultants to the managed care industry have recently pointed out the importance of designing integrated systems that self-consciously consider the needs of the broader population they might potentially serve and that more mature ("third generation") managed care plans and markets do, in fact, serve to model these possibilities.[32–34] Managed care commands a greater use of primary care specialists, which portends profound consequences for the prevention- and community-oriented redirection of medical education and residency training. Methods for training physicians and evaluating their subsequent professional performance also increasingly surface patient-centered norms, interdisciplinary team–oriented care provision, and relational as well as rational-scientific skills development that may be particularly appropriate and effective in dealing with the complex multifaceted needs of the most vulnerable.[35,36]

Models of managed care currently dominating the medical care marketplace cannot be accurately characterized as being substantially leavened with these or other essences of a more community- or population-oriented perspective on health and health care—either in the macrocosm of strategic planning and system design or the microcosm of practice. A not so unrealistic scenario to consider, however, may be that their success in a mature managed care environment might ironically lie with attending to this perspective in their overall mission and design. Stranger things have happened in the dramatically transforming medical care market, as evidenced, for example, by the hungry attention on the part of competing managed care plans in capturing the traditionally shunned Medicaid-eligible individuals. Undergirding such reforms may well be the development of innovative modes of state, local, and perhaps federal financing and risk-sharing arrangements to ensure

that the uninsured and the most vulnerable may also be desired and sought-after managed care market segments. The charge to the public health and health services research communities that remains is nonetheless to vigilantly monitor and evaluate the promises and outcomes of these dramatic changes for the health and health care of the most vulnerable.

Community

Nongovernmental and community-based organizations have provided the institutional and organizational backbone for many grass roots efforts to identify and address community health risks.[37] The concept of "community empowerment" perhaps most directly embodies a perspective and set of approaches mirroring the role that communities themselves play in promoting the health of those residing within them. This philosophic and programmatic thrust, as well as the parallel participatory action research agenda based on the writings of Brazilian social activist Freire,[38] are intended to more authentically and fully listen to and learn from communities and to acknowledge that by the very act of members giving voice to their concerns in their own syntax and semantics, they learn *together* how best to address them.[39] This perspective is manifest in the formulation and implementation of community-based health education and health promotion initiatives as well as institutionally sponsored community development activities.[40,41]

Innovations that may offer the most promise for transforming the disparate array of medical and nonmedical programs and services serving the most vulnerable into a comprehensive, coordinated system of care may be those that attempt to merge a more community-oriented perspective on the health of populations and the delivery of services. Community-oriented primary care (COPC) is a model focusing on the delivery of primary medical care in the context of identified community health needs.[42] The COPC model has, however, played a somewhat limited role in health care delivery in the United States, where the medical care, rather than its broader community and public health, functions have tended to dominate.

A number of new initiatives promise to revitalize and expand a look at the role that a focus on the community can contribute to improving both health and medical care. A historical National Congress on Medicine and Public Health, sponsored by the American Medical Association and American Public Health Association, held in the spring of 1996, sought to explore the possibilities for fruitful collaboration between medicine and public health in education, research, and health care.[43] As mentioned earlier, evidence in more mature managed care–dominated markets suggests that there is an increasing recognition on the part of managed care organizations that the entire community is their target population as they increasingly penetrate these markets or experience a high degree of turnover in plan membership.[44] As public health departments and community providers come to define and redefine their unique role in these environments as well, the promise

of a new form of medical care organization representing a partnership between managed care and public health interests—community-oriented managed care—has emerged.[45,46] It has its counterpart in Canada, which has traditionally had a community health but not a managed care emphasis—a comprehensive health care organization that is currently under development in selected areas in the province of Ontario.[47] These entities have as a primary focus how the health of the population or community as a whole might be enhanced by an integrated array of medical and nonmedical programs and services.

The Kellogg Foundation has played a major role in encouraging community involvement in health care planning and development, including a recent national demonstration of the Community Care Network Vision, in partnership with the American Hospital Association and others, that has a community health focus, community accountability, a seamless continuum of care, and management within fixed resources as defining tenets.[48] A Health Resources and Services Administration national conference on primary care similarly inventoried an array of public and private partnerships in cities and counties throughout the United States that are attempting to integrate medical care and community health providers and interests in the context of the changing managed care–dominated medical care environment.[49]

• • •

Both the government and the market play profound roles in shaping the prospects for health and well-being of those they most directly serve. The central argument that has been presented is that to the extent these or other initiatives manifest a community-oriented perspective on the origins and consequences of poor health, the greater the promise they offer for ameliorating the root causes and consequences of the health risks for the most vulnerable.

REFERENCES

1. Aday LA. *At Risk in America: The Health and Health Care Needs of Vulnerable Populations in the United States.* San Francisco, Calif: Jossey-Bass; 1993.
2. World Health Organization. Constitution of the World Health Organization. In: *Handbook of Basic Documents.* Geneva, Switzerland: WHO; 1948.
3. Habermas J; McCarthy T, trans. *The Theory of Communicative Action,* vol 1. *Reason and the Rationalization of Society.* Boston, Mass: Beacon; 1984.
4. Habermas J; McCarthy T, trans. *The Theory of Communicative Action,* vol 2. *Lifeworld and System: A Critique of Functionalist Reason.* Boston, Mass: Beacon; 1987.
5. Bellah RN, Madsen R, Sullivan WM, Swidler A, Tipton SM. *Habits of the Heart: Individualism and Commitment in American Life.* Berkeley, Calif: University of California Press; 1985.
6. McKnight J. *The Careless Society: Community and Its Counterfeits.* New York, NY: Basic Books; 1995.
7. Putnam RD. *Making Democracy Work: Civic Traditions in Modern Italy.* Princeton, NJ: Princeton University Press; 1993.
8. Mulhall S, Swift A. *Liberals and Communitarians.* Cambridge, Mass: Blackwell; 1992.
9. Etzioni A. *The Spirit of Community: Rights, Responsibilities, and the Communitarian Agenda.* New York, NY: Crown; 1993.
10. Frazer E, Lacey N. *The Politics of Community: A Feminist Critique of the Liberal–Communitarian Debate.* Toronto, Ontario, Canada: University of Toronto Press; 1993.
11. Young IM. *Justice and the Politics of Difference.* Princeton, NJ: Princeton University Press; 1990.
12. Beauchamp TL, Childress JF. *Principles of Biomedical Ethics.* 2nd ed. New York, NY: Oxford University Press; 1983.
13. Aday LA, Begley CE, Lairson DR, Slater CH. *Evaluating the Medical Care System: Effectiveness, Efficiency, and Equity.* Ann Arbor, Mich: Health Administration Press; 1993.
14. *Webster's Ninth New Collegiate Dictionary.* Springfield, Mass: Merriam Webster; 1986.
15. White LC. *Merchants of Death: The American Tobacco Industry.* New York, NY: Beech Tree Books; 1988.
16. Aday LA, Pounds MB, Marconi K, Bowen GS. A framework for evaluating the Ryan White Care Act: toward a *C I R C L E* of caring for persons with HIV/AIDS. *AIDS Public Policy J.* 1994;9:137–144.
17. Airhihenbuwa CO. Health promotion and the discourse on culture: implications for empowerment. *Health Educ Q.* 1994;21:345–353.
18. Coleman JS. *Foundations of Social Theory.* Cambridge, Mass: Harvard University Press; 1990.
19. Kretzmann JP, McKnight JL. *Building Communities from the Inside Out: A Path toward Finding and Mobilizing a Community's Assets.* Chicago, Ill: ACTA Publications; 1993.
20. Becker G. *Human Capital.* New York, NY: National Bureau of Economic Research, Columbia University Press; 1964.
21. Hornbeck DW, Salamon LM, eds. *Human Capital and America's Future.* Baltimore, Md: Johns Hopkins University Press; 1991.
22. National Commission on Excellence in Education. *A Nation at Risk: The Imperative for Educational Reform.* Washington, DC: US Department of Education; 1983.
23. Harvey D. *Social Justice and the City.* Oxford, England: Blackwell; 1993.
24. Mier R. *Social Justice and Local Economic Development Policy.* Newbury Park, Calif: Sage; 1993.
25. Smith DM. *Geography and Social Justice.* Oxford, England: Blackwell; 1994.
26. Aday LA. At risk in America: health and health care for vulnerable populations. In: *Proceedings of the Public Health Conference on Records and Statistics.* Washington, DC: US Government Printing Office; 1995.
27. Sardell A. *The U.S. Experiment in Social Medicine: The Community Health Center Program,*

1965–1986. Pittsburgh, Penn: University of Pittsburg Press; 1988.

28. Lee P. Reinventing public health: President Clinton's Health Security Act. In: Rosenau PV, ed. *Health Care Reform in the Nineties*. Thousand Oaks, Calif: Sage; 1994.

29. Ashton J. The Healthy Cities Project: a challenge for health education. *Health Educ Q.* 1991;18: 39–48.

30. American Public Health Association. *Healthy Communities 2000: Model Standards*. 3rd ed. Washington, DC: APHA; 1991.

31. World Health Organization. *Formulating Strategies for Health for All by the Year 2000*. Health for All Series 2. Geneva, Switzerland: WHO; 1979.

32. Shortell SM, Gillies RR, Anderson DA. The new world of managed care: creating organized delivery systems. *Health Affairs*. 1994;13(5):46–64.

33. Shortell SM, Gillies RR, Devers KJ. Reinventing the American hospital. *Milbank Mem Q.* 1995;73: 131–160.

34. Goldsmith JA. A radical prescription for hospitals. *Harvard Bus Rev.* 1989;67:104–111.

35. Pew Health Professions Commission. *Health Professions Education for the Future: Schools in Service to the Nation*. San Francisco, Calif: Pew Charitable Trust; 1993.

36. Pew Health Professions Commission. *Critical Challenges: Revitalizing the Health Professions for the 21st Century*. San Francisco, Calif: Pew Charitable Trust; 1995.

37. Couto RA. Promoting health at the grass roots. *Health Affairs*. 1990;9(2):144–151.

38. Freire P; Ramos MB, trans. *Pedagogy of the Oppressed*. New York, NY: Seabury; 1970.

39. Robertson A, Minkler A. New health promotion movement: a critical examination. *Health Educ Q.* 1994;21:295–312.

40. Israel BA, Checkoway B, Shulz A, Zimmerman M. Health education and community empowerment: conceptualizing and measuring perceptions of individual, organizational, and community control. *Health Educ Q.* 1994;21:149–170.

41. Labonte R. Health promotion and empowerment: reflections on professional practice. *Health Educ Q.* 1994;21:253–268.

42. Abramson JH. Community-oriented primary care —strategy, approaches, and practice: a review. *Public Health Rev.* 1988;16:35–98.

43. Seeking common ground: leaders of public health, medicine begin process of collaboration. *Nation's Health*. 1996;26(4):1.

44. Public health and managed care organizations—a new era of collaboration? *State Initiatives*. 1996; 18(May/June):2–4;10.

45. Lairson DR, Schulmeier G, Begley CE, Aday LA, Coyle Y, Slater CH. Managed care and community-oriented care: Conflict or complement? In press.

46. Texas Department of Health. *Medicaid Reform: Improving the Health of Texans through Community Focused Managed Care*. Austin, Tex: TDH; 1995.

47. *Comprehensive Health Organization*. Kingston, Ontario, Canada: Ministry of Health; 1996.

48. Bogue R. Community experiments in reconfiguring health care delivery. Presented at the Health Care into the Next Century: Markets, States, and Communities Conference; May 4, 1996; Durham, NC.

49. Health Resources and Services Administration. *Proceedings: Second National Primary Care Conference*, Vols 1 and 2. Washington, DC: Government Printing Office; 1994.

CHAPTER 24

Services Integration for Vulnerable Populations: Lessons from Community Mental Health

Keith G. Provan, PhD

DESPITE GAINS MADE in recent years in identifying the needs of vulnerable populations, the many health and human service agencies that provide the services vulnerable populations require have found it increasingly difficult to do their jobs effectively.[1] In part, this difficulty stems from the chronic and severe problems frequently experienced by vulnerable populations, such as drug and alcohol dependency, chronic poverty, intractable health problems, and severe mental illness. However, problems with how services are delivered in a community often stand in the way of effective treatment, despite the best intentions of individual service providers. Although meager public funding can be blamed for some of the problems in treating clients effectively, particularly in limiting the type and amount of services that can be provided,

This research was funded by a grant from the National Institute of Mental Health (R01-MH43783). The author acknowledges Mike Berren, Brint Milward, and Julie Sebastian for their contributions to the project.

Fam Community Health 1997;19(4):19–30
© 1997 Aspen Publishers, Inc.

community agencies must learn to cope with inadequate funding while still maintaining or improving outcomes.

Probably the most widely accepted approach for community health and human service agencies to serve clients with multiple, severe problems in an era of fiscal frugality has been for agencies to integrate and coordinate the services they provide to vulnerable clients.[2] Integration at the level of client services may occur through referrals, joint programs, or case management, and may occur formally or informally. Thus, for instance, a homeless person who stops at one agency to receive a hot meal might also receive a medical examination from an outreach team from another agency that works closely with the first. Or a mental health agency and a substance abuse agency might regularly coordinate the services they provide to dual-diagnosed clients.

When expanded to multiple agencies providing many different services, an entire system of service delivery becomes available to clients, who can then access the system through any agency in the system. In theory, vulnerable clients could have all their social, physical, and psychological needs met through the coordinated efforts of a diverse group of community provider agencies whose service orientation is client centered rather than program or agency centered. That is, through such activities as joint programs, case coordination, and reciprocated referrals, agencies can work to solve the multiple problems of individual clients by tapping the resources and expertise of many agencies in the community, rather than force fitting clients' needs into the preestablished programs of whatever agency happens to be serving the clients and then releasing them.

Anecdotal evidence about the value of services integration for vulnerable populations is substantial, and intuitively the concept has great appeal. In the area of treatment of deinstitutionalized individuals with severe mental illness the idea has taken on the status of institutionalized myth,[3] and there is evidence that this myth has developed in other areas of health and human services as well, including services to the homeless, substance abusers, the elderly, and people with acquired immunodeficiency syndrome (AIDS).[4,5] The appeal of services integration has become especially strong in recent years as a way for publicly funded health and human service agencies to make the most of resources that have been substantially cut. When integration occurs, community agencies can extend their service reach and clients are served more thoroughly, with little or no additional expense.

Despite the prevalence of the "more integration is better" assumption, there is little empirical evidence that community health and human service delivery systems that are more integrated work any better than systems that are less integrated. The problem is that integration itself is difficult and complex and as a result does not always work as intended. It does seem clear that fragmented services, geographic dispersion, multiple sources of categorical funding, and clients with multiple problems and needs all combine to produce a situation in which at least some integration of services across provider agencies is critical to achieve reasonable outcomes. As a result, it would be highly unusual to find any community-based health and human service delivery system that was not integrated to at least some extent. At the other extreme, it is also clear that total integration of all services into a single, huge provider for a given vulnerable population is probably not feasible and not necessarily desirable. In mental health, for instance, the idea of institutionalizing patients in a single center for treatment, housing, and rehabilitation, like a state mental hospital, has little clinical or political support, even though the services provided could be fully integrated and coordinated.

What is not so clear, however, is whether or not higher levels of integration among independent providers will result in better client outcomes, as most presume, or whether the problems of coordination and the complexities of its management will result in outcomes that are no better, or even worse, than systems having only modest levels of integration. What is also unclear is what forms integration may take and which of these forms are more effective than others.

This chapter will attempt to answer these questions. First, I discuss a number of problems inherent in services integration that may limit its effectiveness for serving vulnerable populations. To assess whether the benefits of integration appear to outweigh the problems, I will then summarize the findings of a major comparative study of services integration in community-based delivery systems for persons with severe mental illness. Finally, I will discuss some of the lessons learned from

this study so that state and community health care planners might improve the likelihood that services integration not only will occur, but will occur in ways that are likely to result in more effective services for vulnerable clients.

PROBLEMS OF SERVICES INTEGRATION

The benefits of services integration are well known and have been discussed and promoted by service professionals, policy makers, and academics for the past 20 years and more.[2,6,7] These benefits include the expectation that the full range of clients' needs can be addressed more readily and effectively through integration than when each need or each type of client is separately addressed by a unique provider. When agencies actively integrate their activities, clients benefit since clients need not be forced to coordinate their own services and access to the system is facilitated, problems that are especially acute for vulnerable populations. In addition, individual providers can focus on what they do best, agencies and communities can become engaged in comprehensive service planning, agencies are less likely to engage in duplication of efforts and competition, information is likely to flow more freely, and, as noted above, limited resources can be used more efficiently. While not all these benefits will be attained, integration has obvious advantages, especially for handling the problems of vulnerable clients who would find it extremely difficult, and potentially intimidating, to transact the intricacies of a loosely connected or unconnected group of service providers.

Despite these benefits, however, there are a number of problems with network integration that limit its desirability and the likelihood that positive outcomes will be attained. First is the potential loss of decision autonomy. Whenever an agency is asked to coordinate its activities with another, some autonomy is sacrificed. When multiple agencies are involved, as would be the case in a truly integrated delivery system, agency decisions regarding resource allocation and treatment must be constrained by the needs and decisions of the other agencies that collectively comprise the service delivery network. The more tightly coupled are the providers, the more interdependent they become, and hence, the more the decisions of any one provider agency will have an impact on the decisions of the others.[8,9] While there may be clear advantages to clients from a tightly linked, highly integrated delivery system, agency staff and administrators may resist what they feel is an intrusion on their right to make the decisions that they deem best for their agency and clients.

A closely related problem is that agencies may resist or be ambivalent about strong attempts to emphasize system versus agency needs. Integrated systems work well only if provider agencies are actively and willingly involved in day-to-day coordination efforts. Because such efforts are difficult, however, systems are often coordinated by a lead agency that provides multiple services in major areas but draws on members of the network for other services. These lead agencies may have little formal authority to impose system thinking on the other agencies, which may engage in integrative activities only if it is clear that benefits will accrue to them and their clients. When such benefits are not obvious, agency staff may become only peripherally involved in integration efforts, making the services delivery system weak in some areas that may be important to a large group of clients.

A third potential problem is what might be referred to as "opportunity costs." Health and human service agencies that are involved in integrated delivery systems must devote time and resources to handling issues and problems related to coordination that could be spent directly on client services. This can be frustrating, particularly when service professionals must deal with problems that they view as ones that should have been dealt with by other agencies in the system. The irony is that a major claim of services integration advocates is that fewer resources are needed to provide better services. While this claim may be true, the costs of integration itself can be substantial.

A fourth potential problem is related to agency and staff commitment. Many agencies provide a variety of types of services to different populations of clients. As a result, integration of the system for a particular client group may mean involving agencies that are only peripherally involved with that client group. Securing the commitment of these agencies and their staff may prove difficult. On one hand, service staff may be eager to be involved with other agencies to help them serve clients that they are not equipped to deal with. On the other hand, the staff of these agencies may view these clients as ones who are "difficult," passing them on too readily to other agencies in the system.

Finally, agencies involved in integrated systems may experience some conflict between the goals and needs of staff professionals and administrators. Those staff professionals who are actually involved with clients are most likely to be willing to work closely with other agencies to coordinate services for their clients. Administrators may not always see the benefits of such cooperation, particularly if resource exchanges are involved. Additionally, administrators may be more interested in developing what might be referred to as institutional-level linkages, rather than service links, which directly benefit clients. These institutional links, like shared board members, joint programs, or shared information about funding, accreditation, and the like, are indeed integrative, but their focus on issues of administration means that client services do not necessarily benefit directly.[10] When administrators are focused on institutional-level linkages, they may deemphasize their support of service links, limiting the extent of formalized integration among agencies regarding client services. Thus, integration efforts among agencies regarding clients may need to be informal and based on such activities as referral exchanges rather than on more formal arrangements like service contracts or joint programs.

In sum, despite what appear to be the clear advantages of a system of integrated health and human services, there are a number of potential problems that

may limit the effectiveness of such systems. Thus, it is not at all obvious that the solution to providing services to vulnerable populations of clients is simply to engage in more integration among provider agencies within a community. Because so little empirical research has been conducted to address this question, some colleagues and I decided to conduct a study of services integration focusing on one particular vulnerable client group: adults with severe and chronic mental illness (SMI). The results of the study have been published elsewhere[11,12] so they will only be summarized here. Based on these results, there are some lessons that can be learned for other vulnerable populations of clients regarding the organization of integrated service systems. I will offer some recommendations on what states and communities might do to facilitate services integration in ways that appear to lead to positive client outcomes.

Although there have been many studies of services integration, the type of research we conducted is extremely rare (except for the work of Lehman and associates[13]). For one thing, the study offers an in-depth examination of the full mental health delivery systems, or networks, in four different but comparably sized US cities, allowing comparisons to be made across cities and systems. In addition, the study focused on the relationship between system structure and client outcomes. The aspect of the system that we were most concerned with was integration among agencies. By linking services integration with client outcomes, it is possible to resolve some of the confusion about the value of integration efforts in general and, more specifically, about which forms of integration structure appear to be most effective.

RESEARCH METHODS AND MEASURES

The research sites were carefully chosen to control for the effects of differences in state funding for the mentally ill, which might have a significant impact on the kinds of services provided and subsequent outcomes. The four cities selected were Providence, Rhode Island, Akron, Ohio, Albuquerque, New Mexico, and Tucson, Arizona; all were midsized with 1990 populations ranging from 369,000 to 667,000. Providence and Akron were in states that had relatively high per capita mental health spending ($52.34 and $45.33, respectively), while Albuquerque and Tucson were in states that had low funding ($23.79 and $19.76), based on 1990 data.

Data on network/system structure and agency characteristics were collected from the 32 to 36 agencies in each system during 1991 and 1992 using structured surveys and in-depth personal interviews of key personnel at each agency. Specifically, each agency was provided with a list of every agency in that city that we determined (through prior interviews) was involved in some way in the provision of services to adults with severe mental illness. These included agencies that were heavily involved with our target population, such as psychiatric facilities, counseling agencies, rehabilitation centers, and group homes. It also included agencies that did not necessarily see themselves as

being major players in the system of adults with severe mental illness but whose involvement in that system was critical if full services were to be available for clients. These agencies included substance abuse centers, legal and law enforcement agencies, homeless shelters, transportation agencies, and general human service agencies.

Key personnel at each of these agencies were asked to indicate which of the agencies listed by us were ones that they had been involved with over the past year in providing services to severely mentally ill adults. Response categories included referrals sent to the agency listed, referrals received by that agency, case coordination, joint programs, and service contracts. Responses were only considered valid if both agencies in the link indicated that that service link did indeed exist. These confirmed responses were aggregated across agencies and across type of link and divided by the total possible number of links in that system. This was our measure of services integration for each site.

Data on clients were collected from structured interviews of a 5% random sample of adults (over 18) at each site who were diagnosed as being severely mentally ill, based on criteria established in the *Diagnostic and Statistical Manual* of the American Psychiatric Association, or DSM-III-R as it is commonly known. Data were also collected from the family members of these clients, whenever family members were available, and from the clients' case managers or therapists. Questions regarding outcomes were primarily modifications of items from several standard assessment instruments, especially the Colorado Client Assessment Record and the New York Functioning Scale. By and large, factor analysis of outcome data revealed that family members and the clients themselves (but not case managers or therapists) had similar views regarding the client's general quality of life, satisfaction with services, psychopathology, and level of functioning. We thought that the views of these two groups would provide a more valid assessment of client well-being than the views of case managers or therapists, whose involvement with clients might be limited. Thus, the perspectives of these two respondent groups (clients and families) were aggregated (from factor scores) and used as our indicator of client outcomes, which represented the effectiveness of each system in delivering needed services to clients.

RESEARCH RESULTS

Results indicated that the clients in Providence had by far the highest outcome scores, while Tucson had the least effective system. The scores for Akron were also low, while Albuquerque's clients had outcomes that fell in the midrange. Although Providence was a relatively well-funded system and Tucson a poorly funded one, funding alone could not explain client outcomes. Albuquerque too had poor funding but moderate outcomes, while Akron was well-funded but had outcomes that were almost as low as Tucson. While we were reluctant to draw any conclusions that might imply that funding had no impact on client outcomes, it was clear that something other than funding was affecting client outcomes. In view of the years of discussion about the value of services integration, we then turned our attention to an examination of integration to see if this important aspect of system structure was as critical for explaining client outcomes as was generally assumed.

Our findings revealed that services integration per se was not related to client outcomes for the sample of vulnerable clients we studied. Instead, we found that certain aspects of system structure and integration seemed quite helpful for enhancing client outcomes while other aspects did not. To summarize our results, we found that systems of providers appeared to be integrated in one of two ways. The first approach was exemplified by Tucson. Tucson, with the poorest outcomes, had the highest level of overall integration of the four systems, a finding that was clearly contrary to the prevailing wisdom about the value of services integration. Tucson was integrated in a decentralized way, so that many of the agencies that provided services to the population of SMI adults dealt directly with one another. Much of the integration in Tucson occurred in the form of many small clusters of agencies that interacted closely with each other, but these clusters, or cliques, had little overlap. Thus, while the overall level of interactions among agencies in Tucson was high, it was because small groups of agencies were integrated with one another. Coordination across the full system was lacking, making meaningful integration of client services across a broad spectrum of agencies quite difficult.

In stark contrast, Providence, which had the best client outcome scores, had the lowest overall integration of the four systems, a finding that was totally unexpected. Unlike Tucson, the agencies in Providence generally did not interact directly with one another to provide services to SMI clients. Instead, the system was integrated and coordinated through a large, multiservice mental health agency. Since most agencies in the system interacted directly with this core provider, clients typically had their service needs coordinated and directed by one agency, even though multiple agencies might be involved. In Tucson, clients might move within clusters of agencies, but the absence of a strong central provider made true coordination of services difficult and encouraged duplication of effort. This resulted in inefficient use of limited resources. Providence not only had more resources, but also integration could be controlled and monitored much more effectively and efficiently. In addition, the core agency in Providence either contracted directly with other key agencies or approved the state's funding of other providers for services related to SMI adults, giving agencies an additional incentive to go along with the core agency's integration efforts.

Findings on integration for Albuquerque were in between Tucson and Providence, and consistent with this position, client outcomes were also in the middle, despite low overall system funding. Like Providence, Albuquerque had a central core mental health provider agency. Because of its importance as a provider of many key services to SMI adults and its involvement with by far the largest number of SMI clients in the city, the core agency received considerable funding and was highly visible, making it the single most integrated agency in the system and the de facto center of the system. Nonetheless, this core agency did not maintain strong control over the system, either through its leadership efforts or through its control over funding, enabling many subnetworks to flourish. Thus, many agencies in the system also interacted directly with one another, as in Tucson, resulting in a system that was integrated but not in the centralized way that facilitated real coordination in Providence.

Findings for Akron were more equivocal. The Akron system had a fairly centralized integration structure, with a strong core mental health provider that was wholly owned and controlled by the local funding entity. Most system agencies were connected to the core provider, some through contractual or funding ties, and direct interaction among providers was only modest. Thus, Akron looked more like Providence than the other two sites. However, client outcomes in Akron were relatively poor, second only to those of Tucson. Based on our extensive interviews, we were able to conclude that much of Akron's problems could be attributed to the recent total reorganization of the system of community care for the mentally ill, leaving many agencies, staff members, and clients unsure about where to go for needed services.

Overall, we concluded from our research that integration among service providers was indeed important for attaining reasonable outcomes for adults who were severely mentally ill, but not in the general way that had been assumed previously. Instead, integration had to be done in a way that allowed client services to be tightly coordinated. It was not enough for small groups of agencies to refer clients to one another or even share joint programs, since the full range of needed services would typically not be included as part of the agencies' integration efforts.

CONCLUSIONS AND IMPLICATIONS

Because our study examined only four cities and focused only on the population of adults with severe and chronic mental illness, conclusions about implications for health and human service delivery systems for populations of other vulnerable clients and in other cities must be made rather cautiously. Nonetheless, in view of the importance of the topic and the fact that so little comparative empirical research is available, it seems reasonable to make some tentative recommendations based on the lessons learned from this study. Such recommendations should be useful to system planners and funders concerned with whether or not and how to integrate a diverse set of provider agencies to enhance the impact of limited funds on vulnerable populations of clients.

The major lesson learned is that while the basic concept of integration of services for vulnerable clients is sound, all approaches to system integration do not have equal impact on client outcomes. The findings from our study suggest that outcomes will be strongest when integra-

tion is coordinated and led by a single, strong core agency that controls the allocation of services to clients and the funding of services provided by the other agencies that comprise the service delivery network. Such agencies cannot provide all services themselves, but they can and should be the ones who actively coordinate the many other community agencies serving the vulnerable client group. It is not enough for these agencies to simply be the largest provider of multiple services for the vulnerable client group and the system's most well-integrated member. These agencies must play a strong leadership role to ensure that system integration is actively coordinated. This role may be resisted by agencies striving to maintain their autonomy, although resistance is likely to be minimized when the core agency also controls access to the funding of the services it is attempting to integrate.

A second, closely related lesson from our findings is that when coordination is not centrally controlled but occurs more naturally through the efforts of the many involved providers, clients may not be well served. As noted earlier, a main problem of services integration is that agencies and their staff are often hesitant to give up decision autonomy so that system needs are placed ahead of agency needs. To avoid problems, it may be tempting for system planners and organizers simply to decentralize integration efforts, encouraging but not coordinating the integration of services among providers. Our findings indicate that integration does indeed occur under these conditions, in part because no one agency can provide all needed services independently and in part because agency professionals are trained and socialized to work closely with each other, even across agency boundaries. Nonetheless, this informal integration tends to produce results that are not necessarily sufficient to help vulnerable clients. The very nature of vulnerability means that clients are more likely to need the help of professionals to guide them through the system. When this integration is left up to the professional staff of multiple agencies, it tends not to be systematic, leaving clients only partially served.

A final lesson is that vulnerable clients apparently do not do well in systems that are undergoing massive change. Our results from Akron suggest that despite a system that appeared to be well integrated through a strong central authority, the disruption of system change can be readily felt by the staff of provider agencies and hence by their clients. Tucson also was in the throes of a major system overhaul, which made it even more difficult for its decentralized system of agencies to integrate their activities. In contrast, Albuquerque, which was poorly funded but had more centralized integration than Tucson, was also a very stable system, enabling agency staff members to know the system well (both positive and negative aspects). This knowledge helped to facilitate coordination of services across agencies, even when the core mental health agency did not play an active role in system integration.

What do these conclusions imply for planning and organizing a system of services delivery for populations of vulner-

able clients? The major recommendation that can be made from this research is that system planners and state funders should take an active role in system development. Since integrated systems seem to work best when highly centralized, funders should channel the lion's share of scarce resources for a particular vulnerable population through a core agency that can then subcontract out for services it does not provide. This core agency should also coordinate the package of other services its clients may need through active case management. When funding is spread across multiple agencies, as we found in Tucson, and to a lesser extent in Albuquerque, meaningful coordination becomes more difficult to achieve. When funding flows through a single core provider, other agencies will be more inclined to link and coordinate with the core provider than with each other, facilitating integration and enhancing the likelihood that clients can receive the coordinated services they need.

For some communities, the shift to a more centralized integration approach may involve little substantive change. For others, however, significant disruption may well occur. Our findings on stability indicate that system change is difficult to absorb and that services for vulnerable clients may suffer. Nonetheless, it is unreasonable to conclude that service delivery systems for vulnerable populations are best left alone. Rather, it seems safe to argue that changes will take some time to implement fully since agencies and their staff may have difficulties adjusting.

It is important that the core provider agency takes a strong early role in working closely with the system of providers both to coordinate service delivery for clients and to assure agencies that a more centralized approach to coordination and integration efforts does not mean attempts to actively control internal agency decisions. It does mean, however, that decisions related to client treatment are ones that individual agencies and their staffs need to make in close consultation with the core provider. In many cases, a core provider may integrate key services through subcontracting. In this way, the core agency can control the types and amounts of services received by other agencies in the system through its control of funds. Such an approach is particularly relevant in a system of managed care, where cost considerations mean that strong control over the number and type of services received is required, and the number of agencies that interact with one another is likely to be limited.

•   •   •

As discussed earlier, there are clear advantages as well as disadvantages to services integration. Whether or not, on balance, integration has the positive effect on client outcomes that most policy makers assume has rarely been addressed in a comparative empirical study. Although a number of conclusions can be drawn from the research we have conducted, it is important to recognize that the study is only a first step in analyzing the relationship between system-level factors and client outcomes. We focused primarily on services integration while also considering the impact of differences in system funding and stability, but there may well be other factors that affect client outcomes. For instance, we did not address the efficacy of one type of treatment or service orientation over another or differences in the capabilities of core provider agencies and their key integration partners. The impact of these factors on outcomes may also differ depending on the particular vulnerable client group being considered and their unique set of needs.

In addition, the political and cultural realities in states and individual communities may make a shift to the highly centralized form of integration that we found in Providence unfeasible or unworkable. In fact, we found this to be the case in Akron. Although we assumed that the system of strong centralized control of funding and integration of services in Akron would ultimately lead to improved client outcomes, continued resistance to this new system structure could mean that client outcomes would remain poor or that there would be an eventual return to a more decentralized system model. There is a great deal of research that is needed to resolve these important questions. What the study reported here has done is to demonstrate clearly both the feasibility of and the need to conduct such research across multiple sites and to collect data on client outcomes, rather than merely to assume that certain aspects of system structure, such as integration, work as intended.

REFERENCES

1. Aday LA. *At Risk in America: The Health and Health Care Needs of Vulnerable Populations in the United States*. San Francisco, Calif: Jossey-Bass; 1993.

2. Alter C, Hage J. *Organizations Working Together*. Newbury Park, Calif: Sage; 1993.

3. Weiss JA. Ideas and inducements in mental health policy. *J Policy Analysis Manag*. 1990;9:178–200.

4. Office of the Inspector General. *Services Integration: A Twenty Year Retrospective*. Washington, DC: US Dept Health and Human Services; 1991.

5. Dill A. Institutional environments and organizational responses to AIDS. *J Health Social Behavior*. 1994;35:349–369.

6. Warren RL, Rose, SM, Bergunder AF. *The Structure of Urban Reform*. Lexington, Mass: Lexington Books; 1974.

7. Rogers DL, Whetten DA. *Interorganizational Coordination: Theory, Research, and Implementation*. Ames, Iowa: Iowa State University Press; 1982.

8. Simon HA. The architecture of complexity. *Proc Am Philosoph Soc*. 1962;106(6):467–482.

9. Weick K. Educational organizations as loosely coupled systems. *Admin Sci Q*. 1976;21:1–19.

10. Bolland JM, Wilson JV. Three faces of integrative coordination: a model of interorganizational relations in community-based health and human services. *Health Services Res*. 1994;29:341–366.

11. Provan KG, Milward HB. Integration of community-based services for the severely mentally ill and the structure of public funding: a comparison of four systems. *J Health Politics, Policy Law*. 1994;19:865-894.

12. Provan KG, Milward HB. A preliminary theory of interorganizational network effectiveness: a comparative study of four community mental health systems. *Admin Sci Q*. 1995;40:1–33.

13. Lehman AF, Postrado LT, Roth D, McNary SW, Goldman HH. Continuity of care and client outcomes in the Robert Wood Johnson Foundation Program on chronic mental illness. *Milbank Q*. 1994;72:105–122.

CHAPTER 25

Partnership Building with Special Populations

W. Jay Strickland, PhD

David L. Strickland, MA

THE PUBLICATION *Healthy People 2000*[1] sets baseline health goals for all Americans but emphasizes the needs of high-risk populations, such as lower-income and minority individuals. In general, high-risk populations have poorer health status than other Americans and face multiple barriers to health services. Even when health services are available and accessible, the manner in which providers and patients interact in the treatment setting can have a negative effect on the attitudes, behaviors, and health status of these patients.[2–6] Health promotion and partnership building are promising strategies for improving the health status of high-risk populations in US society.

Original data were collected by the Center for Rural Health and Research, College of Health and Professional Studies, Georgia Southern University. Funding was received from the Office of Rural Health Policy, Health Resources and Services Administration, PHS Grant HRA-000040-02.

An earlier version of this article was presented at the 1995 annual meeting of the American Sociological Association, Washington, DC.

Fam Community Health 1996;19(3):21–34
© 1996 Aspen Publishers, Inc.

AN INTERACTIONAL MODEL OF PROVIDER–PATIENT PARTNERSHIP

Assumptions

The World Health Organization has defined health promotion as "the process of enabling people to increase control over and to improve their health."[7(piii)] This process is facilitated by provider–patient partnership building. At the community level, partnership involves the "informed, flexible, and negotiated distribution (and redistribution) of power among all participants in the processes of change for improved community health."[8(p257)] At the individual level, partnership is enhanced through provider–patient communication and patient empowerment.

The importance of provider–patient communication in health education and treatment settings has been clearly established. At the very least, providers must elicit sufficient information to make a meaningful diagnosis, prescribe treatment, and encourage patient compliance.[9] To facilitate partnership, providers must also provide a foundation of information pertaining to diagnoses, etiology, treatment options, prognoses, risks, and health prevention and promotion information in a manner patients can understand.[2,8,10,11] Only through full, clear, and understandable disclosure can individuals meaningfully participate in their own health care.

The negative effects of power asymmetry between providers and patients have also been discussed widely, and models of partnership usually reject paternalism for collaboration. Although some models suggest that provider power be reduced as the basis for collaboration, actively enhancing the power and status of patients is more consistent with the ideal of partnership.[10,12] Provider–patient collaboration can enhance partnership in two ways. First, patients can be encouraged to participate in decision making throughout the health education and/or treatment process. Second, as suggested by the symbolic interaction perspective, humans manipulate symbols to confer and withhold respect as they establish, demonstrate, and perpetuate power relationships.[11,13,14] By expressing kindness, respect, and sympathy symbolically, providers communicate that patients are important partners in health care.[15]

Description of the model

Based on the existing literature, the interactional model of provider–patient partnership presented in Table 25–1 includes selected information and socioemotional strategies. Information strategies include explaining diagnoses and treatment options, addressing health promotion issues, and soliciting patient input. Perception of provider competence is included as an information strategy because medical information is more likely to be considered valid if the provider is believed to be competent. Socioemotional strategies use symbols to communicate that the patient is respected and include clean facilities, short waits, polite interaction, and the appearance of concern about patient discomfort. Because health promotion and partnership

Table 25–1. An interactional model of provider–patient partnership

Interaction strategies	Outcome
Information context	Provider–patient partnership
Provider explains diagnosis.	
Provider explains treatment options.	
Provider discusses health promotion.	
Provider solicits patient input.	
Patient considers provider competent.	
Socioemotional context	
Treatment setting is clean.	
Wait for consultation is reasonable.	
Patient is treated politely.	
Provider appears concerned about	
patient discomfort.	

are sociopsychological processes, this chapter examines provider–patient interaction from the perspective of the patient rather than through the objective measurement of provider attitudes and behaviors.

Barriers to partnership building

Poor patients increasingly find themselves at the margins of medical care in part because of contextual barriers which exist in the doctor–patient relationship. Communication between doctors and poor patients fails principally because of inadequately shared information and a power asymmetry in the relationship.[2(p312)]

Although comprising only a small body of research, several studies suggest that patient characteristics, including income and race, affect provider attitudes, interaction, and, ultimately quality of care.[3] Prejudices about poor and minority patients are not uncommon,[2] and providers may subscribe to negative stereotypes by assuming that poor patients are lazy, less knowledgeable about illness, and less likely to follow medical directions.[4] These studies concur that "unlike the ideal prototype of the physician, 'real' physicians are much like the rest of us in their general prejudices and stereotypes of the poor."[3(p620)]

Relative to provider–patient interaction, a meta-analysis of 44 recent studies found that the patients' social characteristics were significantly related to communication patterns in the treatment setting.[5] Although there was no difference in patient desire for information across social classes, upper-middle-class patients received more physician time, more information, more positive talk, and more talk overall than did patients from lower social classes. Moreover, white patients received more information, more positive talk, and better quality care than did black or Hispanic patients.

In light of the importance of provider–patient interaction, this chapter examines interactional barriers to partnership for lower-income black patients in the rural South. Four issues are addressed. First, to what extent do interactional barriers impinge on treatment across private practice, clinic, inpatient hospital, and emergency department settings for this population? Second, to what extent does patient satisfaction vary across these settings? Third, to what extent does this population believe that classism and racism affect provider–patient interaction? Fourth, practice recommendations based on these findings are presented.

RESEARCH DESIGN

Methodological triangulation was employed to examine provider–patient interaction across four treatment settings. Quantitative and qualitative data were collected through 281 household interviews, 20 key informant interviews, and 6 focus group interviews.

Household interviews

Household interviews were conducted with knowledgeable members of 281 lower-income black households in five rural counties in south Georgia. County populations ranged from 5,654 to 42,125, with 26.0% to 63.3% black residents.[16] Because many of the target households did not have telephone service, household interviews were conducted on a house-to-house basis in predominantly black neighborhoods that had been identified by community key informants. Mean household size was 2.8 members (SD = 1.8 members) for a total of 788 individuals, including 133 men, 311 women, and 344 children. Over four fifths (81.0%) of the households were at or below the federal poverty line, and 9.2% were between 101% and 125% of the poverty line. The remaining 9.8% of households were between 126% and 185% of the federal poverty level. Over one fourth of the children, non-elderly adults, and elderly adults did not have private or public health insurance coverage.

Conducted by trained interviewers, household interviews took an average of 45 minutes to complete. Although the interviews addressed a wide range of health issues, this article focuses specifically on provider–patient interaction and satisfaction relative to the most recent visits to four treatment settings during the past year. These include private practice, clinic or health department, inpatient hospital, and emergency department settings. The patient during these visits may have been the respondent or a member of the household for whom the respondent was responsible. Because preventive service utilization among this population is low,[17] the interview items were designed to address the treatment of acute and chronic conditions. Relevant interview items are presented below, and, unless noted otherwise, responses included "no," "yes," and "not applicable."

Information context

Five questions were asked about exchange of information between the provider and the patient: (1) Did the provider explain what was wrong with you [diagnosis]? (2) Did the provider explain different ways your problem could be treated [treatment options]? (3) Did the provider talk to you about how you could prevent some health problems (eg, by eating right, not smoking, not drinking) [health promotion]? (4) Did the provider ask how you wanted to treat the problem [patient input]? (5) Did you feel the provider knew what he or she was doing [provider competence]?

Socioemotional context

Four questions were asked about socioemotional aspects of the setting visit: (1) Were the waiting and examination rooms neat and clean? (2) How long did you wait to be seen (in minutes)? (3) Were you treated politely and kindly? (4) Did you feel the provider was concerned about any pain you were feeling?

Patient satisfaction

Both situational and generalized satisfaction were addressed with two items: (1) Would you like to go back to this place for treatment in the future [situational satisfaction]? (2) Have you ever turned down care because of how you were treated [generalized satisfaction]? Please describe.

Key informant and focus group interviews

In-depth interviews were conducted with 20 community key informants and six focus groups comprising service providers and recipients. Key informants included social welfare program administrators (5); clergy (4); nurses (2); mental health professionals (2); educators (2); general community leaders, including officers of the National Association for the Advancement of Colored Persons (NAACP) (2); social workers (1); attorneys (1); and business owners (1). Focus group interviews were conducted with a local chapter of the NAACP (25 members), two Senior Companion support groups (13 members each), a black businesswomen's association (12 members), a community service group for men (10 members), and a support group for single teenage mothers (4 members). All key informants and focus group members were black and resided and/or worked in one of the five target counties.

Interviews were intensive, semistructured, and audiotaped for transcription. Responses to the following four questions pertaining to health and race were analyzed: (1) Is there any place [that provides medical services] you would not send a black friend who is visiting here? Please explain. (2) What kinds of problems do black people in this community have in getting good health care? (3) Do you think black and white people in this community have the same opportunity for good health care? Please explain. (4) Which groups of black people have the greatest problems getting good health care?

FINDINGS

Data were collected from 281 households regarding 342 discrete treatment episodes in private practice (52.6%), clinic (20.2%), inpatient hospital (13.7%), and emergency department settings (13.5%). Over one fourth of the episodes occurred in a hospital setting (see Table 25–2).

Table 25–2. Patient assessment of treatment episodes

Interaction strategy	Percentage of patients who responded affirmatively					
	Private practice (N = 180)	Clinic (N = 69)	Hospital, inpatient (N = 47)	Emergency department (N = 46)	All settings (N = 342)	Rank
Information context						
Provider explained diagnosis.	92.1	91.2	83.0	75.6	88.5	5
Provider explained treatment options.	72.8	66.1	69.6	48.8	67.8	6
Provider discussed health promotion.	67.8	73.9	57.4	37.0	63.5	7
Provider solicited input.	49.1	53.3	52.2	35.7	48.6	8
Provider was considered competent.	91.7	94.2	83.0	78.3	89.2	3
Socioemotional context						
Treatment setting was clean.	97.8	100.0	93.6	97.8	97.7	1
Wait for consultation (mean, in min)	43.9	45.1	35.6	61.3	45.4	9
SD	51.8	46.1	54.2	62.3	52.8	
Patient was treated politely.	97.8	98.6	87.2	87.0	95.0	2
Provider appeared concerned.	90.9	93.9	84.8	77.8	88.9	4
Patient satisfaction						
Patient would like to return.	92.8	97.1	87.2	78.3	90.9	

Information context

Across the four treatment settings, perceived competence of providers and diagnosis explained received the highest percentage of positive responses of the information variables (89.2% and 88.5%, respectively). In about two thirds of the treatment episodes, providers explained treatment options and health promotion issues (67.8% and 63.5%, respectively), and patient input was solicited in less than half the treatment episodes (48.6%). When examining differences between treatment settings, it appears that providers were most likely to explain diagnoses and to be considered competent in private practice and clinic settings and that health promotion issues were most likely to be discussed in clinic settings. Emergency department providers received the lowest percentage of positive responses for each information variable.

To test hypotheses that significant differences existed between the four treatment settings as a whole, Kruskal-Wallis tests were conducted for each information variable. This test is similar to analysis of variance (ANOVA) but is designed for nonparametric data such as distributions of yes and no responses.[18] Although responses to the information variables did not differ significantly at P .05 using this statistic, this may be due, in part, to the relatively small number of emergency department treatment episodes.

In general, household respondents were interested in receiving health information. Several household informants commented positively about follow-up and health promotion literature they had received during the past year. In addition,

the importance of communicating effectively was illustrated by a 50-year-old woman's distress that she "can't understand the doctoral terms." Although representing extreme situations, two respondents were very frustrated because they felt they had received inadequate information. A 35-year-old farm worker recounted that he was "half castrated" after being treated for an auto wreck. Although "there was no choice on the doctor's part, . . . I didn't know anything until it was over. No one told me anything." Likewise, a woman who had given birth during her teenage years suspected she had received a tubal ligation during the caesarean section without her consent. Although she had asked her physician repeatedly if this was the case, she felt he was being evasive.

Household interviews revealed that confidence in provider competence was related to several factors. Emergency department providers who were interns or foreign born, who appeared irritated with nonemergency conditions, or who did not appear sufficiently sympathetic were considered less competent than other providers. In addition, respondents often assumed that urban physicians were more competent than rural physicians. Concerns about competence centered on the provider's ability to provide an accurate diagnosis and the effects of Medicaid insurance coverage on quality of care. The director of a program for minority children, who was also a "100 Points of Light" national service award recipient, explained that

[Some] physicians are totally dependent on Medicaid. So *these* doctors tell you to keep coming back for frequent visits, so they can get money out of Medicaid. Since reimbursement levels are low, they try to see you more often so they can keep up their income. Another problem is the "bouncing game," where one doctor refers you to someone else, and that person doesn't want a Medicaid patient either, so they refer you to someone else, and you get bounced around so often you finally give up. I've *seen* this happen.

A Medicaid recipient interviewed for this study "[tries] to go to two to three doctors" when she needs medical attention because she is never certain whether local physicians are competent.

Socioemotional context

Socioemotional aspects of interaction received more positive ratings than did information variables. Cumulative affirmative responses included treatment setting clean (97.7%), patient treated politely (95.0%), and provider appeared concerned about patient discomfort (88.9%). Although differences across the four settings as a whole were not statistically significant—in part because of the disproportionate distribution of treatment settings—clinics were most likely and inpatient hospital settings least likely to be considered clean. In addition, patients felt that they were treated more politely and providers appeared more concerned in private practice and clinic settings than in hospital settings.

The average wait for consultation was 45.4 minutes (SD = 52.8 min), with a low of 35.6 minutes for inpatient hospital and a high of 61.3 minutes for emergency department settings. Although

ANOVA analysis revealed that the average wait was not significantly different across the four settings as a whole, t test analyses revealed that the average wait for emergency department service was significantly longer than the average wait for inpatient hospital and private physician services at P .05. In addition, transportation was more likely to be considered problematic than time spent waiting for consultations. Exceptions included respondents who were employed full-time or waited several hours for emergency department services.

Comfort zones and cultural appreciation

Several key informants emphasized that cultural barriers between providers and patients need to be addressed. An attorney who serves as a community advocate stated that these barriers can be as obvious as language differences. He related that rural people "may not even understand the health care provider once they get here." Conversely, "we even have doctors who say, 'Hey, come here —can you interpret this?' when they don't understand a patient." Other cultural barriers are more subtle. For example, an outreach nurse noticed that minority patients can be uncomfortable during medical interviews because "coming from the black culture, you don't tell your business—you don't talk about your problems." The importance of a cultural "comfort zone" was illustrated by an incident related by a local psychologist:

Dr H said that he saw an encounter at a health department where a white nurse was treating a black patient. The patient was silent throughout the treatment. At a later date, he saw the same patient with a black nurse, and a conversation was going the whole time. . . . I do think there is a comfort level here.

A local professor reflected that even middle-class minorities consider social comfort when selecting health care providers, even delaying care until they locate a sympathetic provider.

Perceived discrimination and health service utilization

Inability to pay was typically seen as the primary barrier to receiving health care. A public health counselor observed, "Them that have good insurance, it doesn't matter what your color is—you are welcome anywhere." Other respondents suggested that finances could be used as an excuse for excluding black patients. For example, respondents often perceived that most private practices accepted only a limited number of Medicaid patients—if they accepted any at all. Although one community member did "not begrudge doctors' offices [for refusing Medicaid patients] because the reimbursement rate is so low," others attributed Medicaid ceilings to a desire for profit—or racism. The director of a community action group concluded that "if there's an excuse for not serving [black patients], they'll give us the excuse."

Respondents often perceived that race functioned as a secondary, interactional barrier to quality care. Individuals in their 40s remembered segregated medical practices and, later, segregated waiting rooms. Although they concurred that the situation had improved in recent years, they often believed that black and poor patients were treated worse than white patients and patients who were able to pay without Medicaid. A local clergyman related that "there is a lot of distrust of white people. Racism is everywhere. . . . And we need to see—we have our antennae up—to see if you're sincere, if you're for real. And we'll know right away if we sense racism." His colleague agreed that "race is an issue behind everything in the South" and advocated that "we definitely need more black health care professionals, especially doctors."

Of the 281 household informants, 9.7% stated that they had refused treatment for themselves or another member of their household at some time because they were treated rudely. An adult son explained that his mother once refused treatment because she "got 'assistance' —[the] receptionist in the doctor's office got rough with her." A woman in her 30s once "left the hospital early because the nurse was rude to me—the doctor wanted me to stay longer." Other respondents drew a direct connection between race, class, and quality of care. The local "100 Points of Light" recipient stated that she often observed that "one woman who can pay or has insurance is treated one way. Another woman, who has Medicaid, she's treated another way. It's humiliating, so they don't go for preventive services unless they are *really* sick. They know people look down on them."

A logger's wife described a particular emergency department physician as "racist—he treated me bad because I'm black . . . it happens," and a 42-year-old man who was steadily employed recounted that "a white nurse wouldn't spray me [when I was burned] because I'm black, so I had to do it myself." A 61-year-old woman wished that doctors would not "be biased on looks," referring to the race and social class of the patient.

Respondents described four strategies they employ when providers or support staff treat them rudely. First, some respondents refuse formal services. A psychologist observed that "maybe the white nurses in the health departments, some of the older ones, harbor stereotypes, and it interferes with level of care. That's one of the reasons minorities don't seek services." Second, respondents attempt to locate sympathetic providers. A local NAACP president encouraged "his people" to see racism as the provider's problem, and "then we find them someplace else to go." A local professor concurred, explaining that even a middle-class "black person never just goes through the phone book and picks out a doctor and makes an appointment. You ask someone [how the provider treats black patients], even if that means delaying when you seek care. . . . There is a lot of word-of-mouth referral."

Mentioned less frequently, a third option involved remaining with the current provider and demanding greater respect. One household informant stated that she is treated well because she "knows how to cuss," and the activities director of a black-owned and -operated nursing home confronts people when she hears them say racist things about her. However, she realizes that "many of our people, especially older women, just will not be able to do that."

In other instances, individuals continue with the same provider regardless of how they are treated, in large part because there are few options. When asked if a family member had ever refused care, a woman in her 30s stated, "No. My mom says they treat blacks worse than whites, but she'll go back because she'll die without her [kidney dialysis] treatment." Other respondents remained because it was "the only place that takes Medicaid"; there was only one clinic or few physicians in the county, and/or the patient did not have transportation outside the county.

DISCUSSION

The following observations and recommendations are based on data collected from household respondents, community key informants, and focus group members.

Satisfaction with provider–patient interaction

Overall, 90.9% of the household respondents stated that they "would like to go back" to their most recent treatment settings, with a high of 97.1% for clinics and a low of 78.3% for emergency departments. However, this should not be interpreted as blanket satisfaction with provider–patient interaction for three reasons. First, patient satisfaction may have been skewed positively due to the selection process itself. By the time household interviews were conducted, respondents may have "deselected" unacceptable treatment settings in favor of more supportive settings.

Second, open-ended comments provided by household, key informant, and focus group respondents indicated that rude treatment was not uncommon and that a number of local providers had the reputation of being "not good." By definition, "good" providers were considered competent, treated patients with respect, and provided services even when patients could not pay. Those who were "not good" were less likely to provide a conclusive diagnosis and remedy, to treat patients with respect, and/or to provide care when patients could not pay. Third, willingness to return to specific settings may have been influenced by the dearth of options. Contributing factors included the lower rate of physicians per capita in rural areas,[17,19,20] the fact that the rural South is a site of persistent and intergenerational poverty,[21] and the low insuredness rate of Southern black people.[22]

Training and stress reduction programs

Provider–patient interaction can be enhanced through a four-prong strategy. First, relevant staff training programs can be developed and implemented. These programs can emphasize the importance of patient empowerment and partnership building, summarize research findings pertaining to the effect of patient characteristics on quality of care, identify and increase appreciation of multicultural values and norms, and describe objective strategies for enhancing patient empowerment and quality provider–patient interaction. As noted by Braithwaite and Lythcott,

The health community needs to develop comprehensive and culturally sensitive approaches to address the complex and multifaceted issues of minority health and wellness. . . . Because health behaviors are culture-bound, primary prevention efforts . . . must emerge from a knowledge of and respect for the culture of the target community.[12(p283)]

Second, stressors that affect interaction should be identified for specific categories of providers, such as physicians, nurse practitioners and physician assistants, other nurses, aides, and office staff within specific treatment settings. Stressors may be intrapersonal, such as negative stereotypes of special populations, or contextual, such as being presented with nonemergency situations in emergency department settings.

Third, medical practices should investigate whether they can adjust office routines in ways that will reduce stress and improve interaction. For example, receptionists may find it easier to relate to patients positively if they alternate between front desk and clerical duties and are not responsible for bill collection. Lastly, medical and office staff should make a long-term commitment to cultural sensitivity, patient empowerment, and partnership building. This commitment may be reinforced through staff meetings, guest speakers, circulating relevant literature, periodic self-assessments, and emphasizing interpersonal skills as a formal component of employee evaluation.

Communication within the treatment context

The three notable deficiencies across treatment settings involved providing information, soliciting patient input, and addressing health promotion issues. The manner in which these deficiencies can be remedied varies according to the patient's condition and the treatment setting. In every context, providers can explain the etiology and nature of the patient's condition. In addition, whenever treatment options exist, these can be discussed with the goal of collaboratively developing a treatment plan. In some instances, such as routine screenings and major emergencies, options may not exist if the patient is to be treated effectively. In these cases, discussion can center around diagnostic and treatment procedures, the types of information and results these procedures can provide, and anticipated side effects and prognoses. While patients may not be making treatment decisions per se, the provider and patient become collaborators in the treatment process itself.

Data suggest that rural, poor, and minority individuals use preventive services less frequently and suffer from chronic conditions more frequently than do non-poor, urban, and nonminority individuals.[17,23-25] Consequently, a useful goal would be to incorporate a discussion of health promotion and preventive health issues into every visit possible. A combination of innovative strategies may be used, including video presentations in the waiting room and education sessions led by students, volunteers, or paraprofes-sionals during office visits as appropriate. Because of the high level of functional illiteracy among some special populations, education should not rely exclusively on literature campaigns.

Role of the local emergency department

Across the board, respondents indicated that the most problematic setting for provider–patient interaction and patient satisfaction was the emergency department. In large part, patient frustration with emergency department care has structural roots. Lower-income individuals often visit emergency departments for nonemergency episodes because they cannot afford private practice care and/or their condition is outside the scope of health department services. As a result, emergency department physicians are responsible for heavy caseloads often consisting of nonemergency conditions and patients who cannot pay. This strains emergency department resources and overworks physicians, possibly exacerbating negative stereotypes of poor and minority patients. In return, patients may feel that physicians are not taking their condition seriously and are not sufficiently sympathetic.

Despite the stress created by nonemergency conditions and uninsured patients, the emergency department is sometimes the only source of formal medical care for lower-income minority people in the rural South. For this reason, it is critical to reassess the role of the local emergency department and provide partnership within this setting. Staff training programs about multiculturalism, provider attitudes, and provider–patient interaction are essential, and procedures should be evaluated to see if provider stress can be reduced in any way. Health education strategies may be implemented in emergency department settings and directed to the patient or caretaker, especially if a collaboration between local hospitals and health departments exists.

•　•　•

As an exploratory study based on a convenience sample, the findings presented in this chapter do not necessarily represent other contexts or communities. However, these findings are important for two reasons. First, much of the research on minority health consists of secondary analysis of crude health indicators and insuredness rates. Through the collection of qualitative data, respondents were able to describe health care experiences from their own perspective. Second, health needs vary among subpopulations of black Americans,[24–26] and this study focuses on a specific subpopulation as defined by race, region, and class.

As a special population, lower-income minority patients must penetrate two barriers to health care—the structural barrier of accessing services and the interactional barrier of receiving quality care. This study suggests that patient empowerment and health care partnership are valued by lower-income black people in the rural South. In addition, whether incidents of discrimination were actual or merely perceived, intentional or unintentional, respondents often believed that racism and classism were barriers to quality provider–patient interaction. By refining the interactional model of partnership and related instrumentation presented in this chapter, provider–patient dynamics can be examined more explicitly both within and across special populations with the goal of enhancing patient involvement. With this information, providers "can improve their care of poor patients by paying attention to the contextual problems which exist between them and economically underserved patients."[2(p306)]

REFERENCES

1. U.S. Department of Health and Human Services, Public Health Service. *Healthy People 2000: National Health Promotion and Disease Prevention Objectives*. Washington, DC: Government Printing Office; 1991. DHHS publication PHS 91-50212.
2. Ventres W, Gordon P. Communication strategies in caring for the underserved. *J Health Care Poor Underserved*. 1990;1:305–314.
3. Roter C. Commentary. *J Fam Pract*. 1988;27: 620.
4. Price J, Desmond S, Snyder F, Kimmel S. Perceptions of family practice residents regarding health care and poor patients. *J Fam Pract*. 1988;27: 615–621.
5. Hall J, Roter D, Katz N. Meta-analysis of correlates of provider behavior in medical encounters. *Med Care*. 1988;26:657–672.
6. Waitzkin H. Information giving in medical care. *J Health Soc Behav*. 1985;26:81–101.
7. World Health Organization. The Ottawa charter for health promotion. *Health Promotion*. 1986;1: iii–v.
8. Goeppinger J, Shuster G. Community as client: using the nursing process to promote health. In:

Stanhope M, Lancaster J, eds. *Community Health Nursing: Process and Practice for Promoting Health.* 3rd ed. St. Louis, Mo: Mosby; 1991.

9. Beckman H, Frankel R. The effect of physician behavior on the collection of data. *Ann Intern Med.* 1984;101:692–696.

10. Goeppinger J. Health promotion for rural populations: partnership interventions. *Fam Community Health.* 1993;16(1):1–10.

11. Waitzkin H. A critical theory of medical discourse: ideology, social control, and the processing of social context in medical encounters. *J Health Soc Behav.* 1989;30:220–239.

12. Braithwaite R, Lythcott N. Community empowerment as a strategy for health promotion for black and other minority populations. *JAMA.* 1989;261: 282–283.

13. Collins R. On the micro-foundations of macro-sociology. *Am J Sociol.* 1981;86:984–1014.

14. Collins R. Interaction ritual chains, power and property: the micro–macro connection as an empirically-based theoretical problem. In: Alexander JC, Geisen B, Münch R, Smelser NJ, eds. *The Micro–Macro Link.* Berkeley, Calif: University of California Press; 1987.

15. Greenley J, Davidson R. Organizational influences on patient health behaviors. In: Gochman D, ed. *Health Behavior: Emerging Research Perspectives.* New York, NY: Plenum Press; 1988.

16. Bachtel D, Boatright S, eds. *The Georgia County Guide.* 12th ed. Athens, Ga: University of Georgia; 1993.

17. U.S. Congress, Office of Technology Assessment. *Health Care in Rural America.* Washington, DC: Government Printing Office; 1990. Publication OTA-H-34.

18. Kanji G. *100 Statistical Tests.* Newbury Park, Calif: Sage; 1993.

19. Ryan R. *Rural Health in Georgia.* Atlanta, Ga: Georgia State Office of Rural Health; 1993.

20. Korcyzk S. *Health Care Needs, Resources, and Access in Rural America.* Alexandria, Va: Analytical Services; 1989.

21. Brown D, Warner M. Persistent low-income nonmetropolitan areas in the United States: some conceptual challenges for development policy. *Policy Stud J.* 1991;19(2):22–41.

22. Rowland D, Lyons B. Triple jeopardy: rural, poor, and uninsured. *Health Serv Res.* 1989;23:975–1004.

23. U.S. Dept of Health and Human Services. *Vital and Health Statistics: Current Estimates from the National Health Interview Survey, 1990.* Hyattsville, Md: Department of Health and Human Services; 1991. Publication (PHS) 92-1509.

24. Alcena V. Preface. In: *The Status of Health of Blacks in the United States of America.* Dubuque, Iowa: Kendall/Hunt; 1992.

25. Blendon R, Aiken L, Freeman H, Corey C. Access to medical care for black and white Americans. *JAMA.* 1989;261:278–281.

26. Green V. The black extended family in the United States: some research suggestions. In: Shimkin D, Shimkin E, Frate D, eds. *The Extended Family in Black Societies.* The Hague, The Netherlands: Mouton De Gruyer; 1978.

Research, Policy, and Clinical Perspectives

Directions for the Future

Juliann G. Sebastian, PhD, RN, CS

T HE CHAPTERS in this book delineate a range of issues facing health professionals concerned about improving the health of special populations. Much remains to be learned about effective approaches to reducing disparities between the health status of members of these groups and the population as a whole. Serious challenges exist in the implementation of research findings in clinical practice and health policy. This part will highlight key directions in research, policy, and clinical services suggested by the chapters in this book. The chapter that follows by Maeve illuminates many of the methodologic issues that arise when conducting qualitative research with special populations.

RESEARCH

Fig V–1 depicts a model for conceptualizing research and clinical issues related to vulnerable populations.[1] Flaskerud and Winslow's model highlights the critical relationship between resources and health risk for vulnerable populations.

This model suggests the importance of ongoing research into this relationship. For example, individual clinical interventions might be directed to strengthening the personal and social resources of members of special population groups. However, it is not clear what the most cost-effective approaches are to doing so. Health education is one strategy to strengthen personal resources. However, more needs to be done to understand which educational methodologies are most culturally appropriate and best build on the learning readiness of people who may also be dealing with limited financial resources and other stressors. Working with communities to strengthen the social networks and use those ties to help members of special populations achieve and maintain good health is an important goal. Again, the most culturally appropriate and cost-effective strategies under varying local circumstances are not yet fully delineated.

Fig V–2 outlines a broad approach to mapping a research, clinical, and policy agenda for improving the health of members of special populations. Together, these models suggest that relationships between the characteristics of members of special populations and health professionals are interconnected with clinical interventions, individual and population health status, resilience, health policies, and the community context. The linkage points provide particularly critical areas for future study. Although strong relationships have been found between socioeconomic status and health outcomes, the causal links between social, physiologic, cultural, and economic characteristics and health outcomes are not yet

fully understood. For example, Broyles and her colleagues report in their chapter in this text that while ethnicity accounted for more variance in cardiovascular risk factor profiles of Anglo and Mexican American mothers and children than socioeconomic status, none of the usual demographic variables accounted for much variance overall. She and her team noted that the roles that environmental and genetic factors play in risk status are still not well understood in certain populations.

Neither do health researchers completely understand which processes of care are most likely to improve health status for special populations, nor how those processes relate to helping members of special populations build resilience and personal strategies for improving health and preventing illness. Strickland and Strickland describe the critical role of the relationships between health care professionals and clients on health status of special population groups. The nature of these relationships takes on particular importance with special populations because of the need to more effectively incorporate culturally and linguistically appropriate approaches to care. Taking an ecological perspective on processes of care, it is necessary to better understand what communities can do to support and strengthen special populations, and to build a healthier environment for the populace.

Several chapters in this book report on qualitative studies that aim to better understand the reality of managing health problems and promoting health under difficult circumstances. The findings of these works offer original insights into

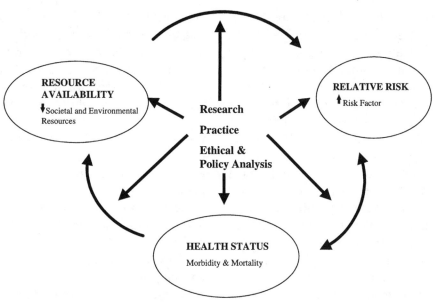

Fig V–1. Vulnerable populations: Conceptual model for research and practice. *Source:* Reprinted with permission from J.A. Flaskerud and B.J. Winslow, Conceptualizing Vulnerable Populations Health-Related Research, *Nursing Research*, Vol. 47, No.2, p. 70, © 1998, Lippincott Williams & Wilkins.

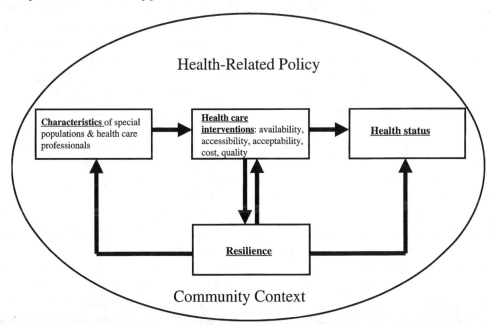

Fig V–2. Framework for directions in research, policy, and clinical improvements in health outcomes of special populations.

the lived experience of health and health care by special populations, and the kinds of strategies that might be most helpful to improving health status in these groups. These qualitative studies provide a theoretically grounded basis for ongoing qualitative and quantitative work to better understand how to reduce health disparities among special populations. A number of the chapters provide insight into the experience of caregiving and chronicity, leading to suggestions for testing the effectiveness of interventions. For example, the chapter by Worcester and Hedrick on respite use by caregivers of frail elders expands the knowledgebase about decision making by caregivers and offers suggestions for immediate clinical applications (eg, the caregiver pamphlet that Worcester and Hedrick describe) and research to quantify respite use and effectiveness. The chapter by Neal et al illuminates how parents with limited financial resources manage when caring for ill children and portrays the meanings and strengths upon which parents drew. Health professionals need deeper understanding of ways to help clients build on their own resilience and find meaning in difficult circumstances and this study adds to that knowledgebase. Neal and her colleagues recommend further investigation into the types of community resources that families need under varying circumstances and how community resources can be used to foster resilience.

Similarly, Peterson and colleagues recommend further study into how families with chronically ill children access health care and development of strategies to use "cultural brokers" to help families access the care they feel is needed. Parker's study of families caring for chronically ill children with tuberous sclerosis complex supports the need for further investigation into the most effective ways to help families coping with rare chronic illnesses. Gramling and colleagues' documentation of the story of one woman with AIDS supports the need for health care professionals to design and test interventions that better link people with the care and resources they need. Together, each of these chapters provides insight into the lived experience of managing health by special populations.

Several of the chapters focus on the unique needs of rural populations. Kidd et al used qualitative methods to develop an understanding of how farm parents teach injury prevention to their children. The findings of this study suggest that research is needed to address the effectiveness of using different approaches to teaching safety behavior, particularly from the perspective of the economic implications of injury prevention. Sullivan and her colleagues report on the experience of living with cancer in rural areas and challenges associated with accessing care and providing community- and family-oriented support for people with cancer.

The study by Affonso et al documents the interplay between rural and cultural belief systems and the impact of those interconnections on stressors during pregnancy. Wing et al's study of Muscogee (Creek) Indian views of alcoholism provides insight into cultural perspectives of this particular group that can be used to design and test culturally appropriate interventions.

Strickland and Strickland report on ways in which lower income minorities cope with the cost of care and how perceptions of when care is needed interact with decisions about seeking care. Similarly, Gifford and Bettenhausen describe subtle barriers to low-income adolescents' receiving prenatal care. These studies demonstrate that more fine-grained analyses of access issues are needed to better understand how to help members of special populations receive the care they want and need.

A number of the chapters in this text focus on populations at high risk of developing health problems, but whose members have found ways to combat the negative impact of socioeconomic forces. For example, Porter noted the potential usefulness of testing perceived self-efficacy to prevent illness among populations at high risk of developing certain health problems. She reported that families whose children were at high risk of lead poisoning were able to mitigate this risk through the actions they took to modify the home environment or the child's exposure to lead within the environment. The likelihood of taking action was related to parental beliefs about the extent of the child's exposure to lead. Villa and colleagues found that the prevalence of chronic disease was not as high among older, lower socioeconomic Koreans as might have been expected and speculate on the lifestyle factors that may have led to relative health advantages. Williams et al share their findings of the perceptions of health promotion held by poor, rural women. These perceptions differ from the assumptions upon which conventional health educational strategies are often based and suggest the need for research into more effective strategies for health promotion with members of special populations. Finally, Ulione found that dual-earner families were able to mitigate the stress of multiple and conflicting demands through job flexibility and social support. These works illustrate the roles that both internal belief systems and external community supports can play in strengthening resilience to health risks.

POLICY

Health policies represent population-based interventions and must account for the needs of special populations in ways that are equitable and that promote social justice. Some of the policy challenges facing the United States require creative solutions to meet these dual goals. For example, the various versions of patients' bills of rights provide patients with more choices of providers and treatments. Managed care organizations are concerned about the impact of these policy proposals on their abilities to control costs with increased options for enrollees to make costly choices. These types of individual decisions may be very important to members of special populations, who often have complex health problems and who may wish to retain relationships with clinicians of their choosing, either because these specialists already know them or because they are more culturally acceptable.

Aday argues for more community-focused policies that better influence the precursors to health of special populations. This is particularly important in view of the particularly strong connections between the social and economic context and the health status of special populations. She agrees with others that stronger collaborative connections between traditional health services and public health are likely to better serve the broad health needs of the populace.[2] Her chapter highlights a growing movement toward greater partnership between health care providers and community agencies and individual citizens.[3-5] Creative new partnerships have the potential to better address local conditions and cultural preferences, strengths, and needs.

One of the most important policy issues is development of creative financing options to increase access to care. With 43.4 million people currently uninsured,[6] this is a critical area for ongoing policy development. The Children's Health Insurance Program is a major initiative that should help achieve this goal for children whose families have not qualified for Medicaid in the past.[7] Paying for uncompensated care for other uninsured and underinsured populations poses continuing policy challenges. For example, gaps exist in reimbursement for the types of care that chronically ill populations need, and especially those with multiple comorbidities. Few mechanisms exist to pay for ongoing health education, family and caregiver support, and related services such as respite or day care. Current efforts[8] to develop financing mechanisms to ensure that chronically ill elderly and disabled populations are able to afford the medications they need exemplify a major policy concern related to those populations who are particularly vulnerable to the adverse effects of chronic illness.

CLINICAL

A number of chapters in this text highlight aspects of the health belief model in relation to individual health-promoting actions. However, rarely do individuals take actions in isolation. More often, people institute multiple health-related activities in varying amounts and at varying times. Health professionals do not always have evidence-based support for recommending particular "doses" of preventive behaviors.[9] The chapter by Cole and Crawford describes a health education program that succeeded in enhancing the knowledge that migrant women have related to health behaviors and in strengthening their self-confidence. Similar programs in the future might build on this design and test which combinations of topics, extent of content coverage, and teaching methods are most effective in reaching critical outcomes related to improving migrant health.

In another example, Powell found that some youth at high risk for violence were able to overcome the impact of the risk factors they faced through a combination of community and personal actions. The next step is better understanding of which interventions have the greatest impact and are the most cost efficient.

Another direction for clinical practice is the use of evidence-based practice with special populations. The chapters in this text provide numerous examples of research findings that could be incorporated into some aspects of clinical practice. One of the key challenges is determination of when and how current clinical guidelines need to be modified to be more consistent with the cultural, economic, and political realities of special population groups. For example, in their study of incarcerated women engaged in behaviors that place them at high risk for HIV infection, Muller and Boyle found that environmental circumstances contributed heavily to individual choices to engage in these behaviors. They emphasize the need to develop population-level interventions to modify the political, cultural, and economic predictors of high-risk behaviors, rather than relying on individually oriented interventions.

Related to this is the need for health professionals to be educated regarding the unique constellations of clinical issues experienced by special populations and strategies for making clinical judgments in complex situations. Miser's study of the clinical judgments made by social workers faced with criminal justice problems illustrates the clinical demands placed on health professionals aiming to provide both comprehensive and specialized care.

Finally, at the organizational level, Plescia and his colleagues describe a successful interdisciplinary model for providing health care to homeless populations. Their team visits sites at which homeless populations gather to receive other health-related and social services and provides care directly on-site at those locations. In this way, they take the care to the population needing it, rather than requiring potential clients to come to them. The Provan chapter also highlights the need to organize services for special populations in ways that best meet their needs. His work suggests that service coordination and coordination of funding streams, as well as clear communication of service policies, are critical for effectively helping members of special population groups promote and maintain health. His chapter indicates that the ways in which services are integrated are important and that policy makers and health professionals cannot assume that any form of service integration is going to be helpful for special population groups. Instead, client outcomes seem to be better when a single core agency coordinates services and funding streams, even though multiple independent agencies may provide the services.

In summary, the chapters in this text delineate a rich array of directions for ongoing research, clinical, and policy interventions to improve the health of special populations. The health needs of special populations are of critical concern given both the ethical imperative to ensure a healthier populace and the demographic shifts that are taking place at the beginning of the twenty-first century.

DISCUSSION QUESTIONS

1. Together with key decision makers in your community, identify the research, clinical, and policy issues your community faces in improving the health of special populations.

What factors are helping move the community toward developing creative responses to those challenges, and what factors serve as barriers to progress? How can you use community/clinical/academic partnerships to overcome the barriers and promote a healthier community?

2. Debate with colleagues whether the research findings that are reported in this text have adequate external validity to be incorporated into practice, or whether they suggest a need for further research prior to incorporation into practice. Evaluate how those ideas that are ready for application can be used to provide fresh, culturally and linguistically competent, and sensitive health services to special populations in your community.

3. What next steps do you and your colleagues need to take to work toward reducing health disparities between members of special populations and the community as a whole? How will you begin? What resources do you need to be successful, and how will you marshall those resources?

REFERENCES

1. Flaskerud JA, Winslow BJ. Conceptualizing vulnerable populations health-related research. *Nurs Res.* 1998;47(2): 69–78.

2. Lasker RD, The Committee on Medicine & Public Health. *Medicine & Public Health: The Power of Collaboration.* New York: The New York Academy of Medicine; 1997.

3. Flynn BC. Healthy cities: toward worldwide health promotion. *Annu Rev Public Health.* 1996;17:299–309.

4. Kretzmann JP, McKnight JL. *Building Communities from the Inside Out: A Path toward Finding and Mobilizing a Community's Assets.* Evanston, Ill: Northwestern University;1993.

5. McKnight J.L. *The Careless Society: Community and Its Counterfeits.* New York: Basic Books; 1995.

6. Bennefield, RL. Health insurance coverage: 1997. *Current Population Reports.* Washington DC: Census Bureau; 1998. pp. 60–202.

7. Hamburg, M. (1998) Eliminating racial and ethnic disparities in health: response to the Presidential Initiative on Race. *Public Health Reports* 113: 372–375.

8. Soumerai SB, Ross-Degnan D. Inadequate prescription drug coverage for Medicare enrollees—a call to action. *N Engl J Med.* 1999;340(9):722–728.

9. Iowa Intervention Project. *Nursing Interventions Classification.* Philadelphia: J.B. Lippincott; 1996.

CHAPTER 26

Methodologic Issues in Qualitative Research with Incarcerated Women

M. Katherine Maeve, RN, PhD

PRISONERS have been designated as a "vulnerable" population by the US Department of Health and Human Services.[1] This additional protection is related to the special constraints prisoners may experience "which could affect their ability to make a truly voluntary and uncoerced decision whether or not to participate as subjects in research."[1(p14)] As more and more persons become incarcerated, it behooves health professionals to include this marginalized group in various kinds of research, particularly research that holds the potential for helping individuals engage in self-nurturing behaviors, and to make changes consistent with remaining free upon their release. While the lack of representation of women in health research has become a national concern, health research regarding incarcerated women is particularly lacking.

The research described in this article was supported by an E. Louise Grant Faculty Scholar Award, Medical College of Georgia.

Fam Community Health 1998;21(3):1–15
© 1998 Aspen Publishers, Inc.

This chapter identifies methodologic issues and concerns encountered while conducting a qualitative participative action research study with incarcerated women. An overview of the issues surrounding incarcerated women is presented along with a brief description of the study currently being conducted. Qualitative methodologic issues are discussed as they pertain to working with incarcerated women. In addition, strategies used by the author to improve the quality of qualitative research with this vulnerable population are presented.

INCARCERATED WOMEN

The number of women entering US prisons has soared over the last two decades. Approximately 117,000 women are currently incarcerated in jails and state prisons in the United States.[2] Studies indicate women in prison are predominantly from economically disadvantaged backgrounds, are less educated, have substance abuse problems, have received inconsistent or no previous health care, and have significant histories of physical and sexual abuse (unpublished data).[3–6] Further, women of color are substantially over represented in this population, comprising about 60% of the total number of women imprisoned.[7] All of these factors, coupled with women's actual imprisonment, imply a particular vulnerability, socially and individually.

Because incarcerated women have not received consistent health care treatment prior to imprisonment, it is not unusual to find newly arriving inmates with

- untreated sexually transmitted diseases;

- undertreated chronic illnesses such as hypertension and diabetes;
- positive skin tests indicating at least exposure to tuberculosis, if not active disease;
- and, at double the rate of men, human immunodeficiency virus (HIV) infection.[7–9]

About 85% of incarcerated women are single mothers of dependent children. Complicating this situation, only about half of these incarcerated women will ever see their children during their imprisonment.[10–12] In part, this is related to the rural, isolated location of many prisons, making the transportation of children more problematic (unpublished data).[4]

One particular difficulty is the number of women suffering from a wide range of mental health conditions, from simple clinical depression to serious mental illness.[6,13,14] Most women newly admitted into the prison system suffer from at least situational depression for obvious reasons, with incarceration just another stress factor.[15] However, because most (75%) have significant histories of physical and sexual abuse, usually beginning as children, many begin their adult lives with long-standing clinical depression and resultant somatic sequelae.[16–19] Girls who live with violence, in its various forms and with its various consequences, grow into adult women who increasingly accept violence and crime as a way of life for themselves and their children (unpublished data).[20] Thus, women become accustomed to living lives that are chronically chaotic, leaving them particularly vulnerable to self-harmful kinds of behaviors and lives that put them in jeopardy for incarceration in the first place (unpublished data).[20,21]

The backgrounds typical of incarcerated women and the nature of prison life make it difficult for women to proactively develop positive ways of nurturing their own health. And, unfortunately, women come to prison with few skills in caring for themselves in the first place (unpublished data). Hence, health research with incarcerated women is vital to understand their ideas about health, to develop strategies whereby women can become more skilled in self-care, and to make decisions consistent with their own health and the health of their communities.

CURRENT STUDY CONTEXT

The study from which the following examples were drawn examines incarcerated women's understanding about health. Participatory action research, utilizing critical hermeneutic techniques, was used to analyze text generated from interviews with incarcerated women over a period of one year (though the study remains ongoing). A total of 20 incarcerated women at a large women's prison in the southeastern United States have participated in the study thus far toward the aims of identifying what health means to incarcerated women and what it takes for them to be healthy and whole. Over the course of the study, 10 women have been paroled or transferred to other prisons, so that at any given time, about 10 women were actively participating. Women met with me weekly to discuss their lives, views on health, current health issues, and concerns about their future well-being. Dialogues and discus-

sions with the women were not tape recorded; rather I took brief notes during our interviews and subsequently wrote extensive field notes. These notes became the primary text, or data, for the study. Other text was derived from journalling notes written about my various experiences and observations while in prison. Within the study, issues of coping, issues of motherhood, relationships with other women, and their histories of sexual and physical abuse, violence, and substance abuse have been emphasized.

QUALITATIVE METHODOLOGIC ISSUES

As noted above, participatory research utilizing critical hermeneutic data analysis techniques were used in the current study. While the intricacies of the conceptual framework and specific methodology of this study are beyond the intent and scope of this article, pertinent commonalities in qualitative research will be discussed. These areas of interest include coercion; consent for participation; access to participants; issues of confidentiality; trust and relationship; the role of the researcher; interviewing issues; intersubjectivity and reciprocity; nontermination; and accuracy of data.

Coercion

Incarcerated populations have been designated as vulnerable populations directly related to their decreased ability to actualize autonomy and freedom of choice.[1] Notions of coercion refer to the idea of encroaching on the natural freedom of individuals. As incarcerated populations have little natural freedom, issues of coercion become especially important.

Undue coercion would exist if a research protocol allowed prison officials, or other prisoners, to decide who should and should not participate. Informed consent procedures, therefore, must be explicit in how the investigator will choose participants outside of the prison bureaucracy, both formal and informal. When the current study began, all inmates at the prison were invited to participate. Notices were placed in dormitories briefly reviewing the study and how it would be conducted. Thirty-five women wrote letters to express their interest, and each was interviewed. Several women who originally indicated interest decided they did not want to become part of the study primarily related to their impending release dates; others did not want to commit to weekly interviews.

This sampling technique, however, clearly led to an elite bias in that only those women who could read and write were able to respond. An alternative method might have been to go to each dormitory, at various times, describe the study, and ask women in person if they had an interest in participating in this kind of research. A list could then have been generated and women interviewed for participation from the list.

Coercion could also exist if proposed research provided participating inmates with necessities or advantages not available to the general population of prisoners. For instance, if medical or mental health services were not generally available to inmates, but were available to research participants, coercion would be clear. However, this can be a potential area of dispute. For example, in this study, inmates who are not participating frequently complain that they have no one to talk to. "Why are they special, why can't you talk to me?" is a question frequently expressed. Although the prison where this study is being conducted has mental health and counseling services and is fully accredited, economic constraints within the state do not provide the fuller, more comprehensive services women often seem to need and want. As qualitative studies typically involve small numbers of participants, this may seem to represent disparity for those not included.

One strategy used to mitigate this feeling for inmates has been to listen to those women expressing concerns by exploring and assessing any acute needs for referrals to the prison counseling system. This has been time consuming but absolutely necessary to support the women as individuals, and to affirm their need to be heard. Women frequently ask me to put their name down in case I have any openings in the future. As participants have been paroled or sent to other prisons, all subsequent participants have come from this list.

Paying participants is also considered as a coercion issue within prisons. Incarcerated persons in large part must buy a substantial portion of their personal possessions, such as snack foods, cigarettes, make-up, stationery, stamps, and the like, from the prison store. These items are deemed necessary by most of us, and no less so for persons in prison. Having an income during incarceration, be it from family or personal resources, is considered vital. The chance to receive any money at all might effect coercion on an inmate who otherwise would not participate in research. Conversely, it is difficult not to offer some kind of payment for the generosity of participants. However, the women in this study have all acknowledged that this "chance to be heard" was of value to them. While researchers must be clear about the consequences of providing tangible goods or money to inmates, reciprocity remains a challenge and obligation that will be discussed later in this chapter.

Coercion might also exist if research participation in any way impacted parole decisions. Therefore, informed consent procedures must apprise potential participants that they will receive no legal benefits or considerations from the parole board by participating in research.

Consent for participation

It is a researcher's responsibility to ensure that participants understand the exact nature of a study and their role in that study. Written consent forms, with their many disclaimers and risk disclosures, should cause any participant in a research study to pause and consider. However, the necessary language within consents is often problematic for incarcerated women. Women in prison tend to have less education; therefore, reading consent forms to and with women is important. Discussing various aspects of the consent form can provide women with the details they need to make a better informed choice.

It is typical for consent forms to provide addresses and phone numbers to access human subjects committees, as well as the investigator. This is problematic in prison where inmates may not make phone calls unless those numbers have been programmed into the computer that monitors the system. As inmates are only allowed a certain number of telephone contacts, adding extra numbers can be difficult. In addition, all calls must be made collect, a difficult accomplishment for universities and committees that are not set up to receive and pay for such calls. In this study, participants were advised that if they chose to add the appropriate numbers, their calls would be accepted. To date, this has not occurred. Because I am at the prison on a weekly basis, questions can easily be directed to me.

The consent process does not end when the form is signed, especially in ongoing studies. Munhall[22] suggested it is difficult in qualitative studies to fully predict issues of risk as dialogue around painful topics might present problems in subsequent interviews not initially anticipated. It remains the researcher's responsibility to ensure that participants continue to understand their right to withdraw from a study, or to refuse to answer questions that make them uncomfortable.

Access to participants

It is quite easy to approach incarcerated women as the "captive" audience they are. However, captive does not in this instance translate into compliance. For understandable reasons, women in prison tend to view the "system" as their adversary. As all research must be approved by a state's department of corrections, it is easy to understand why women might approach any project endorsed by the department with some skepticism.

Second, incarcerated women generally do not come from backgrounds that support the traditional valuing of science and knowledge development. The difficulty researchers face incorporating marginalized populations into studies are widely reported. However, it is clearly not as easy for persons living outside the sphere of privilege of the middle and upper classes to make the connection between science and their lived experience of the world. This is so for incarcerated women. However an additional burden exists in this area. Incarcerated women largely suffer from poor self-esteem, and it is often difficult for the women in my study to comprehend that their lives have any real meaning for any one else in the world, let alone to the scientific community. Yet, without exception, all of the women in this study have expressed their hopes that their stories might help girls and young women.

Issues of confidentiality

In prison, everyone seems to know everyone else's business. Tight confinement and limited socialization opportunities quite naturally lead to people watching people. Watching is a way of life.

The nature of prison life means that everyone knows exactly who is participating in a research study. Currently, all interviews take place in an office with large glass windows, so that women are constantly within view of a corrections officer and of other inmates. Laughter or tears during our dialogues are always on display. This potential was reviewed with

inmates during informed consent procedures. However, while their participation may be clear to others, it is obviously important that the content of their participation remain confidential.

An important strategy used in this study to ensure confidentiality and trust was a certificate of confidentiality from the US Department of Health and Human Services. This certificate relieves investigators from potential compulsory legal demands to connect the identity of any given participant in a research study to specific data, unless the participant specifically gives consent for such disclosure. As I expected that the women might discuss sexual preferences and behaviors, drug and alcohol use, and other kinds of illegal conduct, the certificate allowed me to completely guarantee confidentiality. However, I identified three exceptions. If they told me they were planning to escape, planning to commit suicide, or planning to harm or kill someone else, I would report these issues to prison staff. On two occasions, women have discussed suicidal ideations, and these were reported to staff, with the women's permission. To date, no other problems in this regard have surfaced.

Trust and relationship

Trust and relationship must be established for effective qualitative research. It is not enough for a researcher to have credentials and authority. For women, the role one may assume does not automatically confer trust. Rather, for women, relationship confers trust.[23]

The nature of prison life endorses distrust between staff and inmates, and among inmates themselves.[24] Staff are socialized to scrutinize every action and behavior of inmates as potentially devious. And, most staff members can recount instances where they have been manipulated and lied to by inmates. After all, inmates are in prison because they committed crimes against the society of which staff are members.[24] But, as this essential distrust becomes foundational to all interactions, even those inmates who are genuinely being polite or appropriately asking questions are not granted credibility. In this culture of distrust, inmates also are wary of each other, further complicating the social dynamics of this artificially created community.

Before this study began, I began to build a general relationship with inmates over a period of approximately one year. Beginning a faculty practice at the prison medical unit, I participated in new arrival intakes, developed a prerelease discharge counseling system, and participated in the restructuring of the chronic care clinics. All of these activities involved consistent contact with inmates. In this environment characterized by suspicion and distrust, special attention was paid to following through on all commitments made to inmates and thoroughly listening to their concerns.

This was also a time when I began to understand some of the inherent ethical challenges in providing nursing care to inmates. The greatest challenge to nurses seemed to be around issues of punishment.[24] Although the department of corrections clearly does not expect, nor want, nurses to become part of an inmate's punishment, it is hard to separate oneself from that aspect of prison nurs-

ing. Nurses simply are part of the prison system that is effecting punishment on inmates. Maintaining an awareness of this problem through open discussions with inmate participants has proved valuable for me and for them, raising our individual and collective consciousness.

Believing that nursing identity lies in relationship,[25] the mandate that nurses must not form relationships with inmates was problematic. It takes extraordinary effort on the part of nurses to avoid practicing from a position of punishment, and an equally extraordinary effort to develop therapeutic relationships with incarcerated women. Because I was not directly employed by the department of corrections, inmates were less likely to see me as part of their punishment. I was also not a permanent part of the structure of the medical unit as my faculty practice ended at the time the study began. As medical complaints are the most common cause of inmates' formal disputes with prisons,[3] this separation allowed inmates to perceive me differently. Though I am careful not to enter into efforts of redress against the prison or the medical unit, I nonetheless make it a point to listen to women and try to provide an outside perspective to their views. Because I really am not part of the structures they often feel adversarial toward, I have been able to be their "sounding board" on a number of occasions.

Regardless of one's role in prison, relationships between all persons are expected to be characterized by distance and formality.[24] Fundamentally, through many mechanisms, relationships are forbidden and ultimately punishable. For instance, in the name of preventing homosexual activity, women are forbidden to show physical affection with one another, even if that affection is not based on a sexual interaction. Women are not allowed to visit each other in their rooms where they could presumably have sexual relations. However, this also means that women cannot meet together privately to share the joys and sorrows of their lives, an important component of women's elemental selves, in or out of prison. In these ways, relationships, sexual and otherwise, become pathologized and are frequently the source of disciplinary actions. Therefore, incarcerated women come to expect that meaningful relationships must be covert. In the current study, women approached their dialogues with the same sort of expectations. In the beginning of the study, participants frequently expressed concern that they were sharing too much intimate information with me, wondering if that would somehow harm them, or harm my ability to continue the research. Over time, they have been reassured that the certificate of confidentiality protects me, as well as them. Consistent with ethical considerations, they are reminded that they only need to share what they feel comfortable in sharing, that they are not in any way bound to give me information.

Symbols of trust between incarcerated women and researchers are difficult to identify and nurture within a prison system. Though women in the free world frequently share their lives around food, this is forbidden in prison. Staff, including myself, are not permitted to give anything to an inmate that could be misconstrued.

However, I am permitted to give participants in this study various books that sup-port women's exploration of health issues and education. This has been helpful to individual inmates for their own personal growth and exploration of self, but it has also been extraordinarily meaningful for the research. For instance, bell hooks' *Sisters of the Yam: Black Women and Self-Recovery*[26] has been particularly helpful for women as they explore issues of self-esteem and understanding of their own history. The poetry of Audre Lorde[27] and Marge Piercy[28] has also been meaningful for the women in this study. Participants have been encouraged to share the books with other inmates or to contribute the books to the prison library. Because I am an avid reader, I have also coordinated book drives at my university to donate large numbers of fiction and nonfiction books. This has been viewed as supportive by both inmates and staff, and has allowed me an avenue to "give back" to this community of women.

Role of the researcher

The role of researchers in quantitative and qualitative paradigms is different. For instance, a researcher in quantitative studies might aspire toward neutrality and independence from research participants. In qualitative paradigms, the researcher and participant roles are interrelated, with an expectation that each impacts the other.[29] Traditionally, the role of researchers conducting qualitative interviews has been to develop knowledge, as opposed to conducting therapeutic interviews. However, as qualitative methods become more diverse, the role of researcher and the goal of interviews may be actualized quite differently between methodologies.[30] For instance, ethnographers use interviews to study cultures and subcultures, using interview data to discover cultural themes.

In the present study, the utilization of participative action research and critical hermeneutic data analysis techniques calls for the merging of roles between researcher and participant. The historic "situatedness" of both researcher and participant is crucial to this interpretive method. Therefore, my social class and background as a nurse, friend, lover, mother, sister, scholar, researcher, and the like were not incidental to the study. Each of my roles in life, as the various roles of the women themselves, was fundamental to the research process.[31]

Further, the critical component of this type of methodology explicitly identifies the goals of emancipation, empowerment, and enlightenment for, and with, participants.[32] Interviews serve as a process of "conscientization" or bringing into consciousness that which is missing, or unavailable.[33] For instance in this study, we frequently discuss ways to care for self, knowledge that could potentially empower women to avoid self-harming behavior. Caring for self has included ways to avoid substance abuse when released, how to avoid relationships that lead to criminal behavior, and the like. Interviews were, therefore, therapeutic.

While the role of the researcher with incarcerated women may be viewed within an advocacy framework, researchers must resist any tendency to assume an adversarial role with prison personnel on behalf of women. The development of trusting relationships with security officers is essential to successfully conduct qualitative research and to maintain the researcher's own safety. Like many health care personnel, officers often rotate shifts and may or may not have accurate information on how or why research is being conducted. Officers must not feel the advocacy role of the researcher in any way interferes with their safety concerns, procedural requirements, or authority. Therefore, continued association and dialogue with officers to maintain open lines of communication is essential. Although I frequently receive requests to assist inmates in their disputes with officers, I limit this assistance to dialoguing with women about how they might best approach a positive resolution through their own efforts.

Interviewing issues

As noted above, interviews are foundational to most qualitative methodologies. However, the way qualitative researchers conduct interviews varies with individuals and intentions within the research itself. In this study, based on my experience interacting with incarcerated women, I allowed participants to talk about whatever was on their minds. Specific questions and probes came only after I had heard their "story." Therefore, the women themselves determined the structure of the interviews. Some weeks, interviews and dialogues were brief, discussion superficial. Other weeks, the interviews and dialogues were detailed and intense.

However, taking a slow approach with the participants has allowed for greater depth of information and some surprises. For example, most research reviewed prior to the study indicated that relationships with mothers were the most important feature of incarcerated women's social and family structure. The participants validated that assertion in the first few months of the study. Gradually, however, participants began to describe problematic, dysfunctional relationships with their mothers. Indeed, many noted that their mothers had been directly involved in early childhood physical abuse, and did not protect their daughters from sexual abuse by others. Some women described learning to use drugs with their mothers and that their mothers had also been involved in criminal activity during their childhood.

Still, women seemed to believe they must hang on to idealized versions of the relationships with their mothers for many reasons. The difficulty of mother-daughter relationships was not new to this study, however, two important issues related to children and parole issues were unique. Mothers of incarcerated women are frequently the caretakers of their daughter's minor children. How the women's children might view their mothers upon release likely depended on the good will the women were able to maintain with their mothers during imprisonment. In addition, women believed they would make parole more easily if they were paroling out to their mother's address. However, after many months into the study, women began to express the view that relationships with their mothers were so dysfunctional as to contribute to their own possible relapse and recidivism once they were released. For those inmates who were paroled while the study was being conducted, anxiety over mother-daughter relationships increased as release dates got closer. This insight was only made clear after many months of data collection and demonstrates the necessity of prolonged engagement.

One particular difficulty in conducting interviews in prison is frequent interruptions and the sometimes overwhelming sounds of the prison itself. Listening in prison is a difficult undertaking. Ironically, it is the women who have taught me to ignore the sudden presence of others, the blaring of the loudspeaker, and the sounds of other inmates. Adopting an attitude of patience is requisite, as is the ability to simply tune others out and discretely change the topic of conversation when a stranger bursts into the room.

Intersubjectivity and reciprocity

Notions of intersubjectivity and reciprocity are important within qualitative methodologies. Intersubjectivity has been defined as the sharing of subjectivity between researcher and participant so that each is truly present to the other in mutually validating ways.[29,34,35]

In other words, being in a relationship with a participant, intersubjectively, means sharing the tenor of each individual's experience.[36] Reciprocity within qualitative methodologies subsumes intersubjectivity, but also reflects actions on the part of both researcher and participant. As the participant is clearly engaged in assisting the researcher, how a researcher reciprocates is an important feature within the research relationship.[37]

In the current study, intersubjectivity represented a willingness on my part to listen and be fully present to the anguish of abuse, violence, and disconnection women typically experienced in early childhood, much of which continued until their incarceration. Intersubjectivity also involved sharing anguish women felt over the crimes they had committed, torn relationships with children, and years of addictions. Real intersubjectivity can be very painful, a reality with which qualitative researchers must at some point come to terms.

A consequence of intersubjectivity, and responsiveness to the idea of reciprocity, involved the sharing of my personal and professional understanding about some of the issues with which the women were struggling. Walking a thin line between making inappropriate disclosures about my life, yet sharing lessons I have learned throughout my life as a woman and nurse was, and remains, a challenge. Still, many of the complexities of these women's lives are analogous to the lives of most women, including me.

An example within the study germane to this discussion was the issue of being separated from children. One of the participants in this study had been extraordinarily generous with her time and involvement, and had provided many new insights and perspectives. She had not seen her children, now 12 and 8 years old, for over six years. This was a source of great anxiety and sadness for her, an anxiety and sadness I had once felt in my own life. We shared many conversations about the pain involved in this difficult separation. With her permission, I contacted a charitable foundation that provided services to children of imprisoned mothers in another part of the state. Hearing her story, this extraordinary group of people committed to bring the children to the prison to see their mother immediately, and committed to bring the children every six months until her release some two years from now. Although in a prison setting reciprocity rarely involves such dramatic and immediate results, the notions of intersubjectivity and relationship can be profoundly rewarding for both researcher and participant—and in this case for two innocent children.

Reciprocity is also actualized in more subtle ways. For instance, it has been suggested that relationships with strong women role models are important for women trying to rebuild their lives after prison.[38,39] An important concept I have become increasingly aware of is the role I play as a relatively educated and successful woman within a community of women who have failed, and who are reminded of that failure every minute of every day. Because I have never been incarcerated or even arrested, and because I am not part of their punishment structure, my reactions to problems and conflicts within the prison are often watched closely. For example, before the study began, I was working in the medical unit with a particularly aggressive and obnoxious physician who became angry at me in front of a large group of inmates. As he raised his voice and stood nose to nose with me, I stood unmoved and calmly listened. Then in a quiet but firm voice told him why he was wrong and how he was totally out of line in manner. I then calmly turned away and returned to my work. This physician continued to stand and glare at me and then suddenly kicked an examination stool. Inmates watched silently and with great interest. This incident has been recounted to me many times by inmates who share that they wish they could learn to stand up for themselves, walk away, and not physically react. Indeed, the wish to not react with violence is a frequent topic of conversations in our weekly dialogues. Therefore, what I share with participants through conversations, or how they observe my behavior within their community, has become methodologically important.

Nontermination

Nontermination is another methodologic issue in qualitative research.[37] The nature of qualitative research, and this research in particular, often involves deeply personal and intimate issues. To touch on these issues and enter into relationships with incarcerated women necessitates a long-term and flexible commitment. As Lipson and Meleis[37] discovered with immigrant and ethnic populations, participants in qualitative research interact with researchers primarily based on relationships, not their roles as researchers. Therefore, participants may feel the need to maintain some contact. This may not be an easy transition for some investigators. Discomfort on the part of researchers about "such ongoing involvement necessitates clarifying the assumptions upon which the research is based, such as striving for 'pure objectivity.'"[37(p108)]

Early on in the current study a participant asked, "Am I just going to get myself all worked up over these things and then you'll be done, and I'll be left here?" The answer to that question was, No. This participant, and the others, were assured that barring some unforeseen catastrophe or major change in my life circumstance, I was committed to the research and to their participation until they were paroled or decided to drop out of the study for their own reasons. (For clarity, I anticipated that this study, with minor changes, might last five years and was awarded a certificate of confidentiality for that period of time. To date, none of the participants in the study anticipate being in prison that long.)

Nontermination can also mean maintaining contact outside of prison upon parole. Participants in all research studies have the right to contact investigators with questions. In line with that obligation, the women involved in this study were given the university address where they could contact me. To date, three women who were paroled during the study have written to let me know they made it out OK and were doing well. As a good deal of our conversations have been about how they can be healthy and whole once they leave prison, it is only natural that women might want to maintain some contact. Because the women know I am beginning research with women newly released from prison, they correctly assume that I am interested in their process and progress upon parole.

Accuracy of data

Despite assurances to the contrary, it was expected that incarcerated women might be reluctant to accurately discuss certain aspects of their lives, especially their imprisonment, for fear of reprisals if confidentiality was breached. Because prisons both create and sustain distrust, it was anticipated that data would not always be completely accurate. The self that interviewees present to interviewers often reflects what they believe is acceptable to divulge and what they believe is expected and will be understood.[37] Because of the duration of the current study, these issues largely have sorted themselves out over time. However, some topics wax and wane with accuracy, especially those involving past incidences of violence or self-abusive behavior. For example, when discussing her incarceration for aggravated assault, a participant on some occasions will describe the horror of what she did, and at other times describe the incident in ways that imply she was not at fault. Over time, however, I have learned that this has less to do with her level of comfort in talking with me, as it does her level of comfort in talking with her self. Some days, she simply cannot face what she has done. Therefore, viewed over time, continued dialogue serves as its own "member check." Generally, as women have learned to speak their own truths through dialogue, those same truths have become unavoidable to themselves.[40]

Accuracy and validity of data can also be implied and supported through the research of others. Though limited research, especially qualitative research, has been conducted with incarcerated women, much of what the women in this study describe and discuss is consistent with pertinent literature. For instance, 15 of the 20 participants (75%) describe

sexual and physical abuse beginning in early childhood, and 16 of the 20 participants (80%) describe crimes associated with substance abuse, both data that are consistent with national figures (unpublished data).[4-8] Therefore, in many respects, the context of stories and experiences described by incarcerated women appears consistent with descriptions of other incarcerated and nonincarcerated women.

Although accuracy of data may appear elusive with incarcerated populations, continued interviews over time, compared with extant literature, can validate data as well as suggest new lines of inquiry toward clarification and expansion of the database.

•   •   •

Clearly, health care research with incarcerated women is a challenge, but one well worth the investment of health care researchers. Though women have been convicted of crimes against the society of which we are all members, the vast majority of these women will be released back into our communities. While prisons serve to enforce complete and utter dependence, women will be released back into society that has a shrinking disposition to look kindly upon them, yet has high expectations toward their self-sufficiency and rehabilitation. It is imperative that we begin to understand how to help women help themselves become healthy and whole before and after they leave prison. These issues must be approached systematically beginning with appropriate research. To do otherwise is to risk the well-being of individuals and communities, and diminishing economic resources.

The qualitative, methodologic issues and problems discussed in this chapter can be mitigated by careful planning and the laying of substantive groundwork. In particular, it is important for qualitative researchers to have a real, ongoing interest in the value and well-being of women in prison. Interview times must be extendible and flexible. Incarcerated women must be able to trust that arrangements made with the investigator will be honored in terms of time and the women's need to be heard. Through the articulation of structures to encourage trust and to manage intersubjectivity and structure reciprocity, qualitative research with incarcerated women can be accomplished with meaningful results.

REFERENCES

1. US Department of Health and Human Services. *Protecting Human Research Subject: Institutional Review Board Guidebook.* Washington, DC: US Government Printing Office; 1993.

2. Bureau of Justice Statistics. *Prison and Jail Inmates at Midyear 1997.* Washington, DC; US Dept of Justice; 1998.

3. American Correctional Association. *The Female Offender.* Laurel, Md: Author; 1990.

4. Immarigeon R, Chesney-Lind M. *Women's Prisons: Overcrowded and Overused.* San Francisco: NCCD; 1992.

5. Mullings J. *Victimization, Substance Abuse, and High-Risk Behavior as Predictors of Health among Women at Admission to Prison.* Dissertation. Huntsville, Tex: Sam Houston University; 1997.

6. Singer M, Bussey J, Li-Yu S, Lunghofer L. The psychosocial issues of women serving time in jail. *Soc Work.* 1995;40(1):103–113.

7. Bureau of Justice Statistics. *Special Report: Women in Prison.* Washington, DC: US Dept of Justice; 1994. Publication no. NCJ–145321.

8. Fogel C. Determining risk status in a primary care setting. *Appl Nurs Res.* 1992;5(3):140–145.

9. El–Bassel N, Ivanoff A, Schilling R, Gilbert L, Borne D, Chen D. Preventing HIV/AIDS in drug–abusing incarcerated women through skills building and social support enhancement: preliminary outcomes. *Soc Work.* 1995;19(3):131–141.

10. Bloom B. Imprisoned mothers. In: Gabel K, Johnston D, eds. *Children of Incarcerated Parents.* New York: Lexington Press; 1995.

11. Bloom B, Lind M, Owen B. *Women in California Prisons: Hidden Victims of the War on Drugs.* San Francisco: Center on Juvenile and Criminal Justice; 1994.

12. Taylor S. Women offenders and reentry issues. *J Psychoactive Drugs.* 1996;28:85–93.

13. Fogel C, Martin S. The mental health of incarcerated women. *West J Nurs Res.* 1992;14(1):30–47.

14. Jemelka R, Trupin E, Chiles J. The mentally ill in prisons: a review. *Hosp Community Psychiatr.* 1989;40(5):481–491.

15. Fogel C. Hard time: the stressful nature of incarceration for women. *West J Nurs Res.* 1993; 14(4):367–377.

16. Campbell J, Kub J, Rose L. Depression in battered women. *JAMWA.* 1996;51(3):106–110.

17. Koss M. The impact of crime victimization on women's medical use. *J Women's Health.* 1993; 2(1):67–72.

18. National Commission on Correctional Health Care. *Women's Health Care in Correctional Settings.* Chicago: Author; 1994.

19. Richie B, Johnsen C. Abuse histories among newly incarcerated women in a New York City jail. *JAMWA.* 1996;51(3):111–117.

20. De Zulueta F. *From Pain to Violence: The Traumatic Roots of Destructiveness.* London: Whurr; 1993.

21. Gil-Rivas V, Fioentine R, Anglin M. Sexual abuse, physical abuse, and posttraumatic stress disorder among women participating in outpatient drug abuse treatment. *J Psychoactive Drugs.* 1996;28: 95–102.

22. Munhall P. Ethical considerations in qualitative research. *West J Nurs Res.* 1989;10(2):150–162.

23. Jordan J. The meaning of mutuality. In: Jordan J, Kaplan A, Miller J, Stiver I, Surrey J, eds. *Women's Growth in Connection.* New York: Guilford; 1991.

24. Maeve MK. Nursing practice with incarcerated women: caring within mandated (sic) alienation. *Issues Ment Health Nurs.* 1997;18:495–510.

25. Maeve MK. The carrier bag theory of nursing practice. *ANS.* 1994;16(4):9–22.

26. hooks b. *Sisters of the Yam: Black Women and Self-Recovery.* Boston: Southend Press; 1993.

27. Lorde A. *The Black Unicorn.* New York: Norton; 1978.

28. Piercy M. *Circles on the Water.* New York: Knopf; 1994.

29. Watson J. *Nursing: Human Science and Human Care.* New York: NLN; 1988.

30. Hutchinson S, Wilson H. Research and therapeutic interviews. In: Morse J, ed. *Qualitative Nursing Research.* Newbury Park, Calif: Sage; 1997.

31. Allen D. Hermeneutics: philosophical traditions and nursing practice research. *Nurs Sci Q.* 1995;8(4): 174–182.

32. Henderson D. Consciousness raising in participatory research: method and methodology for emancipatory nursing inquiry. *ANS.* 1995;17(3): 58–69.

33. Holter I. Critical theory: a foundation for the development of nursing theories. *Schol Inquiry Nurs Pract.* 1988;2(3):223–236.

34. Parse R. *Nursing Research: Qualitative Methods.* Bowie, Md: 1985.

35. Paterson J, Zderad L. *Humanistic Nursing.* New York: Wiley; 1976.

36. Maeve MK. Weaving a fabric of moral meaning: how nurses live with suffering and death. *J Adv Nurs.* In press.

37. Lipson J, Meleis A. Methodological issues in research with immigrants. *Med Anthrop.* 1989;12: 103–115.

38. Henderson D. Drug abuse and incarcerated women. Presented to American Society of Criminology; San Diego, California; Nov. 20, 1996.

39. Taylor S. Women offenders and reentry issues. *J Psychoactive Drugs.* 1996;28:85–93.

40. Lorde A. *Sister Outsider: Essays & Speeches.* Freedom, Calif: Crossing Press; 1984.

CHAPTER 27

Hypertext Links Related to Special Populations

The hypertext links listed below provide additional information related to special populations. These links focus on policy information and community-based initiatives aimed toward improving health status of special populations. A number of the links are to federal offices whose missions specifically include providing or ensuring service provision for special populations. Other links are to organizations whose activities are related to the health needs of special populations. Because URL addresses change frequently, it is possible that the reader may need to access the sites through other addresses. Also, web site content changes regularly, so listing sites here does not imply endorsement of the content. However, the reader may find these listings helpful starting points in a search for additional information for use in designing and providing health services for special population groups.

Federal Sites:

1. Healthy People Home Page
   http://odphp.osophs.dhhs.gov/pubs/hp2000/
   Both the Healthy People Home Page and the Healthy People 2010 Home Page describe national goals and strategies for promoting health and reducing illness. Both also include an emphasis on special populations.

2. Healthy People 2010 Home Page
   http://web.health.gov/healthypeople/
   The Healthy People 2010 plan will likely address reduction of disparities between special populations and the population as a whole even more strongly than previous national health plans.

3. President Clinton's Initiative on Race
    http://aspe.os.dhhs.gov/race/racehlth.htm
    This site outlines Clinton's Initiative on Race, in which he focuses the nation's attention on health disparities still existing between selected racial and ethnic groups and the population of the United States as a whole. The Department of Health and Human Services' goals and plans are described.

4. Health United States, 1998
    http://www.cdc.gov/nchswww/releases/98news/huspr98.htm
    This site describes the relationships between income, education, and health status.

5. Office of Disease Prevention and Health Promotion
    http://odphp.osophs.dhhs.gov/
    This site includes wide ranging information about national efforts to reduce diseases and promote health.

6. Health Resources and Services Administration Fact Sheet
    http://www.hrsa.dhhs.gov/Newsroom/factsheets/mngdcare.htm
    This site includes interesting links to managed care information related to special populations.

7. Federal Health Resources and Services Administration
    www.hrsa.dhhs.gov/
    This federal office is part of the Public Health Service. It funds numerous community-based clinical programs aimed at improving health of underserved populations. The web site includes references to recently funded initiatives related to the health of women and children.

8. Federal Bureau of Primary Health Care
    www.bphc.hrsa.dhhs.gov/
    This federal office aims to improve health care for vulnerable and underserved populations.

9. National Health Service Corps
    www.bphc.hrsa.dhhs.gov/nhsc/
    The National Health Service Corps is a program of the Bureau of Primary Health Care that aims to "reduce health disparities in health professional shortage areas by assisting communities with site development and through the preparation, recruitment and retention of community-responsive, culturally competent primary care clinicians" (National Health Service Corps web site, Feb. 16, 1999).

10. Department of Health and Human Services
    www.os.dhhs.gov/
    This federal department focuses on "providing essential human services, espe-

cially for those who are least able to help themselves" (DHHS web site, Feb. 16, 1999). The web site includes links to other federal programs that serve a wide range of special population groups. For example, links are included to the Indian Health Service and the Substance Abuse and Mental Health Services Administration.

11. Indian Health Service
http://www.tucson.ihs.gov/
This office is responsible for providing health care to American Indians and Alaskan Natives. The web site includes detailed information about health programs available for American Indians and Alaskan Natives.

12. Substance Abuse and Mental Health Services Administration
http://www.samhsa.gov/
SAMHSA is the federal office dedicated to preventing and treating substance abuse, and providing services to people with mental health problems.

13. Agency for Health Care Policy and Research
http://www.ahcpr.gov/
This site includes access to clinical and preventive guidelines. AHCPR funds studies of the effectiveness and efficiency of health services delivery models.

14. Centers for Disease Control and Prevention
http://www.cdc.gov/
This federal program focuses on preventing and controlling the spread of disease. The web site contains links to a wide range of resources related to illness prevention.

15. Medicare
http://www.hcfa.gov/medicare/medicare.htm
The Medicare site provides data, programmatic information, and policy updates related to Medicare enrollees.

16. Medicaid
http://www.hcfa.gov/medicaid/medicaid.htm
The Medicaid web site includes access to federal and state data describing the population of people enrolled in Medicaid, as well as programmatic and policy information.

17. Children's Health Insurance Program
http://www.hcfa.gov/init/children.htm
This site provides information about the new Children's Health Insurance Program and state-level activities. This program is a major new effort to ensure that children will have the financial means to access health services.

Organizational Sites:

18. University of Colorado-Boulder Service-Learning Home Page
    http://csf.Colorado.EDU/sl/
    Service-learning is a teaching strategy that incorporates partnerships with communities in designing learning and service activities. This site contains links to numerous resources related to service-learning and community partnerships.

19. American Public Health Association
    http://www.apha.org/
    This site contains a wide range of information related to improving public health and the health of underserved populations.

20. International Healthy Cities Foundation
    http://www.healthycities.org/
    This site provides information about the global healthy cities movement, which aims to include local populations in identifying strengths and needs for promoting community health, and working in partnerships to design locally responsive strategies for promoting healthy communities.

21. Community Campus Partnerships for Health
    http://futurehealth.ucsf.edu/ccph.html
    This organization also emphasizes community-based partnerships, but particularly focuses on partnerships between communities and academia. Many of these partnerships aim to improve the health of special population groups.

Index

N